OSCAR WILDE'S PARIS

Oscar Wilde's Paris

Legends and Legacies

EDITED BY COLETTE COLLIGAN
AND GREGORY MACKIE

UNIVERSITY OF TORONTO PRESS
Toronto Buffalo London

Toronto Buffalo London
utppublishing.com
Printed in Canada

ISBN 978-1-4875-4141-5 (cloth)
ISBN 978-1-4875-4143-9 (EPUB)
ISBN 978-1-4875-4142-2 (PDF)

Library and Archives Canada Cataloguing in Publication

Title: Oscar Wilde's Paris : legends and legacies / edited by Colette Colligan and Gregory Mackie.
Names: Colligan, Colette, 1974– editor. | Mackie, Gregory, 1976– editor.
Description: Includes bibliographical references and index.
Identifiers: Canadiana (print) 20250284669 | Canadiana (ebook) 20250285320 | ISBN 9781487541415 (hardcover) | ISBN 9781487541439 (EPUB) | ISBN 9781487541422 (PDF)
Subjects: LCSH: Wilde, Oscar, 1854–1900 – Homes and haunts – France – Paris. | LCSH: Authors, Irish – Homes and haunts – France – Paris. | LCSH: Authors, Irish – France – Paris – History – 19th century. | LCSH: Irish – France – Paris – History – 19th century. | LCSH: Paris (France) – Intellectual life – 19th century.
Classification: LCC PR5823 .O83 2025 | DDC 828/.809–dc23

Cover design: Val Cooke; John Beadle
Cover image: Toulouse-Lautrec, Oscar Wilde et Romain Coolus 1896 © The Trustees of the British Museum; (title font) iStock.com/OlenaGo

The manufacturer's authorised representative in the EU for product safety is Mare Nostrum Group B.V., Mauritskade 21D, 1091 GC Amsterdam, The Netherlands. Email: gpsr@mare-nostrum.co.uk.

We wish to acknowledge the land on which the University of Toronto Press operates. This land is the traditional territory of the Wendat, the Anishnaabeg, the Haudenosaunee, the Métis, and the Mississaugas of the Credit First Nation.

This book has been published with the assistance of the University of British Columbia, Simon Fraser University, and the Centre Interdisciplinaire de Recherche sur les Patrimoines en Lettres et Langues at the Université d'Angers.

University of Toronto Press acknowledges the financial support of the Government of Canada, the Canada Council for the Arts, and the Ontario Arts Council, an agency of the Government of Ontario, for its publishing activities.

Canada Council for the Arts
Conseil des Arts du Canada

Funded by the Government of Canada
Financé par le gouvernement du Canada

Contents

Illustrations

Acknowledgments

We would like to thank Paris's Institut d'études avancées (IEA), a research centre in the heart of the city specializing in the humanities and social sciences. In the spring of 2020, the IEA agreed to host our symposium on the topic of "Oscar Wilde in Paris" with the aim of bringing together a group of international Wilde scholars, many of whom are featured in this collection. Our plans were frustrated by the pandemic and the subsequent lockdown, but our collaboration persevered and transformed into this volume.

As the project drew to a close, the IEA kindly agreed to give us access to office space in its magnificent seventeenth-century building on Île Saint-Louis, in the very premises where Charles Baudelaire once lived, which Wilde himself would have appreciated. We are extremely grateful for the institutional and collaborative support of the IEA and its excellent team. Thanks to Saadi Lahlou, Simon Luck, Claire Jeandel, and Nadège Bourgeois in particular.

Our thanks also extend to our contributors who have shown remarkable tenacity by sticking with the project despite the pandemic. Our affiliate universities have also offered considerable support. The University of British Columbia awarded the project a Social Sciences and Humanities Research Council Explore Grant that funded a trip to Paris, and a UBC Scholarly Publication Grant helped to cover some publishing costs. The Department of English at Simon Fraser University provided funding for the initial symposium and then the completion of the volume. The Centre Interdisciplinaire de Recherche sur les Patrimoines en Lettres et Langues (CIRPaLL) based at the Université d'Angers helped to cover reproduction costs for images under copyright.

Libraries have also been the backbone of this project. Special thanks go to the Rare Books and Special Collections Library at the University of British Columbia (for providing images), the William Andrews Clark

Memorial Library, UCLA, the Harry Ransom Centre at the University of Texas at Austin, and the Bibliothèque nationale de France in Paris.

Throughout the publication process, it has been a pleasure working with the University of Toronto Press, and particularly with our editor, Mark Thompson and our copy editor, Emily Reiner. We felt in good hands guided by their expert and generous support.

We extend our gratitude to our two research assistants: Anna Lamontagne for their expert assistance proofing translations from the French, and Daniel Geddes for his preparation of the manuscript.

We cannot forget to thank the *incontournable* city of Paris for its inspiration and beauty and many Wildean sites. And of course we are grateful for having been able to trace Wilde's presence through so many sites rich in history. Walking through Paris in his footsteps more than 120 years after his death, amid the streets and buildings he too would have seen, inspired us to think that he was with us in some way.

Our final thanks go to Vin Nardizzi, for his support, advice, and wisdom in guiding us through so many forks in the road.

OSCAR WILDE'S PARIS

Introduction: The Romance of Wilde and the City of Light

COLETTE COLLIGAN AND GREGORY MACKIE

JACK. He seems to have expressed a desire to be buried in Paris.
CHASUBLE. In Paris! I fear that hardly points to a very serious state of mind at the last.

– *The Importance of Being Earnest*

Le fantôme d'Oscar Wilde

Paris remains haunted by the ghost of Oscar Wilde, and even today people flock to the city to be possessed by him.

For residents and visitors alike, Wilde's tomb in the city's storied Père Lachaise Cemetery (installed in 1912), has become a place of pilgrimage marked by a special imaginative and affective power. By the 1990s, a uniquely expressive ritual had developed among visitors to the monument in the twentieth arrondissement: countless of them have recorded their affinity for Wilde's spirit by covering the monument with lipstick kisses and graffiti testimonials. Over time, the stone began to deteriorate under the greasy weight of so much lipstick-and-ink affection. With an irony that Wilde himself would have appreciated, his admirers were killing the thing they loved – or at least its monumental symbol. Since 2011, when the restored tomb was unveiled on the anniversary of Wilde's death, its physical integrity has been protected by the installation of a glass screen in a project funded by the French and Irish governments. But the mythic aura of the writer, in that place, remains so strong that his devotees are undeterred by such protective interventions, and now it is the transparent barrier that records the lipstick affection that once marked, and threatened to destroy, the tomb itself. Although of relatively recent origin, it would appear that this particular ritual has staying power. By making the pilgrimage to the Parisian tomb and kissing *even the glass*, his admirers are trying to get as close as they can to him – or to what he represents to them – and this is crucially a form of intimacy that can only be achieved in the City of Light. Arguably, such an intimate connection to Wilde cannot be experienced in Dublin, the city of his birth and youth, nor in London, the city of his literary ascendance.

Elsewhere in the city, at number 13 in the rue des Beaux-Arts on the Left Bank of the Seine, in the sixth arrondissement, a very different form of contemporary Wildean pilgrimage is available to those seeking communion with the writer's memory and legacy. The building housing the Hôtel d'Alsace – the modest hostelry where Wilde died on 30 November 1900 – still stands, but in recent years it has been transformed and extensively renovated into a luxury, five-star lodging called simply L'Hôtel. Despite the well-documented history of Wide's existence in what he called "a poor little Bohemian hotel"[1] being dominated by debt and pain, his association with the hotel is celebrated extensively. It is marked by two exterior plaques on the building's facade (a third indicates the later residence of the Argentinian writer Jorge Luis Borges, who began his literary career by translating Wilde's story "The Happy Prince" into Spanish at the age of nine). Literary, symbolic, and material associations with Wilde proliferate in the lobby and throughout the hotel. The management has shrewdly placed decorative books, historical photographs of Wilde accompanied by peacock feathers, and even a framed original letter, written in French from that exact address. The decor is appropriately sumptuous and even decadent, with soft lighting, velvets, and silks, calling to mind Wilde in his aesthetic glory rather than his penurious decline. The hotel's lounge is now called Wilde's, and, for a considerable price, one can even sleep in an "Oscar Wilde suite." (That the actual location of Wilde's room in that building is in a different part of the hotel perhaps matters more to literary history than it does to marketing.) Now redecorated beyond recognition into a site of *grand luxe* reminiscent of Whistler's Peacock Room, the aura of Wildean presence and archive persists in a display of photographs and documents, including what seems to be another original letter. Marketing, memorialization, and mythmaking converge in opulent, seductive fashion everywhere at L'Hôtel.

Other Parisian locales also lay claim to Wilde. They include the Hôtel Marsollier, in the second arrondissement, which celebrates that Wilde stayed there in 1899 with a modest plaque and framed quotations from the writer. The signage at that location tactfully does not mention the management's impounding of Wilde's clothing for non-payment of rent. Elsewhere, in the twentieth arrondissement, a branch of the Paris municipal library system, renamed the Bibliothèque Oscar Wilde in

2011, also perpetuates the idea of a site-specific and transhistorical connectedness to Wilde that is afforded by the monumental gravesite and the seductive bookishness at L'Hôtel.

Wilde's ghost wanders the cemeteries, hotels, and libraries in the many arrondissements of Paris, while his admirers continue to seek to be possessed by him. This idyll is perpetuated in Wes Craven's short film for the anthology *Paris, je t'aime* (2006) which takes place at Père Lachaise Cemetery. A bickering British couple, caught up in the trivial matters of the serious world, reaffirm their love after the woman kisses Wilde's tombstone (which is covered with flowers and lit candles) and the man catches a glimpse of Wilde's ghost (played perfectly by Alexander Payne). Wilde's "lightness" infuses their romance as they walk off together from the cemetery into the city and into life. Wilde's ghost and the City of Light once again prove to be an emblematic pairing. Rupert Everett's 2018 film *The Happy Prince*, which concentrates on Wilde's final years after his release from prison, portrays a very different, though no less evocative and definitively Parisian, image of the man. Everett's exiled writer is impoverished, and evidently living on borrowed time; nevertheless, as he is witnessed drinking in insalubrious bars and cafes, conversing with friends, or consorting with sex workers (and speaking a great deal of French in the process), the grittily rendered texture of 1890s Parisian low life becomes part of his story, and he a unique part of its distinctive ambience.

Wilde's pairing with Paris was on full display again for those who visited the Petit Palais in 2016. Dominique Morel and Merlin Holland (Wilde's grandson) curated the first major international exhibition on the writer held in Paris: *Oscar Wilde, L'impertinent absolu* (Insolence incarnate). Along with a rich program of public lectures, the exhibition put a spotlight on Wilde's love of the city, while adding one more bright light to la Ville Lumière. Although the writer's association with Paris was already widely known and remembered through thousands of pilgrimages to his iconic tombstone at Père Lachaise, the exhibition highlighted the combination of academic and public interest in Wilde that is part of the city's famed cultural patrimony, a "wilde" symbol with which the city could fashion itself and its central place in world literature.[2] Wilde's association with the city's cultural history and his "passionate admiration" for its prominent artistic figures was also evoked in the Petit Palais's more recent 2023 exhibition devoted to the legendary Parisian diva Sarah Bernhardt. The exhibition displayed a copy of Wilde's French play *Salomé*, for which Bernhardt had been in rehearsal before it was deemed too blasphemous for the London stage.

Wilde's association with Paris is now a widely recognized commonplace. This short tour of selected Wilde sites – some new, some old, some ephemeral, but all charged with meaning and emotion – shows the persistence and adaptability of the association between Paris and Wilde, as it comes into view in cemeteries and hotels, libraries and museums, cinema screens, hearts, and imaginations. This tour is also the springboard for our volume on *Oscar Wilde's Paris*, which looks back at how Wilde's now mythic association with Paris began.

Situating Wilde in Paris

That Wilde's life, career, and celebrity were built across different national cultures informs important scholarship on the writer. There is the Irish Wilde, explored in Declan Kiberd's *Inventing Ireland* (1995), Jerusha McCormack's collection *Wilde the Irishman* (1998), and Jarlath Killeen's *The Faiths of Oscar Wilde* (2005), who used his difference as an Irish subject to reinvent the language and culture of Shakespeare. There is the Hellenistic Wilde, steeped in classical Greek literature, culture, and philosophy, illuminated by Iain Ross's *Oscar Wilde and Ancient Greece* (2013). There is the American Wilde, brought to life in Michèle Mendelssohn's biography *Making Oscar Wilde* (2018) and John Cooper's *Oscar Wilde in America* website, who used his year-long tour across North America to discover himself abroad as a writer and personality.[3] There is the English Wilde, discussed in Michael Patrick Gillespie's *Branding Oscar Wilde* (2018), who conquered London society and the London stage. And then of course there is the French Wilde, memorably evoked in Richard Ellmann's best-selling 1987 biography of the writer as well as Pascal Aquien's *Oscar Wilde: Les mots et les songes* (2006) – the Wilde who made France, and specifically Paris, the setting for both his exaltation and his exile, while taking a few side trips through Europe and North Africa along the way.[4]

Several studies have likewise brought focus to Wilde's particular ties to Paris. One of our volume's contributors, Nicholas Frankel, has recently published the most comprehensive biography focusing on Wilde's life after his release from prison. The title of his book – *Oscar Wilde: The Unrepentant Years* (2017) – succinctly makes his argument, and challenges the traditionally doom-inflected story of Wilde's final years in Paris.[5] The affiliation of the Irish author and the French capital has also nourished a handful of transnational studies, including David Charles Rose's *Oscar Wilde's Elegant Republic* (2015), Herbert Lottman's *Oscar Wilde à Paris* (2007), and Jens Rosteck's *Die Sphinx verstummt: Oscar Wilde in Paris* (2000).[6]

Our volume embraces this transnational approach in Wilde scholarship, while also extending its temporal parameters. Previous studies have primarily addressed Wilde's association with the city during his lifetime, and not the period after 1900 when publishers, writers, and artists were assessing his value and competing over his memory. *The Reception of Oscar Wilde in Europe* (2010), edited by another one of our contributors, Stefano Evangelista, is a noteworthy exception that moves beyond the strict horizon of Wilde's lifetime to investigate the making of his reputation in Europe after his death.[7] With a nod to this broader remit, but focusing on Paris as a key site for Wildean cultural production, *Oscar Wilde's Paris* not only brings new critical attention to the many facets of Wilde's Parisian adventures when he was alive, but also considers the Parisian afterlife that suffuses his posthumous legacy, tracing a cultural history of the Irish writer in the city over a roughly sixty-year period, from the 1880s to the 1940s.[8]

During these formative years, which include Wilde's rise to literary successes, his trials and imprisonment, his Parisian self-exile and death, and his afterlife as a figure of notoriety and legend, his relationship with the city developed in literature, journalism, and the visual arts, as well as in the city's famous cafes, bars, restaurants, hotels, and cemeteries. This relationship rested on three touchstones. The first was that Wilde passionately pursued the relationship. He called Paris "the most wonderful city in the world, the only civilised capital; the only place on earth where you find absolute toleration for all human frailties, with passionate admiration for all human virtues and capacities."[9] Paris, evoking notions of personal and artistic freedoms, was integral to his self-image as a writer and an aesthetic rebel and as an expatriate Irishman driven out by the English. A second important touchstone was that Wilde's connection to the metropolis had a significant impact on his career and cultural legacy. His orientation towards the city after his 1897 release from prison and his untimely death there at the age of forty-six has shaped how he has influenced literature and been remembered. He had many French disciples, although his influence was not always acknowledged and sometimes resisted. Several of his early biographers were also French, as were some of his early critics, who described him as "l'écrivain français" and "l'homosexuel."[10] That this memory of Wilde has, in turn, become important to the image of Paris itself has become the third touchstone. Wilde's Paris story is important to the larger story of Paris. Whether as ambitious aesthete, Francophile flâneur, or disreputable expatriate, remembered in literature, memoirs, and hotel lobbies, Wilde has become one of the city's achievements and symbols, and one more of its undeniable attractions.

Bringing together Wilde scholars from Belgium, Britain, Canada, France, and the United States to build a transnational understanding of Wilde's association with Paris, *Oscar Wilde's Paris* convenes specialist knowledge and new research to explore these different touchstones of the writer's affiliation with, and affinity for, the French capital that formed during and after his lifetime. Organized into five sections, each containing paired chapters, our volume examines various cultural iterations of "Oscar Wilde's Paris," from his relationship with the city streets, hotels, cafes, restaurants, museums, and inhabitants, to the city journalism that developed around him especially after his fall, to the tangible (and intangible) archival traces he left and generated, to his not-so-straightforward literary influence on Parisian writers, and to the different legends that competed to memorialize his Paris story and shape his legacy.

Wilde City

Our volume opens with a section devoted to the "Wilde City" and the role Paris played in Wilde's own self-fashioning as a writer and artist over his lifetime. If, as Michèle Mendelssohn has argued, Wilde was "made" in North America after a successful year-long tour that turned him into a celebrity, he remade himself again in Paris, the city where he spent several months immediately after his American tour and where he repeatedly returned in the years that followed. In the last two decades of his life, which saw his spectacular rise and fall as a celebrity writer, he spent three extended periods in the city that were formative for his writing, career, and legacy.

Wilde was not the first traveller to be seduced by the city of Paris. Like many others before him, he revelled in the city's distinctive urban environment: its cafes, restaurants, and terraces, kiosks and bookshops, boulevards and parks, museums and exhibitions, dinner parties and salons, and hotels and nightlife. These spaces animated his voluminous correspondence during his many visits and residencies in the city, a complicated mix of glamour and grit. His letters were often written in these spaces, composed on stationery bearing the letterheads of the places he frequented: at the Hôtel Continental in the early 1880s when first flush with cash, fame, and ambition, and later, in the late 1890s, at the more bohemian Calisaya bar when his fame had turned to infamy.

Paris's urban spaces likewise permeated Wilde's literary imagination. In *The Picture of Dorian Gray*, Paris and the queer painter Basil Hallward are envisioned together. Basil is invited to Paris to exhibit his idolatrous painting of the handsome Dorian Gray. Later, it is in Paris that Basil plans to "take a studio" to complete "a great picture." Paris is imagined as having the exhibition spaces and studios that can support

Basil's queer art and provide it a more appreciative public. After Dorian murders Basil, he allows the world to think the artist simply went off to Paris.[11] In *The Importance of Being Earnest*, Paris is again imagined as the place to send incorrigible characters. Jack enlists Paris's Grand Hotel as the place to dispose of his naughty alter ego Ernest, who has supposedly died of some unspoken Parisian debauchery.[12] In the Wildean imagination, Parisian spaces offer alternative artistic and moral lives to what is possible in London. They are also spaces where Londoners can supposedly disappear or be killed off – a preternatural imagining given Wilde's own biography. For Wilde, Paris is forever the site of alternative possibilities.

But long before the London sex trials effectively destroyed Wilde in 1895, confining him to prison, forcing him into exile (mainly in Paris), and eventually leading to his early death in 1900, Wilde thrived on the city's affordances. These affordances were not only its unique spaces, but also the mix of people who lived in and flocked to the city. As "the capital of the nineteenth century," in Walter Benjamin's well-known formulation, people from around the world streamed into the city – business people, travellers, tourists, students, tradespeople, political exiles, some with means and some without.[13] When Wilde came to the city, he sought out social connection; he was a literary networker *par excellence*. During his first long stay in Paris in 1883, he set out to meet the titans of French literature, as part of a campaign to gain literary legitimacy. By his second long stay in the early 1890s, his social connections in Paris grew as he attended soirées hosted by Stéphane Mallarmé and met Marcel Proust. At that point, however, and after the publication of *The Picture of Dorian Gray*, Wilde's ambition to seek out France's cultural notables was matched by aspiring writers and artists who sought to meet him, such as the young André Gide, Pierre Louÿs, and Henry Davray, all of whom would eventually become important to his cultural memory.

Paris was formative for Wilde's life and career, as it was for countless others before him, because of its concentration of spaces and peoples invested in art, culture, and creative freedoms. For Wilde, inhabiting the city at different periods in his career and navigating transnational social networks was a rite of passage. It was a sign of his arrival as a writer on the world stage, as well as a licence to express himself uninhibitedly. He is famous for writing his avant-garde symbolist play *Salomé* during his second long visit to Paris in 1891,[14] a drama that pushed the boundaries of expression by highlighting themes of deviant sexual desire, patriarchy, and femicide. Inspired by the creative vitality of the city and keen to adopt Parisian avant-garde styles and movements, he wrote the play in strange, archaic French, with the famous Parisian actress Sarah Bernhardt in the lead role.[15] His linguistic experimentation with an ornate and decorative French language was a symbolic act of adopting an aesthetic of art for art's sake. A group of young French writers, Pierre Louÿs, Marcel Schwob, and others, lent him a hand, themselves inspired by Wilde's Francophilia and combining it with their own Anglophilia in an erotic dance of transnational aesthetics. With its presumed freedom of expression and moral permissiveness, which allowed art to take precedence over moral judgment, Paris was for Wilde the springboard for a rebellious aesthetics and an erotic imagination that were constitutive for him, both in art and in life.

Of course, Wilde's 1895 trials and imprisonment changed his social standing, even in Paris. Many of the more established artists, writers, and journalists with whom he had fraternized fell away, with the exception of the most loyal. In his last years in Paris, he was no longer an elegant guest, mesmerizing the party with his conversation and quips. He was instead often found drinking and smoking in cafes surrounded by a younger, more bohemian set of artists and writers and picking up passers-by. A resolutely non-conformist, expatriate, and transnational sociability emerged around this outsider Wilde in outings that perhaps afforded him a more liberating and "unrepentant" social life, in Frankel's phrase. At different stages of his life and career, Wilde sought and found affiliations with the various cultural groups of Paris, both when he was in search of literary legitimacy and grandeur, and when he sought refuge and an authentic life. The rich social fabric of Paris, with its different threads of consecration and marginality, made possible because it attracted so many people and so much diversity in the name of art, culture, and expression, drew Wilde to the city time and again, remaining a vital social element in his self-creation as an artist. In a life characterized by remarkable and dramatic transformations, Paris remained a constant object of Wilde's affections, even as his associations with it adapted and changed.

Nicholas Frankel's chapter, "Oscar Wilde and 'the artistic capital of the world,'" introduces the section by attending to how Wilde fashioned himself as a writer during his many sojourns in the French capital. According to Frankel, Wilde conceived of Paris as a city with the power to confer a unique artistic respectability and freedom – a city where he could escape the confines of identity conferred by his Irish birth and English undergraduate education, establishing himself in a cultural field that supposedly recognized no laws and boundaries other than those of art. Frankel shows how Wilde repeatedly drew on the city's complex social environment to gain status, position himself, and deepen ties within the Parisian cultural field in order to establish himself as an artist in this world republic of letters.

If Frankel shows how Wilde counted on his social contacts to position himself as a man of letters, Paisley Mann charts how he also navigated the city's urban spaces to do the same. In her chapter "'I am not really myself except in the midst of elegant crowds': The Role of Paris in Wilde's Identity Formation," Mann investigates how Wilde's encounters with the physical spaces of Paris functioned as a means to craft himself and to assert his cultural knowledge and sense of style. Mann uncovers the hotels, boulevards, and cafes that figure in Wilde's poetry and letters to suggest that he used these urban spaces as socio-spatial markers to fashion an identity as a writer increasingly antagonistic to England and as a Londoner increasingly disillusioned with that city's restrictive mores.

By tracing Wilde's interactions with the social, geographical, and material fabric of the city, Frankel and Mann illuminate the vital historical connections between physical places and lived experience that underlie Wilde's passionate romance with Paris.

Journalistic Advocacy

If Wilde claimed Paris as his own, it could be said that Paris also claimed him as its own. Parisian journalism played a key role in the city's appropriation of the writer and his tragedy as its own to remember and denounce, reinforcing his association with Paris and promulgating the uptake of his legacy. Wilde's three trials in the spring of 1895 were the critical moment in this development. This was, of course, when Wilde sued the Marquess of Queensberry for libel, only to withdraw his charges once the libel trial collapsed. The incriminating evidence produced in that first trial triggered his arrest on charges of "gross indecency" and eventual conviction and sentencing to prison for two years with hard labour.

Even before his trials, as our contributor Rebecca Mitchell has previously documented, the Parisian press took an interest in Wilde and made him known in the city.[16] France's long political history, geographical proximity, and cultural exchanges with Britain meant that British affairs permeated French journalism, and Wilde's insertion into Parisian literary circles in the 1880s and early 1890s helped make him a recognized figure and a ready-to-deploy topic for the city's journalists. Interviewed by *L'Echo de Paris* and profiled in *Le Figaro* in 1891 and translated by Stuart Merrill, Marcel Schwob, and Gaston Bonnefont for the periodical press in the same period, Wilde was an appealing British figure already in the memory of the Parisian press and part of its background reality when the news of his trials broke in spring 1895.[17]

The structure of Paris's media system likewise meant that Wilde's trials were extensively covered. There were over a hundred daily newspapers in the city, pushing and competing with each other to cover his trials day in and day out, from start to finish. Well-capitalized Parisian newspapers employed journalists on the ground in London to sit in the Old Bailey Court and report on the proceedings, while news agencies similarly ensured a steady flow of information. Telegraphic technology enabled such information to be disseminated expeditiously with little delay, and was often able to report on what happened in court the previous day. Not restricted by the same practices of silence as the British press (when it came to "nameless offences" such as homosexuality), Parisian newspapers also printed names of people mentioned during the trials that were suppressed in the British papers, even mentioning the current prime minister, Lord Rosebery, whose name came up during the trials in the form of rumours about his sexual preference for men.[18] As a result, the Wilde trials' coverage by Parisian newspapers was second only to newspapers in London, and sometimes with exclusive and uncensored details.

This coverage was also unique. Parisian journalists wrote differently about the scandal than did British journalists. In addition to reporting on the case, they published lengthy columns by leading journalists who commented passionately on the trials and followed not only the case, but also Wilde's incarceration. Our volume's second section, on "Journalistic Advocacy," highlights the city journalism that took up Wilde's trials as a Parisian news story and then played a key role in championing him, both during his lifetime and afterwards.

Colette Colligan's opening chapter in this section focuses on "How Parisian Journalists Changed Their Minds about the Wilde Scandal." Examining how journalists mobilized opinion during his trials, this chapter accesses the French news archive and previously undiscovered articles. The digitization of these archives makes them legible in new ways, revealing not only the extent to which Parisian journalists reported on the trials, but also the extent to which they communicated about the scandal differently than in Britain and, indeed, elsewhere in the world. By scaling up analysis of Parisian news articles and reading their complex interdependencies through different social theories of scandal, Colligan shows that Parisian journalists collectively turned the Wilde scandal into a larger outcry against moral hypocrisy and carceral injustice and, in the process, centred Paris as a site of queer advocacy and as a stage for Wilde's eventual resurgence.

Petra Dierkes continues the examination of how Parisian journalism championed Wilde's cause after his fall in her chapter "Oscar Wilde and Henry-D. Davray: Reviewing, Translating, and Publishing Wilde for the *Mercure de France.*" If Wilde was no longer a topic of daily news coverage and commentary in Parisian daily newspapers after his trials and prison sentence, he remained a permanent topic, and presence, in the more specialized periodical press. Dierkes argues that the Parisian journal *Mercure de France* strategically used its platform to bolster Wilde's literary reputation after 1895, even as other Parisian friends turned against him. This championing of Wilde was accomplished through the agency of Henry Davray (1873–1944), one of Wilde's most prolific early French translators, and Rachilde (Marguerite Eymery-Vallette, 1860–1953), the journal's co-editor, skilled social networkers with an eye on the future of queer art. The journal benefited from the affordances and reach of journalism as it could publish pieces quickly and continuously and in a variety of formats – such as reviews, essays, translations – to promote Wilde.

As this chapter also reveals, the *Mercure de France*'s support for Wilde lasted well into the 1920s and extended its advocacy beyond journalism to stand-alone volumes devoted to Wilde, such as Davray's translations into French of Wilde's *Ballade de la geôle de Reading* (1898) and *De profundis* (1905); co-translations of critical and biographical titles such as Arthur Ransome's *Oscar Wilde* (1914) and Frank Harris's *La vie et les confessions d'Oscar Wilde* (1928); and his biography *Oscar Wilde: La tragédie finale* (1928).[19] Building on the journalistic advocacy that developed around the trials, the *Mercure de France* thus played a central role in promoting Wilde's legacy in the early years of his obloquy. It was the Parisian counterpart to Robert Ross's work with the London publisher Methuen, which in 1908 had published the *Collected Works of Oscar Wilde* – a monumental project designed to consolidate the author's literary oeuvre and rehabilitate his reputation.[20] Davray was in close contact with many of those involved in the Methuen project, revealing not only how Wilde's London supporters continued their work transnationally with Parisian collaborators, but also the significant impact of Parisian advocacy on Wilde's literary legacy and memory.

Archive and Anecdote

Wilde's association with Paris also has a powerful archival trace. This association is archival in orientation insofar as "archives" can be defined as aggregations of memory, feeling, and legend that persist in material and non-material forms through time. Indeed, the mythic resonance of

Wilde's affiliation with Paris is partly an effect of its being archival: this myth can be understood as a compendium of (sometimes conflicting) memories preserved and promulgated in a variety of unique formats, from the anecdotal to the documentary. To excavate and explore the extraordinary records of "Oscar Wilde's Paris" is thus also to delve into what Ann Cvetkovich would call an "archive of feelings," an accumulation of lore in different modes of materiality – not all of it factually reliable.[21]

Although the written record of this legendary association is imaginatively located in Paris, much of it is documented in English. The lore surrounding Wilde's final, post-prison years in Paris (the period stretching roughly from 1898 to 1900) is particularly rich in anecdotes. Stories about this period animate some of the Wilde legend's most familiar elements: that during those final Parisian years the gifted writer was no longer able to write, but remained a witty and charming conversationalist; that Wilde was lonely and destitute to a degree that imperilled his dignity; and perhaps most importantly, that the city he loved had become a refuge. In the aggregation of these anecdotes, we begin to glimpse a version of the popular image of Wilde the suffering martyr that Parisian journalists had invented when covering his incarceration, an image that Robert Ross further cultivated with his highly edited publication of *De Profundis* in 1905.[22] Located specifically in Paris, this set of associations is organized around the image of Wilde as an embattled secular saint. In this Paris legend, Wilde is an outcast misunderstood by the majority, but one whose tragic life is endowed with special meaning for a privileged minority capable of identifying with the unique – and yet somehow also universal – predicament of the rebel-aesthete. At its core, this mythic image is also defined by loss: the Wilde who lived in Paris at the end of the nineteenth century is a tragic figure who has been reduced in circumstances, in opportunities, and in artistic output: a figure transformed by suffering into a lesser version of himself. In this sense, the post-prison Wilde in Paris is already a creature of memory, one whose best days were even then behind him, though it was the city that had helped make him extraordinary.

In the early memoirs that situate Wilde in Paris, we can trace the origins of many of the stories that got told about the expatriate Irish writer; by propagating and embroidering a nascent mythology, they also perform a critical archival function in recording and preserving a particular narrative. Arthur Ransome's "Oscar Wilde in Paris," which appeared in magazines on both sides of the Atlantic in 1911, is a prime example. Ransome's highly sympathetic article appeared at a critical historical moment in the development of the Wilde myth. It came well after the 1908 publication of Ross's multi-volume edition of Wilde's *Collected Works*, and yet soon enough after the writer's 1900 death for the living memories of those who knew Wilde to have remained vibrant.

Ransome expands on "how intimately Paris was connected with his life," and indeed how the French capital provides an ideal setting for Wildean storytelling: "He was always at home in Paris, and he died there," Ransome observes:

> On the background of that city, rather than of London, the drama of his life stands out, cleared of side issues, far enough away to be seen by us, with its lighthearted, exuberant beginning, its moment of glory [...] its catastrophe, which he turned into a momentary renaissance, its defeat and sombre end.[23]

To understand Wilde's life through the familiar metaphor of theatre, in other words, requires the placement of that drama on a stage set up as "Paris." Ransome's piece makes several other moves that have become hallmarks of Wildean mythologizing. He recounts anecdotes about Wilde's times in the city; he drops the names of multiple French literary figures with whom Wilde had contact; he cites precise information about Parisian daily life, including geographical locations; and he seeks to correct factual errors to the record, noting, for instance, the disagreements over the quality of Wilde's French and the discrepancies between accounts of the composition of *Salomé*. Although Ransome establishes the long duration of Wilde's association with the French capital (beginning in the 1870s), his account nevertheless privileges the 1890s, and the writer's trials and imprisonment remain a narrative fulcrum. "The news of his condemnation roused a ferment in Paris," we are told, as Wilde's French loyalists rallied around an absent and incarcerated Oscar. Once the scandalous writer had become unmentionable, "when English journalists only stopped abusing him to close their lips over his name, [...] when admiration of his books was become a secret thing, like a half-ashamed religion," Wilde retained a virtual presence in the City of Light that anticipated his exile there. "If there is any truth to the saying that we are where we are loved," Ransome suggests, "then Oscar Wilde may indeed be said to have been in Paris."[24]

Laurence Housman's elegiac *Echo de Paris* (1923) goes further still in conceptually suturing Wilde's memory to the city. For Housman, who borrows the name of a prominent French newspaper for his title, place becomes a surrogate for memory itself. In other words, if Wilde is a figure of memory, that memory is inextricable from its location in Paris. Housman's book recalls in "a free rendering of what was actually said" an 1899 cafe conversation featuring himself, Wilde, Robert Ross, and Henry Davray. The memoir's use of the dialogue form pays tribute to the author of *Intentions*, as does its neo-Wildean subtitle, "A Study from Life," which invites the reader to imagine the text along the pictorial lines of a still-life painting. As an imaginative reconstruction of a conversation, Housman takes a certain artistic licence with historical precision, all the while adopting Ransome's gambit of aggregating and preserving anecdotes. For example, Housman endorses the notion that Wilde's talent was primarily verbal, for "as a personality he was more considerable than as a writer," and he labels Wilde "the most accomplished talker I ever met."[25] Housman's approach to memory and history is appropriately Wildean in its prioritizing of the vitality of storytelling over the facts themselves, and yet archival in its evident desire to preserve a cultural legacy defined by a sense of loss. These archival dimensions of Wilde's association with Paris take up this volume's third section.

Narrativizing the past by assembling a patchwork of facts and anecdotes has long troubled accounts of Wilde's Paris death, as Joseph Bristow establishes in "Disputed Memories: Oscar Wilde's Deathbed at the Hôtel d'Alsace." That Wilde "died in terrible circumstances" at the Hôtel d'Alsace on 30 November 1900 is attested to by multiple accounts, but those accounts differ in numerous details, perhaps most sensationally in Frank Harris's much-disputed and grotesque account of Wilde's death being marked by an otolaryngologeous explosion of mucus and blood. The facts surrounding Wilde's deathbed conversion to the Roman Catholic Church have similarly been obscured by competing anecdotes. With access to an untapped archive in the records preserved by the Passionist priest Father Cuthbert Dunne, who was with Wilde in his last moments, Bristow untangles legend from reality with a keen attentiveness to the interests and biases of those whose records have survived. (Wilde, for his part, did indeed become a Catholic.) Just as the memorialization of Wilde's death has been a function of competing and often inaccurate accounts, Bristow shows how one archive of lore and often-partisan mythmaking stacks up against another one animated by scrupulous attention to fact and historical detail.

Information in any archive is often partial and fragmentary, particularly when that archive is distributed across languages and national borders, as Rebecca N. Mitchell shows in "Oscar Wilde's French Fragments," the section's paired chapter. Drawing, like Bristow, on previously overlooked archival sources, she is equally concerned with challenging inaccuracies and misconceptions that distort literary history. Mitchell explores the fragmentary manuscript traces of Wilde's characteristically epigrammatic style of writing in French to suggest that these early French fragments represent still-nascent aspects of his composition practice and literary style, and that their treatment and publication in French venues helped determine the contours of Wilde's reputation there, which persists to this day. Her chapter follows the history of these fragments and their transmission in later works, including the oral tales collected as Wildean remnants by Léon Guillot de Saix (1885–1964), as evidence of the continued commitment to the idea of Wilde's fraternity with Paris and with French language and letters.[26] Bristow and Mitchell excavate the unusual records of Wilde in Paris which aggregated and relayed the writer's memory, sealing his bond with the city. There are, for example, several versions of Wilde's quip about the ghastly wallpaper that covered the walls of the Hôtel d'Alsace as he lay dying – "One of us has to go" – and every transmission of this anecdote continues to build this "archive of feelings" that has given shape to Wilde's association with Paris.[27]

Literary Influence and Appropriation

While the horrors of Parisian wallpaper festooned with chocolate-coloured flowers on a blue background might have inspired one of the aesthete's last quips, it was the marvels of French language and literature that first attracted Wilde to Paris and that gave rise to successful – and sometimes not so successful – transnational literary "cross-pollination" that spread through Paris's "republic of letters" and beyond.[28]

French and Greek, Wilde once said, were the only two languages that mattered. He also gushed about Gustave Flaubert. To Max Beerbohm he reputedly admitted, "I never read Flaubert's *Tentation de St. Antoine* without signing my name at the end of it. *Que voulez-vous*?" and to W.E. Henley, he added, "Yes! Flaubert is my master, and when I get on with my translation of the *Tentation* I shall be Flaubert II ... "[29] Nor was Flaubert the only French writer to have captured Wilde's imagination. Honoré de Balzac, Charles Baudelaire, and Théophile Gautier also shaped the distinctive taste for anti-realism, romanticism, and literary decadence that flavoured all his writing.[30] From Wilde's encounters with established and up-and-coming authors in Parisian restaurants, at dinners, and in salons, he drew inspiration and French cachet. He even found literary collaborators, as shown by his French play *Salomé*, inspired by the French tradition of the femme fatale and corrected with the help of several Parisian writers. Wilde actively profiled himself as a Parisian writer to see his literary greatness realized in that cultural capital. Of course, some criticized him for borrowing too heavily from the French-language writers he loved and admired, such as Alexandre Dumas fils, Guy de Maupassant, and especially Joris-Karl Huysmans. He was an insatiable devourer of French literature, in which he found an inexhaustible source of images, feelings, and turns of phrase to nourish and inspire his own writing. In response to criticism that his appropriations amounted to a form of plagiarism,[31] he quipped: "[W]hen I see a monstrous tulip with *four* wonderful petals in someone else's garden, I am impelled to grow a monstrous tulip with *five* wonderful petals, but that is no reason why someone should grow a tulip with only *three* petals."[32]

As he was inspired by French writing, he too inspired many French writers, both in his lifetime and after. In *Oscar Wilde, écrivain français* (1975), Jacques de Langlade was one of the first critics to draw attention to Wilde's influence on French literature, devoting entire chapters to the impact he had on writers such as André Gide, Marcel Proust, and Jean Cocteau.[33] Tracing this influence introduces certain challenges, however. If Wilde was always prepared to sign Flaubert's works as his own, not all French writers were prepared to sign their names to Wilde's works, or to have their works associated with his style. For some younger Parisian writers especially, association with the writer and acknowledgment of his literary influence proved damaging to their careers. It is as if Wilde's sexual and gender transgressions, in life and in art, had taken on the quality of the "poisonous influences" explored in *The Picture of Dorian Gray*.[34] André Gide felt poisoned by Wilde. So too did Pierre Louÿs, one of Wilde's most important points of contact with literary Paris. Another writer, Catulle Mendès, famously challenged the journalist Jules Huret to a duel when he insinuated in his column published at the time of the trials that he was part of Wilde's literary and social circle. Wilde's literary influence remained a complicated site of struggle for Parisian writers, exposing the pangs that sometimes arose from his romance with French culture.

Our fourth section delves into the troubled literary coordinates of Wilde's association with Parisian culture as writers wrestled over claiming (and disavowing) his influence both when he was alive and after. In "Oscar Wilde and Pierre Louÿs: the Construction of a Literary Friendship," Clément Dessy and Stefano Evangelista offer a detailed analysis of the relationship struck between Wilde and the Belgian-born Pierre Louÿs (1870–1925). They begin by reconstructing the fertile exchange of ideas and formation of ties between Wilde and Louÿs when they met in the early 1890s. Each writer, at first, enthusiastically played up their literary friendship and mutual influence. They referred to each other in their writing, experimented with translating each other, and displayed Anglophilia and Francophilia, each using the other to position himself as a cosmopolitan writer of the world pushing the boundaries of contemporary sexual morality. This literary friendship did not survive more than a couple of years, however, as Louÿs distanced himself from Wilde's homosexuality and the spectacular scandal that surrounded him. Yet, as Dessy and Evangelista demonstrate, even though Louÿs may have abandoned his friendship with Wilde, the Irish writer's influence on him persisted in his choice of themes and literary forms. Wilde's disavowed influence on the writer was even noted by André Gide when he himself was struggling with Wilde's irresistible hold over him and coming to terms with his own position as a young queer writer.

Kristin Mahoney, in the second paired chapter of this section, extends this examination by looking at another facet of the difficulties encountered in claiming – or indeed, inhabiting – Wilde's literary influence. Her chapter on "Oscar Wilde, Jacques d'Adelswärd Fersen, and Cross-Channel Decadence in the Twentieth Century" focuses on the queer writer Fersen (1880–1923) who ventured to claim Wilde as his master, only to face ridicule and derision by other keepers of his legacy. He worked to attract comparisons between himself and Wilde throughout his career. His novel *Lord Lyllian* (1905) is a French revision of *The Picture of Dorian Gray*, just one of his many attempts to reincarnate Wilde, re-enact his transgressions, and reproduce his style and persona.[35] Fersen's appropriations of Wilde's sexual dissidence, as well as his own run-ins with the law, even inspired others to write underground pornography depicting Wilde, Fersen, and others partaking in wild sexual orgies.[36] Fersen's example shows that at least some queer Parisian writers emerging in the years just after Wilde's death imitated both his aesthetic and sexual rebellion.

As Mahoney discovers, however, Fersen's Wildean literary performances were dismissed by writers such as Norman Douglas and Compton Mackenzie as laughable failures. The issue that emerged in their queer expatriate literary circle was not whether to claim Wilde's influence, but whether a writer such as Fersen deserved to claim that influence, or even measured up to it. Mahoney attends to the manner in which the critique of Fersen's uptake of Wildean decadence became an opportunity for French and British writers to generate a mode of Decadent modernism meant to carry forward the Decadent ethos as well as the Wilde legend into the twentieth century, while at the same time cultivating through negative affect how Wilde's transnational literary legacy could and should be passed on.

The Wildean textual entanglements uncovered by Dessy and Evangelista, along with Mahoney, demonstrate Parisian writers' deep allegiance to the Francophile Irishman and their role in building his literary legacy. And yet, at the same time, they show how his influence risked disavowal and suffered from gaps in memory as well as problems of transmission. This also holds true for a later generation of French writers after Louÿs and Fersen. As Emmanuel Vernadakis argues, the writing of the queer French-American writer Julien Green (1900–98) bears the imprint of Wilde's influence, yet remains unacknowledged and unwanted.[37] Of all Wilde's associations with Parisian culture, his literary influence and appropriation raised the most questions, such as whether he should pilfer from the French writers he admired, and whether young Parisian writers wanted to submit to his seductive literary charms, and, in yet another formulation, whether Wilde's Parisian imitators were equal to the Decadent stylings of their master. Either way, Wilde's indelible impact on the Decadent literary turn of fin-de-siècle Paris remains a central component of his legacy.

Legend and Legacy

Our title, *Oscar Wilde's Paris*, implies that "Wilde's" is a particular version of the French capital, palpable in specific geographical sites, in literary networks, in archives, in lore, and in the journalistic record. To rearrange the direction of the title's possessive phrase into "Paris's Oscar Wilde" is to survey this generative association from yet another perspective, and to discover how the storied city turned Wilde into its very own legend.

That Wilde belongs to Paris, in this sense, is best apprehended at a site that is at once unassuming and completely appropriate. It is, above all, to discover a civic version of Wilde – the writer's adoption by the French public and his integration into the contemporary urban fabric of the capital. Paris's Bibliothèque Oscar Wilde, formerly the Bibliothèque St-Fargeau, is a local library serving a largely lower-income community. Located in the twentieth arrondissement, it is remote from better-known Left and Right Bank locations chronicled in our volume's first section on the "Wilde City." Part of the City of Paris's municipal library system, it was renamed in Wilde's honour in November 2011, just as the protective glass barriers were being installed around the writer's tomb in the nearby Père Lachaise Cemetery. A single-storey building surrounded by Brutalist 1970s concrete apartment towers, Wilde's namesake library is neither a sumptuous nor a glamorous place. Its website indicates that it serves the local neighbourhood, and, in clear homage to Wilde's place in dramatic literary history, it also specializes in contemporary theatre.

Despite (or perhaps because of) its humble setting, the *bibliothèque* is a friendly and welcoming place. Like many civic libraries, it offers access to computers and community services for the surrounding population, in addition to a modest but comprehensive collection of books. There are no grand pictorial tributes to Wilde inside the library; instead, Wilde's Parisian legacy is celebrated more quietly with an impressively complete collection of his writings. In this place, we are reminded that Wilde's cultural legacy is ultimately comprised of words. Wilde titles are distributed throughout the library stacks into multiple sections such as Drama, Prose Fiction, and Poetry – a testament to the generic diversity of his writings – and thus fully integrated into the larger context of a civic library. The Drama section boasts multiple copies of the plays, and the various translations of *The Importance of Being Earnest*, for example (rendered as *L'Importance d'être sérieux* in one translation, and the more familiar *L'Importance d'être constant* in another), suggest the vitality of Wilde's uptake in the French language. Works in the original English, along with those in French translation, are shelved together, a testament to Wilde's enduringly bilingual and cross-cultural resonance. The collection is so inclusive that even some speculative and dubious attributions make an appearance: *Teleny*, the anonymously authored 1893 gay erotic novel that has been speculatively attributed to Wilde is there, as is the even more obscure *La chasse à l'opossum*, a title that appears nowhere in (its ostensibly original) English.

In assembling this collection, the City of Paris's librarians have been as inclusive as possible in their presentation of the literary Wilde as a shared cultural resource. For Wilde to belong to Paris, after all, means that he must belong to Parisians. The fact that Wilde is being presented, in the form of the *bibliothèque*, to a community visibly marked by socially and economically disadvantageous circumstances offers us yet another context for understanding the Irish writer's layered and complex mythology in his final home. This is not the decadent Wilde of *Le portrait de Dorian Gray* or *Salomé*, nor is it the comic high society playwright of *Constant*, *Un mari idéal*, or *L'Éventail de Lady Windermere*. At the *bibliothèque*, we encounter instead the Wilde of "The Soul of Man under Socialism" or *The Ballad of Reading Gaol* – a writer committed to critiquing social injustice. That Wilde's literary legacy includes a responsiveness to suffering, inequality, and injustice has not gone unnoticed at the bibliothèque Oscar Wilde, judging by the sheer volume and diversity of his writings on offer there. The tribute signalled by the naming and stocking of this library may be modest and subtle, but it is also, perhaps, the most fitting of all, with Wilde's books being available to be read by the citizens of Paris, and at no charge.

The Wildean legacy proffered at the *bibliothèque* is both tangible and material, if decidedly unromantic. A much more evocative and better-known site that equally affords its visitors a tactile experience of the Wilde legend occupies the same Parisian arrondissement: the monumental tomb located at the eastern end of Père Lachaise Cemetery. The destination of innumerable pilgrimages, transformed by lipstick kisses into a queer shrine, the tomb, as Ellen Crowell observes in the volume's fifth section, "has always, for better or worse, stood in as a proxy for Wilde's physical body." In "Oscar Wilde's Tomb: *Silence* and the Aesthetics of Queer Memorial," Crowell establishes how, in the aftermath of Wilde's death, those individuals closest to the writer sought a suitable funerary monument for him. She explores the interpersonal and aesthetic politics that informed the commissioning of Jacob Epstein as the Paris tomb's sculptor, and how that choice must be understood as integral to how we remember Wilde today.[38] Noting how profoundly the aesthetics of funerary sculpture are in dialogue with both literary and queer history, Crowell also imagines how an alternate monument adorning Wilde's tomb might have differently configured that dialogue. By comparing Epstein's tomb with the radically different aesthetics that guided a rejected design, this one by the writer's close artistic collaborator and friend Charles Ricketts, Crowell considers how aesthetics have shaped twentieth and twenty-first century approaches to queer memory, mourning, and modernity.

The imaginative possibilities of locating queer memory in Paris – albeit of a more abstruse if equally fervent kind – animate Gregory Mackie's chapter, "Un faux parisien: Sylvestre Dorian and *Oscar Wilde's Letters to Sarah Bernhardt*." In the early twentieth century, just as Wilde's tomb achieved the status of the ultimately authentic (indeed, intimate) site of contact with his legacy, competing and less genuine ways of memorializing him proliferated in print. By the 1920s, with the publication of multiple memoirs about his life and collections of his letters, Wilde's posthumous legend was reinforced by a rapidly expanding print corpus. Investigating the overlooked 1924 newspaper articles that initially appeared in the *Detroit Free Press* before being collected as the booklet *Oscar Wilde's Letters to Sarah Bernhardt*, this chapter explores the Parisian coordinates of celebrity, fantasy, and mythmaking in early twentieth-century America that informed Wilde's afterlife. That the Bernhardt letters were fakes contrived by the self-proclaimed "Parisian dramatist" Sylvestre Dorian (pseud. Brett Holland, 1898–1934), a queer American writer and impostor who had also circulated forgeries of Wilde manuscripts from Paris,[39] suggests that Wilde's legacy could continue to inspire new representations, desires, and performances long after the Irish writer's death, and in locations as remote from Paris as Detroit.

As these final chapters argue, the Wilde legend is a product of cultural memory – even in cases, such as Sylvestre Dorian's Bernhardt letters, of memorializing what had never actually existed. The notion of "Oscar Wilde's Paris," moreover, is best apprehended as a posthumous mental location; it is an imaginative construction that evokes loss and recovery simultaneously. As a place, but also as an idea, Paris can be understood as a beneficiary of Wilde's legacy, or, in other words, as the Irish writer's heir.

The Intertwining of Two Mythologies

What ultimately emerges from our cultural archaeology of this association is an understanding of the co-evolution of two mutually constitutive mythologies – the myth of Wilde and the myth of Paris. The myth of Wilde's artistic greatness and terrible martyrdom, that persistently alluring tragic narrative he helped create, was partly born of his ties to Paris. Paris was the city that helped him accumulate much-desired cultural capital and refine his persona as an artist and that also welcomed him when he was an outcast. The myth of Wilde, meanwhile, has been woven into the myth of Paris; it is suffused with a distinctly Parisian aura. In many ways, Wilde's Paris reflects the city's own myth-laden sense of itself: "There is but one Paris, *voyez-vous*, and Paris is France. It is the abode of artists; nay, it is la *ville artiste*," Wilde declared in 1892.[40] The city of freedom, the city of art, the city of the world, the city of revolution, and the city of light – so described by Pascale Casanova – acquired one more "gemlike flame" to further illuminate its own story of greatness.[41]

Intertwined, these two enduringly compelling myths have managed to weave themselves into each other's fabric. As Paris played a crucial role in the making of Wilde's literary career and legacy, so Wilde in turn was appropriated to become a newly resonant symbol for the city. As Wilde's presence in Paris made it an even more special place and paved the way for countless sojourns to the city, so Paris helped make Wilde an extraordinary figure. The myth of Wilde – itself constructed by many expatriate and border-crossing figures steeped in the nineteenth-century mythology of Paris – both anticipated and nurtured the idea of Paris for generations to come – for numerous writers, journalists, artists, and publishers moving through a hostile world and searching for the complex interactions and cultural formations that were possible in interwar Paris at the crossroads of modernity.[42]

Myths are stories of a culture that give it meaning and purpose to drive it forward. They shape belief and imagination and propel action and behaviour. Attentive to unexplored sources and the varied experiences of cultural life, *Oscar Wilde's Paris* elucidates Wilde's persistent and adaptable association with the French capital in the period of its formation to offer a historical paradigm of a larger social process that saw people gathering in certain places charged with myth, and the lived realities and artistic expressions such myth created and reflected. In their totality, the aim of this volume's chapters is, in a manner of speaking, transtemporal. To explore and assess the association of Wilde and Paris is to travel back into the nineteenth century, and through time, to the present. These two myths continue their romance to the present day. Wilde continues to renew the myth of Paris, and Paris reciprocates, co-sustaining an aesthetical orientation towards the world by invigorating an extraordinary life that encompassed both centrality and marginality.

NOTES

1 Wilde to Reginald Turner, 6 December 1898, in *The Complete Letters of Oscar Wilde*, ed. Merlin Holland and Rupert Hart-Davis (New York: Henry Holt, 2000), 1107.

2 See Dominique Morel and Merlin Holland, eds. *Oscar Wilde: L'impertinent absolu* (Paris: Paris-Musées, 2016).

3 See *Oscar Wilde in America: The Definitive Resource of Oscar Wilde's Visits to America*, https://www.oscarwildeinamerica.org. The first in-depth exploration of the American Wilde was Lloyd Lewis and Henry Justin Smith's *Oscar Wilde Discovers America, 1882* (New York: Harcourt Brace, 1935).

4 On Wilde's Irish background, see Declan Kiberd, *Inventing Ireland: The Literature of a Modern Nation* (London: Jonathan Cape, 1995); Jerusha McCormack, ed. *Wilde the Irishman* (New Haven, CT: Yale University Press, 1998); and Jarlath Killeen *The Faiths of Oscar Wilde: Catholicism, Folklore and Ireland* (Basingstoke, UK: Palgrave Macmillan, 2005). This reference to Shakespeare plays on Wilde's famous comment to Edmond de Goncourt, "Français de sympathie, je suis Irlandais de race, et les Anglais m'ont condamné à parler le langage de Shakespeare." See Wilde, *Complete Letters*, 505. On Wilde and ancient Greece, see Iain Ross, *Oscar Wilde and Ancient Greece* (Cambridge: Cambridge University Press, 2013).

On Wilde's American tour, see Michèle Mendelssohn, *Making Oscar Wilde* (Oxford: Oxford University Press, 2018); and on the marketing of his persona to the British public, see Michael Patrick Gillespie's *Branding Oscar Wilde* (New York: Routledge, 2018). For biographies that cover Wilde's deep ties to France, see, for example, Richard Ellmann, *Oscar Wilde* (London: Penguin, 1988), which has sections devoted to Wilde's exaltation and exile; and Pascal Aquien's *Oscar Wilde: Les mots et les songes* (Croissy-Beaubourg: Aden, 2006).

5 Nicholas Frankel, *Oscar Wilde: The Unrepentant Years* (Cambridge, MA: Harvard University Press, 2017).

6 See David Charles Rose's *Oscar Wilde's Elegant Republic: Transformation, Dislocation and Fantasy in Fin-de-Siècle Paris* (Newcastle upon Tyne: Cambridge Scholars, 2015); Herbert Lottman's *Oscar Wilde à Paris* (Paris: Fayard, 2007); Jens Rosteck's *Die Sphinx verstummt: Oscar Wilde in Paris* (Berlin: Propyläen, 2000).

7 See Stefano Evangelista, ed. *The Reception of Oscar Wilde in Europe* (London: Bloomsbury, 2010).

8 For another influential study of Wilde mythmaking, see John Stokes, *Oscar Wilde: Myths, Miracles, and Imitations* (Cambridge: Cambridge University Press, 1996).

9 Evangelista, *Reception*, 427.

10 See Jacques de Langlade, *Oscar Wilde, écrivain français* (Paris: Stock, 1975); and Robert Merle, *Oscar Wilde, ou la "destinée" de l'homosexuel* (Paris: Gallimard, 1955). Also see Léon Lemonnier, *La Vie d'Oscar Wilde* (Paris: Éditions de la Nouvelle Revue Critique, 1931).

11 See *The Complete Works of Oscar Wilde, Vol. 3, The Picture of Dorian Gray: The 1890 and 1891 Texts*, ed. Joseph Bristow (Oxford: Oxford University Press, 2005), 291.

12 See *The Complete Works of Oscar Wilde, Vol. 10, Plays 3: The Importance of Being Earnest; A Wife's Tragedy*, ed. Joseph W. Donohue (Oxford: Oxford University Press, 2019), 800. Wilde had stayed at the Grand Hotel on the Boulevard des Capucines in November and December of 1891.

13 See Walter Benjamin, "Paris, Capital of the Nineteenth Century," in *Reflections: Essays, Aphorisms, Autobiographical Writings*, trans. Edmund Jephcott (New York: Schoken Books, 1978).

14 Wilde stayed in Paris twice in 1891: the first trip was a short visit during part of February and March, and the second a longer stay from late October to late December.

15 On the French of Wilde's play, see Emily Eells, "Wilde's French *Salomé*," *Cahiers victoriens et édouardiens* 72 (Autumn 2010): 115–30. See also William A. Cohen, "Wilde's French," in *Wilde Discoveries: Traditions, Histories, Archives*, ed. Joseph Bristow (Toronto: University of Toronto Press, 2013), 233–59.

16 See Rebecca N. Mitchell, "Oscar Wilde and the French Press, 1880–91," *Victorian Periodicals Review* 49, no. 1 (Spring 2016): 123–48.

17 Mitchell, "Wilde and the French Press," 125. For a timeline of French translations of Wilde's works, see Paul Barnaby, "Timeline of the European Reception of Oscar Wilde" in Evangelista, *Reception*, xxi-lxxxii. The French-American writer Stuart Merrill was the first to translate Wilde into French, with his 1889 translation of "The Birthday of the Infanta." Marcel Schwob translated "The Selfish Giant" in 1891, and Gaston Bonnefont's translation of *Lady Windermere's Fan* appeared in 1892.

18 For an overview of French journalism in the nineteenth and early twentieth centuries, see Ross F. Collins, "Traitorous Collaboration: The Press in France, 1815–1914," in *The Rise of Western Journalism, 1815–1914*, ed. Ross F. Collins and E.M. Palmegiano (Jefferson, NC: McFarland, 2007), 71–105. On the suppression of public information about sex crimes, see H.G. Cocks, *Nameless Offences: Homosexual Desire in the Nineteenth Century* (London: I.B. Tauris, 2003).

19 See Wilde, *Ballade de la geôle de Reading*, trans. Henry-D. Davray (Paris: Mercure de France, 1898); *De Profundis, précédé de lettres écrites de la prison* (Paris: Mercure de France, 1905); Arthur Ransome, *Oscar Wilde*, trans. G. de Lautrec and H.-D. Davray (Paris: Mercure de France, 1914); Frank Harris, *La vie et les confessions d'Oscar Wilde*, trans. Henry-D. Davray and Madeleine Vernon (Paris: Mercure de France, 1928).

20 See Wilde, *The Collected Works*, ed. Robert Ross, 14 vols. (London: Methuen, 1908).

21 See Ann Cvetkovitch, *An Archive of Feelings: Trauma, Sexuality, and Lesbian Public Cultures* (Durham, NC: Duke University Press, 2003).

22 On Robert Ross's rehabilitative intentions for *De Profundis*, see Josephine M. Guy and Ian Small, *Oscar Wilde's Profession: Writing and the Culture Industry in the Late Nineteenth Century* (Oxford: Oxford University Press, 2000), 178–219; and Gregory Mackie, *Beautiful Untrue Things: Forging Oscar Wilde's Extraordinary Afterlife* (Toronto: University of Toronto Press, 2019), 34–40.

23 See Arthur Ransome, "Oscar Wilde in Paris," *T.P.'s Magazine* (London), vol. 2, no. 9 (June 1911): 427.

24 Ransome, "Oscar Wilde in Paris," 433.

25 See Laurence Housman, *Echo de Paris: A Study from Life* (London: Jonathan Cape, 1923), 14–15.

26 For a recent publication of Guillot de Saix's oral tales (*contes parlés*), see *Rien n'est vrai que le beau: oeuvres choisies, lettres*, ed. Pascal Aquien (Paris: Gallimard, 2019).

27 There are many versions of this anecdote. One of the best known, relayed in Richard Ellmann's biography, is that Wilde told his friend, the

Anglo-French writer Claire de Pratz (1866–1934), "My wallpaper and I are fighting a duel to the death. One or the other of us has to go." See Ellmann, *Oscar Wilde*, 581. Ellmann's ultimate source is Léon Guillot de Saix, "Souvenirs inédits sur Oscar Wilde," *L'Européen*, 8 May 1929.

28 On transnational cross-pollination, see Emily Eells, preface to *Two "Tombeaux" to Oscar Wilde: Jean Cocteau's "Le Portrait surnaturel de Dorian Gray" and Raymond Laurent's Essay on Wildean Aesthetics* (Buckinghamshire, UK: Rivendale Press, 2010); and Matthew Potolsky, *The Decadent Republic of Letters: Taste, Politics, and Cosmopolitan Community from Baudelaire to Beardsley* (Philadelphia: University of Pennsylvania Press, 2013).

29 Wilde told Maurice Sisley, writing for *Le Gaulois* in 1892, "To me there are only two languages in the world: French and Greek." See Ellmann, *Oscar Wilde*, 352. On Wilde's avowed admiration for Flaubert, see Max Beerbohm's letter to Reggie Turner from 15 April 1883, quoted in *Palgrave Advances in Oscar Wilde Studies*, ed. Frederick S. Roden (New York: Palgrave Macmillan, 2004), 11–12, and Wilde to W.E. Henley (? December 1888), *Complete Letters*, 372. Wilde never translated Flaubert's *Tentation de saint Antoine*.

30 On Wilde's admiration for these French writers, see John Stokes, "Wilde and Paris," in *Oscar Wilde in Context*, ed. Kerry Powell and Peter Raby (Cambridge: Cambridge University Press, 2013), 60–70.

31 Wilde had been accused of plagiarism throughout his career. See Joseph Bristow and Rebecca N. Mitchell, "On Oscar Wilde and Plagiarism," *Public Domain Review*, 13 January 2016, https://publicdomainreview.org/essay/on-oscar-wilde-and-plagiarism.

32 Wilde quoted in Robert Ross, introduction to *Salome* by Oscar Wilde (London: Methuen, 1912), xxiii.

33 See Jacques de Langlade, *Oscar Wilde, écrivain français* (Paris: Stock, 1975).

34 Wilde, *The Complete Works of Oscar Wilde, Vol. 3, The Picture of Dorian Gray*, 269.

35 See Adelswärd Fersen, *Messes Noires: Lord Lyllian* (Paris: Léon Vanier, 1905).

36 See Dr. A.-S. Lagail [Alphonse Gallais, pseud.], *Les Mémoires du Baron Jacques: Lubricités infernales de la noblesse décadente* (Priapeville [Paris?]: Librairie Galante, 1904).

37 See Emmanuel Vernadakis, "Oscar Wilde et Julien Green: marges, espaces et interlignes," *Études Greeniennes* 10 (2018): 11–26.

38 For a detailed account of the designing of the Epstein monument, see Simon Wilson, "From Greek Youth to Flying Demon Angel: Jacob Epstein's Studies for his Tomb for Oscar Wilde," *The Wildean* 56 (January 2020): 3–62.

39 On Holland's career as the Paris-based forger "Dorian Hope," see Mackie, *Beautiful Untrue Things*, 68–123.

40 See Maurice Sisley, "La *Salomé* de M. Oscar Wilde," *Le Gaulois* (29 June 1892), 1, quoted in E.H. Mikhail, *Oscar Wilde: Interviews and Recollections* (London: Macmillan, 1979), 1:189.

41 This is the myth of Paris, still powerful today, that is discussed in Pascale Casanova's impressive study, *La république mondiale des lettres* (Paris: Éditions du Seuil, 1999), and the remarkable collection of essays *Le Paris des étrangers: depuis un siècle*, ed. André Kaspi et Antoine Marès (Paris: Imprimerie nationale, 1989).

42 See Raymond Williams, "The Metropolis and the Emergence of Modernism," in *Unreal City: Urban Experience in Modern European Literature and Art*, ed. Edward Timms and David Kelley (Manchester: Manchester University Press, 1985), 13–24.

PART ONE

Wilde City

1 Oscar Wilde and "the artistic capital of the world"

NICHOLAS FRANKEL

Paris is the centre of art, the artistic capital of the world.

Wilde, reported in the *Pall Mall Budget*, 30 June 1892[1]

In June 1892, just days after the English censor had refused a performance licence for his play *Salomé*, Oscar Wilde declared that he would no longer call himself a citizen of a country that "showed such narrowness in its artistic judgement" and that he would leave England and settle henceforth in Paris. Paris is "the centre of art, the artistic capital of the world," he told the *Pall Mall Budget*: "There is but one Paris, *voyez-vous*," he told *Le Gaulois*: "it is the abode of artists; nay, it is *la ville artiste*."[2]

This determination to take up residence in Paris cannot have surprised Wilde's friends and acquaintances. Paris was "another fatherland," the Irish-born author declared, "of which I have long been enamoured."[3] He had spent long periods there, most recently the previous autumn, when *L'Echo de Paris* declared him "le great event" of the season and he told one English correspondent "Paris is so charming that I think of becoming a French poet!"[4] He had first visited the city briefly in 1867, accompanied by his mother and brother, and although he continued making short visits periodically right up to his arrest in 1895, the city's attraction for him is explained in part by a series of longer visits in the period 1883–91, during which he forged important relationships with Paris-based writers, artists, actors, salon-hostesses, and journalists. In the course of a three-month visit to the city in early 1883, for instance, he befriended his future biographer Robert Sherard, the fashionable painters Jacques-Emile Blanche and John Singer Sargent, the novelist Paul Bourget, and the actor Benoît-Constant Coquelin, while also cementing an already-firm friendship with the great actress Sarah Bernhardt – later both producer and star of the abortive debut production of *Salomé* in 1892 – whom he had known since the late 1870s. Similarly, during a two-month visit to Paris in the autumn of 1891, Wilde established important relationships with Symbolist writers who circulated in the orbit of Stéphane Mallarmé, France's greatest living poet. During this visit, the French poets Pierre Louÿs, Adolphe Retté, and Stuart Merrill actively assisted Wilde with the composition (in French) of his play *Salomé,* at least where points of French language were concerned; and Wilde presented Mallarmé with an inscribed copy of *The Picture of Dorian Gray,* eliciting from Mallarmé the comment that the novel was a "miracle" and "one of few with the power to move me."[5] (During an earlier trip to Paris in the spring of 1891, the novelist Emile Zola had told Wilde equally forcefully that he considered his visit a great honour.)

As importantly, in the years before publicly announcing his intention to emigrate to Paris, Wilde had composed several literary works there, while also making arrangements for the French publication and translation of others. *The Duchess of Padua,* "The Harlot's House," and most of *The Sphinx* had been composed in Paris, in addition to the already-mentioned *Salomé,* while two of Wilde's prose tales had appeared there in French translation. Plans were also afoot by mid-1892 for the French publication of *Salomé* (in the original French, the proofs corrected by Wilde's friend Marcel Schwob) as well as for translations of *The Picture of Dorian Gray, Intentions,* and *Lady Windermere's Fan.*

From a biographical standpoint at least, it is a matter of considerable regret that Wilde did not carry out his intention to emigrate to Paris in 1892. Within three years he would be arrested in London, convicted, and sentenced to two years with hard labour in an English prison for the crime of "gross indecency." (This vaguely worded sexual offence, newly created in 1885, born of paranoia and aimed squarely at homosexual men, had no parallels on the European Continent, where Wilde would see out the remainder of his life upon release and where same-sex relations were tolerated by law.) Quite apart from the immense personal suffering it caused, Wilde's criminal conviction wrecked his career, precipitated his bankruptcy, made him a pariah, and almost certainly hastened his early death.

If Wilde did not emigrate to Paris in 1892, however, upon his emergence from prison five years later he immediately began making plans to resuscitate his career there. "All I want is to have my artistic reappearance, and my rehabilitation through art, in Paris," he informed Lord Alfred Douglas in a letter tentatively dated 2 June 1897.[6] But he did not immediately take up residence there. He resided initially in Dieppe, on the Normandy coast, and then in the more secluded and private

Figure 1.1 Atelier Nadar, photoportrait of Stéphane Mallarmé, c. 1894–1904, Bibliothèque nationale de France (https://gallica.bnf.fr).

environment of nearby Berneval, where he lived under the assumed name of Sebastian Melmoth so as "to avoid the prying eye and the foolish tongue."[7] "I am frightened of Paris," he confessed to Robert Ross fourteen days after his release: "If I live in Paris, I may be doomed to things I don't desire."[8]

But by this date he had already received a visit from the avant-garde Parisian theatre director and actor Aurélien-Marie Lugné-Poe, a fervent admirer, who had given *Salomé* its theatrical debut at the Theâtre de L'Oeuvre one year previously, while Wilde languished in prison. Lugné-Poe's visit is significant on at least two accounts: first, the two men evidently discussed Wilde's composition of a new play – like *Salomé*, "religious in surroundings and treatment of subject" – that might help facilitate Wilde's artistic rehabilitation.[9] (This would not be "a play for a run," Wilde explained, but rather one fitted for a select audience and for just three performances at most.) Second, Wilde was conscious that Lugné-Poe acted as a representative of the Parisian intelligentsia. "I want him to say ... how grateful I was and am to France for their recognition of me as an artist in the day of my humiliation," Wilde told More

Adey just hours after the Frenchman's departure, "and how my better treatment in an English prison was due to the French men of letters."[10] Lugné-Poe's stage production of *Salomé*, Wilde firmly believed, "was the thing that turned the scale in my favour, as far as my treatment in prison by the Government was concerned."[11]

Even more important for Wilde's "artistic rehabilitation" is the fact that within days of his release Wilde began writing *The Ballad of Reading Gaol*. "I have begun something that I think will be very good," he told Ross on 1 June.[12] "The poem is nearly finished," he told Ross six weeks later: "some of the verses are awfully good."[13] In fact the poem was not nearly finished at all. Wilde would continue working on it well into the fall of 1897, only finally bringing it to completion while residing with Lord Alfred Douglas at Posilippo, near Naples, where the poem's fifth and penultimate canto was composed.[14] (At Posilippo, Wilde laboured over the poem "in a manner which I had never known him to labour before," Douglas later recollected.)[15] In mid-December 1897, Wilde announced "I have got it now to a fairly high standard,"[16] and two months later, on 13 February 1898, the poem was published to warm and surprisingly sympathetic press reviews. Within three months, it had sold over four thousand copies, gone into six editions, and proven itself the bestselling book of Wilde's lifetime. Significantly, around the date (and possibly on the very day) of its publication, Wilde relocated finally to Paris. He would remain there for the final three and a half years of his life, except for relatively short sojourns in Italy, Switzerland, and on the French Riviera. If he had been frightened of Paris at the time of his release, the publication of *The Ballad of Reading Gaol* – which would be translated by the French Anglophile Henry-Durand Davray and published by the *Mercure de France* later in 1898 – gave him the courage to risk his reappearance there. "I shall be in Paris on Sunday next," he wrote four days before the poem's publication: "it is my only chance of working. I miss an intellectual atmosphere."[17] "A poem gives one *droit de cité*, and shows that one is still an artist," he told Robert Ross.[18]

As it turned out, in what remained of his short lifetime, Wilde did not experience the artistic rehabilitation, in Paris or anywhere else, that he longed for upon his release from prison. But this fact is less important for my purposes than the complex of ideas about Paris that drove his migration to the city and his aspirations for himself in the first place. As we have already seen, Wilde's 1898 migration to Paris was the fulfilment of a longstanding desire to pursue his career in "the artistic capital of the world," and as early as 1891 he had remarked that "among the poets of France I shall find my true friends."[19] Over the course of what follows, I shall argue that more than a place where Wilde sought important, sympathetic intellectual and artistic friendships, Paris must be understood critically and symbolically as what the French sociologist Pierre Bourdieu terms a unique *field of cultural production*, a social domain endowed with power to consecrate new and emerging writers not merely as successful authors, but also as distinguished "artists" whose work transcended (as the ideology of art and artistry would have it) the limitations of time and place. To a writer who sought to incarnate the very spirit of art – or at least, to prove, contra Whistler, that the writer was "the supreme artist, ... the master of colour and of form, and ... lord over all life and all arts"[20] – Paris was indispensable to Wilde's self-creation.

At the same time, Paris must be understood not merely as the capital of France but as what the French comparatist Pascale Casanova, echoing Wilde's own description, terms "the capital of the literary world, the city endowed with the greatest literary prestige on earth ... the capital of a republic having neither borders nor boundaries."[21] That is to say, Paris must be understood globally or comparatively, and not merely as the capital of a distinctly French cultural tradition, especially in light of its appeal to writers and artists from a panoply of non-French national traditions. Paris's legendary, mythic status in the eyes of writers and artists born in the margins is clear from Honoré de Balzac's *Les Illusions perdues*; and the city possessed a similar status in Wilde's eyes in the years when he was still aspiring to literary success. It was in Paris that Wilde sought – and in 1891 eventually acquired – the signs of literary distinction that marked him as not merely a global author, but also an "artist" of the very first order.

Entering the Field

Some hints of Paris's importance to Wilde's self-understanding as an author are implicit in his visits to the city prior to his announcement of his intention to migrate there permanently. His three-month visit to Paris in 1883, for instance, is conspicuous for the self-consciousness with which Wilde strove to achieve literary advancement. Despite his fame in the English-speaking world as the self-proclaimed apostle of aestheticism, Wilde could not at this date lay claim to being an established author – he had only the rather questionable 1881 volume *Poems* to his name at this time – and, unlike his two-month visit to Paris eight years later, his 1883 visit was not reported in the French press. Nonetheless Wilde arrived in Paris at the end of January 1883 full of confidence – displaying all "the elegances of Lucien de Rubempré," according to Robert Sherard – determined to make a lasting impression in the world of French letters.[22] As Sherard remarks with dry understatement, Wilde "was not disdainful of the indispensable arts for fostering social advancement" and upon his arrival in Paris he "sent copies of his volume of poems, with letters, to various artists and authors."[23]

The timing of Wilde's 1883 visit, immediately following his yearlong visit to North America, is interesting in its own right. In mid-1881, six months before his departure for America, at a reception held by his mother, he had met his future wife, Constance Lloyd. According to family legend, he reportedly told his mother on this occasion "By the by, mamma, I think of marrying that girl," and as Matthew Sturgis discreetly puts it, "opportunities were soon engineered for them to meet again."[24] But strikingly, upon his return from North America in January 1883, Wilde appears to have made no effort to see his future wife, notwithstanding that his mother carefully nurtured relations with her during his long absence and that within a few months he would be engaged to be married to her. Instead, within days of returning to England, he departed for Paris. Before leaving North America, he had committed himself to composing a five-act tragedy in blank verse for the American actress Mary Anderson, and it is often suggested that Wilde went to Paris in 1883 with the object of composing his play there. (This suggestion benefits in hindsight from the fact that Wilde did indeed compose *The Duchess of Padua* during the early weeks of his visit.) One wonders, nevertheless, how Constance and Wilde's mother felt about the speed of his new departure. For it seems that he had more on his mind than fulfilling his promise to Anderson.

Once installed in the Hotel Voltaire, he donned a white gown with a monkish cowl in imitation of Balzac, Robert Sherard informs us; and in social settings, he carried a turquoise-headed ivory cane, also in imitation of Balzac, while wearing a bright red waistcoat in sartorial homage to another favourite French author, Théophile Gautier. Sherard tells us that biographies of Balzac were strewn around Wilde's hotel room, "textbooks with which to study a part."[25] By adopting the paraphernalia of his favourite French writers, Sherard suggests, Wilde was attempting "to school himself into labour and production"[26] – and to some extent he was successful. On 23 March, he sent Anderson a "Titan" of a letter announcing the completion of *The Duchess of Padua,* which he felt to be "the masterpiece of all my literary work."[27] Anderson promptly – and perhaps wisely – declined the play.

Wilde's 1883 visit to Paris is important, however, for reasons other than his completion of *The Duchess of Padua*. It was distinguished by a measure of both literary and social success, although it would be some time before the fruits of Wilde's productivity were recognized, and his social success was neither so public nor so celebratory in nature as that which would attend his lengthy visit to Paris in 1891. In 1883 Wilde was determined upon proving himself as a Decadent poet in the mold of Charles Baudelaire and Gérard de Nerval, and Sherard witnessed Wilde's composition in Paris in 1883 of arguably his two greatest poems, "The Harlot's House" and *The Sphinx*. There is no doubt that Paris provided the proper atmosphere for these two compositions, remarks Richard Ellmann. Along with the early poems of John Gray, they are perhaps the best examples in English of a kind of poetry associated hitherto primarily with Baudelaire, Nerval, and Paul Verlaine even as it came to be celebrated in the English-speaking world, in the wake of Baudelaire's 1867 death, as epitomizing a transnational Decadent movement.

But it wasn't enough that Wilde was productive. He must be *seen to be* productive, especially in the world of French letters, and he eagerly sought acceptance in the eyes of French writers and intellectuals. Upon his arrival he distributed copies of his own *Poems* to leading cultural figures, just as he would do with *Dorian Gray* in 1891, accompanied by somewhat obsequious letters such as those that survive to the painter Jacques-Emile Blanche, the critic Theodore Duret, the novelist and collector Edmond de Goncourt, and the poet Maurice Rollinat. "It pleases me to think that perhaps there will be a place for my first flowers of poetry near your Watteau, your Boucher, and that treasure which in your *House of an Artist* you have immortalized forever," he wrote to Goncourt.[28] Rollinat's poem "La Vache au taureau" was "the most magnificent hymn" that the "countryside Venus" had ever received, he informed its author, without parallel since Lucretius's *De Natura*.[29] Even without such fawning prose accompaniments, the distribution of *Poems* seems to have had a pronounced effect: Blanche painted – and then rapidly exhibited – a painting of a young woman reading Wilde's poems ("she seems not to want to lift her eyes from my book even for a moment," Wilde jokingly commented when thanking Blanche for the compliment), and Sherard says that twelve years later, at the time of Wilde's arrest, he saw copies of *Poems* ostentatiously "laid out as curios of actuality" at more than one literary salon.[30] "The advances that were made to him by distinguished people in Parisian society had been carefully attracted by himself," writes Sherard: "many doors were opened to him" and "he was frequently in the exclusive society which numbered Edmond de Goncourt among its ornaments."[31] Besides Goncourt, Rollinat, Blanche, and Duret, Wilde is known to have socialized during this visit with the novelists Victor Hugo and Emile Zola, the poet Paul Verlaine, the actors Sarah Bernhardt and Benoît-Constant Coquelin, and the painters Edgar Degas, Camille Pissarro, Giuseppe De Nittis, and John Singer Sargent among others. He was also taken up by the American society hostess Kate Moore, courted by the wealthy society hostess Charlotte Baignères (whose salon was later attended by Marcel Proust and André Gide, among others), and he "found himself invited to literary salons, exhibition openings, and dinner parties."[32]

By contrast, the circumstances in which Wilde visited Paris for two months in the autumn of 1891 were very different. Once again, the visit is notable for its combination of social success and artistic productivity, suggesting the degree to which the two were for Wilde always closely intertwined, but his reputation now went before him and Wilde was feted more publicly than he had been eight years earlier. He now had a number of notable book publications to his name, and indeed the visit is inseparable from the publication in book form the previous spring of *Dorian Gray* and *Intentions*, the two works that Wilde and many others considered the best expressions of his literary artistry to date. Wilde had in fact already arranged for *Intentions* to be translated into French by the time he arrived in Paris in the autumn of 1891, and the debts owed to contemporary French literature by Wilde's only novel *The Picture of Dorian Gray* – called by Arthur Ransome, "one of the first French novels to be written in English" – have been frequently remarked by critics. Together with extracts of "The Soul of Man under Socialism" that appeared in the anarchist journal *La Revolté* in June 1891, both publications ensured that Wilde would be taken seriously as an author when he arrived in the city in October 1891.

As we have seen, Wilde distributed signed, personalized copies of *Dorian Gray* upon his arrival, and he also gifted at least one signed copy of *Intentions* during this visit. The terms with which he presented *Dorian Gray* to the editor, novelist, and literary salon-hostess Juliette Adam, founder of the *Nouvelle revue*, are typical: asking her to accept a personal copy "as a testament of my admiration for the author of *La Païenne*, a book that charmed me greatly with its unsettling and very modern beauty," he told Adam that *Dorian Gray* "contains many of my ideas on modern art and its relations to the life of the individual, as well as social life, philosophy, and morality."[33] The gift was clearly meant from one modern writer to another, and as Wilde had remarked to the French writer Catulle Mendès in 1884, "there is no modern literature outside France."[34]

As Richard Hibbitt has written, Wilde "was now an established writer, whose reputation had spread to France."[35] The visit was reported in *L'Echo de Paris*, *Le Figaro*, and *Le Gaulois*, and he was now taken up by a number of French or French-speaking writers. To be sure,

Figure 1.2 Alfred Le Petit, engraved caricature of Juliette Adam in *Les Contemporaines* (1881) (https://gallica.bnf.fr). The writer, editor, and salon-hostess is identified here by both her married name (Mme. Edmond Adam) and her maiden name (Juliette Lamber[t]).

in the previous spring, in the course of a much briefer visit to Paris, he had attended two of Mallarmé's *mardis* [Tuesday evening soirées], and Ellmann notes that "the disciples took account of Mallarmé's tacit endorsement."[36] However, it is Mallarmé's high opinion of *Dorian Gray*, expressed in an effusive letter to Wilde in the autumn of 1891, that is more likely to have had a pronounced effect on his many followers. (Mallarmé was to praise Wilde's *Salomé* in similarly profuse terms upon its publication – in French – in Paris in March 1893.) As Hibbit writes, only now did Wilde "became acquainted with a younger generation of French writers," including Marcel Schwob, Jean Lorrain, Pierre Louÿs, Adolphe Retté, Stuart Merrill, André Gide, and Henri de Regnier, and he also "began to acquire potential translators of his works."[37] Schwob's translation of "The Selfish Giant" would appear in *L'Echo de Paris* in December 1891, while Merrill's translation of "The Birthday of the Little Princess" (as "The Birthday of the Infanta" was titled before its republication in *A House of Pomegranates* in 1891) had appeared in *Paris illustré* in 1889, simultaneously with the story's first publication in English.[38]

Several young French-speaking writers who became friends in the fall of 1891 – Louÿs, Retté, and possibly Merrill – are known to have corrected or assisted with Wilde's composition in French of *Salomé*. Indeed the play's composition may be regarded as an homage to the French literary establishment of Wilde's day and an instrument for what Ellmann calls "the seduction of Paris."[39] As Wilde would have been well aware, Mallarmé was at work upon *Herodiade* ("the best known unfinished poem since Kubla Khan," says Ellmann), his own Symbolist version of the Salome myth; two of Wilde's favourite French novelists, Gustave Flaubert and Joris-Karl Huysmans, had recently immortalized Salome in fiction; and Gustave Moreau's painting "Salomé Dancing Before Herod," directly and memorably invoked in Huysmans's Decadent masterpiece *A Rebours*, had created a sensation when first exhibited in 1876. Wilde's knowledge of the iconography of Salome was immense, states Ellmann, although "only Moreau satisfied him, and he liked to quote Huysmans's descriptions of the Moreau paintings."[40] The Salome myth has been called "the decadent ideal" or "the icon of the ideology of the decadents," and it was a favourite trope among Parisian artists and writers of the fin de siècle. As the wide circulation among Mallarmé's acolytes of Wilde's draft manuscripts of *Salomé* indicates, Wilde hoped that the play would ensure his ascendance into the pantheon of Decadent literature.

Wilde's fall 1891 visit to Paris is important too for his social and public success, particularly in the literary salons and the eyes of established French authors and journalists. Ellmann writes that the two-month visit

Figure 1.3 Gustave Moreau, "Salome Dancing Before Herod," first exhibited Paris, 1876. Hammer Museum, Los Angeles (Wikipedia Commons). Wilde's own dramatic version of the Salome myth, composed in French and published in Paris in 1893, was given its stage premiere in Paris in 1896 while Wilde was in prison.

was "a continual feast," while the full remark printed by *L'Echo de Paris* concerning Wilde's social success was that he was "le 'great event' *of the Parisian literary salons*" (my emphasis).[41] According to William Rothenstein, who saw much of him at this time, Wilde "was the lion of the season in Paris" and was "invited everywhere."[42] "Princely galas were held in his name," observed Jean Lorrain: "poets and writers organized banquets in honor of the author of *The Picture of Dorian Gray*. Wilde ... was the man of the hour then; people literally fought over him. His voluminous brown frock coats, his triple-knotted ties ... and his jowly, oily face, beardless and groomed like that of a Roman emperor ... were as much of a drawing card in literary circles as they were in society parties; this English poet's books, printed with a sense of artistry unknown in France, were always carelessly yet ostentatiously piled on the side tables that aesthetic baronesses and Yankee princesses reserved for their favorite curiosities."[43] "The newspapers were full of his doings and sayings," says Rothenstein, and "Madame Adam took him up and asked numbers of people to meet him."[44]

L'Echo de Paris played an especially important part: on 6 December, it published a lengthy interview with Wilde, by the journalist Jacques Daurelle, titled "An English Poet in Paris." Here Wilde spoke at length about his love for Paris and French literature, while Daurelle observed silently that "in his demeanour, his tastes and his talent, [Wilde] recalls Théophile Gautier almost exactly."[45] Two weeks later, *L'Echo* published a long open letter from Wilde to Edmond de Goncourt in which the former, while explaining "the intellectual basis of my aesthetic" and giving "an assurance of my complete admiration," took issue with Goncourt's account of an offhand remark concerning the English poet Algernon Swinburne that Wilde had, according to Goncourt, made eight years previously on first meeting the eminent French writer.[46] The occasion for Wilde's letter was the publication in *L'Echo* two days earlier, on 17 December 1891, of extracts from Goncourt's 1883 diary, in which Goncourt not only recorded Wilde as saying that Swinburne was a flaunter of vice, but also slighted Wilde personally as "an individual of doubtful sex, with a ham actor's language and tall stories."[47] Tactfully ignoring the personal insult, Wilde used his letter to correct Goncourt's eight-year-old account, saying that Goncourt must have misunderstood him, and assuring Goncourt of his admiration for Swinburne as the first British poet to voice "the cry of flesh tormented by desire and memory," while simultaneously insisting that "the evenings which one had the happiness to spend with such a great writer as yourself are unforgettable."[48] We do not know Goncourt's reaction. But as his letter's publication indicates, Wilde did not intend Goncourt to be his only reader.

Figure 1.4 Advertising poster for *L'Echo de Paris*, 1890, Bibliothèque nationale de France, https://gallica.bnf.fr. The poster incorporates portraits of distinguished contributors to the paper around this time.

"You will see that he writes with every elegance," *L'Echo* assured its readers.[49]

As the publication of Wilde's letter to Goncourt indicates, the literary and social dimensions of Wilde's success in Paris at this time went hand in hand; and his advances in the eyes of Mallarmé, Adam, and other members of the French literary establishment should be seen as a form of consecration. In the course of interviewing Wilde for *L'Echo de Paris*, Daurelle noticed strewn about Wilde's hotel room "the books

Figure 1.5 Photoportrait of Edmond de Goncourt, c. 1899, Library of Congress, Washington, DC.

which our writers had flocked to give him, with admiring dedications, reviews, [and] photographs of friends."[50] Along with a brief letter to Mallarmé that accompanied the presentation-copy of *The Picture of Dorian Gray*, Wilde's letters to Adam and to the equally important salon-hostess Madame Emile Straus survive, the last of them stating that Wilde was "most touched by your kindness in granting me entrance into your distinguished and artistic salon."[51] Both Richard Hibbitt's and Richard Ellmann's accounts of the visit contain extensive lists of the French writers, both established and emerging, with whom Wilde socialized, with Hibbitt remarking that "the apogee of the initial French interest in Wilde" took place on 15 December 1891, when, about a week before Wilde's departure for London, Maurice Barrès gave a dinner in his honour at which Léon Daudet, Anatole France, Joris-Karl Huysmans, and Jean Moréas were all present.[52] With some justice, Ellmann writes that Wilde "pervaded Paris" in the fall of 1891.[53]

Paris as a Field of Cultural Production

The details of Wilde's lengthy visits to Paris before his conviction have been oft-recounted by Wilde's biographers. But these visits, which do much to explain Wilde's eventual residence, death, and burial in Paris, are of more than biographical importance. As I have already suggested, Paris needs to be understood critically for its structural position and symbolic power within the larger world of letters, pace Pierre Bourdieu, as a specific *field of cultural production.* For Bourdieu, a field of cultural production is a delimited social domain, relatively independent and autonomous from the larger economic and political realms, in which the usual laws of economics are inverted and "the only audience aimed at is other producers (as with Symbolist poetry)."[54] Its dominant figures and institutions – the salon, the critic, the established writer, the literary journalist, etc. – possess in abundance what Bourdieu famously called *symbolic capital,* and for this reason they are effectively endowed with the power both to consecrate and deny those emerging and often marginal figures who in turn aspire to the position of author or artist. But the field is for this reason marked by social friction, and entry to it is by no means assured: Bourdieu describes the field of cultural production as an often contentious site of "struggles in which what is at stake is the power to impose the dominant definition of the writer and therefore to delimit the population of those entitled to take part in the struggle to define the writer."[55] More particularly, the struggle is often between "established figures and the young challengers, ... between those who have made their mark and are fighting to persist, and those who cannot make their mark without pushing into the past those who have an interest in stopping the clock."[56]

Wilde's determination to cultivate Goncourt's good opinion in the face of public disparagement might easily be understood as such a struggle. So too might the effort Wilde put into courting figures such as Mallarmé, Adam, and Straus. For as Casanova further explains, the field of cultural production "has its own mode of operation, its own economy, which produces hierarchies and various forms of violence ... It is equipped ... with its own consecrating authorities, charged with responsibility for legislating on literary matters, which function as the sole legitimate arbiters with regard to questions of recognition."[57] Literary prestige thus depends upon "the existence of a more or less extensive professional 'milieu' ... on salons, a specialized press, and sought-after publishers ... on respected judges of talent, whose reputation and authority as discoverers of unknown literary texts may be national or international, and of course on celebrated writers wholly devoted to the task of writing."[58]

But what makes Paris distinctive as a field of cultural production, it might be asked, especially in light of Wilde's earlier migration from Dublin to London in the late 1870s? Might not those cities be regarded as important fields of cultural production too?[59] One answer to these questions might be sought in Walter Benjamin's famous description of Paris as "the capital of the nineteenth century," as central to the Victorian imagination partly by virtue of its modern urban spaces – its boulevards, arcades, department stores, parks, and luxuriously furnished domestic interiors. But an answer of more direct relevance to Wilde lies in his already-quoted remark that Paris is "the centre of art, the artistic capital of the world." For where late-Victorian London might be termed an imperial city, defined in part by its relation to those territories that the English administered and ruled, late-Victorian Paris was, as Casanova writes, "the capital of a republic having neither borders nor boundaries, ... a kingdom of literature set up in opposition to the ordinary laws of states, a transnational realm whose sole imperatives are those of art and literature"; and it exerted an especially powerful force on "those who proclaimed themselves to be stateless and above political laws: in a word, artists."[60]

In part, Paris's global prestige was a by-product of the French Revolution. Paris "symbolized the Revolution, the overthrow of the monarchy, the invention of the rights of man," explains Casanova.[61] But the city was also "the capital of letters, the arts, luxurious living, and fashion. Paris was therefore at once the intellectual capital of the world, the arbiter of good taste, and (at least in the mythological account ...) the source of political democracy, an idealized city where artistic freedom could be proclaimed and lived."[62] It emancipated writers from their birth-identities and in some cases from their mother tongues, too. Paris was thereby "able to manufacture a universal literature while consecrating works produced in outlying territories – impressing the stamp of *littérarité* upon texts that came from farflung lands, thereby denationalizing and departicularizing them."[63] By promoting "laws of universality" as distinct from "the ordinary political laws of nations," Paris became an ideal for writers from every part of the world who aspired to autonomy – a "place where books – submitted to critical judgment and transmuted – can be denationalized and their authors made universal."[64]

Paris's role in consecrating emerging writers on the seemingly universal plain of art, divorced from local contingencies of national and regional politics, constitutes one important reason why Wilde was so keen to have his works translated into French – in some instances before they had been published in English – and also why he strove to compose *Salomé* in French. (Tellingly, the title page of the first English-language edition of *Salomé*, published in 1894, states that the edition was "translated from the French of Oscar Wilde"). As far as Wilde was concerned, "there are only two languages in the world, French and Greek."[65] But his eagerness to cast his writings in French should not be understood merely as eagerness to identify them with strains in French culture. As Casanova explains, "certain languages, by virtue of the prestige of the texts written in them, are reputed to be more literary than others, to embody literature."[66] And as William A. Cohen has written, "because of the connection, in his mind, between the French language and artistic creation, Wilde understands French as the very language of art; through the use of French, he can conceive of forms of identity and subjectivity organized not around national belonging or linguistic community, but instead around aesthetics."[67] While the literary or artistic prestige conferred by the French language might well have led Wilde personally into what his friend the Nicaraguan poet Rubén Darío called a kind of "mental Gallicism,"[68] it also explains the crucial role played by French translators in Wilde's literary success. As Casanova observes, while the translator is often disregarded by reader and critic alike, he or she is nevertheless an "indispensable intermediary for crossing the borders of the literary world"; and where self-translation is impossible, the translator "assumes a key role, becoming almost a double, an alter ego, a substitute author responsible for carrying over a text from an unknown and unliterary language into the world of literature."[69]

To recognize the prestige and *littérarité* that are conferred on literary texts by the employment of French, whether in the original or in translation, is not to say that Wilde adopted an unproblematic relation to the French language; and Wilde, who was always quick to remind auditors of his Irish origins, referred to himself more than once as bilingual, as straddling different linguistic traditions. *Salomé*, in particular, has often been faulted both for its awkward French and for the awkwardness of its first English translation. (Scholars disagree about the extent to which Wilde himself was responsible for the first English translation, many of them perhaps too quickly and too exclusively attributing its self-conscious diction and intonation to Lord Alfred Douglas, who was identified in Wilde's dedication – though not on the book's title page – as "the translator of my play").[70] Even when performed in French, the play "has to be acted with an English accent," remarked the French art historian and biographer Philippe Jullian, and as I have observed elsewhere, the play is written in a language fundamentally alienated from itself, as if two separate languages were vying for supremacy.[71] As Casanova explains, "assimilated authors, who stand in a relation of foreignness and insecurity to the dominant language, seek by a sort of hypercorrection to make the linguistic traces of their origins disappear, as one does in the case of an accent."[72] But Wilde, who was at home in no single national tradition or language, represents what might be called a *dissimilated* author; and such authors, "whether or not they have another language at their disposal, seek by every possible means to distance themselves from the dominant language, either by devising a distinctive (and therefore to some extent illegitimate) use of this language, or by creating ... a new national (and potentially literary) language."[73] Even as he composed and first published *Salomé* in Paris and in French, Wilde intended his play to possess a "double life," remarks Elizabeth Richmond-Garza: he strove to "defamiliarize his own writing process" and foreground his relationship to language itself.[74] In both its original French and its first English translation, *Salomé* exemplifies "a writing practice constituted outside a national language," agrees Cohen, since it adopts an "extrinsic relation" to language itself, at least as the expression of a distinctly national subjectivity.[75] Wilde himself stated that while *Salomé* contains "modes of expression that no French man of letters would have used," they "give a certain relief or colour to the play" and in this respect he followed the example of the Belgian Symbolist Maurice Maeterlinck, the "curious effect" of whose writing derived "from the fact that he, a Flamand by race, writes in an alien language."[76] "An artist gains his best, his truest inspiration, from the materials he uses," Wilde observed in late 1891 when explaining to a British correspondent that he was presently "in Paris, studying the curious and fascinating development of Art in France."[77] Together with the twentieth-century Algerian author Kateb Yacine, Wilde might easily have said that "I write in French in order to say to the French that I am not French."[78] Yet despite his insistence on his own difference, he needed the Parisian cultural field in order to establish himself as a writer of global artistic significance.

On the Outer Edges of the Literary World

Viewing Paris as the artistic capital of the world enables us to frame Wilde's post-prison migration there not as a pariah's tragic, doomed flight from England, as Richard Ellmann among others has argued, but rather as Wilde's effort to re-establish and reassert the position he had occupied – at least in his own mind – as a literary figure in the years before his criminal conviction. As I have already indicated, long before his completion of *The Ballad of Reading Gaol*, he had expressed a desire to have his "artistic reappearance, and ... rehabilitation through art, in Paris"; he was acutely sensible of the compliment paid him by

Lugné-Poe in mounting the first theatrical production of *Salomé* in 1896, even attributing to Lugné-Poe's production his improved treatment at the hands of the English authorities; he was aware of how many eminent French men of letters had defended him in the Paris press even as he had been vilified by the English as his trials unfolded in the spring of 1895; and he would always be grateful, as he put it, to Frenchmen "for their recognition of me as an artist in the day of my humiliation."

If "a poem gives one *droit de cité*" and "shows that one is still an artist," however, Wilde must have been disappointed by the reception with which he was met upon his arrival in Paris simultaneous with the publication of *The Ballad of Reading Gaol* in February 1898. Before leaving for Paris, he instructed his publisher, Leonard Smithers, to send some twenty-five copies of the poem's first edition to British friends and acquaintances, after he had first signed and returned the unstitched title pages that Smithers had specially mailed him.[79] But within a matter of days, he was complaining that "none of the people to whom I sent copies have written to me. The lack of imagination in people is astonishing."[80] To be sure, he had written the poem partly with the object of advancing the cause of British prison reform, and the poem quickly caught the attention of British newspapers and politicians on account of its exposé of the cruelties and sufferings inflicted on prisoners in the name of justice.[81] Although Wilde was gratified by what we might term the poem's political reception in Britain, even going so far as to remark three months later that "I have been able to deal a heavy and fatal blow at the monstrous prison-system of English justice," it "is not altogether a pamphlet on prison reform," he commented, and "I want the literary papers to criticize it."[82]

If he felt ignored by the English literary and cultural establishment, he had higher hopes of being appreciated by the French. A few days after arriving in Paris, he asked Smithers "why not print some copies on some special paper?," explaining that he wanted to distribute copies to friends in Paris – to "Henri Bauër, [Octave] Mirbeau, and others" – and he didn't like to give second editions.[83] Bauër's and Mirbeau's reactions, if they received copies, are not known, but there is reason to think that within a few weeks of his arrival in Paris, Wilde was being shunned as completely by leading figures in the French intelligentsia as he was by the British. Certainly he was gratified to hear, shortly after arriving, that "there is going to be a recitation in a French translation of some of my poems in prose at the Odéon – at a literary matinée"; and in mid-April 1898 a laudatory notice of *The Ballad* appeared in the avant-garde journal *La Revue blanche,* while a few days later its editor, Félix Fénéon, wrote Wilde "a charming letter begging me to go and see them all."[84]

For a while, unfailing support was also shown by the Symbolist review *Mercure de France*, owned by the novelist Rachilde and edited by her husband Alfred Vallette (to both of whom Wilde inscribed presentation copies of *The Ballad*).[85] In April, the *Mercure* published a laudatory review of the poem, by Henry-Durand Davray, whom Wilde was at this time assisting with an English translation of the poem, and in May, Davray's translation appeared in the magazine too. Although the *Mercure* was to publish Davray's translation in book form in September, with Wilde's English text on facing pages, *The Ballad* did not make a splash in Paris and Wilde seems to have realized quickly that his wished-for "rehabilitation" would not be forthcoming, at least among France's pre-eminent writers. "While the literary people are charming to me when they meet me, we meet rarely," he complained to Robert Ross in mid-May: "my companions are such as I can get, and I of course have to pay for such friendships."[86] "His will had been broken," André Gide later wrote, perhaps with some exaggeration: "the first months he could still delude himself, but he very soon gave way. It was like an abdication. Nothing remained in his shattered life but the mournful musty odour of what he had once been."[87] Where he had previously been invited to literary salons and private parties and his activities had been avidly reported in the French press, Wilde's social life, such as it was, was now confined largely to cafes and wine cellars, where he frequently picked up impecunious young male lovers; and far from being established men and women of French letters, his literary companions now were writers and artists of decidedly bohemian character.

The character and still more the sexual preference of many of his new Parisian associates did Wilde harm in the eyes of many who had previously been loyal supporters. Warned by Robert Ross against being too flagrant in taking young male lovers, Wilde replied: "When you talk morals to me, I always pipe on a reed and a faun comes running out of the thicket."[88] Wilde "was hand in glove with all the little boys on the Boulevard," explained Lord Alfred Douglas years later: "He never attempted to deny or conceal it. Oscar believed, as many other eminent people do, that he had a perfect right to indulge his own tastes ... In fact nothing irritated him more than to meet (as he occasionally did) admirers who refused to believe that he was addicted to the vices for which he was condemned. This used to infuriate him."[89] But the openness with which Wilde "feasted with panthers," to use the famous phrase with which Wilde himself described his penchant for the company of rent boys, was hardly likely to endear him to those who might help rebuild his literary reputation. "French writers were very harsh on Oscar Wilde," observed the expatriate Spanish writer Pío Baroja.[90] "People ...

shut their doors to him," remarked Gide; "they would look the other way if they saw him coming," observed Vincent O'Sullivan; and even among the handful who remained faithful the longest, some were now saying that Wilde was no longer fit to be seen.[91] Paris was "gradually closing itself against him," remarked Ernest La Jeunesse shortly after Wilde's death, proving itself as deaf and heartless as London.[92] "O[scar] W[ilde] whom I have defended so ardently inspires me now only with contempt ... I turn away from his foul odour; he no longer exists for me," wrote Henry Bauër (who had bravely defended Wilde in the pages of *L'Echo de Paris* in June 1895) privately in August 1898.[93]

Wilde's existence on the margins of Parisian society – bohemian, impecunious, and promiscuous – over the final three-and-a-half years of his life has been described by many biographers, but one feature of this existence is especially deserving of comment and emphasis here. Whereas before his imprisonment Wilde had kept the company of French men and women of letters, many such men and women now steered clear of him, and instead his literary associates were, with one or two exceptions, transplanted foreigners who had come to Paris to advance their own careers. Besides the already-mentioned Baroja, his friends included the Guatemalan poet Enrique Gómez-Castillo, the Nicaraguan modernist Rubén Darío, the Francophile Greek Symbolist Ioannis A. Papadiamantopoulos (long resident and famous in Paris as Jean Moréas), and the Spanish poet Manuel Machado. They met at the Calisaya Bar, an American-style bar in the Boulevard des Italiens. This was "a place he never would have dreamed of entering in his best days," says Vincent O'Sullivan, and frequenting it "did him harm with the censorious."[94] Wilde kept further visits to the Calisaya a secret from O'Sullivan, but he was nonetheless unashamed of his association with the bar and its cosmopolitan inhabitants: "Kalisaya, the American bar near the Credit Lyonnais, is now the literary resort of myself and my friends; and we all gather there at five o'clock – Moréas, La Jeunesse, and all the young poets," he proudly told Reginald Turner.[95]

Machado has left a memorable portrait of the Calisaya Bar:

> Containing a huge countertop of shiny mahogany, with a copper rail for resting the arms, the *bar*, properly-speaking, was filled with drinkers, yankee-style, half of them standing, half of them seated on high wicker stools, who sipped their concoctions and then quietly slipped away, while the bartenders mixed the 132 cocktails that were on offer. More sybaritic, we Parisians slowly consumed our absinthes – this lasted all evening – lounging on plush couches surrounding an elegant pedestal. I say "we Parisians" – Jean Moréas, the Greek, the Anglo-Irish Oscar Wilde, and myself, born in

> the Macarena [a neighbourhood of the Spanish city of Seville] – because in Paris there are no foreigners. Or, if you prefer, in Paris there are only Parisians![96]

If Machado's account is to be believed, Wilde's relations with these expatriate writers were alcohol-fueled and debauched. But Machado, Darío, and Gómez-Carrillo would all redefine their national literary traditions when they returned to their homelands, and Wilde's friendships with them are no less important a signifier of Paris's global stature than his earlier friendships with French men and women of letters such as Mallarmé, Louÿs, and Goncourt. Casanova writes that, while some expatriate writers turned to Paris "to escape the restrictive conventions" of their native countries, others "came to the center to equip themselves with the knowledge and technical expertise of literary modernity in order to revolutionize the literature of their homelands."[97] Casanova would call writers such as Machado and Darío "'eccentric' cosmopolitans on the outer edges of the literary world," as distinct from "cosmopolitans of the center," although no less than the latter, she says, such "eccentric" cosmopolitans assist "the diffusion of the great revolutions carried out in the center and so [share] in the universal credit of the innovations they help transmit."[98]

Certainly it is debatable whether Wilde fits this description exactly: unlike Machado, Darío, and the young Colombian poet Guillermo Valencia (whom Wilde also met at the Calisaya),[99] Wilde would not go on to produce any new work after 1898, much less anything that would directly transform literary traditions in his native Ireland, and within three years of the *Ballad's* publication he would be dead. But Wilde's offhand reference to the Calisaya as the "literary resort" of himself and his new friends cannot be regarded as entirely facetious, and Machado's account of the Calisaya speaks to the respect and camaraderie with which Wilde was viewed by a small cadre of non-French authors temporarily domiciled in Paris in the late 1890s.

Wilde's involvement with such expatriate writers, in short, testifies to the central structural position of Paris within the global economy of literature no less eloquently than his earlier involvements with the "respectable" French men and women of letters whose imprimatur he courted before his arrest. While the city was undoubtedly renowned for its permissiveness and tolerance as well, Paris, as we have seen, was a uniquely powerful field of cultural production in and through which Wilde could, in the years leading up to his imprisonment, participate in the seemingly autonomous, transnational world of literature; and Wilde felt that residence there was essential to his artistic rehabilitation

Figure 1.6 Advertising poster for the Calisaya Bar, c. 1890s, Bibliothèque nationale de France (https://gallica.bnf.fr).

following his imprisonment and social disgrace. In the latter respect, of course, Wilde himself was to be disappointed, as the pitiful attendance at his funeral, and still more the general silence surrounding his lonely death in 1900, indicates. But his grave is now a French National Monument, while in his own lifetime Paris played a critical role in the creation of some of Wilde's most enduring works. As importantly, through the attention paid to Wilde by French authors, translators, critics, journalists, and salon-hostesses in the wake of the publication of *Dorian Gray* and *Intentions* in 1891, as well as through Lugné-Poe's widely reported staging of *Salomé* there in 1896, in defiance of the English censor and the English justice system, Paris contributed markedly to Wilde's global standing in his own lifetime as a transnational "artist" of the very first order.

NOTES

1 "The Censure and *Salomé*," *Pall Mall Budget*, 30 June 1892, repr. in *Oscar Wilde: Interviews and Recollections*, ed. E.H. Mikhail (London: Macmillan, 1979), 1:188.
2 "La *Salomé* de M. Oscar Wilde," *Le Gaulois*, 29 June 1892, trans. E.H. Mikhail as "I Adore Paris," in Mikhail, *Oscar Wilde*, 1:189.
3 "I Adore Paris," in Mikhail, *Oscar Wilde*, 1:189.
4 Oscar Wilde, *The Complete Letters of Oscar Wilde*, ed. Rupert Hart-Davis and Merlin Holland (New York: Henry Holt, 2000), 493.
5 "J'achéve le livre, un des seuls qui puissent émouvoir" (quoted in Wilde, *Complete Letters*, 492n3). All translations mine unless specified.
6 Wilde, *Complete Letters*, 873.
7 Wilde, *Complete Letters*, 864.
8 Wilde, *Complete Letters*, 869.
9 Wilde, *Complete Letters*, 873.
10 Wilde, *Complete Letters*, 847.
11 Wilde, *Complete Letters*, 872. Although Wilde may well have believed that Lugné-Poe's staging of *Salome* "was the thing that turned the scale in my favour," he almost certainly exaggerated its influence on the treatment he received in jail. The production was widely reviewed in the French press and cemented Wilde's reputation in Paris. Although it was noticed in a couple of London papers, there exists no evidence to suggest that it created greater sympathy for him in British governmental circles.
12 Wilde, *Complete Letters*, 869.
13 Wilde, *Complete Letters*, 915.
14 "Canto" is Wilde's own term for each of the numbered sections of *The Ballad*. See his letter to Leonard Smithers, 4 September 1897, in Wilde, *Complete Letters*, 933. Wilde probably used this term because of its associations with Dante's *Inferno*, which he had reread avidly in prison.
15 Lord Alfred Douglas, *Oscar Wilde and Myself* (New York: Duffield, 1914), 123.
16 Wilde, *Complete Letters*, 1007.
17 Wilde, *Complete Letters*, 1013.
18 Wilde, *Complete Letters*, 1022. *Droit de cité* means "citizenship rights." See too Wilde's comment, made roughly one week after arriving in Paris: "the

intellectual atmosphere of Paris has done me good ... I now have ideas, not merely passions" (Wilde, *Complete Letters*, 1023).

19 "J'espère que les jeunes poètes de France m'aimeront un jour" (Wilde, *Complete Letters*, 497).

20 *The Critical Writings of Oscar Wilde: An Annotated Selection*, ed. Nicholas Frankel (Cambridge, MA: Harvard University Press, 2022), 48.

21 Pascale Casanova, *The World Republic of Letters*, trans. M.B. DeBevoise (Cambridge, MA: Harvard University Press, 2004), 24, 29.

22 Robert H. Sherard, *Oscar Wilde: The Story of an Unhappy Friendship* (London: Greening, 1909), 21.

23 Sherard, *Oscar Wilde: The Story of an Unhappy Friendship*, 70.

24 Matthew Sturgis, *Oscar: A Life* (London: Head of Zeus, 2018), 176.

25 Sherard, *Oscar Wilde: The Story of an Unhappy Friendship*, 29.

26 Sherard, *Oscar Wilde: The Story of an Unhappy Friendship*, 27.

27 Wilde, *Complete Letters*, 196.

28 "Je serai bien content de penser qu'il y aura une place, peut-être, pour mes premières fleurs de poésies, près de vos Watteau, et de vos Boucher, et de ce trésor ... que dans votre *Maison d'un artiste* vous avez pour toujours immortalisé." Wilde, *Complete Letters*, 207.

29 "C'est l'hymne le plus magnifique que la Vénus des Champs a jamais reçu." Wilde, *Complete Letters*, 208.

30 "elle ne veut pas lever ses yeux de mon livre, même pour un instant." Wilde, *Complete Letters*, 206; Sherard, *Oscar Wilde: The Story of an Unhappy Friendship*, 70.

31 Sherard, *Oscar Wilde: The Story of an Unhappy Friendship*, 70; Sherard, *The Life of Oscar Wilde* (London: T.W. Laurie, 1906), 229.

32 Sturgis, *Oscar: A Life*, 275–6.

33 "*Le Portrait de Dorian Gray* ... contient beaucoup des mes idées sur l'art moderne, et ses rapports avec la vie individuelle, et la vie sociale, la philosophie et la moralité ... [D]e ma faire l'honneur d'accepter un examplaire en temoignage de mon admiration sincère pour l'auteur de *La Païenne,* livre qui m'a tant charmé avec sa beauté troublante et modern." Wilde, *Complete Letters*, 500.

34 Quoted in Richard Ellmann, *Oscar Wilde* (New York: Knopf, 1988), 252.

35 Richard Hibbitt, "The Artist as Aesthete: The French Creation of Oscar Wilde," in *The Reception of Oscar Wilde in Europe*, ed. Stefano Evangelista (London: Continuum, 2010), 68.

36 Ellmann, *Oscar Wilde*, 336.

37 Hibbitt, "The Artist as Aesthete," 68.

38 The exquisitely printed Parisian weekly *Paris illustré* ran from 1883 to 1890. For just over a year of its existence, from October 1888 to November 1889, it was published simultaneously in both English and

French editions. Although printed in Paris along with the French edition, the English edition was published in London and New York by the International News Company. See Stuart Mason [Christopher Millard], *Bibliography of Oscar Wilde* (London: T.W. Laurie, 1914), 174.

39 Ellmann, *Oscar Wilde*, 346.

40 Ellmann, *Oscar Wilde*, 342.

41 Ellmann, *Oscar Wilde*, 346.

42 William Rothenstein, *Men and Memories* (New York: Coward-McCann, 1931), 92.

43 Jean Lorrain, "Salomé et ses poètes," *Le Journal* (11 February 1896), 1, quoted and translated in Nancy Erber, "The French Trials of Oscar Wilde," *Journal of the History of Sexuality* 6, no. 4 (April 1996), 557.

44 Rothenstein, *Men and Memories*, 92. David Rose has questioned Ellmann's and Rothenstein's accounts, among others, of Wilde's social success in Paris. See "Pervading Paris," chapter 8 of his *Oscar Wilde's Elegant Republic* (Newcastle, UK: Cambridge Scholars Press, 2015), 151–89. But Rose confuses and conflates Wilde's visits of 1883 (when Wilde was not taken seriously in many quarters) and 1891 (when Wilde was an established and widely respected author).

45 Jacques Daurelle, "Un Poète anglais à Paris," *L'Echo de Paris*, 6 December 1891; trans. as "An English Poet in Paris," in Mikhail, *Oscar Wilde*, 1:170.

46 "La base intellectuelle de mon esthétique," "l'assurance de toute mon admiration." Wilde, *Complete Letters*, 504–5, 506.

47 "cet individu au sexe douteux, au langage de cabotin, aux récits blagueurs." Wilde, *Complete Letters*, 504n2.

48 "le cri de la chair tourmenteée par le désir et le souvenir," "Les soirées qu'on a eu le bonnheur de passer avec un grand écrivain comme vous l'êtes sont inoubliables." Wilde, *Complete Letters*, 505.

49 "on verra du moins qu'il l'écrit en toute élégance." Wilde, *Complete Letters*, 504n2.

50 Daurelle, "An English Poet in Paris," 170.

51 "je suis on ne peut plus touché de votre bonté en m'accordant l'entrée de votre salon si célèbre, si artistique." Wilde, *Complete Letters*, 496.

52 Hibbitt, "The Artist as Aesthete," 70.

53 Ellmann, *Oscar Wilde*, 351.

54 Pierre Bourdieu, "The Field of Cultural Production; or, The Economic World Reversed," in *The Field of Cultural Production: Essays on Art and Literature*, ed. and trans. Randal Johnson (New York: Columbia University Press, 1993), 39.

55 Bourdieu, *The Field of Cultural Production*, 42.

56 Bourdieu, *The Field of Cultural Production*, 60.

57 Casanova, *World Republic*, 12.

58 Casanova, *World Republic,* 15.

59 Casanova writes that "London is, of course, ... the other great capital of world literature ... Its power of recognition, which extends from Ireland to India, Africa, and Australia, is unquestionably one of the greatest in the world" (*World Republic,* 117–18). But Casanova also observes that London's literary power partly derives from "the immensity of its former colonial empire," and while it continues to confer "real literary legitimacy upon writers from Commonwealth nations, successors to the territories of the old empire," London "has seldom imposed itself outside the linguistic jurisdiction of the British Empire (now Commonwealth)." Casanova, *World Republic,* 118–19.

60 Casanova, *World Republic,* 29.

61 Casanova, *World Republic,* 24.

62 Casanova, *World Republic,* 24.

63 Casanova, *World Republic,* 87.

64 Casanova, *World Republic,* 87, 127.

65 "I Adore Paris," in Mikhail, *Oscar Wilde,* 1:190.

66 Casanova, *World Republic,* 17.

67 William A. Cohen, "Wilde's French," in *Wilde Discoveries: Traditions, Histories, Archives,* ed. Joseph Bristow (Toronto: University of Toronto Press, 2013), 233–4.

68 Quoted in Casanova, *World Republic,* 19, 96.

69 Casanova, *World Republic,* 142–3. While not denying the importance and global influence of literature composed originally in English, Casanova instances Shakespeare, Byron, Richardson, Sterne, and Scott as examples before Wilde's day of "English authors [who] enjoyed truly universal recognition ... only through the translation of their writings into French" (146).

70 See Nicholas Frankel, review of *Salome: A Tragedy in One Act,* by Oscar Wilde, trans. Joseph W. Donohue, illustr. Barry Moser (Charlottesville: University of Virginia Press, 2011), *Journal of Pre-Raphaelite Studies,* n.s. 22 (Spring 2013), 110–14.

71 Philippe Jullian, *Oscar Wilde,* trans. Violet Wyndham (London: Constable, 1971), 209. For discussion of the play's linguistic self-alienation, see Nicholas Frankel, *Oscar Wilde's Decorated Books* (Ann Arbor: University of Michigan Press, 2000), 56.

72 Casanova, *World Republic,* 255.

73 Casanova, *World Republic,* 255–6.

74 Elizabeth Richmond-Garza, "The Double Life of *Salomé,*" in *Refiguring Wilde's Salomé,* ed. Michael Y. Bennett (New York: Rodopi, 2011), 26

75 Cohen, "Wilde's French," 241, 238.

76 "The Censure and *Salomé,*" 188.

77 Wilde, *Complete Letters*, 499.

78 Quoted in Casanova, *World Republic*, 260.

79 Some thirty signed presentation copies of the *Ballad*'s first edition are known to exist today, representing nearly 5 per cent of the edition's print run. However, the number actually dispensed by Wilde and his publisher may be higher. My gratitude to Mark Samuels Lasner for details about surviving presentation copies.

80 Wilde, *Complete Letters*, 1022.

81 See Nicholas Frankel, *Oscar Wilde: The Unrepentant Years* (Cambridge, MA: Harvard University Press, 2017), 183–4, 199–200.

82 Wilde, *Complete Letters*, 1080, 1023.

83 Wilde, *Complete Letters*, 1022.

84 Wilde, *Complete Letters*, 1030, 1057.

85 For details of the *Mercure*'s support as well as of Wilde's friendships with Rachilde and the translator Henry-Durand Davray, who was in charge of reviewing work by British authors for the *Mercure*, see Petra Dierkes-Thrun, "Oscar Wilde, Rachilde, and the *Mercure de France*," in *Wilde's Other Worlds*, ed. Petra Dierkes-Thrun and Michael Davis (Milton, UK: Routledge, 2018), 220–41.

86 Wilde, *Complete Letters*, 10.

87 André Gide, *Oscar Wilde: In Memoriam*, trans. Bernard Frechtman (New York: Philosophical Society, 1949), 30.

88 Wilde, *Complete Letters*, 1105–6.

89 Alfred Douglas, letter to Robert Sherard, 17 September 1932, British Library, add. MS 81705.

90 "Los escritores franceses se mostraron muy severos con Oscar Wilde." Pío Baroja, "Un Juicio Severo," in *Los amigos españoles de Oscar Wilde*, ed. José Esteban (Madrid: Reino de Cordelia, 2012), 30.

91 Gide, *Oscar Wilde: In Memoriam*, 31; Vincent O'Sullivan, *Aspects of Wilde* (New York: Holt, 1936), 51.

92 Ernest La Jeunesse, "Oscar Wilde" (1900), repr. and trans. in Mikhail, *Oscar Wilde*, 2:479.

93 Quoted in J. Robert Maguire, *Ceremonies of Bravery: Oscar Wilde, Carlos Blacker, and the Dreyfus Affair* (Oxford: Oxford University Press, 2013), 137.

94 O'Sullivan, *Aspects of Wilde*, 164. Marcel Schwob and Stuart Merrill had complained privately to O'Sullivan that Wilde "was ruining what sympathy was left for him by showing himself ... in such a place as the Calisaya Bar."

95 Wilde, *Complete Letters*, 1108. *Calisaya* is a liqueur derived from the Peruvian bark *Cinchona calisaya*. Wilde spelled "Calisaya" with a "K" ("Kalisaya") to make it sound more Greek.

96 Manuel Machado, "La última balada del poeta inglés," in Esteban, *Los Amigos Españoles de Oscar Wilde*, 51. By a "yankee-style" bar, Machado means that customers were seated or standing at the bar, rather than occupying separate tables. Similarly when Wilde himself refers to the Calisaya as an "American bar," he means that it was an American-style bar, with barmen serving behind a long countertop, not that it was popular with Americans.

97 Casanova, *World Republic*, 99–100.

98 Casanova, *World Republic*, 100.

99 See Ana Rodríguez Navas and Nathalie Bouzaglo, "Oscar Wilde's Forgotten Legacy in Latin America," *Journal of Latin American Cultural Studies* 28, no. 3 (2019): 321–8.

2 "I am not really myself except in the midst of elegant crowds": The Role of Paris in Wilde's Identity Formation

PAISLEY MANN

In 1883, after his lecture tour in North America and brief stay in London, the twenty-eight-year-old Oscar Wilde travelled to Paris. Aiming to befriend artists and writers, he sent copies of his volume *Poems* to Edmond de Goncourt, Victor Hugo, and Maurice Rollinat and visited with Jacques-Emile Blanche and Théodore Duret.[1] Wishing to insert himself within Paris's artistic circles, Wilde also sought to reinvent himself as a French writer and used fashion to communicate a break with his earlier self, "the gentleman who wore long hair and carried a sunflower down Piccadilly."[2] He adopted the silk hat and tailored coat worn by the French and, consciously styling himself like Balzac, wore a "white wool dressing gown" when writing and carried a turquoise-studded ivory cane when walking through the city.[3] It was also during this three-month visit that he had his hair cut like the Roman Emperor Nero, marking the occasion by famously declaring, "[t]he Oscar of the first period is dead."[4]

Throughout his life, Wilde was a frequent visitor to and resident of Paris, and his love of France and penchant for self-invention are well known. Prior to this 1883 trip, he had visited the French capital with his mother and brother in 1867 and 1874, passed through in 1875 and 1877 as part of longer European tours, and returned in 1880 on his way back from the Loire Valley. In 1884, he and Constance spent three weeks in Paris on their honeymoon; he visited twice in 1891, once in both 1892 and 1894, and, from 1898 until his death in 1900, Wilde spent the majority of his time in Paris. Acknowledging his affinity with the French capital, he described himself to Edmond de Goncourt as "Français de sympathie, ... Irlandais de race et les Anglais m'ont condamné à parler le langage de Shakespeare" ("French by sympathy ... Irish by nationality, and the English have condemned me to speak the language of Shakespeare").[5]

As Michael F. Davis and Petra Dierkes-Thrun suggest, Wilde was a "great self-fashioner" and these frequent journeys between London and Paris allowed to "fashion, refashion, and perform" various identities.[6] Indeed, monographs about Wilde – from memoirs and tributes by Robert Sherard, Arthur Ransome, Frank Harris, and André Gide to biographies by Richard Ellmann, Herbert Lottman, Nicholas Frankel, and Matthew Sturgis – have covered the periods that Wilde spent in Paris, stressing the impact that these stays had on his artistic and personal development. Over the course of his lifetime, the French metropolis offered him opportunities for friendships with leading artists and writers, increased artistic freedom and recognition, favourable press coverage, greater opportunities for sexual exploration, and, later, a place of sanctuary.

Like Wilde, Paris was itself in a process of reinvention and identity consolidation, having been transformed during Haussmannization (1853–70) from an "overgrown [and] medieval" city into one that would be "seen and admired."[7] In these two decades, Baron Georges-Eugène Haussmann (1809–91) replaced slums and narrow streets with uniform apartment blocks and wide boulevards and greatly increased the size and number of the city's green spaces.[8] New streets were often positioned to culminate at either pre-existing, culturally significant landmarks, such as the Arc de Triomphe, or newly commissioned ones, such as the Opéra Garnier, linking the new city and the Second Empire with French glory and innovation.[9] Nineteenth-century Paris's regular hosting of *expositions universelles* (1855, 1867, 1878, 1889, and 1900) further solidified its connection to urban innovation, as each exhibition brought opportunities to showcase French achievement. During the nineteenth century, Paris became *the* modern metropolis, and the city functioned as fertile ground for Wilde's own personal and artistic self-fashioning.

Although scholars have considered the impact of Wilde's sojourns in Paris, many of these studies have tended to focus on Paris more as a cultural than a physical space, with less sustained attention given to the significance of landmarks and specific sites that he frequented. The precise locations of Wilde's Paris, however, offer insight into how he used the city to fashion his identity (or identities) and to assert his cultural knowledge and sense of style. In point of fact, there is a spatial dimension to the much-quoted anecdote about Wilde's 1883 hairstyle that critics sometimes omit or leave unexplored: this coiffure did not merely imitate Nero, but rather a specific bust of the emperor that he saw in the Louvre, a location that continued to fascinate him. Such a realization – that Wilde patterned his appearance after a specific object in a site endowed with cultural capital – sparked this chapter's investigation into the ways in which Wilde drew inspiration from the Parisian urban landscape. Consequently, this chapter focuses on the parks, boulevards, and cafes that figure in Wilde's poetry and letters as well as the neighbourhoods and hotels in which he stayed, in order to trace his relationship to and self-fashioning within the French capital.

Wilde's Neighbourhoods: A Geography of Wilde in Paris

Wilde's initial encounter with Paris – a holiday in 1867 with his mother and brother that offered a distraction from their grief over his sister Isola's recent death – was shaped by Haussmann's modernized vision for the ancient city.[10] At this point, most of Haussmann's major projects had been completed; that this visit occurred during the 1867 *exposition universelle* would have heightened Wilde's sense of Paris as a place of architectural wonder. The Wildes attended the fair, which was situated on the Champ de Mars (where the Eiffel Tower now stands) and which included amusement parks and restaurants in addition to purpose-built pavilions displaying works of art and industry. Though we do not have Wilde's own account, Lady Wilde wrote that the family left Paris with a sense that Dublin was a "little provincial town" compared to "the brilliance of Paris."[11] Her dichotomous approach anticipates Wilde's own, as he later repeatedly aligned himself with Paris's cultural brilliance and distanced himself from British culture.

There is little information available about Wilde's earliest trips to Paris, and until recently, scholars assumed his 1874 visit, also with his mother and brother, was his first.[12] While Herbert Lottman mentions that Wilde visited Paris briefly in 1875, 1877, and 1880 en route to or from other parts of France or Europe, we do not know where he stayed or what landmarks he visited.[13] In light of this limited knowledge, this chapter concentrates on fin-de-siècle Paris, dividing Wilde's trips into three distinct periods – the early 1880s, the early 1890s, and the late 1890s.[14] These successive visits reveal the evolving role that the French capital played in Wilde's self-fashioning as an author, cultural critic, flâneur, and reluctant British subject increasingly disillusioned with London's urban aesthetics and its social strictures. Given the chapter's spatial focus, I have mapped out the specific locations of the accommodations where he stayed and the cafes, restaurants, and bars that he visited during these three periods (Figure 2.1).[15] As Franco Moretti points out, such a process "bring[s] to light relations that would otherwise remain hidden."[16] In this case, mapping these key landmarks reframes our understanding of how Wilde inhabited Paris and how, with each subsequent visit, he used particular neighbourhoods to refashion himself.

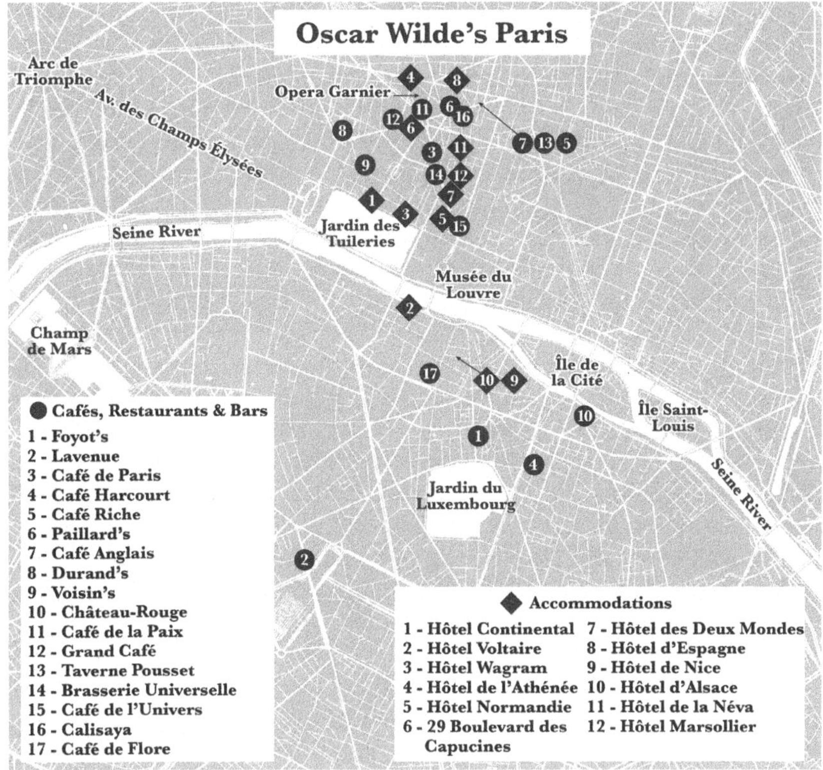

Figure 2.1 A map of Oscar Wilde's Paris.

In attending to the precise locations of Wilde's accommodations, this chapter counterbalances the importance that has been placed on his last residence – the dreary Hôtel d'Alsace in the sixth arrondissement – that has become infamously associated with him. Wilde-themed tours of Paris include a stop here, and while the now-upscale hotel obscures its insalubrious origins, it capitalizes on its sensational status as "the last home of Oscar Wilde."[17] Guests can sleep in the "[h]istoric, unique, and indulgent Oscar Wilde suite" in which he died – a room that is marketed with one of his witticisms taken out of context: "I have the simplest taste. I am always satisfied with the best."[18] Given that he resignedly stayed there only when funds were limited, this enduring association between Wilde and the Hôtel d'Alsace has created a distorted perspective on the types of accommodation and neighbourhoods he inhabited – a mischaracterization that is accentuated because his relationship to many of his earlier hotels has also been underexplored.

Mapping Wilde's locations, however, reveals that he preferred to reside in the area between the Jardin des Tuileries and the Opéra Garnier and moved to the sixth arrondissement only near the end of his life. Even within this relatively small radius, however, Wilde's urban preferences did shift over time, and these choices for lodging and cafes, both in terms of location and specific establishment, offer insight into his evolving relationship to the modernized city as well as into his emerging sense of himself as a writer and cosmopolitan cultural critic. In the 1880s, he stayed in the historic centre of Paris and chose accommodations and restaurants for their literary significance and cultural capital, creating a symbolic and geographic link between himself and France's past and present literary establishment. In the following decade, he moved to newer, Haussmann-designed neighbourhoods and used their hotels and cafes as inroads into Paris's current literary circles while also exploring the city's seedier quartiers. With his broadening knowledge of Parisian neighbourhoods and street culture, Wilde began to fashion himself as an urban expert. After his incarceration, he attempted to resurrect his literary and personal reputation by renewing his connection to the Opéra district even as his dwindling finances often forced him to stay in the cheaper sixth arrondissement on the Left Bank. Now in exile, Wilde sought refuge in the public spaces of Paris as he distanced himself from English culture. With each series of visits, Wilde repositioned himself both within the city itself and in relation to his previous episodes of self-fashioning, using the new urban space as an opportunity for continual self-transformation.

1880s: Wilde in the Historic Centre of Paris

Flush with the earnings of his North American lecture tour, Wilde stayed for the first several nights of his 1883 visit in the first arrondissement at the Hôtel Continental, a lavish accommodation that positioned him in a select group of travellers.[19] Built only five years earlier and listed in *Baedeker's Paris and Environs* (1881) as one of Paris's three large luxury hotels, the Continental was a "magnificent [edifice] ... replete with every comfort."[20] Its location – 3 rue de Castiglione – placed Wilde in close proximity to cultural landmarks as well as at the nexus of historical and evolving Paris. Across the street was the Jardin des Tuileries, created in the sixteenth century for Catherine de' Medici and expanded throughout the seventeenth to the nineteenth centuries as it opened to the public. The Louvre, housed in a former palace, was within walking distance, and the south side of the hotel faced the recently completed rue de Rivoli, a fashionable street with hotels and shops that British travel literature described as "broad and luxurious ... all modern gaiety and radiance" and "one of the handsomest streets in Paris."[21] Moreover, that the hotel was designed by Henri Blondel, the son-in-law of the Opéra Garnier architect, would have linked it – and its guests – to the grandeur of the Second Empire.[22] Such a hotel choice seems strategic; in staying at the Continental, Wilde could align himself with Parisian refinement.

Though spread out across the city, the restaurants that Wilde patronized in 1883 also demonstrate his attempts to imagine himself as a successful literary celebrity. With Robert Sherard, he went to Foyot's at 33 rue de Tournon (sixth arrondissement) and to Lavenue, a cafe near the Gare Montparnasse (fifteenth arrondissement, just south-west of the sixth). Lottman notes their cultural relevance: the "ultrachic" Foyot's was one of the Left Bank's finest restaurants, and Lavenue was patronized by artists and literary figures.[23] Further contributing to his sense of his own literary success was the fact that Wilde often paid for these meals with the advance he received for *The Duchess of Padua*, boasting to Sherard that they would be "din[ing] with the Duchess."[24] Wilde sought out extravagant establishments, eating only breakfast at his hotel and cultivating the "impression ... that he was a man of considerable fortune."[25] He insisted upon taking Sherard to the Café de Paris (39 avenue de l'Opéra, ninth arrondissement), using its reputation for being "exclusively patronised by millionaires" to fashion his own identity as a successful, sophisticated writer.[26] Indeed, Wilde was keenly aware of how key landmarks could confer status and shift perception. As he told Sherard, it was "a duty" of "the artist and *littérateur* to show the *bourgeois* ... that the man of letters" is not always "a needy Bohemian dwelling in a garret and for the most part starving."[27]

The cost of a stay at the Continental meant that for the remainder of his three-month visit, Wilde relocated to the more modest Hôtel Voltaire, a second-class hotel that both *Murray's Handbook for Visitors to Paris* (1879) and *Baedeker's Paris* (1881) recommended.[28] Located just across the river at 19 quai Voltaire (seventh arrondissement), the Voltaire still afforded Wilde access to the city centre's key sights; from his room, he could see the Seine and the Louvre, though when Sherard remarked on this view, Wilde, presenting himself as knowing and dispassionate, told him that "a gentleman never looks out of the window."[29] He did, however, include this geographical detail in a letter to Clarisse Moore, stating that he was "deep in literary work" and "[could not] stir from [his] little rooms over the Seine."[30] Here, Wilde seems to delight in situating himself as a writer whose artistic output develops alongside a key landmark; like his Balzacian robe, the Seine's proximity acts as a literary talisman.

The Voltaire also held literary and personal significance: Charles Baudelaire lived there during the 1850s, and Wilde stayed there with his family in 1874 when he had begun writing *The Sphinx*.[31] Being in the same physical location seems to have reinvigorated the poem's imaginative territory, and he returned to work on it. In a letter to Sherard after returning to London, Wilde attributed his artistic productivity to the French capital, lamenting, "the splendid whirl and swirl of life in London sweeps me from my Sphinx ... I wish I was back in Paris, where I did such good work."[32] The poem's content is also deeply connected to the hotel and its location: John Stokes calls it Wilde's "most Baudelairean poem," and Sturgis notes the sphinx nearby in the Louvre.[33] There were also two sphinxes flanking an entrance to the adjoining Jardin des Tuileries.[34] The poem's immortal sphinx, who oversees "[a] thousand weary centuries" and observes key events in Egyptian, Roman, and Christian history, mirrors these sculptures, which stood as silent observers to the political and architectural changes Paris underwent.[35] In a fitting tribute, one final sphinx – the Jacob Epstein-designed funeral monument in the Père Lachaise Cemetery (twentieth arrondissement) – hovers over Wilde's grave and oversees the generations of admirers who have transformed the tomb into a shrine.

Wilde was fascinated by landmarks at the physical and symbolic centre of historical Paris, and he returned to them in poetry and daily excursions. The Louvre, in addition to providing inspiration for *The Sphinx* and his Nero haircut, became a frequent destination; Wilde told Sherard of his "habit of spending long hours" contemplating the museum's Venus de Milo statue.[36] Outdoor sculptures – including a dancing boy in the adjoining Jardin des Tuileries and the Egyptian obelisk in the nearby Place de la Concorde – also became regular sites of pilgrimage.[37] Sherard noted Wilde's "real delight" at the dancing boy statue, suggesting that, although Wilde "often talked about Art with his tongue in his cheek," he believed Wilde spoke truthfully when he said he visited it daily.[38] These regular visits to the Jardin des Tuileries also placed Wilde as an observer of quotidian Parisian life. *Murray's Handbook* (1879) describes the garden as "a favourite resort of Parisians of every class," where "[a]t all times of the day children and their nurses swarm, and ... the walks and chairs are filled with crowds of gaily dressed people, enjoying the fresh air and the pleasure of seeing and being seen."[39] The sight of children playing seems to have captivated Wilde the most, resulting in "two little 'Impressions' of the children flying balloons in the Tuilery [*sic*] gardens" that he sent to Edmund Yates while still in Paris.[40] These two pieces became "Le Jardin des Tuileries," published in 1885 as a fundraiser for the North-Eastern Hospital for Children, and

"Les Ballons," the second part of "Fantaisies Décoratives," which was included in an 1887 edition of the *Lady's Pictorial*.[41]

The poems rest on small, everyday joys found within the park, highlighting movement and imagination. The speaker of "Le Jardin des Tuileries" delights in watching children at play, contrasting their energy with the "winter air [that] is keen and cold."[42] As he sits, children race "[l]ike little things of dancing gold," "hide/In the bleak tangles of the bosk," and, when their nurses are distracted, "steal across the square,/ And launch their paper navies where/Huge Triton writhes in greenish bronze."[43] The speaker remains entranced by their excitement and marvels that the "cruel tree" remains "black and leafless" while children climb its branches; if he were the tree, he would participate by " break[ing]/Into spring blossoms white and blue!"[44] In "Les Ballons," Wilde again concentrates on carefree movement, narrowing his focus to the "light and luminous balloons" played with in the park.[45] While in the first poem the speaker's actions are minimal, here, the speaker is non-existent, dissolving as he contemplates the spectacle around him. Similarly, the children who presumably play with the balloons are unmentioned; the poem instead traces the balloons' subtle actions as they "dip and drift like satin moons" and "silken butterflies," "rise and reel like dancing girls," and "fall and float like silver dust."[46] Despite their relative simplicity, these poems situate Wilde's speaker as an urban observer; like Baudelaire's flâneur, he becomes a "passionate spectator" who finds "immense joy ... in the heart of the multitude, amid the ebb and flow of movement."[47] To notice the balloons' small movements and the intricacies of the children's games, Wilde's speaker must linger; like a series of Monet's paintings that capture subtle changes of light and motion in the same landscape over a period of time, these poems meditate on the iterative activities that accrue meaning within Parisian public space.

Wilde visited Paris one last time this decade, with Constance on their honeymoon in 1884. Their accommodation, the Hôtel Wagram on the rue de Rivoli (first arrondissement) was near the Continental and again offered a view of the Jardin des Tuileries. A smaller hotel than the Continental, the Wagram still ranked highly in guidebooks.[48] Both hotel and location impressed Constance, who described them in a letter to her brother: "We have an *appartement* here of three rooms, twenty francs a day: not dear for a Paris hotel: we are *au quatrième* and have a lovely view over the gardens of the Tuileries: the ruins of the palace are, alas, no more."[49] This reference to the Tuileries Palace (Figure 2.2) – a former royal residence attached to the gardens that the Communards destroyed in 1871 and that lay in ruins until being demolished in 1882–3 –

Figure 2.2 Ernest Landrey, "View of the Tuileries Palace in Paris after the Paris Commune Fire, 1871" (Rijksmuseum, Amsterdam; www.rijksmuseum.nl).

hints at what I want to suggest motivated Wilde's recursive journeys to and stays near this historic area.[50] Though at the heart of Paris and still bearing the marks of its royal past, the first arrondissement also represented flux and transformation: the Continental was built on the site of the former Ministère des Finances (also destroyed by Communards); the Place de la Concorde was previously the Place de la Révolution, where the guillotine stood; and of course the Louvre and the Jardin des Tuileries had been reserved for monarchy before opening as a museum and public garden. Wilde would have seen the Tuileries Palace in its earlier stages – still standing in 1867; in ruins in 1874, 1875, 1877, and 1880; and in the process of being removed in 1883. He celebrated the ideological significance of this material change, remarking to Sherard in 1883 that each "little blackened stone" represented "a chapter in the Bible of Democracy."[51] While the first arrondissement provided Wilde with both an elegant location from which to explore Paris and a sense of being, like Baudelaire, at home "in the heart of the multitude," its material changes during his initial visits took on added personal resonance, as both the city and the writer were involved in a process of self-fashioning and renewal.[52] In the city to shed the "Oscar of the first period"[53] and armed with the physical markers of this transformation – the Neronian hairstyle and Balzacian cane and cowl – Wilde could draw inspiration from Paris's spatial transformation and the ideological evolution it symbolized.

Early 1890s: The Opéra District

Wilde did not return to the French capital until 1891 – seven years after his honeymoon – and his accommodation choices in the first half of this decade reveal a progression in his relationship to Paris. Moving slightly north-east, Wilde stayed at the nexus of the first, second, and ninth arrondissements in hotels clustered near the Opéra Garnier and the avenue de l'Opéra that were, like his previous accommodations, recommended for their proximity to key sights and popularity with upper-class English guests.[54] From February to March 1891, he stayed at the Hôtel de l'Athénée (15 rue Scribe, ninth arrondissement) across from the Opéra; when he returned at the end of October, he stayed briefly at the Hôtel Normandie on the rue de l'Echelle (first arrondissement), a small street near the south-east end of the avenue de l'Opéra; by November, he had moved to an apartment in a hotel at 29 boulevard des Capucines (second arrondissement), a short walk from the Opéra.[55] On his brief 1892 visit, he returned to the boulevard des Capucines apartment, and in 1894, he stayed at the Hôtel des Deux Mondes (22 avenue de l'Opéra, first arrondissement).

Although not far from previous hotels, Wilde's new neighbourhood represented a greater symbolic and material break with pre-Haussmannized Paris. Renovated extensively, the area was largely a mid-nineteenth-century creation, with only some of its small streets retaining a look of "old Paris."[56] Unlike the Louvre and the Jardin des Tuileries, which had accrued centuries of cultural meaning, the ninth arrondissement's landmarks – the diagonal avenue de l'Opéra and Opéra Garnier – were newly constructed, begun in 1861 and 1864 and completed in 1875 and 1879, respectively. They were, therefore, less palimpsestic, offering a modern urban text without traces of monarchical, classical Paris. Together, these landmarks represented the pinnacle of Haussmann's vision and remade the ninth arrondissement into an entertainment and luxury district, as large cafes and department stores soon clustered around the Opéra Garnier and the streets radiating from it.[57] Moving to this neighbourhood placed Wilde more solidly at the new "centre of gravity of smart Paris."[58]

Guidebooks drew attention to the lively atmosphere that the neighbourhood's cafes, *grands magasins*, and boulevards provided. *Baedeker's*

Paris (1891) described the Opéra district as a place of "indescribable animation and brilliancy," and *Murray's Handbook* (1890) highlighted its sensory abundance, noting "the hosts of people sitting outside cafés, the throng of loungers along the pavement, the lofty houses, the splendid shops, the brilliantly lighted cafés, and the numerous theatres," all of which "will be quite new to an Englishman."[59] Wilde's "The Sphinx without a Secret" (1887) begins with a similar perspective on the neighbourhood's vibrancy and singularity: at an outdoor table at Café de la Paix (across the street from the Opéra), the English narrator sits "watching the splendour and shabbiness of Parisian life, and wondering over [his] vermouth at the strange panorama of pride and poverty that was passing before [him]."[60] Wilde himself was particularly drawn to this energy and saw his new district as offering him a reconstituted, more sophisticated sense of self. Standing in front of his rue des Capucines accommodation, he gestured to the vibrant street life and remarked to the writer Ernest Raynaud, "how all this outdoes the languishing beauty of the countryside. The solitude of the country stifles and crushes me ... I am not really myself except in the midst of elegant crowds, in the exploits of capitals, at the heart of rich districts, or amid the sumptuous ornamentation of palace-hotels."[61] His phrasing – that he is "not really [himself]" when not ensconced in "elegant crowds" and "rich districts" – demonstrates his desire to belong in and to be associated with his new fashionable surroundings, such that he crafts his persona as inextricable from them.

Indeed, Wilde seems to have recognized and capitalized upon the role that the built environment played in his identity formation. In addition to using his stays around the Opéra to become a participant in fashionable Parisian life, Wilde attempted to cultivate and to reinforce geographically his deepening ties to Paris's artistic establishment through these new socio-spatial preferences. As Richard Hibbitt suggests, Wilde's 1891 visits marked "a crucial change in his social and literary position": prior attempts at friendships were rewarded, and he attended Stéphane Mallarmé's soirées, befriended André Gide and Pierre Louÿs, and met Marcel Proust.[62] Though Wilde did dine at places across the city, including the Café d'Harcourt at 47 boulevard Saint-Michel (fifth arrondissement),[63] the cafes and restaurants in and adjacent to the ninth arrondissement were key in developing these literary connections and in cultivating a reputation for cultural sophistication. He first met Mallarmé at Café Riche (16 boulevard des Italiens, ninth arrondissement), and during these visits in the early 1890s, he dined at other famed establishments in the vicinity, including Paillard's (38 boulevard des Italiens, ninth), Café Anglais (13 boulevard des Italiens, ninth), Durand's (intersection of Place de la Madeleine and rue Royale, eighth), and Voisin's (corner of rue Saint-Honoré and rue Cambon, first).[64] These restaurants had significant cultural cachet: Durand's was "one of the most fashionable and most expensive restaurants in Paris;" and "scarcely any foreigner of distinction visit[ed] ... without dining ... at the Café Anglais."[65] In much the same way as on previous visits, where he used his accommodation and sartorial choices to align himself with older generations of writers such as Baudelaire and Balzac, Wilde's relocation to the Opéra district suggests a deliberate effort to position himself alongside the nation's contemporary writers and cultural elite, using these establishments as geographic metonyms for social and artistic belonging.

At the same time, however, even if Wilde concentrated his time around the Opéra, he was keen to establish himself as someone who knew Paris extensively. In an 1891 interview, he stressed his connections to establishments of all kinds: "Je fréquente aussi bien le Château-Rouge que le café Anglais" (I frequent the Château-Rouge as well as the Café Anglais).[66] By mentioning the Château-Rouge, "a *cabaret* and doss-house" on the Left Bank at 57 rue Galande (fifth arrondissement) "frequented by thieves, prostitutes, pimps, ruffians and down-and-outs," Wilde positioned himself as a liberal-minded authority on the city, suggesting – perhaps not entirely accurately – that his geographic and leisure preferences were broad and varied, guided not by morality or fashion but by a desire to find places where he could "éprouver une émotion" ("feel an emotion").[67] This emphasis on disreputable places is connected to his denigration of London mores. Immediately prior to mentioning his patronage of all kinds of establishments, he defined the French capital against London: while one must "cache tout" ("conceal all") in London, one can "montre tout" ("reveal all") while in Paris.[68] Mentioning his connections to seedier establishments, therefore, furthered this dichotomy and offered socio-spatial proof of his greater affinity with Paris.

In an 1891 letter to the editor of the *Speaker*, Wilde again used features of the French city – in this instance, its newspaper kiosks – to critique England. Made of iron and painted a dark green, these kiosks, with their dome and spire, became a recognizable feature of the Haussmannized city that matched its benches, lamp posts, and water fountains; for Wilde, they were also material signifiers of France's superior aesthetics (Figure 2.3). The letter begins, "Sir, I have just ... purchased a copy of the *Speaker* at one of the charming kiosks that decorate Paris, institutions, by the way, that I think we should at once introduce into London."[69] Despite seeming like an aside, Wilde's thoughts on the kiosks overtake the letter's intended purpose; only after expounding on their aesthetic significance did Wilde clarify that he was writing "not ... about the ... kiosks" but "to correct a statement" about *A House of Pomegranates*.[70] "The kiosk is a delightful object," Wilde declared, "and, when illuminated at night from within, as lovely as a fantastic Chinese lantern, especially when the transparent advertisements are from the clever pencil of M. Chéret."[71] This enthusiastic celebration of Parisian urban aesthetics soon turned to a critique of Britain's analogous spaces: "In London we have merely the ill-clad newsvendors, whose voice, in spite of the admirable efforts of the Royal College of Music to make England a really musical nation, is always out of tune, and whose rags, badly designed and badly worn, merely emphasise a painful note of uncomely misery, without conveying that impression of picturesqueness which is the only thing that makes the spectacle of poverty of others at all bearable."[72] Consequently, Wilde stressed, "the establishment of kiosks in London ... is a thing that the County Council should at once take in hand."[73]

This aesthetic critique is perhaps connected to his larger frustration with English newspapers; in "The Decay of Lying" (initially published in 1889 and republished in 1891), Wilde censured British journalists' impulse to provide "the bald, sordid, disgusting facts of life" and suggested that France "manage[d] [to protect people's privacy] better" because it "limit[ed] the journalist, and allow[ed] the artist almost perfect freedom" while England "allow[ed] absolute freedom to the journalist, and entirely limit[ed] the artist."[74] For Wilde, both the content within the newspaper and the manner in which it was sold betrayed English aesthetic and moral deficiencies. Davis and Dierkes-Thrun suggest that Wilde often "styled himself ... [as a] continental *flaneur*" and "aesthete" who performed the "apostolic work of bringing the good news of art and aesthetics .... to the British."[75] Wilde's excursus on the kiosk and the lack of a London counterpart demonstrates this apostolic impulse, and the letter is structured so as to imply that he is such a keen urban observer that he cannot help but insert his wisdom into a letter on an unrelated (albeit literary) subject. Alongside his recursive visits to key, fashionable spaces within Haussmannized Paris during the early 1890s, this commentary on the newspaper kiosk suggests Wilde's desire to cultivate an identity as an expert on Parisian street culture and as an active participant in the city's artistic circles.

Late 1890s: The Opéra District and the Left Bank

When Wilde left England upon his 1897 release from prison, he intended to settle in Berneval-sur-mer, a small village in Normandy, fearing that if he lived in Paris, he might "be doomed to things [he didn't] desire."[76]

Figure 2.3 Newspaper Kiosk Number 242 (Ville de Paris / Bibliothèque historique; https://bibliotheques-specialisees.paris.fr).

Despite this plan, he returned to Paris multiple times: he stayed briefly in 1897 while en route to Italy; returned in 1898 after an extended stay in Naples (with Alfred Douglas) had proven "fatal" for his writing; and, aside from short trips to the South of France, Switzerland, and Italy, remained in Paris until his death in 1900.[77] His first accommodation was the Hôtel d'Espagne at 4 rue Taitbout (ninth arrondissement).[78] While geographically near to where he stayed a few years previously, this hotel choice indicated his reduced means: *Murray's Handbook* (1890) noted that hotels on this street were "less frequented by English than by French, Italians, Spaniards, and commercial people generally."[79] Upon returning in February 1898, Wilde stayed across the river at the Hôtel de Nice on rue des Beaux-Arts (sixth arrondissement), an accommodation that *Baedeker's Paris* (1896) described as "well spoken of" despite being, like all Left Bank hotels, "less conveniently situated" than accommodations on the Right Bank.[80] By the end of March, he had moved to the less expensive Hôtel d'Alsace on the same street, remaining there until December.[81] That spring, Wilde told Robert Ross that he was considering looking for accommodation "in some of the streets close to the *near* end of the Champs Elysées," an area that was, as Frankel points out, Paris's "most popular homosexual meeting place."[82] He never managed to move into an apartment of his own, however, partly because of finances and potentially, as he told Ross, because of his "name."[83]

A restlessness characterizes Wilde's accommodation choices in this period. In May 1899, he returned to the Opéra district, staying at the Hôtel de la Néva (9 rue Monsigny, second arrondissement), but by the end of the month, he had moved to the Hôtel Marsollier on rue Marsollier, also in the second.[84] While Wilde rarely mentioned his accommodations in earlier correspondence, his precarious finances and the resulting need for ever cheaper accommodation became frequent themes in his post-incarceration letters. Lamenting that he "[could not] stay in Paris; it [cost] too much," he often requested money to pay his hotel debts.[85] When he returned to the less expensive Hôtel d'Alsace in August 1899, the Hôtel Marsollier's "evil proprietor detained [his clothes]" on account of his unpaid bill.[86] Apart from a visit to Rome, Wilde remained until his death in November 1900 at the Hôtel d'Alsace, "a poor little Bohemian hotel, only suited for those Sybarites who are exiled from Sybaris."[87] There was a rather cruel irony in that this "wretched inn," as Sherard termed it, was "barely three minutes' walk" from the Hôtel Voltaire (where he had stayed in 1883), yet it symbolized exile and defeat rather than artistic productivity and personal transformation.[88]

Once again, mapping the locations of Wilde's Paris offers insight, this time into the ways that he attempted to reconstruct his identity. While scholars have rightly highlighted the prosaic, downward trajectory that these increasingly shabby hotels convey, his choices in these final years also need to be viewed within the broader context of his previous socio-spatial relationship with Paris and his aspirations for his return. Prior to resettling in Paris, Wilde wrote to Lord Alfred Douglas, "All I want is to have my artistic reappearance, and my own rehabilitation through art, in *Paris*, not in London. It is a homage and a debt I owe to that great city of art."[89] As Frankel points out, Wilde "had good reason for thinking Paris would embrace him warmly once again" given French newspapers' sympathetic coverage of his trials, the public support of leading writers, and a recent Parisian production of *Salomé*.[90] Instead, many of the artistic circles he hoped would welcome him were shut to him, and the rehabilitation he wanted did not materialize.[91] In light of his hopes for the future, these frequent moves and, more particularly, his oscillation between the cheaper sixth arrondissement and the Opéra district tell a concurrent but counter narrative, one of resolute and continued attempts to return – geographically and socially – to the Paris to which he used to belong and to where, "in the midst of elegant crowds" he was "really [him]self."[92]

Indeed, the crowd played an important role in Wilde's attempts at identity re-formation, and in the late 1890s, he increasingly sought refuge in public spaces that could impart a sense of self and social belonging. Avoiding his hotels, which were too "cold and uncomfortable" to host guests and which reminded him of how far he had fallen, Wilde often met friends in cafes which were, as he told George Ives, the city's "ordinary meeting-places" where "nobody bothers" to "listen to the conversation of others."[93] Cafes provided Wilde with respite from solitude, and there are multiple accounts of him wandering from cafe to cafe late into the night to avoid returning home.[94] Jean-Joseph Renaud recalled one such attempt to combat loneliness through the public cafe: "Wilde would go to another place, searching for other people to talk to. Then to another ... In these different cafés, night restaurants, brasseries, he kept talking, talking all the time, and as prodigiously, for all people who cared to listen ... At last, when there was nobody left to talk with, he used to walk home slowly, heavily, in the empty Paris streets."[95] Perhaps in a similar effort to avoid solitude, Wilde frequently wrote letters from cafes whereas much of his earlier Parisian correspondence was written in his hotels. Despite insisting that he could no longer afford "places like the Café de la Paix" – the legendary, Second-Empire-era establishment that he referenced in "The Sphinx without a Secret" – he wrote often in the fashionable cafes nearby, including the Grand Café at 14 boulevard des Capucines (ninth), Taverne Pousset at 14 boulevard des Italiens (ninth), Brasserie Universelle at 31 avenue de l'Opéra (second), and Café de l'Univers at 1 place André Malraux near the avenue de l'Opéra (first).[96] Even when staying across the river in the sixth arrondissement, he travelled to these cafes regularly, enacting a sort of pilgrimage that reversed his previous journeys from the fashionable centre to less reputable areas of the city.

In the evenings, Wilde travelled to more Bohemian cafes that connected him to artists and writers. Despite his friends' concerns about the Calisaya's popularity with "sodomist outcasts," this ninth-arrondissement bar (27 boulevard des Italiens) became a favourite spot for meeting with the poets Jean Moréas and Ernest La Jeunesse.[97] He frequented "the low dives of the Latin Quarter" – places where, as he told Ross, he went "under the wing of a poet [to] talk about art."[98] Wilde also spent time in sixth-arrondissement cafes including the Café de Flore at 172 boulevard Saint-Germain (popular with Joris-Karl Huysmans and Charles Maurras), and he travelled to Montmartre for a poetry reading held in a cafe.[99] There were, however, limits to the areas and types of establishments to which Wilde would go: in a series of letters to Ives, he expressed repeated shock at Ives's "appalling" suggestion to meet not in "proper, seemly restaurants" but "in a cabaret [on] the other side of the Arc de Triomphe, frequented ... by *cochers de fiacre*" (cab drivers).[100] Increasingly shut out of fashionable Parisian society, Wilde seemed eager to demarcate the boundaries of his Paris.

In a similar impulse, Wilde channelled his frustrations with English culture into a sort of geographic gatekeeping. Having been snubbed by "middle-class English" in Nice, Wilde took particular issue with the "dreary English" who visited Paris.[101] In an August 1898 letter to his publisher, Leonard Smithers, Wilde complained, "Paris is hot and empty. Even the charming people of bad character have gone away. Perspiring English families are all that can be seen. Pray don't desert me in this crisis."[102] A few days later, he wrote: "the English are very unpopular in Paris now, as all those who are over here [are] under Cook's direction."[103] Asserting himself as an authority over a landscape that had seemingly pushed him aside, Wilde tried to quell the apparent "indignation on the Boulevards" by stressing that these types of English tourists "are our worst specimens."[104] His complaints continued in a letter to Frank Harris the following day: "Paris is terrible in its heat. I walk in streets of brass, and there is no one here ... [T]he *gendarmes* [French police] yawn and regret their enforced idleness. Giving wrong directions to English tourists is the only thing that consoles them."[105] Wilde's presence in Paris was somewhat liminal – in exile and neither a French citizen nor a vacationing Englishman. By aligning himself with those who knew the city well, however, Wilde attempted to distance himself from the casual English tourists he derided and cast himself as a more legitimate urban presence.

During the final months of Wilde's life, the 1900 Exposition Universelle acted as his last neighbourhood, a space that both hinted at the city's futurity and, for Wilde, recalled his first visit during the 1867 fair. Set on the Champ de Mars and extending along both sides of the Seine, the Exhibition became "a meeting place for the world" and welcomed fifty-one million visitors over seven months.[106] Despite feeling some tension with the fair's English tourists, Wilde visited often, "amus[ing] himself ... like a big child."[107] In addition to displaying an array of new goods and inventions, including a Ferris wheel, films by the Lumière brothers, and X-ray photographs, the Exhibition previewed objects and technologies that would become part of the modern cityscapes that Wilde would not live to see: visitors could view automobiles and bicycles, ride an escalator and electric trolley, and stand on a moving walkway called, appropriately, the "rue de l'avenir" ("street of the future") (Figure 2.4).[108] Many of the Exhibition's purpose-built structures – the Porte Monumentale, the Globe Céleste, the Palais de l'Electricité, and the Château d'Eau – were temporary, vanishing from the landscape soon after the fair closed. However, other buildings and infrastructure – the Grand and Petit Palais, the Paris Métro and its Art Nouveau entrances, the Pont Alexandre III, and three railway stations (the Gares de Lyon, des Invalides, and d'Orsay) – remained and remade the city of Paris once again. To Ernest La Jeunesse, the Exhibition's physical structures gave Wilde one last opportunity for identity formation:[109] In his final neighbourhood, among the technologies and buildings that continue to shape Paris today, Wilde gained a brief, proleptic glimpse into the future structure and appearance of his beloved city and one last opportunity to reinvent himself.

Parisian Self-Fashioning: A Conclusion

In a 1911 article, Arthur Ransome traced the various stages in Wilde's relationship to Paris: "its lighthearted, exuberant beginning, its moment of glory, ... its catastrophe ... its defeat and sombre end."[110] In spite of this downward trajectory, Ransome suggested that Wilde "was always at home in Paris" and that "[o]n the background of [Paris] rather than of London the drama of his life stands out, cleared of side issues."[111] Though he recognized Wilde's greater affinity with Paris, Ransome's phrasing – that Paris was the "background" on which pivotal moments in Wilde's life occurred – implies a merely incidental relationship between the physical

Figure 2.4 "Exposition Universelle - Plateforme mobile, station du pont des Invalides," photograph, *Paris: Capital of the 19th Century*, Brown Digital Repository.

spaces of the French city and Wilde's personal development. Instead, the material spaces of Paris – its neighbourhoods, accommodations, parks, cafes, and streets – played a critical creative role, as Wilde sought out areas and architecture that would aid in his process of self-fashioning as a writer and aesthete. In the early 1880s, he situated himself within the historic centre of the city; through his accommodations as well as repeated visits to the Louvre, the Jardins des Tuileries, and the city's expensive restaurants, he connected himself to both culturally significant landmarks and literary figures. Through his Opéra-district hotels and cafes in the first half of the 1890s, Wilde deepened his relationship with modern, Haussmannized Paris and its literary establishment. He also used his knowledge of Parisian public space to fashion himself as a cultural critic and urban expert, taking on a more antagonistic posture towards England's social-spatial values. Finally, despite staying in less desirable locations in the late 1890s, Wilde clung to the spatial markers of his past life through recursive journeys to the cafes and, when possible, stays in the hotels around the Opéra. While Wilde was himself conscious of the role that Paris played in shedding the first Oscar, the French capital repeatedly provided him the urban material with which to evolve into various new Oscars. An inheritor of

Haussmann's Paris whose stays in the metropolis were bookended by Expositions that foregrounded urban renewal and cultural display, Wilde borrowed the city's impulse to innovate and constructed his own identities in dialogue with a city that was itself in flux.

NOTES

1 Richard Hibbitt, "The Artist as Aesthete: The French Creation of Oscar Wilde," in *The Reception of Oscar Wilde in Europe*, ed. Stefano Evangelista (London: Continuum, 2010), 67; Oscar Wilde, *The Complete Letters of Oscar Wilde*, ed. Rupert Hart-Davis and Merlin Holland (New York: Henry Holt, 2000), 206–9.

2 Robert H. Sherard, *The Real Oscar Wilde* (London: T.W. Laurie, 1916), 200.

3 Ellmann, *Oscar Wilde*, 220, 215.

4 Wilde, *Complete Letters*, 195.

5 Wilde, *Complete Letters*, 505.

6 Petra Dierkes-Thrun and Michael Davis, eds., *Wilde's Other Worlds* (Milton, UK: Routledge, 2018), 5.

7 David Pinkney, *Napoleon III and the Rebuilding of Paris* (Princeton: Princeton University Press, 1972), 24; Priscilla Parkhurst Ferguson, *Paris as Revolution: Writing the Nineteenth-Century City* (Berkeley: University of California Press, 1994), 74. Successive governments completed Haussmann's unfinished projects and erected new buildings in a similar architectural style; see François Loyer, *Paris Nineteenth Century: Architecture and Urbanism*, trans. Charles Lyon Clark (New York: Abbeville, 1988), 373.

8 The scale and speed of these changes was staggering: by 1870, Haussmann had built one fifth of Paris's roads, and the number of acres of municipal green space had grown from 47 to 4,500. See T.J. Clark, *The Painting of Modern Life: Paris in the Art of Manet and His Followers* (Princeton: Princeton University Press, 1984), 37; Pinkney, *Napoleon III*, 104.

9 See Shelley Rice, *Parisian Views*, (Cambridge, MA: MIT Press, 1997), 43.

10 For a discussion of this trip, see Matthew Sturgis, *Oscar: A Life* (London: Head of Zeus, 2018), 26.

11 Jane F. Wilde, quoted in Sturgis, *Oscar: A Life*, 27.

12 Matthew Sturgis's access to additional archives uncovered this 1867 visit. See *Oscar: A Life*, 26–7.

13 Herbert Lottman, *Oscar Wilde à Paris* (Paris: Fayart, 2007), 10–11.

14 I have found accommodation details for all but his 1867, 1875, 1877, and 1880 visits.

15 This map was designed for this chapter by Sally Hutcheon.

16 Franco Moretti, *Atlas of the European Novel, 1800–1900* (London: Verso, 1998), 3.

17 "L'Hotel, Paris." For sample itinerary, see "Oscar Wilde's London and Paris Tour," Oscar Wilde Tours, accessed 23 February 2022, https://www.oscarwildetours.com/gay-londongay-paris/.

18 "Oscar Wilde Suite," L'Hotel, accessed 23 February 2022, https://www.l-hotel.com/. Such marketing of course ignores the oft-repeated, though apocryphal, story that Wilde's last words were against the hotel room's hideous wallpaper.

19 See Ellmann, *Oscar Wilde*, 213.

20 *Baedeker's Paris and its Environs* (Leipzig: Karl Baedeker, 1881), 4. It is now the Westin Paris – Vendôme.

21 Augustus J.C. Hare, "Walks in Old Paris," *Good Words* 28 (December 1887), 105; *Baedeker's Paris* (1881), 79.

22 For more details about the hotel, see Elaine Denby, *Grand Hotels: Reality and Illusion* (London: Reaktion, 1998), 85–7.

23 Lottman, *Oscar Wilde à Paris*, 14, 17.

24 Lottman, *Oscar Wilde à Paris*, 235.

25 Sherard, *Real Oscar Wilde*, 219.

26 Sherard, *Real Oscar Wilde*, 220.

27 Sherard, *Real Oscar Wilde*, 220.

28 *Murray's Handbook for Visitors to Paris* (London: John Murray, 1879), 28; *Baedeker's Paris* (1881), 9. The hotel is still operational.

29 Ellmann, *Oscar Wilde*, 215.

30 Wilde, *Complete Letters*, 204.

31 Sturgis, *Oscar: A Life*, 55. There is some debate over whether Wilde began the poem at Oxford or on this trip.

32 Wilde, *Complete Letters*, 211.

33 Stokes, "Wilde and Paris," in *Oscar Wilde in Context*, ed. Peter Raby and Kerry Powell (Cambridge: Cambridge University Press, 2013), 65; Sturgis, *Oscar: A Life*, 55.

34 *Murray's Handbook* (1879), 246.

35 Oscar Wilde, *The Sphinx*, in *The Complete Works of Oscar Wilde*, ed. Bobby Fong and Karl Beckson (Oxford: Oxford University Press, 2000), 1:181, line 17.

36 Sherard, *Real Oscar Wilde*, 208. Wilde's interest in the statue remained: he later had a replica in his Tite Street home. Stokes, "Oscar Wilde in France," 66.

37 See Stokes, "Oscar Wilde in France," 66; Sherard, *Real Oscar Wilde*, 336.

38 Sherard, *Real Oscar Wilde*, 392.

39 *Murray's Handbook* (1879), 246. For a similar description, see *Baedeker's Paris* (1881), 159.

40 Wilde, *Complete Letters*, 206.

41 See Wilde, *Complete Letters*, 206n2.

42 Wilde, "Le Jardin des Tuileries," in *The Complete Works of Oscar Wilde*, ed. Bobby Fong and Karl Beckson (Oxford: Oxford University Press, 2000), 1:159, line 1.

43 Wilde, "Jardin," 159–60, lines 3, 7–8, 10–12. I have not been able to locate this statue. Children do launch toy boats in the Grand Basin near the western entrance, and there are two fountains containing sculptures of Triton and sea nymphs in the Place de la Concorde, just to the east of this entrance. Perhaps Wilde has conflated pond and fountain.

44 Wilde, "Jardin," 160, lines 17, 16, 19–20.

45 Wilde, "Les Ballons," in *The Complete Works of Oscar Wilde*, ed. Bobby Fong and Karl Beckson (Oxford: Oxford University Press, 2000), 1:163, line 2.

46 Wilde, "Ballons," 163–4, lines 3, 4, 6, 8.

47 Charles Baudelaire, *Painter of Modern Life and Other Essays*, ed. and trans. Jonathan Mayne (New York: Phaidon, 1995), 9.

48 It was described as one of the area's "most comfortable hotels" and was "much frequented by English travellers." *Murray's Handbook* (1879), 28; *Baedeker's Paris* (1881), 4.

49 Wilde, *Complete Letters*, 227.

50 See Louis J. Iandoli, "The Palace of the Tuileries and Its Demolition: 1871–1883," *The French Review* 79, no. 5 (2006): 986–1008.

51 Sherard, *Real Oscar Wilde*, 36.

52 Baudelaire, *Painter of Modern Life*, 9.

53 Wilde, *Complete Letters*, 195.

54 *Baedeker's Paris* (1891), 5–6; *Murray's Handbook* (1890), 44.

55 Lottman, *Oscar Wilde à Paris*, 41.

56 David P. Jordan, "Haussmann and Haussmannisation: The Legacy for Paris," *French Historical Studies* 27, no. 1 (Winter 2004), 110, 90.

57 David P. Jordan, *Transforming Paris: The Life and Labors of Baron Hausmann* (New York: Free Press, 1995), 207.

58 Michael Barker, "Brasseries, Restaurants and Cafés in Paris, and a Gazetteer of Establishments of Decorative Interest," *The Journal of the Decorative Arts Society 1850 – The Present*, no. 22 (1998), 83.

59 *Baedeker's Paris* (1891), 70; *Murray's Handbook* (1890), 102.

60 Oscar Wilde, "The Sphinx without a Secret," in *The Complete Works of Oscar Wilde*, ed. Ian Small (Oxford: Oxford University Press, 2017), 8:78. Café de la Paix opened in 1862 and soon became the Opéra district's most fashionable establishment. See Colligan, *A Publisher's Paradise*, 201.

61 Ellmann, *Oscar Wilde*, 348.

62 Hibbitt, "Artist as Aesthete," 68–70. Rebecca N. Mitchell similarly argues that "1891 marked a watershed in Wilde's career and in his critical

reception in France." Rebecca N. Mitchell, "Oscar Wilde and the French Press, 1880–91," *Victorian Periodicals Review* 49, no. 1 (2016), 126.

63 Ellmann notes that Wilde went with Gide and Louÿs to Café d'Harcourt. Ellmann, *Oscar Wilde*, 353. Near the Sorbonne (fifth arrondissement), the cafe was popular with students. *Harper's Guide to Paris and the Exposition of 1900* (London: Harper and Brothers, 1900), 66.

64 Horst Schroeder, "Oscar Wilde's and Stéphane Mallarmé's First Meeting and Mallarmé's Presentation Copy," *The Wildean*, no. 41 (2012), 75. Marcel Schwob mentions Wilde dining at Durand's. Lottman, *Oscar Wilde à Paris*, 43. In a letter, Wilde reminds Lord Alfred Douglas of their meals at Voisin's and Paillard's. Wilde, *Complete Letters*, 696.

65 George Augustus Sala, *Paris Herself Again in 1878–9* (London: Vizetelly and Co., 1884), 213; H. Sutherland Edwards, *Old and New Paris: Its History, Its People, and Its Places* (London: Cassell and Company, 1893), 123. Durand's hosted "a glittering crowd of artists, politicians, and writers, including ... Anatole France and Émile Zola." Alec Lobrano, *Hungry for Paris* (New York: Random House), 387.

66 Jacques Daurelle, "Un Poète anglais à Paris," *L'Écho de Paris*, 6 December 1891, 2, *BnF Gallica*.

67 Richard Griffiths, "The Château-Rouge and the Père Lunette: Insights into the 'Slumming' Culture of Late Nineteenth-Century France," *French Cultural Studies* 24, no. 1 (2013), 5, https://doi.org/10.1177/0957155812464160.; Daurelle, "Un Poète anglais," 2. For an account of their visit to the Château-Rouge, see Sherard, *Oscar Wilde*, 94–7. See Frankel for details of Wilde's earlier visits to brothels with Sherard during his honeymoon and his visits to Montmartre's bars with Sherard, William Rothenstein, and Henri de Toulouse-Lautrec. Frankel, *Oscar Wilde*, 193.

68 Daurelle, "Un Poète anglais," 2.

69 Wilde, *Complete Letters*, 501.

70 Wilde, *Complete Letters*, 501.

71 Wilde, *Complete Letters*, 501.

72 Wilde, *Complete Letters*, 501.

73 Wilde, *Complete Letters*, 501. Wilde's beloved kiosks are currently endangered: in 2016, Paris's mayor proposed a redesign that would offer more comfortable working conditions for newsvendors but that lacked the original's charm. In an unknowing nod to Wilde, one commenter suggested that the modernized kiosk would make Paris "as ugly as London." Henry Samuel, "Parisians Say City Will Be 'As Ugly As London' if Romantic Newspaper Kiosks Replaced with Modern 'Sardine Tins,'" *The Telegraph*, 8 July 2016, https://www.telegraph.co.uk/news/2016/07/08/parisians-say-city-will-be-as-ugly-as-london-if-romantic-newspap/.

74 Wilde, "Decay of Lying," in *The Complete Works of Oscar Wilde*, ed. Josephine M. Guy (Oxford: Oxford University Press, 2007), 4:190, 256.
75 Davis and Dierkes-Thrun, *Wilde's Other Worlds*, 5, 7.
76 Wilde, *Complete Letters*, 869.
77 Wilde, *Complete Letters*, 1023.
78 Street address listed in *Baedeker's Paris* (1896), 5.
79 *Murray's Handbook* (1890), 45. In contrast, his 1894 accommodation, the Hôtel des Deux Mondes, was "well kept, and suited to English tastes" (44).
80 *Baedeker's Paris* (1896), 7.
81 The Hôtel d'Alsace was classed in the "tenth category [of hotels], although its proprietor was convinced that it ought to be fifth" and notes that it was "more spacious" and "far cheaper" than the Hôtel de Nice. Frankel, *Oscar Wilde*, 205, 221.
82 Wilde, *Complete Letters*, 1074; Frankel, *Oscar Wilde*, 209.
83 Wilde, *Complete Letters*, 1078.
84 Street address mentioned in *Baedeker's Paris* (1896), 6.
85 Wilde, *Complete Letters*, 1149. See his letters to Leonard Smithers and Robert Ross for representative examples. *Complete Letters*, 1026, 1174.
86 Wilde, *Complete* Letters, 1162. Wilde was only able to retrieve them because the Hôtel d'Alsace's owner paid the Marsollier's bill. Frankel, *Oscar Wilde*, 258.
87 Wilde, *Complete Letters*, 1107.
88 Sherard, *Real Oscar Wilde*, 198.
89 Sherard, *Real Oscar Wilde*, 873.
90 Frankel, *Oscar Wilde*, 192, 196.
91 Frankel, *Oscar Wilde*, 206. See also Sturgis, *Oscar: A Life*, 675.
92 Ellmann, *Oscar Wilde*, 348.
93 Wilde, *Complete Letters*, 1172.
94 See Ellmann, *Oscar Wilde*, 564–5 and Frankel, *Oscar Wilde*, 260–1.
95 Jean-Joseph Renaud, "The Last Months of Oscar Wilde," unpublished typescript, The William Andrews Clark Memorial Library, University of California, Los Angeles, quoted in Frankel, *Oscar Wilde*, 261.
96 Wilde, *Complete Letters*, 1072. His statement about the Café de la Paix is not entirely accurate: Douglas took him there in 1899, and he spoke of a "luncheon" there in 1900 (1152, 1177).
97 Vincent O'Sullivan, undated letter to A.J.A. Symons, in *Some Letters of Vincent O'Sullivan to A.J.A. Symons* (Edinburgh: Tragara Press, 1975), quoted in Frankel, *Oscar Wilde*, 255. See also 241, 255–6 and Sturgis, *Oscar: A Life*, 690–1.
98 Sturgis, *Oscar: A Life*, 692; Wilde, *Complete Letters*, 1072.
99 Barker, "Brasseries," 86; Sturgis, *Oscar: A Life*, 692.

100 Wilde, *Complete Letters*, 1196, 1172. Wilde's aversion to meeting at a location frequented by male prostitutes (here euphemized as cab drivers) perhaps stemmed from the circumstances surrounding his downfall in 1895.

101 Wilde, *Complete Letters*, 1125, 936.

102 Wilde, *Complete Letters*, 1092. August is the month in which French citizens typically go on holiday. In a letter to Ross during the 1900 Exhibition, Wilde extended this disapproval: "Paris is full of second-rate tourists. German and American are the only languages one hears. It is dreadful." Wilde, *Complete Letters*, 1195.

103 Wilde, *Complete Letters*, 1093. The tour operator Thomas Cook made excursions to the Continent accessible to a wider range of Victorians.

104 Wilde, *Complete Letters*, 1093.

105 Wilde, *Complete Letters*, 1094. Wilde reused the first half of this comment in a letter to Ross a few days later.

106 Colette Colligan, *A Publisher's Paradise: Expatriate Literary Culture in Paris, 1890–1960* (Amherst: University of Massachusetts Press, 2014), 228; "Expo 1900 Paris," *Bureau international des expositions*, accessed 12 March 2022, https://www.bie-paris.org/site/en/1900-paris.

107 Stuart Merrill, "Some Unpublished Recollections of Oscar Wilde," in *Oscar Wilde: Interviews and Recollections*, ed. E.H. Mikhail (London: Macmillan, 1979), 2:470. At one point, Wilde feared "he was responsible for the failure of the Exhibition, the English having gone away when they saw him there so well-dressed and happy" (1212). He told Ross that "[t]he only ugly thing at the Exhibition is the public" (1189).

108 See Frankel, *Oscar Wilde*, 292; "Expo 1900 Paris." There was also an exhibit that looked backwards through its recreations of old Paris; Colligan describes Charles Hirsch's chance encounter with Wilde in Vieux Paris, calling it a "fitting" space to find the "broken man in semi-exile." *A Publisher's Paradise*, 228.

109 Ernest La Jeunesse, "Oscar Wilde," in *Oscar Wilde: Interviews and Recollections*, ed. E.H. Mikhail (London: Macmillan, 1979), 2:480.

110 Arthur Ransome, "Oscar Wilde in Paris," *Bookman* 33, no. 3 (1911), 268–9.

111 Ransome, "Oscar Wilde in Paris," 268.

PART TWO

Journalistic Advocacy

3 How Parisian Journalists Changed Their Minds about the Wilde Scandal

COLETTE COLLIGAN

The three trials of Oscar Wilde in 1895 at the Old Bailey Court in London were the most publicized sex scandal of the nineteenth century. The scandal was triggered when Wilde was at the height of his literary celebrity, known for his plays, poetry, essays, and novel *The Picture of Dorian Gray*. But his three trials in April and May of 1895 had a cataclysmic effect on his life and career. The key players in the court drama were the Marquess of Queensberry, who was scandalized by Wilde's affair with his son; Lord Alfred Douglas, who was Queensberry's son and Wilde's lover; and Wilde, who initially sued Queensberry for libel after the Marquess left him an abusive message on his calling card at his club in London. Wilde lost this case, a loss that immediately turned him from a plaintiff to a defendant, prosecuted for "gross indecency," a Victorian-era legal framework for criminalizing homosexuality. After two trials, Wilde was finally convicted and sentenced to two years' imprisonment with hard labour.

Newspapers around the world reported and commented extensively on the trials. Looking on from the other side of the English Channel, Parisian newspapers were especially active in following how they unfolded. Nancy Erber and Pascal Aquien have previously noted the intensity of the coverage by the Parisian press.[1] In 1994, a France-based bookseller-publisher, in the name of the association of friends of Hugues Rebell, even published a booklet entitled *Pour Oscar Wilde* that compiled a handful of articles that had been written in defence of the writer.[2] This booklet, however, selectively picked articles from the archive, overlooking many others as well as key aspects of Parisian journalistic activity.

The mass digitization of newspaper archives has made it possible, where previously it was not, to rediscover the Parisian media coverage of the trials and situate this coverage within a larger journalistic milieu. Delving into the Parisian news archive, I propose to reframe how articles on the Wilde trials have been read thus far, considering them as more than the sum of their parts. These articles were a complicated mix of each other, highly responsive to each other, and path dependent. More than just stand-alone articles, they were written in response to other articles and written to elicit new ones, as one journalist after another opined about the Wilde trials while looking around to see what the other was thinking.

Being able to read these news articles as more than the sum of their parts helps us appreciate how their authors collectively took part in larger communication rituals that take place when a scandal breaks, such as staging opinion about exposed wrong acts. Scandal, according to social theory, can be defined as collective public outrage against social transgression. Ari Adut has already applied classic scandal theory to the Wilde trials, building on the work of Max Gluckman in particular, who argues that the outrage scandal brings triggers normalization work in society to maintain social order.[3] What I bring to Adut's excellent analysis is, first, data-intensive material insight into the Parisian journalistic response to the scandal, and, second, Damien de Blic and Cyril Lemieux's reconceptualization of scandal as a *test* of social structures and values.[4] Scandal is, in my understanding, a test: it pushes communities to evaluate their attachment to values. In so doing, it carries a certain risk that the denunciation from which it erupts will not be affirmed in the end. This state of risk opens up a potential for the transformation of values as well as moral revolution and revaluation.[5] Long before the Wilde trials, French pamphleteers and journalists were known to test and challenge the terms of a scandal, repeatedly turning howls of outrage against alleged malefactors into cries of indignation against their accusers. This possibility of a shift in opinion within the French media system, when a scandal enters a later stage of its development known as an "affair," paved the way for the Wilde scandal to develop into something new and different in the hands of Parisian journalists. Because the news coverage within its wider communications milieu has been overlooked, this shift has largely gone undetected until now.

By expanding the analysis of journalists' opinions in the Parisian press and reading the interdependent relationships between articles through social theories of scandal, I aim to show how journalists collectively changed their minds about Wilde, transforming what was initially a scandal into a widespread outcry against intolerance and injustice that had a lasting effect on Wilde's Parisian and international legacy.

The Parisian News Archive in the Digital Age

This story of how Parisian journalists changed their minds about the Wilde scandal can be told thanks to digital access to historical newspapers. The Bibliothèque nationale de France's (BnF) digitization of its vast newspaper archives has revealed the staggering number of Parisian newspapers published in the city in the late nineteenth century, as well as their intense interest in Wilde's trials. This is not only a story of access and recovery, however, but also of new digital methods for reading newspapers. An online database called the *Wilde Trials International News Archive*, developed in partnership with the Digital Humanities Innovation Lab at Simon Fraser University, offers several new ways to read how these old newspapers covered Wilde's three trials and prison sentence.[6] Of most importance, it enables news articles to be read sequentially and comparatively to reveal how they participated in collective communication around the Wilde scandal.

Using this database, I have consulted seventy-one Parisian daily and weekly newspapers and collected over 1,500 articles on the Wilde trials, from the beginning of the trials to the end of 1895. A bar chart of these articles shows three major waves of coverage, each corresponding unsurprisingly to one of the three trials (Figure 3.1). Some of these articles were well-known vectors of opinion, such as editorials (*articles de tête*) and columns (*chroniques*), which were distinguished by their length and which gave the French press its reputation as the press of opinion (*la presse d'opinion*).[7] More recent journalistic genres also appeared at the end of the nineteenth century, such as interviews and reportage (a form of investigative journalism imported from America) which could be seen as new tools to solicit and structure opinion. I turn to these four journalistic genres to analyse the mise en scène of journalistic opinion around scandal, while recognizing that the plasticity of genres and the mixing of texts can blur the boundary between opinion and information in the press.[8]

When these four journalistic genres are visualized against other types of newspaper articles covering the trials (such as telegraphic dispatches and standard news articles), we see that they not only appeared during the three trials in April and May 1895, but also during the summer and again towards the end of the year. It is intriguing that opinion-driven articles continued even as more information-heavy news articles dropped significantly, and the intrigue deepens further when one considers their high word count (Figure 3.2). Why did this form of journalism persist in Paris well past the trials themselves?

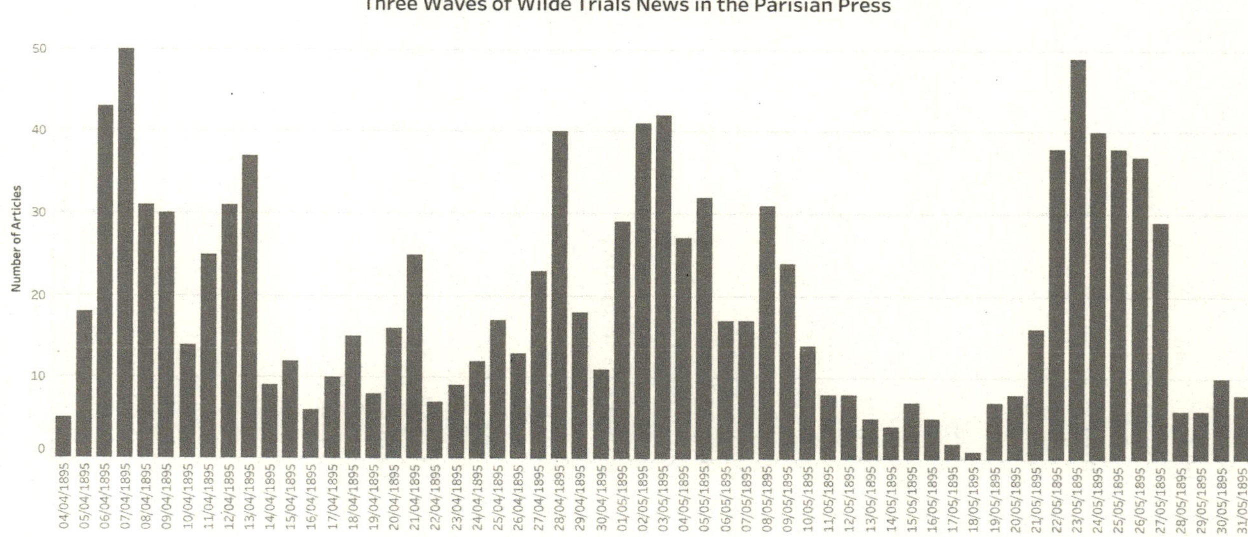

Figure 3.1 Three waves of Wilde trials news in the Parisian press. Data source: *The Wilde Trials International News Archive.*

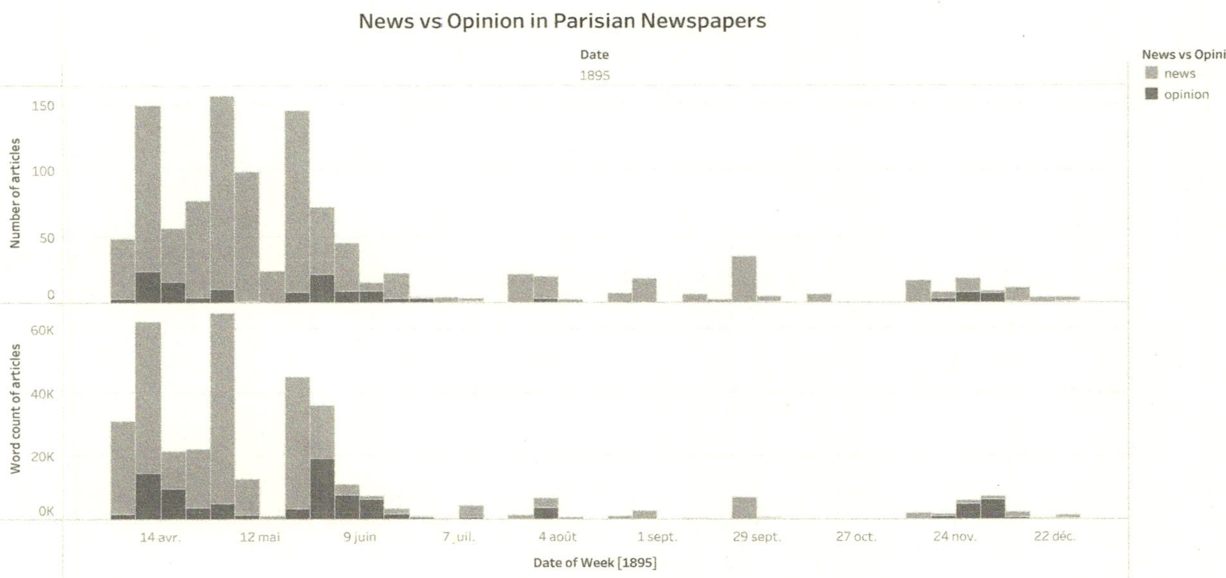

Figure 3.2 News vs. opinion in Parisian newspapers. Data source: *The Wilde Trials International News Archive.*

To answer this question, this chapter looks at three moments (during the trials, just after Wilde's conviction, and towards the end of the year) to examine how Parisian journalists expressed their opinions within a larger journalistic milieu of scandal, and how those opinions evolved to transform Wilde's trials from a sex scandal into a cause of injustice that called for a different judgment and sentence than those rendered by Judge Wills on 25 May at London's Old Bailey Court.

Journalistic Opinion during Wilde's Trials (5 April–27 May)

In the first wave of opinion, forty-seven articles consisting of editorials, columns, and interviews passed judgment on Wilde. Most of these articles were against him and expressed strong collective condemnation.

A first target of indignation focused on the Aesthetic movement. The position taken on both sides of the Channel was that the aesthetic principles of art for art's sake led to moral degeneration. This was the position put forward by the cultural theorist, Max Nordau, who had recently published his book *Dégénérescence* and was interviewed by *Le Gaulois*.[9] A second subject of indignation was British moral hypocrisy. It was sweet revenge for the French, often accused of immorality by their neighbours, to redirect their moral outrage onto the British. As a *Gil Blas* columnist wrote, "It's no secret for anyone that virtuous English society, which gets nauseous and indignant when it talks about 'French vices,' is simply the most rotten in the world. The Marquis de Sade has a veritable army of disciples in London who have, it is said, perfected the refinements of the demonic master."[10] To expose British moral hypocrisy, Parisian columnists took the opportunity to evoke references to pornography, sex work, and sodomy and, in so doing, made sexual practices, notions, and stories much more explicit than other national presses.

A third subject of indignation was directed at Wilde himself, with a changing emphasis on his lack of talent, his plagiaristic tendencies, and his effeminacy (symbolized by the image of him carrying a lily in his hand).[11] There were also comments about press standards, the public nature of sex trials in Britain, and the problem of prosecuting literature, but on the whole journalists rallied against Wilde, Aestheticism, and British moral hypocrisy in a general expression of homophobia wrapped in anti-British sentiment.

The classic theory of scandal helps to explain the almost unanimous denunciation of Wilde in the Parisian press during the two months of his trials. In his essay on gossip and scandal, Max Gluckman argues that scandal is one of the primary means by which social groups confirm their values and establish alliances. For Gluckman, it is this aspect of scandal that makes it a universal phenomenon, one that is even associated with "joyful feelings."[12] By participating in the public punishment of Wilde and circulating identical sentences and images, Parisian newspapers of all political and cultural horizons echoed each other, collectively expressing their indignation against Wilde, according to the communication practices confirming scandal.

Such was the intense wave of indignation and outrage over the scandal that a duel was fought in the forest of Saint-Germain-en-Laye outside Paris. The duel, which took place on 17 April, was provoked by the well-known journalist, Jules Huret, who had written a short, but devastating article in *Le Figaro supplément littéraire* that named certain Parisian men of letters who knew Wilde. These were all young men – Jean Lorrain, Marcel Schwob, and Catulle Mendès – the latter of whom challenged Huret to the duel.[13] Little blood was shed, and honour was ritualistically restored, but the fight revealed the intense feelings driving the scandal.

Intensity also lends itself to absurdity, however, which created an opening for a handful of journalists to critique how the scandal was playing out. Right after the duel, approximately ten days after the end of the libel trial, a few journalists called for calm.[14] Others went further and started to question whether Wilde was being judged fairly. Among these, a newspaper called *Le Gil Blas* stood out for its exceptional positioning, which has gone unnoticed until now. *Gil Blas* was the very same newspaper that had evoked the idea of de Sade's disciples walking the streets of London. But in addition to this negative article, it published a few other articles by a little-known journalist called Julien Despretz who had expressed some sympathy for Wilde, describing his behaviour as courageous in face of blackmailers.[15] After the foolhardy duel, Despretz came back onto the scene of judgment, and this time, he was far more critical of how the scandal was unfolding in Paris and in London. He noted the hypocrisy of those Parisians who had once associated with Wilde now denying any connection with him and suggested that journalists were condemning his works without having read them. Turning his attention to the London scene, he found a reign of terror where untalented hypocrites were attacking Wilde and other British men in order to raise themselves up before their peers.[16]

Even more strikingly, just after the conclusion of Wilde's first trial for "gross indecency," *Gil Blas* published an article that openly defended Wilde, pointing out that he was being scapegoated for a common "sin" of a mass of others.[17] Noting, moreover, that other men were mentioned as Wilde's companions or partners during the trials, the article's writer asked: "Why this one and not those ones? Why Wilde and not the others? Why Wilde and not Douglas (whom his father accuses as much as the writer and who does not even defend himself)? Why Wilde and not Lord ***, whose name was mentioned, and twenty others whose names were passed around by lawyers in writing, so that they would not be named out loud and made public? ... "[18]

By commenting on the sexual insinuations made about other men during the trials, reported on in the press, the journalist addressed not only the arbitrary application of the law, but also a certain tolerance towards intimacy between men, insofar as some names remained unpublished and unpunished.

Cyril Lemieux's sociological insights on the key role of rumour and gossip in the development of scandal help explain the significance of this article as well as the two preceding ones in *Gil Blas*. In an important collection on the history and theory of scandal, entitled *Affaires, scandales, et grandes causes,* Lemieux writes that rumour and gossip are primary forms of scandal that permit the development of tolerance towards social transgressions, allowing the evolution of a scandal to be checked and various opinions to emerge within a closed circle. As he writes, "It is a way for individuals to relativize some of their official norms [and] gradually under the radar allow a new sense of justice to emerge and become valued."[19] In other words, by highlighting a certain level of tolerance around sexual transgression that protected other men, this article revealed cleavage lines in social attitudes about homosexuality and its punishment as well as a local sense of justice. It can thus be seen as the opening note of the transformation of the media scandal into another journalistic form, forecasting the potential for a reversal of opinion about Wilde.

Wilde himself seems to have understood the importance of gossip in testing moral standards. In his play *Lady Windermere's Fan* (first performed in 1892 and published in 1893), one of the characters says:

> I never talk scandal. I only talk gossip. What is the difference between scandal and gossip? Oh! Gossip is charming! History is merely gossip. But scandal is gossip made tedious by morality.[20]

That said, the articles in *Gil Blas* did not immediately trigger any larger shift in opinion in the Parisian press. Articles published the same day continued to denounce Wilde, and commentary on the trials diminished to little more than a couple of interviews that were undertaken of Queensberry and Douglas during Wilde's final third trial.[21] Considering the public dynamics of scandal, where denunciation rests as much on how others handle the scandal as on the transgression itself,[22] it was risky for *Gil Blas* and its journalists not to join in Wilde's chastisement. Perhaps it was its reputation for levity and irreverence in journalistic circles that allowed *Gil Blas* to stand apart from others amid the intense outrage that prevailed.

Notably, Jean Ajalbert was the signed author of the 3 May article in *Gil Blas* that claimed Wilde had been scapegoated. He was one of the principal pens who would defend Captain Dreyfus during the Dreyfus Affair (an affair that centred on a French army captain unjustly accused and convicted of passing on military secrets to the Germans) and was also one of the first to call out the antisemitic nature of the attacks against Dreyfus in an article that appeared just months before the Wilde trials began.[23] He was not yet seen as an opinion leader, and his article on Wilde does not seem to have had observable impact, but in both the Dreyfus and Wilde affairs, he played the role of the canary in the coal mine warning others about the world's dark places. With Ajalbert in the mix, this raises the question: did the Wilde scandal have the potential to become a larger cause of iconic injustice as would the Dreyfus Affair just a few years later?

Journalistic Opinion after Wilde's Conviction (28 May– 31 July)

The answer is yes. Indeed, a sudden change of opinion, almost unanimous, occurred in the Parisian press, which saw the scandalous phase of the Wilde trials pass into a new phase. This change can be seen in the data, specifically the subsequent wave of editorials and columns that were published in the early summer after Wilde's sentence of two years of hard labour. The ingredients for this reversal were already there, as we have just seen. But the reversal was triggered by an important work of English reportage ("reportage Anglais") published by *Le Temps*.

On 28 May, three days after Wilde's conviction, *Le Temps* published a hard-hitting article entitled "Hard Labour" that not only described Wilde's first days of incarceration, but also explained in detail what this sentence would entail for him, and others, in Britain's prison system. The article included descriptions of prisoners walking the treadmill (otherwise known as the everlasting staircase), as well as oakum picking (which involved picking apart old rope for the fibrous material used in shipbuilding). Hard labour had no real equivalent in France, the article observed, but was instead a form of state-sanctioned torture, both physical and mental in its effects, a torture which it brought vividly before the mind's eye in a harrowing description of the treadmill:

> Imagine a gigantic wheel whose spokes reach four metres and whose circumference is divided into paddles, much like the circumference of a steamboat wheel. There is this difference between the wheel and the treadmill, that the wheel acts on the water by virtue of an internal propulsion, while the treadmill receives its propulsion from outside and owes it only to the men forced to hard labour. In the upper part of the circumference, the paddles lead to narrow cells where they appear, in passing, as the receding steps of a staircase.
>
> Brought into one of these cells, the condemned man is obliged to suspend himself with both hands from two rings dangling above his head, and to put his weight with his feet on the paddles that move, in order to activate the movement of this great wheel that he does not even see. If he hesitates, a guard placed behind him can apply a whip to him; if he stops, the wheel, in its continuous movement, hits him hard on the feet; if he stumbles, he risks paying for his failure with a broken leg. If he refuses, he is punished with the whip, the "cat with nine tails." This weapon of thin braided leather takes away the skin at the first blow and digs into the living wound at the second.[24]

Likening the punishment to a martyrdom, the article concluded by exposing its cruelty and calling for its abolition: "Such is the punishment of hard labour, the terror of all English criminals. It shows such a disproportion between the cruelty of the punishment and the crimes it punishes that one cannot hesitate to wish for its abolition."[25] The source of the article's information remains unclear. Its author, who remained unnamed, seems to have visited an English prison and been keenly aware of recent controversy over penal policies in local prisons, although this person made no mention of London's *Daily Chronicle* articles on "Our Dark Places" or the recent prison commission report recommending changes to penal policy.[26]

It was not necessarily the intention of *Le Temps* to shift opinion on Wilde, but it did. It was the most authoritative general-information daily in Paris at the time, giving its journalism special weight. It also brandished the power of reportage, which was a genre of heightened journalistic value at the time. According to Guillaume Pinson, it enlarged and shook up the geographic enterprise and critical reflection of French journalism, which in Wilde's case, moved opinion beyond the usual Anglo-French cultural rivalries.[27] The impact and influence of *Le Temps* reportage was clear. More than 60 per cent of the article was subsequently repeated verbatim in at least eighteen other French-language newspaper articles.

Over the next month, June 1895, this article also triggered the publication of thirty-two other articles in the Parisian press, in the form of editorials, columns, and interviews, all overwhelmingly in Wilde's favour. These articles appeared in newspapers of all political stripes, including the most widely circulated in Paris, as well as in newspapers that had previously denounced Wilde. Together they created an echo chamber that amplified opinion in favour of the author, revealing the interconnectedness of Parisian journalism, and showing how, despite their political differences, newspapers in the Parisian news system were a complicated mix of each other.

As for the content of the hard labour articles, there were two types. There were those that generalized the cry of injustice, and those that focused on Wilde's suffering in particular. In the first case, many newspapers, even if they did not copy the *Temps* article, reformulated it, using it as a template for their own descriptions of the treadmill, oakum picking, hard board and fare, and solitary confinement, some of which were in turn copied and cited by other newspapers.

Such was the case of an article that appeared in *Le Jour*, which reformulated the article in *Le Temps* to sensationalize the physical pain and cruelty of hard labour and to awaken humanitarian feeling. Under a banner headline across its front page "La Torture en Angleterre," it published an article that dwelt on the cries of the condemned: "And in the dreary silence of the prison, the wheel turns, turns; and one hears, mixed with the dull roar of the propeller, the sighs, the muffled complaints of the condemned ... The atrocious task must go on; the machine must run, tearing off toes, flaying skin, breaking something if necessary if the movement of the condemned man is too slow or clumsy."[28]

The article also concluded with a call to action, to redirect public outrage from the accused onto the accuser: "And in the face of such legal infamy, I wonder if this is happening in Europe, at the end of a century that claims to be civilized. Should we, in the presence of this torture, ... despise the judges who ordered it or be indignant with those who tolerate it."[29]

This outrage was taken up and enlarged the next day by Henry Rochefort, the well-known editor of *L'Intransigeant*. A former Communard who had been imprisoned in a French penal colony in New Caledonia, he used the rising indignation against the British penal system to shed light on the cruelty and torture of France's penal colonies.[30] Other journalists also picked up and passed on these arguments, connecting the Wilde case to a larger cross-Channel cause for prison reform in the name of humanity and restorative justice.[31] This sentiment, however, did not yet extend to Dreyfus, imprisoned in the infamous Devil's

Island penal colony in French Guiana since the beginning of January 1895. A journalist for *Le XIX siècle* claimed that Wilde's sentence, which was tantamount to being killed a little at a time, was even worse than Dreyfus's: "Dreyfus is a happy man of the earth next to Oscar Wilde, who did not betray his country."[32] It was Wilde's case that justified the pleas for prison reform, not Dreyfus's.

While articles such as these generalized the call for prison reform, others undertook Wilde's defence more directly. This happened quickly: it became permissible, just a couple of days after *Le Temps* published its reportage, to relativize Wilde's so-called crime. Referring to the harrowing descriptions of the treadmill from *Le Temps*, Henry Fouquier, for example, published an article in *L'Echo de Paris* that denounced the barbarity of the punishment as well as the iniquity of a law that punished a crime that harmed no one. During the trials, he had published an article that participated in Wilde's condemnation, but he now explained, in a remarkable shift, how his feelings about Wilde had changed: "And I confess without embarrassment that the disgust that the aesthete could cause me, I feel today for those who condemned him."[33] He acknowledged his initial disgust for the writer, but then redirected it to Wilde's accusers. He would remain one of Wilde's most ardent defenders in Paris, as would *L'Echo de Paris*.

With these expressions of sympathy for Wilde, many other articles followed over the next month protesting the conditions of Wilde's imprisonment, while passing arguments in defence of his sexuality. Jean Ajalbert re-emerged in *Gil Blas* to provide context on male sex workers.[34] Another journalist for *La Justice* offered French sexological explanations for Wilde's sexuality, citing Jean-Martin Charcot and Valentin Magnan, introducing a variety of vocabulary to describe such desires (such as "l'inversion du sens genital" and "les perversions sexuelles") and also describing Magnan's own admission that he too felt this kind of same-sex desire.[35] In foregrounding historical context and scientific knowledge to protest Wilde's harsh sentencing, these articles generated a great deal of information and publicity about such desires.

As these articles about Wilde's hard labour circulated and reversed opinion, along with worrisome reports about his failing health in prison, his iconization as a martyr began to crystallize. Images of him as the man who carried the lily in his hand were replaced with images of him as a "squirrel in a cage" and as a convict walking the treadmill. The popular daily *Le Quotidien illustré* even furnished a cover illustration of Wilde on the treadmill suspended from rings above him and outfitted in prison garb marked with broad arrows (Figure 3.3). The accompanying article claimed that the illustrator had visited an English prison and witnessed such scenes.[36]

Figure 3.3 Louis Sabattier,"Oscar Wilde aux travaux forcés" [Oscar Wilde at hard labour], *Le Quotidien illustré*, 7 June 1895, cover illustration, Bibliothèque nationale de France.

This story sparked further journalistic enterprise, as other journalists sought to get a glimpse into English prisons and the dreaded treadmill that had become a symbol of Wilde's suffering. *Le Gaulois* interviewed an English barrister supposedly with close knowledge of the case who detailed how Wilde endured the treadmill. Excerpts from this interview were then recopied in at least four separate Parisian newspapers, solidifying this image of Wilde even further.[37]

The fact that this series of repetitions from one article to another was intentional is confirmed by the journalist Henry Baüer in *L'Echo de Paris*. He insisted on the importance of the reproduction of these articles to stimulate social transformation: "They must be reproduced by all the newspapers, known in Europe, in the whole civilized world."[38] In so doing, he not only revealed the intention behind these acts of copying, but also an effort to extend the outcry in Paris throughout Europe. The same day, Octave Mirbeau wrote his powerful cry for pity for Wilde in *Le Journal*: "The vision of this unfortunate man, and of a thousand other obscure martyrs, turning the wheel of torment, with this constant terror of death, if, at the end of their strength, at the end of their courage, they stop, for a moment, turning, obsesses me like an awful nightmare."[39] Mirbeau's use of the term "martyr" to characterize Wilde's punishment would have lasting effect on his legacy. Just two weeks after *Le Temps*'s initial reportage, the Parisian press had thus opened the door for demanding another conclusion to the trials, one that would push for Wilde's release from prison and agitate for prison reform.

Amid this public outcry against Wilde's sentencing, only four newspapers printed a counter-opinion. *Le Figaro* called into question whether Wilde had been forced to walk the treadmill.[40] *Galignani's Messenger*, an English-language newspaper in Paris, picked up the question, drawing on a source who claimed to have visited Wilde in prison, who denied he ever walked the treadmill, and who accused the French press of circulating "false accounts" and "inexact statements."[41] This article was, in turn, translated and reprinted by *La Presse* and *Le Siècle*, which ridiculed Wilde and mocked the tears of the French journalists.[42] These articles imported the virulent anti-Wilde sentiment of the British. In doing so, they tested the French news system's ability to transmit accurate information. Whether Wilde ever walked the treadmill during the first month of his prison sentence in Pentonville prison is in fact in doubt, unverifiable in the prison records and disputed by biographers.[43] Regardless, these articles did not shift opinion again, nor did they polarize it. In the Parisian press, the image of Wilde on the treadmill became the single most potent image driving journalistic opinion against penal injustice and generating the idea of Wilde's martyrdom.

The pre-existing conditions for this reversal as well as the influence of *Le Temps*, whose widely circulated article exposed the cruelty of British hard labour and drew a vivid picture of Wilde's punishment, helped shift journalistic opinion. They altered what was permissible public response and pushed the evolution of the scandal. All scandals have the potential to shift in this way, according to de Blic and Lemieux's sociology of scandal. As a ceremony of social degradation that tests a community's existing structures and values, scandals always carry the risk of non-consensus and potential reversibility.[44]

Their theory builds on Élisabeth Claverie's concept of the affair, which she developed in the context of reading Voltaire's campaigns against religious intolerance. Whereas a scandal raises indignation against the accused, an affair redirects indignation onto the accuser, reversing the situation by showing a schism in opinion.[45] As Lemieux writes elsewhere, developing this idea, the affair is the later stage of the scandal.[46] This concept of the affair as the later stage of scandal not only provides an analytical framework for understanding how the Wilde scandal transformed into an affair in Parisian newspapers, but also explains how journalism gave voice to an alternative sense of justice by revealing a lack of consensus on moral values.

I think it is also possible to observe something of even more radical significance in the transformation of the Wilde scandal to an affair in the Parisian press. In his elaboration of Claverie's concept of the affair, Lemieux emphasizes how it allows a schism of opinion to be revealed, and one that is often pre-existing, though not openly expressed or perhaps fully understood. But it is also possible to see how the reversal of scandal can also provoke a change of opinion, which is perhaps an even more difficult social act than expressing non-consensus. As the Wilde scandal moved into the affair stage, Henry Fouquier acknowledged as much when he said, as I quoted earlier, that the disgust he felt for Wilde shifted from the writer onto his accusers. He also claimed agency over his change of opinion and perceptual shift of the world. Nor was he alone: several journalists as well as many newspapers altered their positions.

In a public forum, it is difficult to change one's mind, as it can be viewed as a sign of fallibility and weakness. Cognitive psychologists have also shown how humans resist changing their minds, regularly showing confirmation bias and even experiencing a rush of good feelings when their beliefs are confirmed.[47] The transformation of the scandal into an affair, however, provides a cultural mechanism for changing one's mind (as well as expressing a counter-opinion) that also confers a sense of agency over one's actions. The affair, moreover, has a rich history in France and its press, and is socially legitimated through historical iteration. Since Claverie first theorized the affair, numerous studies have followed to describe its media history, with the Dreyfus Affair, which was brewing just as the Wilde case was boiling over, as the paradigmatic example.

In short, then, the enabling conditions were already there for the Wilde scandal to transform into an affair in the Parisian press. A few things then happened that helped the affair take hold. An influential and disinterested intermediary intervened directing indignation away from

Wilde to a new target. This indignation spread via rapid replication and reformulation. Rhetorical tactics were mobilized to raise the cry of injustice and expand sympathy for Wilde. And these actions were legitimated by the cultural memory of previous affairs. Together, they created a journalistic environment for people to renegotiate their attachment to moral values and powerful feelings surrounding sexuality and penal justice to forge a new consciousness in a period of intolerance. Parisian journalism thus made it possible to change one's mind about Wilde.

Was the particularly French communication ritual of the affair – and the opinion-making it made possible – transferable and replicable elsewhere? It was certainly transferable as the article that triggered the transformation of the Wilde scandal in Parisian newspapers spread widely via a globalized press. Thus far, fifty-seven copies of the *Temps* article on hard labour have been found in the francophone press of France, Britain, Europe, North America, and indeed elsewhere in the world.[48]

One Dutchman was so moved by the horror of Wilde's hard labour (which he learned about from reading Dutch newspapers that were reprinting the *Temps* article and publishing commentary on criminality, sexuality, and the carceral state) that he wrote a letter to the chaplain of Pentonville prison (preserved in the Prison Commission records on Wilde). In this letter, he communicated his sense of moral outrage and connected it to the humanitarian movement to abolish slavery: "I cannot conceive that the government of this high-minded Nation, that was the first in coming up for the poor slaves, would tolerate such treatment, let alone order convicts to be whipped, if they show signs of fatigue."[49]

A Failed Petition (23 November– 31 December 1895)

With so much opinion turning towards Wilde in the Parisian press, the question that remains is why this outrage dissipated after June, and disappeared from the news by the beginning of August, failing to develop into a larger journalistic cause and planetary outcry, as it did with the Dreyfus case just a few years later. A failure in social tactics is partly to blame.

In late November, the affair did seem to pick up again. Having received news of Wilde's dire state of health, Stuart Merrill, a young French-American poet, announced joint plans to launch a petition with Robert Sherard, a Francophile Briton, to Queen Victoria to have Wilde released early from prison on the grounds of humanity and art.[50] They solicited signatures of eminent French and British writers, even naming them, including the influential French novelist, Émile Zola. This petition, which was reprinted in the daily press, mobilized the same journalists as before, as well as a few new ones, to write a last flurry of articles and interviews on Wilde's sentence of hard labour.

Petitions are written documents addressed to an authority that solicit signatures to demand a favour or redress an injustice. As such, they mobilize opinion by asking people to take a stand. They also make positions public through the act of attaching a signature, materializing what Ari Adut observes are the social dynamics of publicity that move scandals forward.[51] The act of signing one's name can reveal one's attachment to a value as much as the act of not signing one's name: as Adut puts it, actors "respond more to others' prior public handling of disgrace than to the transgression underlying the scandal."[52] The Parisian newspapers were immediately interested to learn which writers would and would not sign the petition.

One newspaper, *Le Gaulois*, was even able to get an interview with Zola to see where he stood.[53] Zola refused to sign, on the grounds that he did not understand its terms or know its petitioners, and he feared being taken for a dupe. Other major writers followed suit. It might be said, then, that Zola, one of the principal voices behind the pro-Dreyfus campaign with his 1898 "J'Accuse" article in *L'Aurore*,[54] put the nail in the coffin of the Wilde affair, as an issue for the mass daily press. It is true that some journalists chose to defend Wilde again, including Jean Ajalbert, one of Wilde's first defenders.[55] One of the most striking opinion pieces, by the writer Marcel Fouquier and published in *Le XIX siècle* and *Le Rappel*, concluded that Voltaire and Victor Hugo would not have hesitated to sign the petition.[56] In so doing, he legitimized the cause by putting the Wilde scandal into a longer history of French affairs, in which writers such as these intervened against perceived injustice. In the eighteenth century, Voltaire spoke out against the persecution of Protestants, and just a few decades before the Wilde scandal, Hugo spoke out against the imprisonment of the Communards. But the petition to release Wilde ultimately failed, with mostly only minor writers willing to sign it.

The Wilde affair failed to materialize into a larger journalistic outcry against injustice likely because it was a foreign news story and did not involve the French courts and system of justice, and perhaps because it lacked polarized opinion to drive it forward and generate controversy, but another important element was a mishandling of the social dynamics of publicity. The affair phase of the story had made it permissible for journalists to defend Wilde publicly and even change their minds about him. It did not mean, however, that others could be publicly named as people who would defend Wilde and others like him. Merrill may have misread the mood of the general public, mistaking the turnaround in the newspapers for an accurate reflection of public sentiment and ignoring generalized homophobia. According to Christophe Charle, careful social strategy is needed to launch successful petitions.[57] Petitions need to solicit signatures that seem neither too elitist, as to seem out of touch with larger social questions, nor too inconsequential or compromised, to lack credibility. Merrill played his hand too early, only soliciting the names of the key authors of the day, which he subsequently failed to gather, and thus ended up connecting the petition, and arguably the larger Wilde affair, to a minor group of Parisian writers sympathetic to Wilde, many of them associated with the literary and social margins of Decadence, Symbolism, anarchism, pornography, and homosexuality.

Conclusion

In the Parisian press, the Wilde scandal turned into an affair that called for pity for Wilde, both in the context of prison reform and tolerance for same-sex intimacies. That certain partisan writers spoke up for Wilde in the Parisian press was already known, but the extent of the outcry in the Parisian press, the significance of *Le Temps*'s reportage on hard labour, the evolution of the scandal into the more critical mode of the affair, and the emergence of a cultural mechanism justifying a change of minds and hearts are all new discoveries. It is the mass digitization of the news archive that has brought the larger patterns of Wilde journalism into view as well as the textual interactions and sequences that mobilized journalistic opinion around the scandal with the systems and technologies of the day.

The Wilde affair may have failed to develop fully in the Parisian press to become a much larger outcry against Wilde's suffering and British penal injustice, but the images of his martyrdom and the memory of journalistic outrage and enterprise persisted. They persisted in more peripheral cultural platforms in Paris – on the stages of avant-garde Parisian theatres (with the 1896 performance of his French play *Salomé* at the Théâtre de l'Oeuvre) and on the pages of niche literary reviews (like the *Mercure de France* discussed by Petra Dierkes in the following chapter). Journalism on the trials was also remembered and handed down. *Le Temps*'s article on hard labour recirculated in the French press in 1897, possibly connected to Wilde's recent release from prison. Its description of the treadmill also appeared in *La Revue encyclopédique*, bearing witness to one of the horrors of English local prisons that was abolished in the 1898 Prison Act. *Le Gaulois*'s interview with the eminent barrister describing Wilde's ordeal on the treadmill (who was presumed to be Wilde's lawyer Edward Clarke) was also recovered and reprinted, reappearing in Charles Grolleau's introduction to the 1906 Paris edition of *The Trial of Oscar Wilde*. Journalism about the trials was also retransmitted and preserved in the form of newspaper clippings.[58] Neither the scandal nor the affair leaves things as they were at their origin. Instead of seeing scandal simply as a form of sensationalism or violence mediated and exploited by newspapers, we can also see it as an inoculation to non-normativity and as an aid to social tolerance and social change. In the words of one critic, scandal can be the aperitif of revolution ("l'apéritif de la révolution").[59] In Wilde's case, Parisian journalism staged a negotiation and reconsideration of values, and invites us to consider how journalistic installations can function as a laboratory for the change of opinion and the formation of a new consciousness.

NOTES

1 Nancy Erber, "The French Trials of Oscar Wilde," *Journal of the History of Sexuality* 6, no. 4 (April 1996): 549–88; Pascal Aquien, *Oscar Wilde: Les mots et les songes* (Croissy-Beaubourg: Aden, 2006); Marco Wan, "From the Rack to the Press: Representation of the Oscar Wilde Trials in the French Newspaper *Le Temps*," *Law and Literature* 18, no. 1 (2006): 47–67.

2 Hughes Rebell, *Pour Oscar Wilde: des écrivains français au secours du condamné* (Rouen: Elisabeth Brunet, Association des amis d'Hugues Rebell, 1994).

3 Ari Adut, "A Theory of Scandal: Victorians, Homosexuality, and the Fall of Oscar Wilde," *American Journal of Sociology* 111, no. 1 (July 2005): 213–48; Max Gluckman, "Papers in Honor of Melville J. Herskovits: Gossip and Scandal," *Current Anthropology* 4, no. 3 (June 1963): 307–16.

4 Damien de Blic and Cyril Lemieux, "Le scandale comme épreuve: Éléments de sociologie pragmatique," *Politix* 3, no. 71 (2005): 9–38.

5 De Blic and Lemieux, "Le scandale," 13.

6 *Wilde Trials International News Archive*, last updated 25 March 2025, https://dhil.lib.sfu.ca/wilde/index.html.

7 Michael B. Palmer, *Des petits journaux aux grandes agences: Naissance du journalisme moderne, 1863–1914* (Paris: Aubier, 1983).

8 For a discussion of journalistic genres in the nineteenth-century press, see Dominique Kalifa, Philippe Régnier, Marie-Ève Thérenty, and Alain Vaillant, eds., *La civilisation du journal: histoire culturelle et littéraire de la presse française au XIXe siècle* (Paris: Nouveau Monde, 2011); and Guillaume Pinson, *La culture médiatique francophone en Europe et en Amérique du Nord: De 1760 à la veille de la Seconde Guerre mondiale* (Montreal: Presses de l'Université Laval, 2016), 67–8, 202–10, on reportage specifically.

9 Paul Roche, "Oscar Wilde jugé par le docteur Max Nordau," *Le Gaulois*, 10 April 1895; Max Nordau, *Entartung* (Berlin: Duncker, 1892); Max Nordau, *Dégénérescence* (Paris: Alcan, 1894).

10 Adolphe Tavernier, "Chronique parisienne," *Gil Blas*, 11 April 1895. "Ce n'est un secret pour personne que cette bonne société anglaise, qui

a des nausées indignées quand elle parle des 'vices française' est tout simplement la plus pourrie du monde. Le marquis de Sade compte à Londres une véritable armée de disciples qui ont, dit-on, perfectionné les raffinements du maître démoniaque."

11 For example, on plagiarism. (cf. *L'Intransigeant*, 22 April 1895).

12 Gluckman, "Gossip and Scandal," 313; cf. de Blic and Lemieux, "Le scandale comme épreuve," 13.

13 Jules Huret, "Petite chronique des lettres," *Le Figaro supplément littéraire*, 13 April 1895. Duels were still practised in France at the end of the nineteenth century, including among journalists, but the practice was declining.

14 Henry Fouquier, "La Barbarie," *L'Echo de Paris*, 30 May 1895; Henry Baüer, "Oscar Wilde en prison," *L'Echo de Paris*, 15 June 1895.

15 Julien Despretz, "Le procès Oscar Wilde," *Gil Blas*, 15 April 1895.

16 Julien Despretz, "Oscar Wilde littérateur," *Gil Blas*, 25 April 1895.

17 Jean Ajalbert, "L'Avocat d'Oscar," *Gil Blas*, 3 May 1895. "L'on fait de lui la bête émissaire du péché d'une masse d'autres."

18 Ajalbert, "L'Avocat d'Oscar." "Pourquoi celui-ci et pas ceux-là? Pourquoi Wilde et pas les autres? Pourquoi Wilde et pas Douglas (que son père accuse autant que l'écrivain et qui ne se défend même pas)? Pourquoi Wilde et pas lord ***, dont le nom a été prononcé, et vingt autres dont les avocats se font passer les noms écrits, pour qu'ils ne soient pas prononcés, publiés?" "Lord ***" was likely Lord Rosebery, the prime minister at the time, to whom the article referred. The Marquess of Queensberry had written a letter, which was read in court, that had insinuated that he had relations with other men.

19 Cyril Lemieux, "L'Accusation tolérante: Remarques sur les rapports entre commérage, scandale et affaire," in *Affaires, scandales et grandes causes: De Socrate à Pinochet*, ed. Luc Boltanski, Elisabeth Claverie, Nicolas Offenstadt, and Stéphane Van Damme (Paris: Stock, 2007), 378. "C'est une manière pour les individus de relativiser certains de leurs normes officielles [et] progressivement souterrainement de faire apparaître et valoir un nouveau sense du juste."

20 Wilde, *Lady Windermere's Fan* (London: Elkin Mathews and John Lane, 1893).

21 "Marquis and Son Come to Blows," *New York Herald* (European edition), 22 May 1895; George Docquois, "Entretien avec Lord Alfred Douglas," *Le Journal*, 25 May 1895.

22 Adut, "A Theory of Scandal," 238.

23 "Crime et châtiment," *Gil Blas*, 9 January 1895. By a strange coincidence, Wilde came to know the man who was the real traitor in the Dreyfus Affair (Charles Marie Ferdinand Walsin-Esterházy). The intersections

between Wilde and Esterházy are taken up in J. Robert Maguire, *Ceremonies of Bravery: Oscar Wilde, Carlos Blacker, and the Dreyfus Affair* (Oxford: Oxford University Press, 2013), and by Nicholas Frankel, *Oscar Wilde: The Unrepentant Years* (Cambridge, MA: Harvard University Press, 2017).

24 "Le 'Hard Labour,'" *Le Temps*, 28 May 1895.
"Imaginez une roue gigantesque dont les rayons atteignent quatre mètres et dont la circonférence est divisée en palettes, à peu près comme la circonférence d'une roue de bateau à vapeur, d'une aube. Il y a cette différence entre l'aube et le tread mill, que l'aube agit sur l'eau en vertu d'une propulsion intérieure, tandis que le tread mill reçoit sa propulsion du dehors et la doit uniquement aux hommes frappés de hard labour. Dans la partie supérieure de la circonférence, les palettes aboutissent à des cellules étroites où elles figurent, en passant, les marches fuyantes d'un escalier.
"Amené dans une de ces cellules, le condamné est tenu de se suspendre de ses deux mains à deux anneaux ballottant au-dessus de sa tête, et de peser de tout son poids avec ses pieds sur les palettes qui défilent, afin d'actionner le mouvement de cette grande roue qu'il n'aperçoit même pas. S'il hésite, un gardien placé derrière lui peut lui appliquer un coup de fouet; s'il s'arrête, la roue, dans son mouvement continu, l'atteint rudement aux pieds; s'il trébuche, il s'expose à payer sa défaillance d'une jambe cassée. S'il refuse, c'est la peine disciplinaire du fouet, du 'chat à neuf queues.' Cette arme de mince cuir tressé emporte la peau au premier coup et fouille la plaie vive au deuxième."

25 "Le 'Hard Labour.'" "Telle est cette peine du hard labour l'effroi, la terreur de tous les malfaiteurs anglais. Elle accuse une telle disproportion entre la cruauté du châtiment et les délits qu'elle châtie qu'on ne saurait hésiter à souhaiter son abolition."

26 "Our Dark Places," *Daily Chronicle*, 23, 25, and 29 January 1894.

27 Pinson, *La culture médiatique francophone*, 204.

28 "La Torture en Angleterre," *Le Jour*, 29 May 1895. "Et dans le morne silence de la prison, la roue tourne, tourne; et l'on entend, melés au grondement sourd de l'hélice, les soupirs, les plaintes étouffées des condamnés ... Il faut que l'atroce besogne continue; il faut que la machine marche, arrachant les orteils, écorchant la peau, brisant au besoin quelque chose si le mouvement du condamné est trop lent ou maladroit."

29 "La Torture en Angleterre." "Et devant une pareille infamie légale, je me demande si cela se passe en Europe, à la fin d'un siècle qui se prétend civilisé. Faut-il, en présence de ce supplice, que l'Inquisition oublia, mépriser les juges qui l'ont ordonné ou s'indigner contre ceux qui le tolèrent."

30 Henri Rochefort, "Supplicieurs et suppliciés," *L'Intransigeant*, 30 May 1895.
31 cf. *Le Petit Parisien*, 30 May 1895.
32 "'Dur Travail': Le châtiment d'Oscar Wilde," *Le XIX siècle*, 4 June 1895. "Dreyfus est un heureux de la terre auprès d'Oscar Wilde, qui n'a pas trahi sa patrie."
33 Henry Fouquier, "La barbarie," *L'Echo de Paris*, 30 May 1895. "Et j'avoue sans embarras que le dégoût que pouvait me causer l'esthète, je l'éprouve aujourd'hui pour ceux qui l'ont condamné."
34 Jean Ajalbert, "Article additionnel," *Gil Blas*, 31 May 1895.
35 Léon Millot, "Hard Labour," *La Justice*, 7 June 1895.
36 "Oscar Wilde, au moulin de discipline," *Quotidien illustré*, 7 June 1895.
37 "Oscar Wilde, à la prison de Pentonville," *Le Gaulois*, 13 June 1895; see also *Le Soir*, 14 June 1895; *L'Echo de Paris*, 15 June 1895; *La France*, 15 June 1895; and *L'Intransigeant*, 15 June 1895.
38 Henry Baüer, "Oscar Wilde en prison," *L'Echo de Paris*, 15 June 1895. "Il faut qu'ils soient reproduits par tous les journaux, connus de l'Europe, de tout le monde civilisé."
39 Octave Mirbeau, "À propos du 'Hard Labour,'" *Le Journal*, 16 June 1895. "La vision de cet infortuné, et de mille autres martyrs obscurs, tournant la roue de supplice, avec cette terreur constante de la mort, si, à bout de force, à bout de courage, ils s'arrêtent, un instant, de tourner, m'obsède comme un affreux cauchemar."
40 "À travers Paris," *Le Figaro*, 15 June 1895.
41 "Mr. Oscar Wilde at Pentonville," *Galignani Messenger*, 25 June 1895.
42 "Une visite à Oscar wilde," *La Presse*, 26 June 1895; "Au jour le jour, L'Esthète martyr," *Le Siècle*, 28 June 1895. It also seems to have been reprinted in the British press: *Edinburgh Evening News*, 28 June 1895.
43 The treadmill was one of the punishments which was designated first-class hard labour. Upon admission to a prison, a medical examiner would determine the fitness of a prisoner sentenced to hard labour. Biographers do not agree whether Wilde was found fit for this form of hard labour or not. Harford Montgomery Hyde, in his *Oscar Wilde: The Aftermath* (London: Methuen, 1963), claims to have seen Pentonville prison admission records that show that Wilde was not put to work on the treadmill, but was assigned light labour such as oakum picking instead (4). This record is not among the Prison Commission documents related to the Wilde case in the National Archives in London (P COMM 8/432–435). Whether or not Wilde ever served his hard labour working on the treadmill remains in doubt. Wilde himself never spoke of the specific prison labour he endured.
44 De Blic and Lemieux, "Le scandale comme épreuve," 13.

45 Élisabeth Claverie, "Procès, affaire, cause. Voltaire et l'innovation critique," *Politix* 2, no. 26 (1994): 76–85; and De Blic and Lemieux, "Le scandale comme épreuve," 16.

46 Lemieux, "L'Accusation tolérante," 369.

47 Elizabeth Kolbert, "Why Facts Don't Change Our Minds," *The New Yorker*, 20 February 2017; Hugo Mercier and Dan Sperber, *The Enigma of Reason* (Cambridge, MA: Harvard University Press, 2017).

48 For a list of French reprints, see *Le Temps*'s article on hard labour from 28 May 1895 transcribed in *Wilde Trials International News Archive*, https://dhil.lib.sfu.ca/wilde/view.html?f=flt_3387.

49 The National Archives, London, P COMM 8/432.

50 *La Plume*, 15 November and 1 December 1895.

51 Adut, "A Theory of Scandal," 218.

52 Adut, "A Theory of Scandal," 240.

53 "Interview-express," *Le Gaulois*, 26 November 1895.

54 Émile Zola, "J'Accuse ... !," *L'Aurore*, 13 January 1895.

55 Jean Ajalbert, "L'Avocat d'Oscar," *Gil Blas*, 3 May 1895.

56 Marcel Fouquier, "Chronique, par Marcel Fouquier," *Le XIX siècle*, 3 December 1895; *Le Rappel*, 3 December 1895.

57 Christophe Charle, *Paris, fin de siècle: Culture et politique* (Paris: Seuil, 1998), 69.

58 Charles Grolleau, *The Trial of Oscar Wilde* (Paris: C. Carrington, 1906).

59 Eric de Dampierre, "Thèmes pour l'édude du scandale," *Annales: economies, sociétés, civilizations* 9, no. 3 (1954): 335.

4 Oscar Wilde and Henry-D. Davray: Reviewing, Translating, and Publishing Wilde for the *Mercure de France*

PETRA DIERKES

When Oscar Wilde's body was laid to rest on 3 December 1900, only a few dozen mourners attended the funeral. Out of those who came to the church service at Saint-Germain-des-Prés in Paris, thirteen set off to accompany Wilde's funeral hearse to the Cimetière de Bagneux, but "only six or so [of those] arrived" at Wilde's initial burial site.[1] Among the few who were still in attendance when the coffin was lowered into the earth was one man who played an important role for Wilde's literary career in Paris: Henry-D. Davray (1873–1944), a gifted translator and key contributor to the respected literary journal *Mercure de France*. He was accompanied by Paul Fort, the former founder and director of the Théâtre d'Art, which, by then, had been renamed Théâtre de l'Oeuvre (and staged the 1896 world premiere of *Salomé*). Both Davray and Fort had been among the few close friends who paid Wilde their final respects at the Hôtel d'Alsace.[2] They also represented the community of writers and journalists associated with the respected literary journal *Mercure de France*, which sent a wreath to the funeral to honour Wilde.[3]

In this chapter, I wish to call attention to the importance of the *Mercure de France*'s championing of Wilde's work in France from the 1890s to the 1920s, and specifically the still relatively unknown role that Henry-D. Davray played in the transnational literary and cultural effort to rebuild Wilde's reputation. As I have argued elsewhere, in the wake of Wilde's 1895 crisis when he was tried and imprisoned for "gross indecency," the *Mercure de France* provided an important public intellectual forum for protesting Wilde's imprisonment and vouching for the artistic merit of his work.[4] As a periodical publication able to react to current news and trends, spearheaded by the writer Rachilde's editorial prowess and personal support for Wilde, the *Mercure de France* strategically intervened at key moments of crisis to advance a sympathetic story of Wilde to French readers. They were aided in no small measure by the tireless, quiet, steady efforts of Henry-D. Davray, who championed Wilde's work literally for decades, from the mid-1890s to the late 1920s. Davray not only translated two of Wilde's works for the *Mercure* (the *Ballad of Reading Gaol* and *De Profundis*), he also collaborated directly with Wilde and Robert Ross on his translations, and was in touch with key players in England involved with Methuen's 1908 publication of the *Collected Works of Oscar Wilde,* such as Christopher Millard and Walter Ledger. In addition, Davray reviewed Wilde's work and wrote his obituary in the *Mercure*. After Wilde's death, Davray co-translated and published various Wilde-focused monographs by André Gide, Arthur Ransome, and Frank Harris under the *Mercure de France* publishing imprint, culminating in his own, well-received 1928 account of Wilde's last years, *Oscar Wilde: La Tragédie finale*. This work effectively made Davray Wilde's first French biographer. With it, he tried to demonstrate, once and for all, that Wilde's death had robbed the world of a great artistic talent.

Strategic Interventions: The *Mercure de France*'s Protests against Wilde's Mistreatment

Around 1900, the *Mercure de France* was still a young, but already well-respected, French literary journal. Founded by its general editor Alfred Vallette and a group of journalists and writers in Paris in December 1889, the *Mercure* "started as a relatively small journal consisting of 32 pages with a print-run of 600 copies" but "soon became one of the biggest and most influential French periodicals. By 1914, a typical issue consisted of 240 pages and reached an audience of 40,000 readers."[5] The *Mercure de France* attracted a sophisticated audience: it "was read mostly by educated people and even by some writers, as evidenced by their correspondence or by their works."[6] Initially, the *Mercure* appeared twice monthly, then only once a month as it also started publishing monographs. In the summer of 1995, the Bibliothèque nationale de France even housed an exhibition detailing the *Mercure*'s history as a revered Parisian literary institution.[7] While the journal ceased publication in 1965, it continues as a publishing house that still has the same address today: 26, rue de Condé, Paris.

As general editor, Alfred Vallette was responsible for the business operations of the *Mercure*, but his wife and collaborator, Rachilde (Marguerite Eymery-Vallette, 1860–1953), was the journal's true literary brain. At the journal's founding in 1889, Rachilde was an established avant-garde author known for a series of scandalous Decadent novels, particularly *Monsieur Vénus* (1884), which earned her an obscenity trial

Figure 4.1 Jean Veber, H.-D. Davray, c. 1890s, Bibliothèque nationale de France (https://gallica.bnf.fr).

in Belgium. Called a "distinguished pornographer" by Jules Barbey-d'Aurevilly and nicknamed "Mademoiselle Baudelaire" by Maurice Barrès for her gender-defying boldness (her visiting cards famously read, "Rachilde – Homme de lettres"), Rachilde straddled the line between literary genius and Decadent erotica. As literary reviews editor for the *Mercure* from 1889 to 1924, when she retired from the journal, Rachilde picked and reviewed new, noteworthy works of literature for the *Mercure*, all the while keeping a steady pace as a writer herself, publishing over sixty novels and plays in total. Rachilde also held weekly literary salons for the *Mercure* that soon became a crucial networking place for young French avant-garde writers such as Alfred Jarry, André

Gide, Jean Lorrain, Marcel Schwob, Jean Moréas, Félix Fénéon, and others. Rachilde used her salons as recruiting ground for authors and trends the *Mercure* was eager to publish, and these salons contributed in a major way to the *Mercure*'s resounding success as a journal and publishing house.[8]

While it is difficult to reconstruct when exactly Wilde first attended Rachilde's salon, it is likely that he would have done so in 1891, when he actively entered the Paris literary scene and met, among others, some members of Rachilde's circle: Marcel Schwob, Pierre Louÿs, Adolphe Retté, and Stuart Merrill, who helped Wilde with the French text of *Salomé*. Wilde was familiar with Rachilde's *Monsieur Vénus*, which he read on his honeymoon in 1884. He admired it so much that it influenced his original conception of the yellow book in *The Picture of Dorian Gray*.[9] Decades later, Rachilde recalled Wilde's first attendance at her salon. An amused Rachilde writes that Wilde had asked another guest if their hostess had really written *Monsieur Vénus*, as he evidently had trouble reconciling her appearance with her provocative penmanship: "Cette énigmatique créature en robe de laine noire a-t-elle écrit vraiment *Monsieur Vénus*?" ("Did that enigmatic creature in a black wool dress really write Monsieur Vénus?").[10]

Clearly, by 1895, the *Mercure* already treated Wilde as a respected author. When the 1895 "gross indecency" scandal hit, the journal was extremely vocal in protesting Wilde's treatment by the English. In August 1895, it published one of the fieriest of all defences of Oscar Wilde in the French press, Hugues Rebell's "La Défense d'Oscar Wilde." The *Mercure* also made the strategic decision not only to protest Wilde's legal misery but to emphasize his artistic genius by discussing and reviewing his work, sometimes simultaneously. In the "Livres" section of the same issue in which Rebell's article appeared, the *Mercure* also published a highly complimentary review by Camille Mauclair (pseudonym of Séverin Faust) of the first French translation of *The Picture of Dorian Gray* by Eugène Tardieu. The *Mercure* thus delivered a strong coordinated message that Wilde's work was of the highest artistic caliber and his imprisonment an outrageous miscarriage of justice. Rebell deplored that Wilde was treated like an enemy of the state, as if he had assassinated the queen or overthrown Parliament.[11] Similarly, in his review of Wilde's translated novel, Mauclair came out swinging at those writers who had abandoned Wilde: "M. Oscar Wilde est un artiste, et ses collègues ont manqué l'honneur vrai en le lâchant" ("Mr. Oscar Wilde is an artist, and his colleagues have missed true honour by dropping him").[12]

A few months later, with Wilde still languishing in prison, the Théâtre de l'Oeuvre defiantly introduced the world premiere of *Salomé*, under Aurélien-Marie Lugné-Poe's direction and with Lina Munte as Salome and Lugné-Poe himself playing Herod, the other leading role. *Le Journal* reported that Mauclair as well as Henry Bauër had a role in bringing this production about,[13] but that is probably not the complete picture: it is likely that Paul Fort and Rachilde were directly involved as well. Making sure that *Salomé* got staged was probably the most meaningful way Wilde's friends at the *Mercure*, including Mauclair and Fort, could support Wilde in prison. Rachilde herself was a longstanding member of the theatre's play selection committee and probably played a central role in picking *Salomé* for the stage that year. She had also written her own Symbolist plays for the Théâtre d'Art (specifically *La Voix du Sang*, 1890, dedicated to Fort; and *Madame La Mort*, 1891). Rachilde clearly admired *Salomé* and even included indirect references to it in two of her own works, her Symbolist play *L'Araignée de Cristal* (1894) and her 1900 novel *La Jongleuse*.[14] In his memoir, Paul Fort fondly includes *Salomé* in a lineup of "ces grandes et fortes oeuvres" ("those great and powerful works") the Théâtre d'Art and Théâtre de l'Oeuvre had been proud to produce, such as Marlowe's *Dr. Faustus*, Shelley's *The Cenci*, Maeterlinck's *Pelléas et Mélisande*, as well as works by Ibsen, Strindberg, Hofmannsthal, and Jarry.[15]

The reviews of *Salomé* in the Paris press were mixed, as Emily Eells has pointed out. They were also intertwined with reviewers' opinions on Wilde's trials: "the reception of *Salomé* cannot be dissociated from events in Wilde's life."[16] The *Mercure de France*'s stance towards *Salomé* was uniformly positive and supportive of Wilde, however. Jean de Tinan's review of the play appeared in the issue immediately following the premiere (March 1896). Tinan praised Lugné-Poe's production, the actors, and Wilde's artistic talent, calling *Salomé* a play "si profondément imprégnée d'une superbe passion de beauté" ("so deeply imbued with a superb passion for beauty").[17] Tinan stated his hope that the imprisoned Wilde would find encouragement in the resounding success of *Salomé*'s opening night, especially since Wilde had been unable attend the premiere himself.[18] A grateful Wilde wrote to Robert Ross on 10 March 1896 about what this production meant to him:

> Please write to Stuart Merrill in Paris, or Robert Sherard, to say how gratified I was at the performance of my play: and have my thanks conveyed to Lugné-Poe; it is something that at a time of disgrace and shame I should be still regarded as an artist. I wish I could feel more pleasure: but I seem dead to all emotions except those of anguish and despair. However, please let Lugné-Poe know that I am sensible of the honor he has done me.[19]

Henry-D. Davray as Wilde's Loyal Interlocutor and Advocate

While the *Mercure* was particularly active in its targeted journalistic support of Wilde during his trials and imprisonment (1895–7), Henry-D. Davray's main contributions came when he became a crucial collaborator and strategic advocate for Wilde in the years that followed (Figure 4.1). The professional connection the two men developed was one of the most important ones Wilde formed in France, and the most direct working relationship Wilde had with any staff member of the *Mercure*. Davray was the *Mercure*'s anglophone books review editor, publishing his long running "Lettres anglaises" ("English letters") section for an astonishing four and a half decades, from 1896 until 1940. Birgit van Puymbroeck writes, "[w]ith an average of seven or eight books reviewed per month, Davray informed the French reader about the latest works of drama, poetry and prose, about new editions of canonical works, about literary criticism and the periodical press," contributing to the *Mercure*'s "encyclopaedic character" and its indexing of "key tendencies in a rapidly developing literary market."[20] In his "Lettres anglaises," Davray reviewed major realist and modernist authors alongside middlebrow, mass-market writers from Thomas Hardy to Mary Augusta (Mrs. Humphry) Ward, Virginia Woolf, and Victoria Cross. Annie Escuret states that Davray was one of the founders of the Anglo-French Society in 1917 and acted as "a distinguished comparative scholar and cultural mediator between England and France for many years."[21] Importantly, Davray was also an excellent translator: besides Wilde, he translated Kipling, Conrad, Yeats, Gosse, and particularly H.G. Wells, whose work he first brought to French readers' attention.

It is likely that Davray first got to know Wilde during the latter's 1891 Paris visit, when Wilde made the rounds among many writers who were affiliated with Rachilde and the *Mercure de France*. Richard Ellmann writes that Davray had Wilde and the author Yvanhoe Rambosson over for lunch that year.[22] In 1895, Davray was certainly familiar with the details of Wilde's scandal, since he was translating an essay by Lord Alfred Douglas that the *Mercure de France* had solicited to drum up support for the imprisoned Wilde. The manuscript of the French translation, presumably in Davray's hand, with corrections in another hand (probably Rachilde's or Vallette's), is now at Princeton.[23] Despite these efforts, the *Mercure de France* ended up not publishing Davray's translation of Douglas's essay, since Wilde himself had implored the editors not to go ahead with it.[24] It is to Rachilde's and Vallette's credit that they chose to honour Wilde's wishes, even though they themselves had solicited Douglas's article and Davray had already spent time translating it. Douglas took his article, minus Wilde's letters, to *La Revue blanche* (June 1896). Rachilde nonetheless graciously supported both him and Wilde in her essay "Questions brûlantes" ("Burning questions"), which appeared in the same journal in September, where she publicly upheld their relationship (and same-sex love in general) by calling it "a great Love" worthy of respect. The *Mercure* followed up to further support Douglas by publishing a beautiful French and English-facing edition of Douglas's first book, *Poèmes* (October 1896), this time translated by Eugène Tardieu, the first translator of Wilde's *The Picture of Dorian Gray*.

When Wilde was released from prison several months later and trying to regain his literary standing, he was clearly hoping that Paris would help his literary phoenix rise from the ashes. As Wilde wrote to Douglas on 2 June 1897, "[a]ll I want is to have my artistic reappearance, and my own rehabilitation through art, in Paris, not in London. It is a homage and a debt I owe to that great city of art."[25] The sympathetic *Mercure de France* wished to offer Wilde a chance to regain his artistic footing in France, and Davray was among the first to reach out. He started corresponding with Wilde and then went to visit him in Naples in September 1897. Knowing that Wilde had lost his beloved library in his bankruptcy sale, Davray kindly took it upon himself to solicit and collect contemporary French books that were personally inscribed to Wilde by their authors. According to Thomas Wright, "Wilde was overjoyed at receiving the books: 'I am greatly touched,' he said, 'by the sympathy and attention shown to me by you and other French writers. I hope to thank each of the authors individually.' These gifts demonstrated to Wilde that the French continued to regard him as an artist, and not simply as a notorious ex-convict."[26] Davray's kind gesture offered proof positive to Wilde that his French literary network still cared about him.

Encouraged by Davray's visit, Wilde wrote to him in December 1897, asking whether Davray could connect him with "brilliant and interesting" friend, the German artist Paul Herrmann (Héran), to see whether this "good artist" might illustrate a potential luxury edition of the English *Ballad of Reading Goal*, to be published by Leonard Smithers.[27] Wilde's hope did not pan out, however. At some point, Wilde sent a presentation copy of Smithers's first edition of his *Ballad* to Rachilde, the *Mercure*'s literary reviews editor. It is likely that Wilde gifted this rare copy to Rachilde (one of only about twelve Wilde was afforded by Smithers) in an effort to have his new work reviewed by her in the prestigious *Mercure*.[28] Around the same time, Davray became very interested in *The Ballad of Reading Gaol* and discussed a potential French translation with Wilde. In March 1898, Wilde wrote to him: "My dear Davray, I must write a line to you to tell you again how touched and gratified I am by your appreciation of my *Ballad*, and by the interest you take in it. I would greatly like to have it published with a translation by you, for no French man of letters can render English as you can, and either in a review or as a separate volume."[29] But first, in April 1898, Davray published a review of Smithers's English edition of *The Ballad of Reading Gaol* in the *Mercure*, just as Wilde had hoped when he sent it to Rachilde. In his review, Davray praised Wilde's work, noting with empathy that Wilde's literary representation of prison life allowed Wilde to touch readers with his deeply felt range of difficult and raw emotions ranging from deep anguish to self-pity.[30] Following his review, Davray also kept trying to reconnect Wilde to French authors such as Alfred Jarry (author of the scandalous *Ubu roi* and one of Rachilde's most prized protégés) to help him re-establish himself in the French literary world.

Continuing his engagement with Wilde, Davray then went on to collaborate directly with Wilde on the French translation and publication of the *Ballad* for the *Mercure*. Davray gives a detailed account of the conversations with Wilde that helped shape his French translation, in an essay that was originally published in 1913 and later republished in Davray's *La Tragédie finale* (1928). In this account, Davray recalls that when he originally proposed the idea to Wilde, Wilde was sceptical because he thought Davray was proposing a verse translation, an enterprise for which Wilde thought Davray lacked poetic talent.[31] When it became clear that Davray was actually suggesting a translation in prose, Wilde was still reluctant but finally agreed. Davray recalls Wilde's detailed critique of many of his word choices and his suggestion that Davray was incapable of capturing the nuances of the prison experience, since he had never been to prison. According to Davray, many weeks passed before they could agree on a final version: "[c]haque mot fut soupesé, chaque terme fut discuté, chaque phrase fut lue, relue, scandée, avec toutes les intonations possibles" ("each word was weighed, each term was discussed, each sentence was read, reread, recited with all the possible intonations"). At some point, Davray recalls, Wilde even joked that Davray should do his work in a prison cell in Reading so he could do a better job at translating the prison experience.[32] Finally, in October 1899, the inaugural French-language edition of *The Ballad of Reading Gaol* by Davray was published, first in the pages of the *Mercure de France* journal and a few months later as a stand-alone volume in the *Mercure*'s list of monographs, with Wilde's English text and French translation facing each other.[33]

Tragically, Wilde died just a little over one year later, on 30 November 1900. Davray's support did not end with Wilde's death, however. First, Davray wrote a heartfelt and enthusiastic obituary of Wilde for his "Lettres anglaises" column in the *Mercure* (February 1901), in which he praised Wilde for being a "causeur merveilleux, écrivain charmant, auteur dramatique à succès, ... une des plus belles intelligences dont pouvait se faire gloire l'Angleterre" (a "marvelous conversationalist, a charming writer, a successful playwright, ... one of the finest minds of which England could boast").[34] He sharply criticized those who had abandoned Wilde and stressed that Wilde's brilliant work would survive the catastrophe of his final years:

> Le carrière d'Oscar Wilde fut courte, mais, dès ses débuts, le succès lui sourit et ce fut vite le triomphe. Des vers, des essais: *Intentions*, et d'autres inédits encore, des poèmes en prose, *The House of Pomegranates*, *The Portrait* [*sic*] *of Dorian Gray*, avaient affirmé qu'il était un pur artiste et un grand écrivain, car certaines de ses pages sont aussi belles que tout ce qu'il y a de plus beau dans la prose anglaise. Mais ces oeuvres n'étaient pas pour lui que des amusements, et son esprit si versatile, si brillant, si finement ironique, si paradoxical trouva un moyen d'expression qui convenait parfaitement à ses dons si peu communs; c'était le théâtre.[35]

> Oscar Wilde's career was short, but success smiled on him from the start and quickly turned into triumph. Poems, essays: *Intentions*, and still other unpublished prose poems, *The House of Pomegranates*, *The Picture of Dorian Gray*, had established him as a pure artist and a great writer, for some of his pages are as beautiful as all the finest in English prose. But these works were but amusements for him, and his spirit, which was so versatile, so brilliant, so finely ironic, so paradoxical, found a means of expression perfectly suited to his unusual gifts: the theatre.

Transnational Networks: Henry-D. Davray, Robert Ross, and the Anglophone Guardians of Wilde's Legacy

One of the most important yet least known aspects of Davray's championship in France is his active contact and collaboration with Wilde's most ardent posthumous anglophone defenders, particularly Robert Ross, Christopher Millard, and Walter Ledger, as well as Arthur Ransome and Frank Harris. Just like Davray, these men shared an urgent sense of purpose in laying a permanent foundation for Wilde's enduring reputation as a great artist and human being, through a project Gregory Mackie has called "restorative bibliography."[36] While Ross and this circle of men were engaged in editing, collecting, cataloguing, and indexing, often straightwashing Wilde's work, and became embroiled in various libel trials, Davray quietly and steadfastly continued to find ways to collaborate with them to translate, explain, and commend Wilde's oeuvre to French readers. If Ross, Millard, and Ledger were interested in creating "a textual, as opposed to sexual, register for apprehending Oscar Wilde" in England,[37] so did Davray in France.

The first and most important such collaboration with Ross came soon after Wilde's funeral, when Davray managed to receive Ross's approval to translate Ross's recently published Methuen edition of Wilde's *De Profundis* (so titled at a Methuen editor's suggestion). An unpublished letter from 4 July 1905 testifies to the two men's cordial relationship. Ross writes affectionately: "My dear Davray. Many congratulations on your admirable and scholarly translation. I am not enough of a French scholar to appreciate some of the difficulties you have overcome, but you preserve the 'lilt' of Wilde's prose in a wonderful way." Ross says he remembers Wilde's dissatisfaction with another French translator: Wilde "used to say of some translation of his fairy stories that he had written them in purple or red," but that in that particular French translator's version, to Wilde's chagrin, "they came out mauve and pink."[38] By contrast, he asserts, Davray has "preserved the purple and red of *De Profundis*" very well, and deserves praise as "a man of letters with a real feeling for the literary value of the subject." Ross's letter confirms Davray's translation as officially "authorized" and thanks Davray for having shown "*great good taste* and *reserve*" in his preface (subtly hinting that Davray's translation mirrored Ross's own editorial decisions to obscure any direct references to Bosie, Lord Alfred Douglas).[39] Considering the publication dates of Ross's Methuen edition and Davray's French translation of *De Profundis*, it seems likely that Davray was already working in close contact with Ross at that time. The proceeds of Davray's French *De Profundis* probably also contributed to Ross's efforts to take care of Wilde's outstanding debts through monetizing Wilde's works. In a letter from 3 October 1905, Ross tells Davray that "Wilde died owing about £450 to French tradesmen, his doctor, and several friends in Paris. A few weeks before he died he asked me to see that they were paid if I possibly could do so. Half of them have been paid and I was going to use the proceeds of *De Profundis* to pay the remainder of them. I was then going to buy a grave at Père Lachaise," Paris's celebrity cemetery.[40] In 1908, having finished the Methuen project for Wilde's *Collected Works*, Ross was finally able to do so.

Davray and Ross continued to be in contact even beyond *De Profundis*, and it was important to Davray to continue to be in good standing with Ross. This is evident in a letter Davray wrote to Ross in August 1909. Ross had objected to an unflattering, off-the-cuff comparison Davray had made between Wilde and George Meredith, and questioned Davray's devotion to Wilde's memory. Davray writes:

> [E]n lisant la phrase de votre lettre où vous dîtes croire que je ne suis pas un admirateur de Wilde, j'ai eu comme un mouvement de colère et si je vous avais répondu sur le champ [*sic*], je ne l'aurais pas faite [*sic*] sans violence. Mais ... j'ai attendu pour pouvoir réfléchir. De plus, ma peine eût été vive d'avoir une querelle avec vous. En tout cas, j'admettrai difficilement d'être exclus du nombre des admirateurs d'Oscar Wilde, malgré quelques phrases acrimonieuses. Je l'ai assez souvent affirmée, mon opinion, et en termes qui n'ont rien d'ambigü [*sic*]! Et je pense que le meilleur tribut d'admiration qu'on puisse payer à un auteur qu'on admire c'est de le traduire et de l'interprêter [*sic*] avec une fidélité aussi jalouse que je l'ai fait dans "De Profundis" et la "Ballade." Il serait à souhaiter que tous ceux qui ont osé toucher à l'oeuvre de Wilde l'aient fait avec autant de révérencieuse fidélité.[41]

> When I read the sentence in your letter where you say that you believe that I am not an admirer of Wilde, I felt anger stir in me, and if I had answered you on the spot, I would not have done so without violence. But ... I waited to be able to reflect. Besides, I would have been very sorry to have a quarrel with you. In any case, I will hardly permit you to exclude me from the number of admirers of Oscar Wilde, based on a few acrimonious phrases. I have stated my opinion often enough, and in unambiguous terms! And I think that the best tribute of admiration one can pay to an author one admires is to translate and interpret him with such jealous fidelity as I did in "De Profundis" and the "Ballad." One should only wish that all who dared to touch Wilde's work had done so with such reverential fidelity.

"Jealous, reverential fidelity": Davray insists that he put a lot of work into getting Wilde's words exactly right, as a tribute to him. This is very true. Davray's excellent translations were indeed among the chief vehicles that turned francophone public opinion around. In *Oscar Wilde: A Critical Study* (1912) – which Davray also co-translated and published for French readers in 1914 – Arthur Ransome acknowledged the huge impact that translations of Wilde's works had for the author's posthumous recognition by the public:

> Only after his death, upon the appearance of *De Profundis*, and translations of his writings into French, German, Italian, Spanish, Swedish,

> Yiddish, Polish, and Russian, did popular opinion recognize (if it has yet recognized) that the Old Bailey, the public disgrace and the imprisonment were only circumstances in Wilde's private tragedy that would have been terrible even without them, and that they were no guarantee of the worthlessness of what he wrote.[42]

Davray's translation of Wilde's *De Profundis* as well as of the *Ballad* were powerful tools to advocate for Wilde's literary worthiness. It is important to note here that in addition to his translations of Wilde, Davray also went on to translate and publish key posthumous biographies and recollections by others, which helped keep Wilde's name front and centre. Davray was able to do so when in 1898, he was granted a brand-new monograph series of his own at the *Mercure de France*: the *Collection des auteurs étrangers* series, which let him choose, edit, and publish monographs about or by foreign authors, while also acting as the series's main translator. According to Annie Escuret, "Davray had often told Vallette that the *Mercure de France* should publish translations in volume form, but Vallette refused because it was too expensive."[43] When Vallette finally relented, Davray used his new role to publish six monographs that were focused on Wilde's works or life. First, he republished his own translations of *The Ballad of Reading Gaol* (1898) and *De Profundis* (1905, to which he added the *Ballad*). Next came André Gide's *Oscar Wilde: In Memoriam* (1910). Then, Davray published two works by authors from the inner circle of Wildean supporters: Arthur Ransome's *Oscar Wilde* (co-translated by Davray and Gabriel de Lautrec, published 1914) and Frank Harris's *La Vie et les confessions d'Oscar Wilde* (co-translated by Davray and Madeleine Vernon, published 1928). Translating Ransome's work, for which Bosie had just sued Ransome in a messy libel trial in England, was another act of advocacy, both for Ransome and also for Robert Ross, who had spearheaded Ransome's defence. Finally, Davray topped off this intense publishing streak with his own biographical work, *Oscar Wilde: La Tragédie finale – suivi de Episodes et Souvenirs et des Apocryphes* (1928, see below).

In addition to working with Ross and publishing these works by and on Wilde in his *Mercure* series, Davray was in communication with two bibliographers and collectors of Wilde's work: Christopher Millard and Walter E. Ledger. Supporting their efforts to protect and uphold Wilde's reputation from his own influential vantage position in France, Davray reported in the *Mercure* on Millard's recent discovery of a masterful Wildean forgery, Mrs. Chan-Toon's 1921 *For Love of the King*.[44] Mackie calls this "the holy grail" of Wildean forgeries since Mrs. Chan-Toon was able to deceive everyone so well that she became "the only forger to add a title to the list of Wilde's works under the imprint of his authorized publisher, Methuen."[45] Davray published a detailed account of Millard's subsequent investigation and results in the *Mercure de France* in the October 1925 and March 1926 issues, stating with evident satisfaction that the unmasking of this forgery would finally put an end to such deplorable practices as collectors of Wilde were now definitely put on their guard.

When Davray published his own comprehensive retrospective on Wilde's life and career under the *Mercure de France* imprint in 1928, he effectively became the first French biographer of Wilde. In his preface, Davray writes that it was the collector and bibliographer Walter E. Ledger's idea to put together these reminiscences in book form. Besides naming Ledger as his inspiration, Davray also pays tribute to Ross, Ransome, Harris, and Stuart Mason (the pseudonym of Christopher Millard). His careful public acknowledgments of these five key people illustrate how closely Davray really worked with and alongside his anglophone counterparts, and the decades-long transnational connections Davray maintained for solidifying Wilde's legacy.

Davray's book has three parts, the first of which contains Davray's story of the trials and Wilde's relationship with Bosie, as told through the lens of *De Profundis*; the second, "Episodes et Souvenirs," includes the already mentioned earlier essay on Davray's and Wilde's collaboration on the *Ballad of Reading Gaol*'s prose translation, as well as some poignant fragments from Wilde's notebook and other letters. The third part, "Les Apocryphes," contains Davray's (republished) report on Mrs. Chan-Toon's forgery *For Love of the King*. In part one, the longest, Davray paints a vivid picture of Wilde's state of mind in prison, which amounts to a dramatic telling of his suffering. Davray dives deeply into Wilde's text, calling it "un terrible soliloque qui est à la fois réquisitoire impitoyable, tour à tour méprisant et indulgent, un panégyrique d'une altière dignité, un plaidoyer fier et humilié ... Le document, c'est vrai, manque d'unité, mais n'en est-il pas plus humain?" ("a terrible soliloquy which is also a pitiless indictment, by turns contemptuous and indulgent, a public speech of lofty dignity, a proud and humiliated plea ... it is true, the document lacks unity, but doesn't that make it more human?").[46] Davray also recounts the 1895 trial for French readers who, at the time of Davray's writing, might either have needed to be reminded of the decades-old scandal, or were being introduced to Wilde's story for the first time. Davray summarizes how Wilde and Lord Alfred Douglas met, as told in Frank Harris's *Life and Confessions of Oscar Wilde* (a book that Davray had just co-translated and published for the *Mercure*).[47] Quoting from Wilde's early private letters to Bosie, which were read publicly by the Prosecution during the trial, Davray is sympathetic and emphasizes the fallible humanity this relationship shares with *all* other passionate romantic relationships, putting them on an equal footing in this regard:

> D'après ces extraits, qui témoignent d'une passion et d'une tendresse extrêmes, il est possible de s'imaginer que l'amour uranien donne des joies pures et des satisfactions parfaites. Mais la réalité s'écarte de ce tableau enchanteur: le contraste est aussi lamentable ici que dans toutes les liaisons où intervient la passion cérébrale et sensuelle.[48]

> With regard to these excerpts, which testify to an extreme passion and tenderness, it is possible to imagine that Uranian love provides pure joys and perfect satisfactions. But the reality differs from this enchanting picture: the contrast is as regrettable here as in all the liaisons where cerebral and sensual passion intervene.

Davray goes on to relate Wilde's release from prison on 19 May 1897, his immediate departure for France, his arrival in Dieppe and Berneval, and his lonely and fearful state of mind at the time as well as Bosie's incessant, initially unwelcome, efforts to contact him, his inevitable reunion with Bosie in Rouen and Naples in late August or early September that year, and Wilde's continual troubles with money. Davray narrates Wilde's ups and downs to great dramatic effect, making sure to acknowledge and humanize Wilde's suffering. In Davray's account, Wilde's "final tragedy" is ultimately transformed and surpassed by the beauty of his art: "Mais le bel esprit et la belle âme survivent. Le scandale passé s'efface devant la gloire de l'artiste" ("But the beautiful spirit and the beautiful soul survive. The past scandal gives way to the glory of the artist").[49]

One interesting facet of this account is that Davray liberally integrates and quotes from letters Wilde wrote to Ross between May 1897 and January 1898 (34–79).[50] These private and, at the time, yet-to-be-published letters could only have been furnished to Davray either by Ross himself, or perhaps by his other English interlocutor Ransome, who had received "broad access" to Wilde's unpublished letters by Ross himself. Robert Ross had died in 1918. Davray included several personal letters to Ross in which Wilde openly and unapologetically references the sexual nature of his relationship with Bosie.[51] The fact that Davray had such unfettered access to and editorial power over these sensitive letters at all, either through Ross or Ransome, is further proof of Davray's extremely close collaborative relationship with the inner circle of Wilde's anglophone defenders around Ross.

Through his decades-long influence as a reviewer, translator, and series editor for the respected *Mercure de France*, Davray was able to call attention not only to Wilde's work, but also to other English-writing authors he admired, translated, and worked tirelessly to champion in France. At the time of his death on 21 January 1944, Davray was a respected and beloved man of letters whose work was widely recognized and admired. Escuret writes, "many people felt that they had lost an old friend and a lover, critic and patron of literature, the finest liaison officer between French and English letters imaginable, a man whose work had earned him the rank of Chevalier of the Legion of Honour in France, as well as the CBE from the British Government and the Silver Medal of the Royal Society of Arts."[52] The *Times of London* published an obituary of Davray on 25 January 1944, acknowledging his importance to the French and English literary worlds.

Wrapping Up: The *Mercure*'s Last Interventions

Well beyond Wilde's death, Davray's steady work as translator and series editor aligned directly with the *Mercure*'s and Rachilde's own occasional strategic journalistic interventions. Together, they helped counteract the punitive legal narrative and defended Wilde's artistic name for the French public. While Davray was focused on publishing monographs, the *Mercure* as a periodical publication intervened, as necessary, at crucial cultural moments when Wilde's legacy was threatened publicly. For instance, when Lord Alfred published his tell-all book *Oscar Wilde and Myself* (originally written in 1911, translated into French in 1917), Rachilde immediately spoke up against it. In her fiery eleven-page essay satirically entitled "Oscar Wilde et lui" ("Oscar Wilde and he," alluding to Douglas's book's French title, *Oscar Wilde et moi*, "Oscar Wilde and myself"), Rachilde called Douglas cold and self-righteous. She even went as far as comparing his holier-than-thou ravings to the ridiculous gestures of an orang-utan at the feet of a beautiful statue ("les gestes d'un orang-outang devant le socle d'une belle statue").[53] Passionately defending Wilde, Rachilde proudly affirms that "[e]n France, on n'aurait pas pu acquitter Oscar Wilde, tout simplement *parce qu'on n'aurait pas fait le procès*" ("[i]n France, Oscar Wilde could not have been acquitted, simply because he would never have been put on trial").[54]

It seems no coincidence that Rachilde published her essay in the July–August 1918 issue of the *Mercure*, to neatly coincide with the end of the Pemberton-Billing trial in London. In this outrageous libel trial that focused on Wilde's *Salomé* (a work Rachilde herself had helped to bring to the stage and admired), the popular Canadian-American dancer Maud Allan and the well-known avant-garde theatre producer J.T. Grein unsuccessfully accused MP Noel Pemberton-Billing of defamatory criminal and obscene libel, regarding Allan's performance as Salome at London's Royal Court Theatre. The trial ended with a verdict that exonerated Pemberton-Billing and effectively ended Allan's career in England. Besides that, however, the trial once again indicted Wilde, and featured Bosie as star witness who now publicly called Wilde a "great evil" in court.[55] The *Mercure de France* once again stood at the ready to defend Wilde and even sent its own reporter in London to cover the trial. Claude Cahun, née Lucy Schwob, was a niece of Rachilde's friend Marcel Schwob, who had translated Wilde's "The Selfish Giant" into French in 1891 and also helped Wilde with the French of *Salomé*. Cahun's moving, pro-Wilde article "La 'Salomé' d'Oscar Wilde, le procès Billing et les 47,000 pervertis du 'livre noir'" ("The 'Salome' of Oscar Wilde, the Billing trial, and the 47,000 'black book' perverts") was strategically placed in the very same *Mercure* issue that also contained Rachilde's attack on Douglas's tell-all book. Rachilde was clearly up in arms that summer to come to Wilde's defence. In the decade between 1918 and 1928, when Davray published his co-translation of Harris's book as well as his own book on Wilde, Rachilde, Davray, and the *Mercure* seem to have prepared to wrap up their sustained activism on behalf of Wilde. Almost three decades after Wilde's death and burial in his beloved city, Paris, the goal was accomplished: Wilde's artistic imprint on literary history was successfully established and could no longer be easily ignored or stamped out.

As I hope to have shown in this chapter, under the strategic and proactive journalistic, editorial, and translation-focused leadership of Henry-D. Davray and Rachilde, the *Mercure de France* played a crucial and very successful role in redeeming Wilde and keeping his artistic legacy alive. According to Nancy Erber, "the sustained attention given to Wilde's work by literary journals like the *Mercure de France* served to keep [Wilde's] name before the reading public and solidify his reputation as a writer."[56] Davray in particular made an invaluable contribution to Wilde's standing today by translating and explaining Wilde's works, collaborating with Wilde himself as well as joining a transnational literary effort with Ross, Ransome, Millard, Harris, and Ledger, to reclaim and celebrate Wilde's life and art. As Davray lucidly predicted in his February 1901 *Mercure* obituary of Oscar Wilde, many foolish and inappropriate things would be written about Wilde after his death ("[i]l est certain que l'on écrira sur son compte une quantité d'inepties"), but Davray was also sure that time and history would eventually redeem Wilde.[57] It was not only the larger workings of time and history, though, that turned the tide in France and elsewhere. The meticulous, persistent, unwavering personal and professional support of Oscar Wilde by Henry-D. Davray, Rachilde, and the *Mercure de France* built a very strong foundation for today's appreciation and understanding of Wilde the artist and the man.

NOTES

1 Nicholas Frankel, *Oscar Wilde: The Unrepentant Years* (Cambridge, MA: Harvard University Press, 2017), 287.

2 According to Arthur Ransome, "Paul Fort saw [Wilde] just before his death and just after" ("Oscar Wilde in Paris," *T.P.'s Magazine*, June 1911, 435). Ransome also recalls that Fort "was almost the only French poet of whom in his last illness Wilde spoke with affection" and who "spent much time with him" (*Oscar Wilde: A Critical Study* [London: Martin Secker, 1912], 198). As for Davray, Robert Ross, writing to More Adey on 14 December 1900, reported that "Henry Davray came just before they had put on the [coffin] lid. He was very kind and nice" (Oscar Wilde, *The Complete Letters of Oscar Wilde*, ed. Merlin Holland and Rupert Hart-Davis [New York: Henry Holt, 2000], 1222).

3 Richard Ellmann, *Oscar Wilde* (New York: Knopf, 1988), 584.

4 Petra Dierkes-Thrun, "Oscar Wilde, Rachilde, and the *Mercure de France*," in *Wilde's Other Worlds*, ed. Michael F. Davis and Petra Dierkes-Thrun (New York: Routledge, 2018), 220–41.

5 Birgit van Puymbroeck, "Cross-Channel Mediations: Henry-D. Davray and British Popular Fiction in the *Mercure de France*," in *Transitions in Middlebrow Writing, 1880–1930*, ed. Kate Macdonald and Christopher Singer (Basingstoke, UK: Palgrave Macmillan, 2015), 184–5.

6 Annie Escuret, "Henry-D. Davray and the *Mercure de France*," in *The Reception of H.G. Wells in Europe*, ed. Patrick Parrinder and John S. Partington (New York: Continuum, 2005), 46.

7 See the exhibition catalogue, Marie-Françoise Quignard, ed. *Le Mercure de France: cent un ans d'édition* (Paris: Bibliothèque nationale de France, 1995).

8 Claude Dauphiné, "Rachilde et le 'Mercure,'" *Revue d'Histoire littéraire de la France* 92, no. 1 (January–February 1992): 17, 21.

9 See Petra Dierkes-Thrun, "Decadent Sensuality in Rachilde and Wilde," in *Decadence and the Senses*, ed. Jane Desmarais and Alice Condé (London: Legenda, 2017), 55–7.

10 Rachilde, *Alfred Jarry* (Paris: Bernard Grasset, 1928), 12. All translations mine unless specified otherwise.

11 Hugues Rebell, "La Défense d'Oscar Wilde," *Mercure de France*, August 1895, 182.

12 Camille Mauclair, "Le portrait de Dorian Gray, par Oscar Wilde," *Mercure de France*, August 1895, 237–8.

13 See Emily Eells, "Naturalizing Oscar Wilde as an *homme de lettres*: The French Reception of *Dorian Gray* and *Salomé* (1895–1922)," in *The Reception of Oscar Wilde in Europe*, ed. Stefano Evangelista (London: Continuum, 2010), 84.

14 Dierkes-Thrun, "Decadent Sensuality," 58–63.

15 Paul Fort, *Mes mémoires: toute la vie d'un poète, 1872–1943* (Paris: Flammarion, 1944), 40–1.

16 Eells, "Naturalizing Oscar Wilde," 84.

17 Jean de Tinan, "Salomé," *Mercure de France*, March 1896, 415.

18 De Tinan, "Salomé," 417.

19 Wilde, *Complete Letters*, 652–3.

20 Puymbroeck, "Cross-Channel Mediations," 185.

21 Escuret, "Henry-D. Davray," 29–30.

22 Ellmann, *Oscar Wilde*, 341.

23 See Wilde, *Complete Letters*, 646n.

24 Douglas had planned to include some previously unknown personal letters from Wilde. Horrified at the prospect, Wilde asked Robert Sherard from prison to intervene on his behalf.

25 Wilde, *Complete Letters*, 873.

26 Thomas Wright, *Built of Books: How Reading Defined the Life of Oscar Wilde* (New York: Henry Holt, 2009), 278. At the time of Wilde's bankruptcy sale, Wright estimates that "the volumes of French fiction comprised around a quarter of Wilde's library – easily the best-represented genre in his collection" (125).

27 Wilde, *Complete Letters*, 1000 and 1000n1.

28 See Dierkes-Thrun, "Oscar Wilde, Rachilde, and the *Mercure de France*," 229–30.

29 Wilde, *Complete Letters*, 1028.

30 Henry-D. Davray, Review of *The Ballad of Reading Gaol*, *Mercure de France*, April 1898, 324.

31 Davray, *Oscar Wilde: La tragédie finale* (Paris: Mercure de France, 1928), 89.

32 Davray, *Oscar Wilde*, 94–5.

33 The first illustrated French edition of the *Ballad*, with artwork by Jean-Gabriel Daragnès, was only published in 1918.

34 Davray, obituary of Oscar Wilde in "Lettres anglaises," *Mercure de France*, February 1901, 559.

35 Davray, obituary, 559.

36 Gregory Mackie, *Beautiful Untrue Things: Forging Oscar Wilde's Extraordinary Afterlife* (Toronto: University of Toronto Press, 2019), 34.
37 Mackie, *Beautiful Untrue Things*, 35.
38 Ross does not mention any translator by name here, but it could be Marcel Schwob, who translated "The Selfish Giant" in 1891.
39 Letter from Ross to Davray, dated 4 July 1905. Eccles Collection, British Library, London. Emphasis in original.
40 Letter from Ross to Davray, dated 3 October 1905. Eccles Collection, British Library, London. Emphasis in original.
41 Letter from Davray to Ross, dated 28 August 1909. *Oscar Wilde and His Literary Circle Collection: Correspondence, Ms. Wilde* (Box ms. Wilde 14, Folder 14, D267 R825 1909 August 28), William Andrews Clark Memorial Library, UCLA.
42 Ransome, *Oscar Wilde*, 22.
43 Escuret, "Henry-D. Davray," 30. The first book Davray published in his new series was his own translation of H.G. Wells's *The Time Machine*.
44 For a detailed discussion of this forgery, see Mackie, *Beautiful Untrue Things*.
45 Mackie, *Beautiful Untrue Things*, 162.
46 Davray, *La Tragédie finale*, 12–13 and 14.
47 Frank Harris was not a reliable biographer. Among the many inaccuracies, here recounted by Davray, is that Wilde died of syphilis. See Frankel, *Oscar Wilde*, 277–8.
48 Davray, *La Tragédie finale*, 28–9.
49 Davray, *La Tragédie finale*, 80.
50 Davray quotes these letters in *La Tragedie finale*, 34–79.
51 Davray's translated excerpt from Wilde's letter to Ross includes references to well-known classical male homosexual figures, such as Heliogabalus and Antinoüs, and directly mentions "l'amour uranien" ("Uranian love"). See *La Tragédie finale*, 73.
52 Escuret, "Henry-D. Davray," 47.
53 Rachilde, "Oscar Wilde et lui," *Mercure de France*, July–August 1918, 62.
54 Rachilde, "Oscar Wilde et lui," 60.
55 For a detailed account of Wilde's *Salomé* and the Pemberton-Billing trial, see Dierkes-Thrun, *Salome's Modernity: Oscar Wilde and the Aesthetics of Transgression* (Ann Arbor: University of Michigan Press, 2011), 83–124.
56 Nancy Erber, "The French Trials of Oscar Wilde," *Journal of the History of Sexuality* 6, no. 4 (April 1996): 552.
57 Davray, obituary, 560.

PART THREE

Archive and Anecdote

5 Disputed Memories: Oscar Wilde's Deathbed at the Hôtel d'Alsace

JOSEPH BRISTOW

I am not sure one can be too much of a slave to truth.

Reggie Turner to Robert Harborough Sherard

Oscar Wilde died in terrible circumstances. There is no question that he succumbed to an attack of encephalomeningitis at 1:50 pm on Friday, 30 November 1900, in the insalubrious Hôtel d'Alsace at 13 rue des Beaux-Arts, Paris. At the time, he had amassed considerable debts, not least to the hotel proprietor, Jean Dupoirier, who countenanced unsettled invoices amounting to some £112 for many months of lodging.[1] Still, there were for decades contesting viewpoints about the specific events that not only led up to his demise but also those that immediately followed, once his body was prepared for the casket. Although the widely reported notices in both the French and British press concurred on the precise nature of the illness that took Wilde's life, the records of those who watched over him during his final hours soon diverged on several questions. They disagreed, among other things, on the underlying cause that led to the infection of his brain tissue, on the condition of his partly shaved corpse, and on the plausibility of his conversion to Roman Catholicism by a Passionist priest, who was called upon to perform the last rites.

In this chapter, I return attention to the central position that Robert Ross, who assumed the role of Wilde's executor, held among the small group of bystanders who kept vigil before their friend expired. I look, too, at the most contentious assertions that originated with Ross regarding Wilde's final moments soon after his friend's demise. Thereafter, I focus on the disputes that arose in the *St. James's Gazette* during early 1905 about the initiatives that Ross took for Wilde's deathbed conversion and the subsequent funeral arrangements. Many years later, aspects of Ross's account of Wilde's last hours proved disputable to two other eyewitnesses, Reggie Turner and Father Cuthbert Dunne, whose records are explored in some detail towards the end of this discussion.

Ross, however, was hardly alone in circulating questionable stories after Wilde's coffin was lowered into a temporary rented plot in the suburban cemetery at Bagneux on the Monday following his death. As I will show, the legends about Wilde in extremis increased in their fancifulness during the early twentieth century. Even Dupoirier, who spent much time in Wilde's rooms during his remaining hours, went on record several times with distorted claims about his treasured *locataire*. Tall tales about Wilde's death persisted for many decades afterwards. Despite the wealth of scholarship on Wilde's life that flourished in the postwar period, it took until 2000 before one of the most widely touted myths about the origins of the pathology that killed Wilde was at long last laid to rest.[2] Yet it remains the case that two sets of little-known documents by Turner and Dunne on Wilde's deathbed have received scant attention. In these manuscripts, we discover a lasting wish to put straight the record of the nerve-racking episodes that took place in the hotel rooms where Wilde's health went into decline. The testimonies of both Turner and Dunne, whose different connections with the deceased require some explanation, assist in rebalancing Ross's at times misleading reports on Wilde's death.

The first is a batch of correspondence, dating from the 1930s and held at the Clark Library, that Turner sent to three recipients – Thomas Hastie Bell, Robert Harborough Sherard, and A.J.A. Symons, each of whom had specific investments in their knowledge of Wilde's death. As these detailed letters show, Turner kept close to Wilde's bedside during the last week of November 1900. Apart from Stanley Weintraub's engaging biography *Reggie* (1965), comparatively little has been written on the close relationship that led to the weeks that Turner dedicated to Wilde's infirmity. The illegitimate son of the press magnate Edward Levy-Lawson, Turner studied at Merton College, Oxford between 1888 and 1891, before training for the bar. As he told A.J.A. Symons in 1935, he met his contemporary Alfred Douglas at Oxford in his "last year in 1892."[3] It took, however, a while before he entered Douglas's social circle. It was during a sojourn in Egypt in the winter of 1893–4 that Turner, who had the support of a modest allowance from his adoptive family, enjoyed close acquaintance with the young Scottish lord. Douglas had travelled to Egypt ostensibly to assist the British Consul-General, Lord Cromer, in the name of securing a diplomatic position. (Douglas, who found the work uncongenial, promptly returned home.) Hereafter, Turner joined a group of young professional queer men who became Wilde's most loyal companions.

In spring 1895, Turner played a crucial role after Wilde's libel action against John Sholto Douglas, ninth Marquess of Queensberry came to grief. (Wilde's counsel, Sir Edward Clarke, in the face of an unexpected barrage of incriminating evidence from Queensberry's defense, Edward Carson, withdrew the charge.) Both Turner and Ross, whom Douglas had introduced to each other, quickly realized that the police were about to arrest the playwright. They moved briskly to urge Wilde, who was languishing at the Cadogan Hotel, to abscond to the Continent. When Wilde refused to budge, they remained there until the police escorted him to the Bow Street Magistrates' Court. Soon after, the two friends, like many other gay men terrified that they might be subpoenaed, decamped to Calais.

During Wilde's two-year prison term, Turner corresponded with him at some length. Moreover, it was a sign of Turner's steadfast affections that he presented Wilde with a dressing-case not long before the inmate was released. At the same time, Turner made it clear that he could not meet Wilde's request that he accompany his friend from Her Majesty's Prison Pentonville, where the prison sentence ended at 6:00 am on 19 May 1897: "were my presence to be made known by any means to my people my allowance would be stopped, and that I could not afford."[4] Nonetheless, Turner felt sufficiently confident about escaping unwanted gossip in England that he soon availed himself to Wilde on the other side of the Channel. Flanked by Ross, he greeted his friend at Dieppe once *La Tamise* had ferried the ex-convict to permanent exile on the Continent, where Wilde resided under the incognito "Mr. Sebastian Melmoth." Later, Turner fulfilled several urgent requests from Wilde for money for Arthur Cruttenden, a "good chap" with "a sweet nice nature" he had met in prison, as well as gifts, including a "little clock, for my writing table" – "a sort of nickel Waterbury affair."[5]

Always attentive to his friend's needs, Turner exchanged plenty of queer chitchat. Turner provided news about such beloved young men as Charlie Hickey (he "always asks after you most affectionately"), while later Wilde asked after the former soldier Maurice Gilbert, whom he likely paid for sex in Paris, about the time this French pal had been spending with Ross and Turner in London ("I suppose he is wildly loved").[6] Some months after Turner quit his job as a gossip columnist on Levy-Lawson's *Daily Telegraph*, he learned through Ross that Wilde had undergone an expensive mastoidectomy on his right ear. As Wilde told Harris, the bill for the operation, by Dr. Paul Cleiss, which took place on 10 October 1900, came to a substantial "1500 francs (£60)."[7] In these stressful conditions, Turner made his way to Dupoirier's hotel on 16 October 1900 (Wilde's forty-sixth birthday), with Ross arriving the next day. From that moment onward, Turner and Ross went to see Wilde on a daily basis, taking their friend out for rides through the Bois de Boulogne and visits to a local cafe, where the infirm writer sipped on the absinthe that did no favours for his health. Ross, however, departed on 13 November 1900 to join his mother vacationing at Mentone on the French Riviera, since he convinced himself that Wilde's life was not in imminent danger.

Towards the end of November 1900, the bedridden Wilde grew agitated as he slipped in and out consciousness: "from time to time he recited in delirium some piece of Greek or Latin or French, and I could not but notice that his French accent was marked by a sort of Irish brogue, never to be heard when he talked English."[8] Understandably, Turner became increasingly worried as he maintained watch with two nurses, a *garde malade*, and Dupoirier. (Wilde's valet from Brittany, Henri, was also present part of the time.) On occasion, Turner and the hotel landlord administered morphine to Wilde through a Pravaz syringe. Together, they also applied ice to the shaved part of Wilde's head to relieve pain. Even though Turner held out hope that Wilde might recuperate, by Monday, 26 November 1900, he wrote to Ross that during the previous twenty-four hours "the doctors gave very little hope of Oscar's recovery."[9]

As the intense week wore on, Turner faced the prospect of the difficult negotiations that would take place when Wilde expired. To begin with, there were the large sums of monies owing, including one for book purchases from Brentano's, that needed to be covered.[10] Moreover, as Turner explained to Ross, Wilde's doctor, Maurice A'Court Tucker, could "not have consultations with no money."[11] There were, in addition, the costs of hiring an undertaker, obtaining a coffin, securing a burial plot, and defraying the fees for the church service. Furthermore, several individuals would need to be informed. "Dupoirier," he says in a letter to Ross, "wanted to know if [Wilde's] children should not be written to."[12] The only succour was that Wilde was "not in want of anything," since his "mind wanders and he sleeps."[13] Four further urgent letters to Ross followed. In an especially urgent one dated 5:30 pm, Wednesday, 28 November 1900, Turner notes that Wilde, who had a "very high" temperature, "understands the doctor more or less."[14] "You cannot be wrong in coming to Paris," he tells Ross, even if "it may be too late."[15]

Ross returned in time. The minute he reappeared mid-morning on the Thursday, it was obvious that Dupoirier's *locataire* had not much longer to live. Immediately, Ross recognized that there was one further complication that it was his responsibility to resolve. A Catholic convert, Ross believed that in these trying conditions Wilde would at last embrace, after several previous delays, the opportunity to be received into the Church of Rome. This, as he later explained to Adela Schuster, was a promise he had made to Wilde should the writer find himself in such frightful straits: "In March or April this year [1900], he came to Rome where I was wintering with my mother and I noticed that a great change had come over his health ... he wanted me to introduce him to a priest with a view to being received into the Church, and I reproach myself deeply for not having done so."[16] Ross wanted to make good on his word. He promptly sought a priest at St. Joseph's Catholic Church on the nearby avenue Hoche.

The second set of documents under discussion in this chapter, dating from the 1940s and also held at the Clark Library, comes from the priest who answered Ross's request for a deathbed conversion, a thirty-one-year-old Irishman, Father Cuthbert Dunne. Close to the end of the Second World War, when he was in his mid-seventies, Dunne had reason to revive his memories of Wilde's last moments, largely because a Jesuit priest from Missouri had issued a pamphlet mistakenly claiming that the deceased's body was riddled with a distinctly sexual malady. Prior to his death in 1950, Dunne dedicated time to reconstructing the taxing period when he attended Wilde's deathbed. He went to the National Library in Dublin to locate obituaries, and he reviewed the file of the correspondence that he had gathered over the years relating to Wilde's conversion.

"[T]he appalling *débris* which had to be burnt": Ross on Wilde's Dying Hours

Ross bore the greatest burden of responsibility for ensuring not only Wilde's conversion; he also, in the face of potential difficulties, managed the prompt and safe burial of Wilde's body. The artist Will Rothenstein captured Ross's heroic actions as those of a "big-souled" man; "how few men there are," Rothenstein told Ross after learning of Wilde's death, "who will do for a difficult friend what you have done for him."[17] No sooner had Wilde perished than Ross embarked on a demanding series of tasks that involved restoring the copyrights to the Wilde estate, removing all the debts that Wilde had left behind, and editing the fourteen-volume *Collected Works* (1908) that assisted in re-establishing Wilde's literary reputation.

Ross's dedication was all the more remarkable because his intimacy with Wilde had only developed seriously when other friends kept their distance from him. Certainly, he had known Wilde through his family since 1886, when he was still a teenager. During this time, he likely became Wilde's first male lover. The next year, when he was at a London crammer preparing for his Cambridge entrance examinations, Ross lodged for two months at Wilde's family home on Tite Street, Chelsea. Even so, there were long gaps in their acquaintance. As Ross told Schuster, he renewed his contact with Wilde "when he was writing *Lady Windermere*" in 1891.[18] Afterwards, they were seldom in touch "until after the downfall" in spring 1895, when he took special interest in Wilde's welfare once the libel case foundered.[19] Still, for reasons that have been open to some question, Ross – who remained scrupulous in every other respect – also took it upon himself to embellish Wilde's deathbed passion.

The most significant document that presents his view of the taxing period immediately before and after Wilde's demise is the well-known letter, dated 14 December 1900, to More Adey. (Adey, a close friend and roommate of Ross's who was based in London, had done much to safeguard Wilde's legal affairs during the jail sentence.) The highly detailed correspondence reveals that Wilde remained "very talkative," even though he "looked very ill," at the end of October 1900.[20] Wilde's wit was in fine fettle. During a visit from Lily Teixeira (the widow of his brother Willie), he declared, in two well-known quips, that "he was 'dying above his means'" and "would never outlive the century."[21] Still, Ross questioned Tucker's wavering opinions. Tucker at first claimed that the bedbound patient "was much better."[22] Perhaps out of concern that too many words of warning might induce panic, Tucker declared that Wilde "was getting well now," though "he could not live long unless he stopped drinking."[23]

As Ross observes, one of the pressing matters that had made Wilde frantic was his mounting debts. The sum was "something over more than £400": about a tenth of Wilde's annual income before his prison term.[24] The amount roughly translates into $40,000 USD in today's money, and is somewhat higher than the salary of a middle-class man at the time. A particular bugbear was another old friend, Frank Harris, who had been put in the position of paying off multiple individuals to whom Wilde had unscrupulously sold play scenarios several times over – Kyrle Bellew, Cora Brown-Potter, Louis Nethersole, Ada Rehan, and Horace Sedger. Before Ross left for the Riviera, Wilde made it clear to him that he believed Harris was defrauding him. Not long before, Harris had developed one of these dramatic outlines into the successful society comedy *Mr. and Mrs. Daventry*, which had opened on 25 October 1900 in London. The play, which depicts a wife's decision to commit adultery with a younger man, ran for 116 performances until the national mourning for Queen Victoria closed the theatres temporarily in late January 1901.

All the same, amid this financial panic Wilde continued to make wisecracks about his impending demise. "Oscar," Ross recalls, "asked me if I had chosen a place for his tomb."[25] Just before Ross departed for the South of France, Wilde wished to bid farewell to his friend in private. Once Turner and the nurse left them together, Wilde beseeched Ross not to leave him "because he felt that a great change had come over him during the last few days."[26] Ross had no time for the "violent sobbing" that broke from Wilde's lips.[27] Besides uttering "harrowing things" that Ross refused to repeat, Wilde's final request was that his friend should "[l]ook out for some little cup [i.e., nook] in the hills near Nice," where he could retire once he had recovered his health.[28] "Those," Ross recollects, "were the last articulate words he ever spoke to me."[29]

The next part of Ross's long letter focuses on his return to Paris and the Hôtel d'Alsace. Once he found "after great difficulty" Father Cuthbert Dunne, the priest duly administered baptism and extreme unction, although it proved impossible for Wilde to "take the Eucharist."[30] Straight away, Ross began sending several urgent messages, including one to Harris. Ross also communicated with the solicitor Martin Holman, who handled the affairs of Adrian Hope, the somewhat aloof guardian of Wilde's two teenage sons, neither of whom had enjoyed any contact with their father since his imprisonment. As Ross knew, it was imperative to wire Douglas, not least because the Scottish lord, who had recently come into a large inheritance, had the means to defray the substantial expenditures that would follow Wilde's decease.

Together, Ross and Turner spent the night at the d'Alsace. At this juncture, Ross presents a vivid spectacle of Wilde's agonizing death-throes:

> We were called twice by the nurse, who thought Oscar was actually dying. About 5:30 in the morning a complete change came over him, the lines of the face altered, and I believe what is called the death rattle began, but I had never heard anything like it before it sounded like the horrible turning of a crank, and it never ceased until the end. His eyes did not respond to the light test any longer. Foam and blood came out of his mouth, and had to be wiped away by someone standing by him all the time. At 12 o'clock I went out to get some food, Reggie mounting guard. He went out at 12:30. From 1 o'clock we did not leave the room; the painful noise from the throat became louder and louder. Reggie and myself destroyed letters to keep ourselves from breaking down. The two nurses were out, and the proprietor of the hotel had come up to take their place; at 1:45 the time of his breathing altered. I went to the bedside and held his hand, his pulse

> began to flutter. He heaved a deep sigh, the only natural one I had heard since I arrived, the limbs seemed to stretch involuntarily, the breathing came fainter; he passed at 10 minutes to 2:00 pm. exactly.[31]

In principle, this is a painstaking account that pays the closest attention to the precise time and distressing conditions when Wilde's life came to an end. Many years later, Turner confirmed that for "the whole of Thursday morning there was the so-called death-rattle, or heavy breathing, in his throat."[32] Nonetheless, the "foam and blood," not to say "the appalling *débris* which had to be burnt" once the corpse underwent "washing and winding," raised some eyebrows after they appeared in Arthur Ransome's *Oscar Wilde: A Critical Study* (1912), which relied extensively on Ross for information. Moreover, the 1912 volume for the first time introduced a different explanation for the cause of Wilde's fatal decline. Although Ransome concedes that Wilde's demise "was directly due to meningitis," he adds this was "the legacy of an attack of tertiary syphilis."[33] Here, too, Ross was responsible for this claim.

A further elaboration ensued. By 1916, when Harris brought out the two-volume *Oscar Wilde: His Life and Confessions,* he not only reproduced Ross's letter in full but also inserted his own moralizing commentary on the "dreadful disease from which [Wilde] was suffering, or from the after effects of which he was suffering," which "weakens all the tissues of the body." Without any ado, Harris proceeds to make Wilde's final agony into the eruption of a sexually ravaged body, one whose physical ruin was the foregone conclusion of a life squandered in lust:

> Suddenly, as the two friends sat by the bedside in sorrowful anxiety, there was a loud explosion: mucus poured out of Oscar's mouth and nose, and –
>
> Even the bedding had to be burned.
>
> If it is true those who draw the sword shall perish by the sword, it is no less certain that those who live for the body shall perish by the body, and there is no death more degrading.[34]

By invoking Matthew 26:52, Harris suggests that Christ's wisdom shows that those who have revelled in sexual abandon must ultimately pay the price of death through the depredations of a sexually transmitted disease.

In the remainder of the detailed letter to Adey, Ross covers the events that followed the cleaning of Wilde's corpse: "Reggie and myself and the proprietor started for the Mairie to make the official declaration."[35]

Thereafter, Ross had no joy with the officials: "Dying in Paris is really a very difficult and expensive luxury for a foreigner."[36] The fact that Wilde had been living under a false identity threatened to complicate matters as well. So, Ross took Father Dunne's advice and contacted an undertaker at the British Embassy. Moreover, he found two Franciscan nuns to watch the body. As word spread about Wilde's decease, Turner "stayed at the hotel interviewing journalists and clamorous creditors."[37] Soon, the district doctor appeared. He wished to know if Wilde "had committed suicide or was murdered."[38] Once the medical man had inspected Wilde's body, he agreed to a fee for the burial. Meanwhile, a stream of visitors poured in, many of them "poets and literary people," with some signing themselves under "assumed names" in the guest book.[39] By this point, Wilde's cleaned and washed body "looked calm and dignified."[40] "Around his neck," Ross recalls, "was the blessed rosary which you gave me, and on the breast a Franciscan medal given me by one of the nuns."[41]

Before the lid was placed on the casket, Ross asked Maurice Gilbert (who had also come to Wilde's bedside) to take what turned into an "unsuccessful photograph," since "the flashlight did not work properly," and in which we can see the white shirt that was draped over Wilde's corpse (Figure 5.1).[42] We can also make out what Claire de Pratz (the pen name of Solange Cadiot) called "the dreadful 'modern-style' wallpaper of chocolate-colored flowers on a blue background."[43] Recalling her visit to the d'Alsace, which likely occurred several weeks before Wilde's death, de Pratz remembered that he had quipped: "You see, my dear child ... there's a duel to the death between myself and my wallpaper. One of us must remain here. It'll be me or him."[44] After Wilde's coffin was carried out of the bedroom on Sunday, 1 December 1900, the funeral took place the next day. Dunne led the service, with Douglas as the chief mourner. There were two dozen wreaths, including "a pathetic bead trophy" inscribed "*A mon locataire*" from Dupoirier.[45] Fifty-six people, Ross claims, attended the funeral, although the number in attendance was likely much smaller.[46]

Five Years after: Divulging "disgusting" Details in the *St. James's Gazette*

Besides focusing on clearing Wilde's estate of debt, Ross remained dedicated to rehabilitating his friend's literary reputation. One of Ross's greatest feats was to bring before the public a carefully edited version of the long, often recriminatory letter that Wilde composed in Reading Gaol to Douglas during the concluding months of the prison term.

Figure 5.1 Maurice Gilbert, photograph taken by flashlight of Oscar Wilde at approximately 3:50 pm on Friday, 30 November 1900, Hôtel d'Alsace, 13 rue des Beaux Arts, Paris. Stamped, in ink, on verso: "To the appointment to T.M. The King and Queen, William E. Gray, 92, Queen's Rd., Bayswater, W. Fine Art Photographer." William Andrews Clark Memorial Library, University of California, Los Angeles, Wildeiana, Box 20, Folder 4.

Ross's edits ensured that no reference was made to Douglas. Instead, Ross presented those sections of the letter in which Wilde meditates upon suffering in prison. In February 1905, he published the work as *De Profundis*, a title taken from Psalm 129 in the Vulgate Bible. Many sections of the press focused on the most heart-rending aspects of the letter. They were particularly impressed by Wilde's haunting description of solitary confinement: "Outside, the day may be blue and gold, but the light that creeps down the thickly-muffled glass of the small iron-barred window beneath which one sits is both grey and niggard."[47] They were struck, too, by Wilde's penitent voice: "The gods had given me almost everything. But I let myself be lured into long spells of senseless and sensual ease."[48] The *Daily Mirror*, to give a representative example, stood in awe of this "wonderful book" about one of the greatest calamities in living memory: "Of all the pitiful, mysterious tragedies of our time none was more miserable or harder to understand than that of Oscar Wilde."[49] The volume went rapidly into many editions. Its commercial success assisted in ensuring that the "English creditors," as Ross observed, were "paid off ... in full, by the middle of 1906."[50]

Even the conservative *St. James's Gazette*, which had refused on moral grounds to publish any of the evidence relating to Wilde's trials in 1895, acknowledged both the deep integrity and literary quality of *De Profundis*: "Beautiful, supremely beautiful, it is; but that it merely represents a *tour de force* of hypocrisy is not to be believed."[51] A few days later, the *St. James* reiterated the growing interest in Wilde by reprinting from the *Daily Telegraph* a short notice of Jean-Joseph Renaud's recent French edition of Wilde's 1891 volume *Intentions*. The brief report reproves Renaud for omitting any references to "Wilde's last dying epigram": "As he lay at the point of death in a squalid lodging-house bed-room a doctor called in consultation with his colleague already in attendance whispered to the latter some dubious remark about fees of which, to judge by circumstances, there seemed little likelihood. Oscar Wilde, who the doctors thought past hearing, made an effort to speak. 'Gentlemen,' he gasped, 'I am afraid I am dying beyond my means.' It was his last jest."[52]

These two notices spurred Douglas, under the semi-anonymous initial "A.," to provide his own account of Wilde's death. Even though he commends Renaud for producing "an able and carefully-executed French translation" of Wilde's *Intentions*, he finds fault with Renaud's memory of meeting Wilde at a bar on the boulevard des Italiens (most likely, the Calisaya).[53] "Nothing remained of him," Renaud says of Wilde, "but his musical voice and his large childlike blue eyes."[54] As Douglas observes, "Oscar Wilde's eyes were curious – long, narrow, and green. Anything less childlike would be hard to imagine."[55] There are other aspects of Renaud's record that Douglas seeks to demystify. Exceptionally irksome to Douglas is the widespread belief that Wilde suffered material hardship during his declining months in Paris: "The stories of his supposed privations, his frequent inability to obtain a square meal, his lonely and tragic death in a sordid lodging, and his cheap funeral are all grotesquely false."[56] Certainly, Douglas admits that Wilde found it insufferable to adjust from his annual earnings of £5,000 as a dramatist to less than a tenth of that sum on leaving prison. Nevertheless, Wilde "had ... far too many devoted friends in Paris ever to be in need of a meal."[57] As for the supposed tawdriness of the funeral, Douglas asserts that it "was not cheap."[58] "I happened to have paid for it," Douglas observes indignantly, "in conjunction with another friend of his, so I ought to know."[59]

No doubt Douglas was mindful of statements like the one that had recently appeared in *Reynolds's Newspaper*, which claimed that Wilde "went from prison to die in abject poverty in Paris, and that he lies there in an almost unnoted grave."[60] *Reynolds's*, the left-leaning Sunday broadsheet that treated Wilde's downfall with great latitude, had already published articles by Sherard, who claimed that the hard-to-locate gravesite had a "neglected look," since "weeds covered" the mound.[61] In response, Ross explained the reasons that the author was buried in such a modest plot: "It seemed to the two friends who were with him in last illness that it would be inappropriate – in bad taste even – to spend large sums on a costly monument and expenses until these debts were paid, particularly as the creditors had been extremely patient, and had abstained from taking legal action or giving trouble during a very distressing time."[62] Ross adds the reassurance that "there is not the smallest chance of the remains being thrown out into the ditch."[63] Instead, at a later point "they will be removed to one of the more accessible cemeteries in Paris – if possible to Père-Lachaise – where a perpetual concession can be secured."[64] (It took until summer 1909 before Wilde's remains were at last removed to the site designated for the tomb designed by Jacob Epstein and installed three years later at the desired cemetery.[65])

The deep antagonisms that put Douglas and Ross at loggerheads in the 1910s, resulting in many rounds of legal actions between them, have some of their origins in these accounts of Wilde's demise. Perhaps the clearest attack on Ross in the *St. James's* arose when Douglas stated that it was inconceivable that Wilde could have converted to Rome on his deathbed: "Oscar Wilde did not become a Roman Catholic before he died."[66] In Douglas's view, conversion remained impossible because Wilde had "been unconscious for many hours, and he died without ever having any idea of the liberty that had been taken with his unconscious body."[67] Douglas, though, based his opinion on hearsay, since he arrived in Paris the day after Wilde died.

Ross fired back on the disputed conversion, especially as Douglas's repudiation appeared undignified:

> I do not think his consciousness at a particular moment is a matter for discussion. It was in fulfilment of an old promise that I brought a priest to his death-bed. On two former occasions he had contemplated being received – once as young man, and again on his release from Reading. If Father Cuthbert Dunn[e], of the Passionists, was perfectly satisfied, I feel your Catholic correspondent may feel reassured. This does not prevent "A." from holding to his own view because, as he says, not being a Catholic, an act

> of faith and what constitutes an act of faith cannot have much meaning for him.[68]

One might have imagined that these quarrels over Wilde's deathbed experiences and the funeral at which Douglas was chief mourner would have ended there.

The following day, however, matters escalated when Sherard, who had published the first full-length biography of Wilde in 1902, entered the fray. On this occasion, Sherard – whose inclination to "talk morality" on Wilde's queer intimacies put severe pressure on their friendship – claimed to have garnered vital information about the deathbed from Dupoirier.[69] Sherard, assuming he had inside knowledge, sought to rebut those like "A.," who in his view turned Wilde's "death into a jest and seek an advertisement in the amount of the undertaker's bill."[70] He proceeded to itemize a list of sundry details that imply that Dupoirier had an interest in capitalizing on Wilde's memory:

> 1. That he one night found Wilde in the streets of Paris without a domicile. He had been turned out of the room he was living in the rue Marsollier, and had no money for a night's lodging;
> 2. That Wilde was constantly in his debt and that there is still over a thousand francs owing to him on his account;
> 3. That Wilde's gold-mounted teeth which he has on sale were left him as dédommagement [i.e., compensation] by the people who settled Wilde's affairs;
> 4. That towards the end of his life Wilde was engaged in hackwork for a taskmaster who was very irregular in his payments;
> 5. That Wilde died after weeks of great pain (the Pravaz syringe which was used to allay his agony is also on sale), and that only one other person was present.[71]

These five emphatic points contain a tangled mixture of truth and untruths. We know for sure that Wilde moved from the Hôtel de Nice to the d'Alsace in late March 1898 ("Much better," he told Ross, "and half the price"),[72] and his correspondence also shows that he remained there until mid-December before Frank Harris, who had plans for a hotel business in Monaco, settled him in the village of Napoule, near Cannes. On his return to Paris from touring Switzerland with Harold Mellor, a young Englishman he befriended on the Riviera, Wilde lodged first in April 1899 at Hôtel de la Nevá before moving the following month to the Hôtel Marsollier. By July, however, the hotel management impounded his luggage. "I'm in a dreadful state," he informed his publisher Leonard Smithers, "as all my clothes are the Hôtel Marsollier, where I owe a bill."[73] Whether Dupoirier found Wilde roaming the streets at night is an open question. Whatever may have occurred, he nonetheless welcomed his *locataire* back to the d'Alsace, where Wilde remained until his next journey with Mellor, this time to Italy in March 1900. By at least June that year, Wilde returned for the final time to Dupoirier's hotel, where he stayed until his death five months later. Exactly what the "hackwork" was that Wilde supposedly undertook finds no corroboration in any other document.

Still, Sherard's eager attention to these coarsening details proved too much for Teixeira, who right away condemned the "distasteful ... correspondence" that had transpired in the *St. James's*: "Nothing could have horrified" her brother-in-law "more than that men calling themselves his friends should publish concerning his latter days details so disgusting as those appearing in your issue of yesterday, or dispute of any change in his religion to which he may have assented on his deathbed."[74] Even though her caution brought these exchanges to an end, it hardly prevented Sherard from promptly reiterating many of these cheerless details in *Twenty Years in Paris* (1905).

"No one was shocked by anything unseemly or squalid": Reggie Turner, the Mid-1930s, and Memories of Wilde's Death

After Turner had resided for almost two decades in Florence, he entered into a correspondence with the unrestrainable Sherard. The letters that Turner wrote between 1933 and 1937 shed significant light on Wilde's final weeks in Paris. At the time, Turner lived comfortably in the Florentine colony of English expatriates. Sherard, who had issued no fewer than three biographies of Wilde,[75] had been in touch with Turner about the dinner that Ross had organized at the Ritz Hotel, London, to commemorate the publication of Wilde's *Collected Works*. (Douglas had refused to attend.) Turner no doubt knew about Sherard's opinionated views. By this time, Sherard had set himself firmly against anything Harris had claimed about Wilde's sexuality. In 1931, for example, when he had been in touch with A.J.A. Symons, who was beginning his research for a projected biography of Wilde, Sherard made some headstrong comments on his former friend as well as Ross:

> Oscar was no Sodomite but a masochist homosexual, who fell in love malgré lui with young men and got no satisfaction out of the business beyond some insane mental gratification, similar to that of Voltaire devouring his own excrement matter purely for the psychopathologists. The syphilis

> he contracted at Oxford when he was 20, which broke out again in 1886 and destroyed his married life accounts for most of the rest of the deplorable gesta. But I must warn you that Ross DELENDUS EST [i.e., must be destroyed] by any biographer that wishes to speak the truth.[76]

Turner was clearly addressing a man whose impulsive misapprehensions (not to say resolute homophobia) about Wilde and Ross compounded the difficulties in setting the record straight. As Turner's letters unfold to the combative Sherard, he politely comments that he believes *Twenty Years in Paris* to be "of entertaining interest," even if the "'Oscar' part" is not to his mind "the most satisfactory."[77] Turner opened up even more after Sherard sent him a copy of a pamphlet castigating the French author André Gide's "wicked lies" about Wilde in *Si le grain ne meurt* (1924). Especially questionable to Turner is the passage in Gide's 1924 memoir that describes "Oscar as procuring Gide a boy & exulting with satanic laughter" during a visit to Algeria in 1895.[78] "The whole thing," Turner observes, "is fantastic."[79]

Still, as Turner remarks, such tale-telling is not at all unusual: "it is wonderful what inaccuracies even the most honest people will fall into with Oscar."[80] Here, Turner had in mind a graphic episode in Edward Marjoribanks's recent *Carson the Advocate* (1932), which presents a horrifying tableau of Wilde's debility. According to this source, sometime in mid-November 1900 Edward Carson, who had successfully defended Queensberry against Wilde's libel charge, had to avoid a fiacre racing through the streets of Paris:

> He stepped back quickly on to the pavement, and knocked someone down. Turning round to apologise, he saw a man lying in the gutter, and recognised the haggard, painted features of Oscar Wilde ... The eyes of the two men met, and they recognised each other. Carson turned round and said, "I beg your pardon." Wilde, under the name of Sebastian Melmoth, was living in Paris, dying of a terrible disease, "beyond his means," as he observed with the wit which never deserted him, preying on the generosity of his friends: in a week or two he was dead.[81]

On reading this, Turner was aghast: "It is inconceivable that this is true. Someone would have heard of it, certainly I or Ross, who were in Paris at the time. And Oscar never painted his face. Nor was he, I think, on the boulevards, a fortnight before his death, unless he got up out of bed unbeknownst to anyone."[82]

Yet there is one aspect of Wilde's death that Turner felt obliged to depict correctly. He rebuffs Sherard's belief that "Harris interpolated the passage" in the letter from Ross to Adey that appeared as an appendix in his 1916 biography.[83] Turner is referring to Harris's infamous elaboration of the "appalling *débris*" that Ross mentioned. "I saw the letter," Turner remarks. "One didn't think so much of its possible importance at the time or that it would even be reproduced. In any case I know that it /represents\ Ross's views roughly, though of course views change with time."[84] Turner had already made much the same point to Harris ten years before: "the whole scene is an invention of Robbie's."[85] As their correspondence on this topic drew to a conclusion, Turner wanted Sherard to know the truth about Wilde's corpse: "From the moment Oscar died he was decently laid out on his bed, the bald patch on his head to which the leeches had been applied properly covered, & on the white shirt that covered his body were laid, on his breast, some sprigs of herbs, & a crucifix, &, I think, a rosary, placed there by Father Cuthbert Dunne."[86] Once friends soon arrived to pay their respects, there was nothing out of keeping with Wilde's corpse: "No one was shocked by anything unseemly or squalid."[87]

Sherard's tendency to dismiss claims about Wilde's death gave pause to Thomas Hastie Bell, a Scottish anarchist now resident in Los Angeles. In 1930, Bell, who once served as Harris's secretary, published "Oscar Wilde's Unwritten Play" in the *Bookman*. For the most part, the article recounts the backstory to Harris's composition of *Mr. and Mrs. Daventry*. Towards the close of his discussion, Bell asserts that he arrived at the d'Alsace on the afternoon of 30 November 1900 to deliver, on Harris's behalf, a cheque for £10 to Wilde. Once inside the hotel, Bell went upstairs to Wilde's rooms on the first floor and "stepped in at the door" where he saw [a] white-coiffed nun ... sitting at one side with candles burning before her."[88] On the bed was the deceased Wilde. Bell proceeds to mention that he met Dupoirier, who was "nervous about" the sum owed to him.[89] Later, "the two men who had been with Wilde in his illness came back."[90] "One of them," Bell adds, "was Robert Ross," while he did not know who Turner was at the time.[91] On reading Bell's article, Sherard disregarded it as "pure fake."[92] "Harris," Sherard asserts, "never sent him to Paris."[93] Bell's response to Sherard's headstrong remarks was to contact Douglas, who in turn passed his letter along to Turner, which initiated a thoughtful correspondence.

Turner furnished Bell with gracious responses that once more sought to rebalance the record. Importantly, Turner observes that in Ross's letter to Adey "there is no mention of the absolutely untrue & revolting detail of the explosion which Mr. Harris put into his account of the last moments."[94] "When I asked him," Turner adds, "how such a monstrous untruth came to appear, he assured me that Ross had told him, but I am sure Ross could not have done so."[95] There are, too, further matters that Turner wishes to settle. Ross, he says, was confused when he said: "Reggie and myself and the proprietor started for the Mairie": "I never," Turner observes, "went to the Mairie. Nor do I know to this day where it is."[96] Yet Turner reserves some of his strongest criticisms not for Ross but for Dupoirier, who had granted an interview to the Parisian daily *L'Intransigeant* on the thirtieth anniversary of Wilde's death. Besides wrongly claiming that Wilde died in the morning, the hotel landlord declared that he slept in a room adjacent to Wilde's. He claimed as well that that *curé* of St-Germain-des-Prés tended to Wilde. Worse still, Dupoirier recalls: "I washed him & dressed him in his good light brown suit."[97] "All these statements," Turner remarks, "are untrue."[98]

The letters to Sherard and Bell relate to a broader matter that Turner confided to Symons. "I have," Turner confesses, "been asked to write my memories of Wilde."[99] Yet at each attempt, Turner abandoned the project. It appears that the tensions that gathered between Ross and Douglas in the early 1910s made it painful to intervene in Wilde's legacy. In any case, as Turner had already told Sherard, his criticism of Ross broke up their friendship: "When he was criticized or opposed, he lost his heart & his head."[100] Still, Turner held no grudges against Ross, who died just before the end of the Great War: "Ross was a splendid & wonderfully courageous person ... but he had his faults, & grave faults."[101] One of his greatest faults, Turner says, was the impulse to tell lies. The same is true of Douglas, he confesses, though he still "preserve[s] an affection" for him.[102] "I have," he confides to Symons, "come to believe that people can tell lies really believing at the moment that they are truth."[103]

"Divine Mercy brought him in": Father Cuthbert Dunne's Memories, 1945–50

Several months before the end of the Second World War, Father Cuthbert Dunne wrote a letter to the Revd. Father Daniel Lord, SJ, whose pamphlet, *The Pure of Heart*, had recently been reprinted in a fresh edition by the Catholic Truth Society of Ireland. Dunne was startled to learn that Lord had included a blighting reference to the state of Wilde's dying body at the d'Alsace: "I wish we could drag the young generation to the death bed of Oscar Wilde, deserted by his nearest friends, who fled from the stench of his lust-rotten body."[104] This description, as Dunne swears "truthfully before God," is "wholly untrue to facts."[105] In the course of explaining Wilde's longstanding interest since his Oxford days in the Catholic faith, Dunne remarks that, soon after his release from jail, Wilde "got from [Ross] a promise of bringing a priest to him at once – should he ever find him in danger of death."[106] To Dunne, an earlier conversion would have doubtless saved Wilde "from the disasters that subsequently ruined his brilliant career."[107] "At any rate," Dunne goes on, "when the end came, he found his way back to the door which as a youth he did not enter, and Divine Mercy brought him in."[108] In response, Lord agreed to remove the offending passage, which embroiders the unlikely explosion of Wilde's dying body in Harris's biography.

Thereafter, in another document he drafted Dunne made some further level-headed comments about the implausibility of Wilde's body exploding from venereal disease in a respectable Parisian hotel: "[T]here is not to-day in Paris nor was there in Paris in the year 1900, any hotel-keeper anxious for the good name of his house and for the safety and comfort of his other clients who would allow a man dying in a state of rottenness from venereal disease – a source of disgust and danger to others – to remain even for five minutes in his house."[109] Dunne composed, too, a long article that he considered sending to the Catholic Truth Society. In this moving account of Wilde's deathbed, Dunne recalls accompanying Ross "back to the hotel where Wilde lay."[110] (The archives of the Passionist Church on the rue Hoche record that Fr. Cuthbert arrived at the d'Alsace "towards 4 in the evening" of Thursday, 29 November 1900.)[111] "When I reached his bedside," he says, "he was half-conscious, trying indeed to speak, yet not able to utter an articulate word, and I remarked at once that on his head, above the forehead, there was a leech on either side – put there to relieve the pressure of blood upon the brain."[112] Once he turns to the conversion, Dunne explains that he introduced himself to Wilde as a "priest, come to receive him into the Catholic Church and give him the sacraments of the Sick."[113] Wilde, Dunne recollects, gave "signs and answers that satisfied" that there were no doubts about the ailing man's "happy consent": "The attendants left the room and Mr. Ross alone remained, and, assisted by him, I administered the Sacraments, beginning with Baptism – sub conditione. When I spoke near his ear the Acts of Faith, Hope, Charity and Contrition and words to express Resignation to the Divine Will, he attempted all through to repeat these acts and words with me."[114]

Apart from mentioning that he officiated at the Requiem Mass, Dunne focuses on two other notable events that involved him after Wilde's decease. Among Dunne's papers are several letters from Stonyhurst College, the private Catholic school near Blackburn, Lancashire, where Wilde's youngest son, Vyvyan, was a pupil. The head teacher, Father Rector Joseph Browne, SJ, had learned about Dunne's deathbed ministrations. Five days after Wilde's death, Browne asked Dunne if he "was happy enough to reconcile poor Oscar to the Church."[115] Browne adds: "we have a son of [Wilde's] – whom he should not have had – who is of a sensitive and affectionate nature, is most anxious to be reassured about his father's happy end."[116] Dunne's reply, which has gone missing, elicited a compassionate letter from the fourteen-year-old schoolboy, who had converted to Catholicism in Monaco two years before. Respectfully, Holland thanks Dunne for "speaking words of courage and consolation that had a great deal to do with [his] father's conversion."[117] "I beg you," Holland continues, "to thank Mr. Ross for all he did. I have never heard of him but from all accounts he must have been a very good man."[118] This touching correspondence is all the more significant because Ross himself was unaware that it had taken place. "I do not," he informed Adey on 14 December 1900, "suppose the children know that their father is dead."[119]

Dunne, too, preserved an item of correspondence relating to the controversy that arose in the *St. James's Gazette* in 1905. Abbot David Oswald Hunter-Blair contacted Dunne to rebut Douglas's claim that Wilde was not converted because he was "absolutely unconscious" on his deathbed. The abbot, who counted Wilde among his "dearest friends" at Magdalen College, had converted to Catholicism in 1875, and at the time of writing to Dunne he resided at the Benedictine Hall (later known as St. Benet's Hall) for Catholic students attending Oxford.[120] "What I wish to know," Hunter-Blair wrote in 1905, "is, if you could <u>yourself</u> testify, and if you would be willing to do so, that O.W. was <u>not</u> unconscious ... when he received your ministrations, in fact that /he\ received them by his own will, and was <u>knowingly</u> received in to the Church."[121] He concludes by asking Dunne for permission to quote the Passionist priest's assurance that Wilde died a Roman Catholic. Dunne naturally obliged. In his memoir, *In Victorian Days* (1939), Hunter-Blair discusses at length the conflicts Wilde suffered as an undergraduate when contemplating conversion. He then confirms that Dunne received Wilde in the Church "at his own urgent wish ... whilst fully conscious, though unable to speak, and exhibiting every sign of genuine penitence."[122] "One can only be thankful," the abbot concludes, "that, at long last, what one may call his lifelong wish found its fulfilment."[123]

Without doubt, the extraordinary events that led up to Wilde's death understandably aroused such intense passions that some of the individuals closest to him lost perspective on what happened. As we have seen, Ross – who was, as Turner put it, "afflicted with a dramatic imagination" – continued to weave far-fetched tales.[124] He also went so far as to inform Harris that at the time of the funeral the doctors had instructed him "to put Wilde's body in quicklime ... The quicklime, they said, would consume the flesh and leave the white bones – the skeleton – intact, which could then be moved easily."[125] On this basis, Harris believed it was true that when Wilde's remains were moved to Père Lachaise, "Ross found that the quicklime, instead of destroying the flesh, had preserved it."[126] It took until 1925, when Douglas and Turner had taken issue with Ross's claims, before Harris retracted this fabrication along with the one that intimated that "all Oscar's bowels came away in the end."[127] Still, as students of Wilde's life know well, it proved hard for many years to lay this matter to rest. In 1987, Richard Ellmann, in a biography that did much to strengthen Wilde's cultural and literary significance, reprinted the report that Cleiss and Tucker wrote three days before Wilde's demise: "The diagnosis of encephalitic meningitis must be made without doubt."[128] Yet even this document failed to undermine Ellmann's conviction that "Wilde had syphilis," since the venereal disease remained "central to his conception of Wilde's character."[129] In the end, the one matter on which we can agree is that Wilde died before his time. And Wilde did so in such trying straits that those who remained close to his deathbed were compelled to dispute one another's memories of his final hours for decades to come.

No wonder, then, that for many years Dupoirier chose to preserve Wilde's room as a shrine for a stream of visitors who wished to honour the memory of the much-lamented author. The hotel proprietor, according to Sherard, kept the furniture exactly as it had been placed when Wilde died, and he had also saved the deceased's "three hundred odd volumes" in his "two trunks," along with the Pravaz syringe in a "leathern case."[130] Sherard revealed that the devoted landlord informed him that "hardly a week passes but that some visitor from foreign lands comes to the hotel and asks to be shown the room where Oscar Wilde died."[131] Dupoirier went on to add: "One gentleman – he is a wealthy manufacturer from the Midlands – always insists on occupying this room, although it is one of the least cheerful in the none too cheerful house."[132] "It has," he remarked, "become quite a place of pilgrimage."[133] Just before the thirtieth anniversary of Wilde's death, when Dupoirier invited the journalist from *L'Intransigeant* into the room, he opened a bureau from which he retrieved a precious item wrapped in paper: "Apparait un appareil dentaire en or. A la mâchoire supérieure, seules les grosses molaires sont remplacées" (There appeared a gold set of dentures. In the upper jaw, only the large molars were replaced).[134] Dupoirier's hands, we learn, trembled as he held this treasured item.

Much more recently, the Alsace itself has undergone a complete transformation. These days it is known as L'Hotel, an exclusive boutique residence, where it is possible to reserve the "Oscar Wilde Suite": a 337-square-foot room with a private terrace, separate bath, walk-in shower, mini-bar, fine period chairs, desk, and tables, and gold-embossed Whistler-like peacocks adorning the wall above the bed. Scarcely anything about the room resembles the one that Dupoirier safeguarded.[135] Still, L'Hotel has preserved several documents that are displayed in the suite. These items include the final total of the debts owed to Dupoirier. But then so much that the landlord kept has disappeared over time. Some "half a dozen of the most interesting" of Wilde's books were taken, with Dupoirier's permission, by the sculptor Lady Kennet, when she visited the hotel in 1902.[136] There was a coat and waistcoat of Wilde's on top of the wooden box housing some fifty or so items. The proprietor, it appears, also offered her the syringe for administering morphine, which she said should be thrown away. Meanwhile, the gold-capped set of artificial teeth, on which Wilde likely expended a considerable sum during the final year of his life, appear to be in the hands of Dupoirier's descendants.[137] Perhaps one day, they, too, will be put on display.

NOTES

I wish to express my thanks to Yvonne Ivory for guidance on the materials relating to Claire de Pratz. The archivist at the Passionist Provincial Office, Mount Argus, Dublin, provided information on Fr. Cuthbert Dunne. Iain Ross and John Cooper shared their thoughts on the photographs of Wilde's deathbed. Martin Burns of the Oscar Wilde House, Dublin, pointed me to the staff of L'Hotel, who photographed for me the last bill that Jean Dupoirier issued to Wilde. Yvonne Ivory directed me towards W.B. Yeats's letters. The staffs of the William Andrews Clark Memorial Library, University of California, Los Angeles, were unfailing in their assistance.

Epigraph: Reggie Turner, "To Robert Harborough Sherard," ALS, 29 October 1933, Clark Library, Wilde T951L S988, box 68, folder 10.

1 One of the invoices that Dupoirier issued to Wilde in October 1900 shows that monthly room and board came to 90 francs a month. Additional charges for items including tea, lemonade, chocolate, and cognac coffees brought the bill to 180.40 francs. See Robert Harborough Sherard, *The Life of Oscar Wilde* (London: T.W. Laurie, 1906), opp. 420, and (for a slightly different reproduction of the total amount owing to Dupoirier) H. Montgomery Hyde, *Oscar Wilde: A Biography* (New York: Farrar, Straus, and Giroux, 1976), endpapers. The original is held at the L'Hotel, 13 rue

des Beaux-Arts, Paris. In 1902, Robert Ross, who took responsibility for clearing Wilde's debts, stated: "Dupoirier is still owed £56 half of his original bill." "To Adela Schuster," 3 January 1902, in *Robert Ross, Friend of Friends*, ed. Margery Ross (London: Jonathan Cape, 1952), 74. £112 in 1900 equates roughly with a real-price value of £12,500 in today's money. Many years later, Dupoirier claimed that at the time of death Wilde owed him 2,600 francs, which is correct, since the total in the final bill comes 2,643.40 francs. See Immanuel de Rudbeck, "Oscar Wilde était-il subventionné par la reine Victoria?" *L'Impartial*, 23 May 1933, 2.

2 See Ashley H. Robins and Sean L. Sellars, "Oscar Wilde's Terminal Illness: Reappraisal after a Century," *The Lancet* 356 (December 2000): 1841–3. This essay states that Wilde's death was from encephalomeningitis and not any other underlying cause such as syphilis.

3 Reginald Turner, "To A.J.A. Symons," ALS, 11 August 1935, Clark Library, Wilde T951L S988, box 68, folder 10.

4 Reginald Turner, "To Oscar Wilde," [18 May 1897], in *The Complete Letters of Oscar Wilde*, ed. Merlin Holland and Rupert Hart-Davis (London: Fourth Estate, 2000), 836.

5 Wilde, "To Reginald Turner," [? 7 June 1897], and [22 July 1897], in *The Complete Letters*, 887 and 917.

6 Turner, "To Oscar Wilde," [18 May 1897], and Wilde, "To Reginald Turner," [11 May 1898], in *The Complete Letters*, 837 and 1066.

7 Wilde, "To Frank Harris," [? 12 October 1900], in *The Complete Letters*, 1200. In the same letter, Wilde informed Harris that the French-trained doctor, Maurice A'Court Tucker from the British Embassy, who visited Wilde over a period of ten weeks, managed to reduce Cleiss's bill to 750 francs.

8 Frank Harris, "New Preface to 'The Life and Confessions of Oscar Wilde,'" in *New Preface to "The Life and Confessions of Oscar Wilde"* by Frank Harris and Alfred Douglas (London: Fortune Press, 1925), 15. Harris states that he received this information from Turner at a meeting they had at Nice in February 1925.

9 Turner, "To Robert Ross," [26 November 1900], in *The Complete Letters*, 1214.

10 The bill from Brentano's, 37 l'avenue de l'Opera, is dated 3 December 1900; it is made out to "Mr. Oscar Wilde," and it comes to 22.50 francs. The eight titles include a copy of Arthur Morrison's novel, *A Child of the Jago* (1896). Clark Library, Wilde, B839Z W6721, box 6, folder 35.

11 Turner, "To Robert Ross," 27 November 1900, 1215. After Wilde's death, Tucker presented Ross with a bill for 1,350 francs to cover some sixty-eight consultations that had taken place since September. Tucker's bill was sold as Lot 174 at a December 1990 sale at Sotheby's, London. The

number of Tucker's consultations is mentioned in Robins and Sellars, "Oscar Wilde's Terminal Illness," 1842.

12 Turner, "To Robert Ross," [26 November 1900], 1214.

13 Turner, "To Robert Ross," [26 November 1900], 1214.

14 Turner, "To Robert Ross," [28 November 1900], in *The Complete Letters*, 1219.

15 Turner, "To Robert Ross," [28 November 1900], 1219.

16 Ross, "To Adela Schuster," 23 December 1900, in *The Complete Letters*, 1225.

17 Will Rothenstein, "To Robert Ross," 5 December 1900, in Ross, *Robert Ross, Friend of Friends*, 60, 59.

18 Ross, "To Adela Schuster," 23 December 1900, 1229.

19 Ross, "To Adela Schuster," 23 December 1900, 1229.

20 Ross, "To More Adey," 14 December 1900, in *The Complete Letters*, 1212.

21 Ross, "To More Adey," 14 December 1900, 1212.

22 Ross, "To More Adey," 14 December 1900, 1212.

23 Ross, "To More Adey," 14 December 1900, 1213.

24 Ross, "To More Adey," 14 December 1900, 1213.

25 Ross, "To More Adey," 14 December 1900, 1213.

26 Ross, "To More Adey," 14 December 1900, 1214.

27 Ross, "To More Adey," 14 December 1900, 1214.

28 Ross, "To More Adey," 14 December 1900, 1214.

29 Ross, "To More Adey," 14 December 1900, 1214.

30 Ross, "To More Adey," 14 December 1900, 1219–20.

31 Ross, "To More Adey," 14 December 1900, 1220.

32 Harris, "New Preface to 'The Life and Confessions of Oscar Wilde,'" 15.

33 Arthur Ransome, *Oscar Wilde: A Critical Study* (London: Martin Secker, 1912), 199.

34 Frank Harris, *Oscar Wilde: His Life and Confessions*, 2 vols. (New York: privately printed, 1916), 2:539.

35 Ross, "To More Adey," 14 December 1900, 1220.

36 Ross, "To More Adey," 14 December 1900, 1221.

37 Ross, "To More Adey," 14 December 1900, 1221.

38 Ross, "To More Adey," 14 December 1900, 1221.

39 Ross, "To More Adey," 14 December 1900, 1221.

40 Ross, "To More Adey," 14 December 1900, 1221.

41 Ross, "To More Adey," 14 December 1900, 1221.

42 Ross, "To More Adey," 14 December 1900, 1222.

43 "l'épouvantable papier 'modern-style' à fleurs chocolat sur fond bleu." Claire de Pratz, who had contributed to Wilde's *Woman's World* many years before, is quoted in Guillot de Saix, "Souvenirs inédits sur Oscar Wilde," *L'Européen*, 9 May 1929, 2. Although de Saix became notorious for

inventing stories about Wilde, de Pratz's recollection is confirmed in W.B. Yeats, "To Lady Gregory," [17 December 1908], in *The Collected Letters of W.B. Yeats*, ed. John Kelly and Ronald Schuchard, 5 vols. (Oxford: Oxford University Press, 1986–), 5:359.

44 "Voyez-vous, ma chère enfant, me disait-il, il y a un duel à mort entre moi et mon papier de tenture. L'un de nous deux doit y rester. Ce sera lui ou ce sera moi." In de Saix, "Souvenirs inédits sur Oscar Wilde."

45 Ross, "To More Adey," 14 December 1900, 1222.

46 According to the journalist Miriam Aldrich, the number in attendance at the "low mass" was no more than twenty. Her manuscript memoir, "The Burial of a Fallen Poet," is quoted in Nicholas Frankel, *Oscar Wilde: The Unrepentant Years* (Cambridge, MA: Harvard University Press, 2017), 186.

47 Oscar Wilde, *De Profundis*, ed. Robert Ross (London: Methuen, 1905), 12–13.

48 Wide, *De Profundis*, 22.

49 "Pages from the Prison Diary of Oscar Wilde," *Daily Mirror*, 23 February 1905, 11.

50 "The Speech of Robert Ross," 1 December 1908, in Ross, *Robert Ross, Friend of Friends*, 154. Ross's speech was delivered at the dinner held at the Ritz Hotel to celebrate the Methuen edition of Wilde's *Collected Works*.

51 "Oscar Wilde in Prison," *St. James's Gazette*, 23 February 1905, 19.

52 "Oscar Wilde's Death-Bed Jest," *St. James's Gazette*, 28 February 1905, 10.

53 "A." [Alfred Douglas], "Oscar Wilde: His Last Book and His Last Years," *St. James's Gazette*, 2 March 1905, 5.

54 [Douglas], "Oscar Wilde: His Last Book," 5. "Il ne restait de Lui que sa voix musicale et ses grands yeux bleus enfantins": J.-Joseph Renaud, Preface to Oscar Wilde, *Intentions*, trans. Renaud (Paris: P.-V. Stock, 1905), xx.

55 [Douglas], "Oscar Wilde: His Last Book," 5.

56 [Douglas], "Oscar Wilde: His Last Book," 5.

57 [Douglas], "Oscar Wilde: His Last Book," 5.

58 [Douglas], "Oscar Wilde: His Last Book," 5.

59 [Douglas], "Oscar Wilde: His Last Book," 5. Douglas shared the costs of the funeral.

60 "Oscar Wilde's Prison Cry," *Reynolds's Newspaper*, 26 February 1905: 2.

61 Robert H. Sherard, "At Oscar Wilde's Grave," *Reynolds's Newspaper*, 21 June 1903, 2. Sherard wrote at greater length about the gravesite as well as Wilde's rooms at the d'Alsace in "Oscar Wilde's Tomb," *Reynolds's Newspaper*, 31 July 1904, 4.

62 "The Lessee of the Grave at Bagneux" [Robert Ross], *Reynolds's Newspaper*, 7 August 1904, 7.

63 [Ross], *Reynolds's Newspaper*, 7 August 1904, 7.

64 [Ross], *Reynolds's Newspaper*, 7 August 1904, 7.

65 As it turned out, once Epstein's monument was transported from London, where it had been on view, to Père Lachaise in August 1912, the cemetery authorities placed a tarpaulin over it because the sculpture, which features a winged sphinx, had protruding genitals. Epstein designed a butterfly-shaped cache-sexe to cover the offending parts. Two years later, the monument was unveiled. See Ellen Crowell's chapter in this volume, "Oscar Wilde's Tomb: Silence and the Aesthetics of Queer Memorial."

66 [Douglas], "Oscar Wilde: His Last Book," 5.

67 [Douglas], "Oscar Wilde: His Last Book," 5.

68 [Robert Ross], "The Writer of the Preface to 'De Profundis,'" *St. James's Gazette*, 8 March 1905, 18.

69 Wilde, "To. R.H. Sherard," [c. 16 October 1897], in *The Complete Letters*, 963.

70 Robert Harborough Sherard, "Oscar Wilde," *St. James's Gazette*, 9 March 1905, 6.

71 Sherard, "Oscar Wilde," 6.

72 Wilde, "To Robert Ross," [28 March 1898], in *The Complete Letters*, 1050.

73 Wilde, "To Leonard Smithers," [August 1899], in *The Complete Letters*, 1161.

74 Lily Teixeira, "Oscar Wilde," *St. James's Gazette*, 11 March 1905, 18.

75 Sherard had issued the following biographies: *Oscar Wilde: The Story of an Unhappy Friendship* (London: Hermes, 1902); *The Life of Oscar Wilde* (1906); and *The Real Oscar Wilde, To Be Used as a Supplement to, and in Illustration of "The Life of Oscar Wilde"* (London: T. Werner Laurie, 1916).

76 Robert Harborough Sherard, "To A.J.A. Symons," 24 April 1931, ALS, Clark Library, Wilde S551L S988, box 62, folder 25.

77 Turner, "To Robert Harborough Sherard," 22 June 1933, ALS, Clark Library, Wilde T951L S551, box 68, folder 10.

78 Turner, "To Robert Harborough Sherard," ALS, 18 October 1933, Clark Library, Wilde T951L S551, box 68, folder 10. Turner has in mind the passage where André Gide recalls Wilde accosting him in a back alley in Algiers in early 1895: "Dear, voulez-vous le petit musicien" (Dear, would you like to have the little musician). Gide spluttered an affirmative. Once they took a seat in the carriage "Wilde commença de rire, d'un rire éclatant, non tant joyeux que triomphant; d'un rire interminable, immaîtrisable, insolent" (Wilde burst out laughing – a dazzling laugh, more of triumph than pleasure; an interminable, uncontrollable, insolent laugh). *Si le grain ne meurt*, new ed., 3 vols. (Paris: Éditions de la nouvelle revue française, 1924), 3:135.

79 Turner, "To Robert Harborough Sherard," 18 October 1933.

80 Turner, "To Robert Harborough Sherard," 18 October 1933.

81 Edward Marjoribanks, *Carson the Advocate* (New York: Macmillan, 1932), 231.

82 Turner, "To Robert Harborough Sherard," 18 October 1933. Harris reprinted Ross's letter to Adey, dated 14 December 1900, as "Oscar's Last Days," in *Oscar Wilde: His Life and Confessions*, 2:595–603.

83 Turner, "To Robert Harborough Sherard," 29 October 1933, ALS, Clark Library, Wilde T951L S551, box 68, folder 10.

84 Turner, "To Robert Harborough Sherard," 29 October 1933. The insertion is Turner's.

85 Harris, "New Preface to 'The Life and Confessions of Oscar Wilde,'" 22.

86 Turner, "To Robert Harborough Sherard," 9 December 1937, ALS, Clark Library, Wilde T951L S551, box 68, folder 10.

87 Turner, "To Robert Harborough Sherard," 9 December 1937.

88 T.H. Bell, "Oscar Wilde's Unwritten Play," *Bookman* 71 (1930): 149.

89 Bell, "Oscar Wilde's Unwritten Play," 149.

90 Bell, "Oscar Wilde's Unwritten Play," 149.

91 Bell, "Oscar Wilde's Unwritten Play," 150.

92 Robert Harborough Sherard, *Bernard Shaw, Frank Harris and Oscar Wilde* (London: T. Werner Laurie, 1937), 306.

93 Sherard, *Bernard Shaw, Frank Harris and Oscar Wilde*, 306.

94 Turner, "To Thomas H. Bell," [1937], ALS, Clark Library, Wilde T951L B35, box 68, folder 8. The likely date is 1937, not 1935, which has been inserted in pencil on the letter.

95 Turner, "To Thomas H. Bell," [1937].

96 Turner, "To Thomas H. Bell," [1937].

97 Turner, "To Thomas H. Bell," [1937]. Dupoirier's remarks are recorded in Michelle de Boyer, "Oscar Wilde mourait dans mes bras," *L'Intransgéant*, 30 November 1930, 1–2.

98 Turner, "To Thomas H. Bell," [1937].

99 Turner, "To A.J.A. Symons," 11 August 1935.

100 Turner "To Robert Harborough Sherard," 29 October 1933.

101 Turner, "To A.J.A. Symons," 11 August 1935.

102 Turner, "To A.J.A. Symons," 11 August 1935.

103 Turner, "To A.J.A. Symons," 11 August 1935.

104 Rev. Daniel A. Lord, *The Pure of Heart* (Dublin: Catholic Truth Society, 1945), 21.

105 Father Cuthbert Dunne, "To Revd. Daniel A. Lord," 10 May 1945, ALS (copy), Clark Library, Father Cuthbert Dunne Papers, box 1, folder 19.

106 Dunne, "To Revd. Daniel A. Lord," 10 May 1945.

107 Dunne, "To Revd. Daniel A. Lord," 10 May 1945.

108 Dunne, "To Revd. Daniel A. Lord," 10 May 1945.

109 Dunne, draft letter to the Catholic Truth Society, 1945, Clark Library, Dunne papers, box 1, folder 2. A shortened draft of Dunne's previously unpublished memoir of Wilde's last days appeared in Rev. Edmund Burke, C.P., "Oscar Wilde: The Final Scene," *London Magazine* 1, no. 2 (1961), 37–43. Rupert Hart-Davis reprinted the document in his pathbreaking edition of Wilde's *Letters* (1963), and the same text reappeared in Merlin Holland's *Complete Letters* (2000). This document is not among Dunne's papers at the Clark Library.

110 Dunne, draft letter to the Catholic Truth Society, 1945.

111 John Thornhill, "From the Archives," *Passion: The Journal of Passionist Life* 12 (2023): 56.

112 Dunne, draft letter to the Catholic Truth Society, 1945.

113 Dunne, draft letter to the Catholic Truth Society, 1945.

114 Dunne, draft letter to the Catholic Truth Society, 1945. To administer a sacrament *sub conditione* means to offer on the condition that the individual is sufficiently aware to receive it.

115 Father Rector Joseph Browne, "To Father Cuthbert Dunne," 5 December 1900, ALS, Clark Library, Dunne papers, box 1, folder 5.

116 Browne, "To Father Cuthbert Dunne," 5 December 1900.

117 Vyvyan Holland, "To Father Cuthbert Dunne," 14 December 1900, ALS, Clark Library, Dunne papers, box 1, folder 6. Holland signs his name as "Vivian."

118 Holland, "To Father Cuthbert Dunne," 14 December 1900.

119 Ross, "To More Adey," 1221. Ross communicated with both of Wilde's sons. Cyril Holland, a student at Radley College, Oxfordshire, thanked him for his letter: "It was very kind of you to send flowers from us [i.e., from him and his brother Vyvyan to Wilde's funeral]. I am glad you say that he loved us ... Vivian told me you had written to him ... I first read of his death in a paper at breakfast." Cyril Holland, "To Robert Ross," TS (copy) of ALS, undated [? December 1900], Clark Library, MS Wilde, box 32, folder 19.

120 Abbot David Oswald Hunter-Blair, "To Father Cuthbert Dunne," 6 March 1905, Clark Library, Dunne papers, box 1, folder 7.

121 Hunter-Blair, "To Father Cuthbert Dunne," 6 March 1905.

122 Rt. Revd. Sir David Hunter-Blair, *In Victorian Days, and Other Papers* (London: Longmans, Green, 1939), 141.

123 Hunter-Blair, *In Victorian Days*, 142.

124 Harris, "New Preface to 'The Life and Confessions of Oscar Wilde,'" 22.

125 Harris, *Oscar Wilde: His Life and Confessions*, 2:540.

126 Harris, *Oscar Wilde: His Life and Confessions*, 2:540.

127 Harris, "New Preface to 'The Life and Confessions of Oscar Wilde,'" 22.

128 The document is reprinted in Richard Ellmann, *Oscar Wilde* (New York: Knopf, 1988), 582. The British edition of Ellmann's study appeared in 1987.

129 Ellmann, *Oscar Wilde*, 92. Matthew Sturgis devotes a detailed note to Ellmann's claims in *Oscar Wilde: A Life* (New York: Alfred A. Knopf, 2022), 798–9.

130 Robert Harborough Sherard, *Twenty Years in Paris: Being Some Recollections of a Literary Life* (London: Hutchinson, 1905), 457, 456.

131 Sherard, *Twenty Years in Paris*, 456.

132 Sherard, *Twenty Years in Paris*, 456.

133 Sherard, *Twenty Years in Paris*, 456.

134 Boyer, "Oscar Wilde mourait dans mes bras," 2.

135 See "Oscar Wilde Suite," L'Hotel, Paris, https://www.l-hotel.com/rooms/oscar-wilde-suite/.

136 Kathleen Scott, *Self-Portrait of an Artist: from the Diaries and Memoirs of Lady Kennet, Kathleen, Lady Scott* (London: John Murray, 1949), 47.

137 I am grateful to Mathis Lainé, who has informed me that Wilde's false teeth remain in the hands of Jean Dupoirier's descendants. Wilde appears to have obtained the teeth towards the end of his life. In 1923, the journalist T.P. O'Connor recalled that the Irish MP John O'Connor had met Wilde at a restaurant during the writer's final years in Paris; the politician noticed that "all Wilde's front teeth were gone" ("T.P.'s Table Talk," *T.P.'s and Cassell's Weekly*, 27 October 1923, 10). Meanwhile, in 1928 the French writer Gustave Le Rouge recalled meeting Wilde at the Calisaya cafe on the boulevard Montmartre, one of Wilde favorite haunts until he became bedridden: "Nous fûmes surpris de sa bonne humeur qui n'était pas feinte, de son rire qui sonnait franchement, découvrant une denture presque entièrement dorée qui lui donnait une vague apparence d'idole" (We were surprised by his good humor, which was not affected, his laughter that sounded honest, revealing a set of almost entirely gold teeth that gave him the appearance of an idol). "Verlainiens et Décadents: souvenirs inédits de Gustave Le Rouge," *Les nouvelles litteraires*, 3 November 1928, 5.

6 Oscar Wilde's French Fragments

REBECCA N. MITCHELL

> C'est à la fragile, la fluide, la pieuse mémoire des hommes que je me suis adressé afin de transcrire, traduire ou reconstituer les restes des beaux récit oubliés, mais qui ressusciteront d'eux-mêmes quelque jour sur les lèvres d'autres hommes, lesquels croiront les avoir inventés, quand leur cerveau n'aura fait que capter les ondes magiques que laissent vibrer longtemps encore les voix chères qui se sont tues.
>
> It is to the fragile, the fluid, the pious memory of men that I have addressed myself in order to transcribe, translate, or reconstitute the remains of these beautiful forgotten stories, but which resurrect themselves someday on the lips of other men, who believe they have invented them, when their brains only captured the magic waves that let the dear voices that have fallen silent still vibrate for a long time.
>
> Léon Guillot de Saix, *Le Chant du cygne*[1]

Oscar Wilde's literary career was bookended by visits to France. He visited the country in 1883, years before he would write his best-known works. Although the final years of his life were marked by upheaval and trauma that had a profound effect on his literary production and, ultimately, his legacy, in those years Wilde also returned to France, where he spent the last years of his life in exile and, eventually, died. Among the minor tragedies occurring in the wake of his ill-fated lawsuit against the Marquess of Queensberry and subsequent trials was the haphazard dispersal of his manuscripts. Some were sold at the April 1895 auction of Wilde's household goods, an event necessitated to cover the author's significant debts at the time. Entering the marketplace through varied routes, manuscript materials were disassembled, notebooks broken up; some eventually made their way into libraries and archives, while others fell into private hands. In the decades following Wilde's death, as his reputation began to be resuscitated, interest in these often-fragmentary documents surged, especially by those devoted supporters interested in recuperating any vestiges of Wilde's spirit.

Among the tantalizing holograph evidence of Wilde's unpolished writing available today is a series of undated sheets which seem to have been written during Wilde's 1883 visit to France. Written in an imperfect French, they apparently document scraps of conversation between him and various interlocutors and are best described as notes, not a coherent manuscript. Their slippery generic status makes them difficult to define. On the one hand, with their pithy turns of phrase and staccato constructions, these fragments are open to interpretation and can be understood as early examples of Wilde's development of the epigram form. In the years following their composition, Wilde would go on to develop his dialogic style, refine his epigrammatic wit, and polish his command of written French. On the other hand, they are among the earliest accounts of Wilde's travels in France, encounters that would shape his career, his life, and his oeuvre, and they have been used as documentary evidence of those travels by Wilde's biographers.

These fragments, which have long escaped scholarly scrutiny, at least in English,[2] other than to fill in Wilde's biography, also play a curious role in shaping the dissemination of Wilde's works in France through the mid-twentieth century, in part by establishing a precedent for attributing reported speech to Wilde himself. One manifestation of that tradition is the life's work of the eccentric writer and radio host Léon Guillot de Saix (1885–1964), whose dedication to Wilde's memory resulted in the publication in French of scores of oral tales and short stories attributed to Wilde, most of which were based solely on the memories – what Guillot de Saix described as "the fragile, the fluid, the pious memory" – of those who encountered the author. This chapter explores Wilde's fragmentary writings in French to argue that they represent still-nascent aspects of his composition practice and literary style, and that their treatment and publication helped determine Wilde's legacy, which persists to this day. It follows the history of these fragments and their transmission in later works as evidence of the continued commitment to the idea of Wilde's fraternity with Paris and with French language and letters.

Wilde's French Fragments

The six manuscript folios of Wilde's French fragments are loose, not in their original order, and split between the Eccles Bequest held in the British Library (BL) and the New York Public Library (NYPL). They seem to record Wilde's conversations with people that he met, as well as some quips of his own, and feature few of the corrections and revisions evident in Wilde's drafts of his published works. Wilde himself did not date them, but the context suggests that at least some of these fragments originate with the conversations he had during his extended trip to Paris in spring 1883, following his successful lecture tour of North America, where he served as advance publicity for a touring production of Gilbert and Sullivan's comic operetta *Patience*. In that role, he self-consciously amplified the Aesthetic manners and clothing satirized in *Patience*. Yet, on his return to Europe, at the time when he would have written the fragments, he was moving away from that high Aesthetic character into something more nuanced, and these fragments therefore document an important point for Wilde's personal and authorial development.

In the process of their accession into archival institutions, the documents have been named and catalogued. The five NYPL pages are listed as "Holograph Notes and Epigrams, unsigned and undated," and their custom case is labelled "Autograph Manuscript Notes, Epigrams, etc." The single folio in the British Library is catalogued as "Miscellaneous epigrams, including 'Epigrams for Constance Wilde.'" The label "epigrams," applied to both, confers a status that is for the most part unwarranted by the contents of the pages. Rather than lists of epigrams, they evidence the literary and artistic network Wilde began to build while in Paris as well as his democratic interest in recounting turns of phrase from unlikely quarters. "La poesie c'est la grammaire idealisee" reads one line; "pour ecrire il me faut de satin jaune," reads another, both happily ignoring all pretense of accents and capitalization. His French might be imprecise, but the sentiments – "poetry is grammar idealized"; "to write I need yellow satin" – are thoroughly Wildean.[3]

Consider the first folio from the Berg collection at the New York Public Library: a rapid-fire conversation between "Coquelin" – one of a pair of acting brothers – and "Ego" – Wilde himself, that reads as a proto-dialogue of the kind he depicts in his dinner party scenes in *The Picture of Dorian Gray* or on the stage in the Society plays:

COQUELIN. qu'est-ce-que c'est la civilization, monsieur Wilde?
EGO. l'amour du beau.
C. qu'est-ce-que c'est le beau?
EGO. ce que les bourgeois appellent le laid.
C. et ce que les bourgeois appellent le beau?
EGO. cela n'existe pas.[4]

COQUELIN. what is civilization, monsieur Wilde?
EGO. the love of beauty.
C. what is beauty?
EGO. what the bourgeois call the ugly.
C. and what the bourgeois call the beautiful?
EGO. that does not exist.

The recorded speech has the same ring of the rapid-fire back-and-forth between Lord Henry and the Duchess of Monmouth in *Dorian Gray:* "'What of art?' she asked. 'It is a malady.' 'Love?' 'An illusion.' 'Religion?' 'The fashionable substitute for belief.'"[5] That dialogic formulation, while redolent of much of Wilde's prose writing, does render the content as something other than epigrams, a form dependent on the completeness of thought, not of conversational give and take.

The contents of another manuscript folio sheet record the musings of Maurice Rollinat, the French Decadent poet and follower of Baudelaire, whom Wilde met in 1883.[6] In his letters, Wilde praised Rollinat's poem "La Vache au Taureau" from his 1883 collection *Les Névroses*: "c'est un chef d'œuvre. Il y a dedans un vrai souffle de la Nature" ("it is a masterpiece. It has a real breath of Nature").[7] Rollinat's table talk, as recorded in Wilde's notes, captures his preference for epigrammatic paradox, along with his blasé wit: "j'admire les chaises Japonais parce-que ils n'ont pas etait faits pour s'asseoir" ("I admire Japanese chairs because they were not made for sitting").[8] Excerpted as such, it is the kind of one-liner that one might easily imagine finding its way into "The Decay of Lying" or another of Wilde's essays, and perhaps comes closest to achieving the catalogued title of "epigram."

Looking beyond that single line, though, the remainder of Rollinat's ideas – as recorded in Wilde's notes – are less brilliant: "Il n'y a q'une forme pour le beau: mais pour chaque chose chaque individu a un formule: ainsi on ne comprend pas les poëts" ("There is only one form for the beautiful. But for each thing each individual has a formula; so one cannot understand the poets"); "je ne crois pas au progres: mais je crois au stagnation de la perversite humaine" ("I do not believe in progress: but I believe in the stagnation of human perversity"). Whether the fault is Rollinat's, or Wilde's memory, or even Wilde's imperfect French transcription, is unclear. But there is little particularly evocative in the statement, nor in the final note on the manuscript page, written in English – "his idea of music continuing the beauty of the poetry without its idea." There are, though, echoes of Walter Pater's claim in "Giorgione," in *The Renaissance: Studies in Art and Poetry* (1873), that "*All art constantly aspires towards the condition of music*," which means the fragment falls in line with Wilde's broader engagement with aesthetic philosophy at the time.[9]

The single page held at the British Library seems to have come from the same notebook, written like the NYPL pages on unlined cream paper, approximately 8x10", and with the same watermark. Another reason to think that the BL folio comes from the same group as the New York Public Library sheets is that transcriptions from both documents appear together in the art dealer Martin Birnbaum's memoir, *Oscar Wilde: Fragments and Memories*, which he published in 1914. Birnbaum provides the first full transcription of the pages, and while he does not explicitly detail how he came to possess them, he writes that the pages include the dialogue with Coquelin, which "is followed by some French 'phrases and philosophies' and scraps of criticism, all taken from a large common-place book, bought at the sale of Wilde's effects, printed here exactly as they were left."[10]

The commonplace book might have been bound when Birnbaum saw and transcribed it, but was – like so many of Wilde's manuscripts – thereafter broken up into separate pages, which were often sold off by booksellers, as Birnbaum confirms: "The book from which these fragments were taken contained much more," he writes, "but the dealer into whose hands it fell was in the habit of tearing out the sheets and inserting them into copies of first editions of Wilde's books, to enhance their value for the many bibliophiles who collect his works."[11] Perhaps more significantly, Birnbaum is a rare voice in questioning the value of offering up the jottings for public consumption: "The propriety of publishing such scraps, left behind without an author's final revisions, is open to question, but the French fragments quoted above seem exceptional, for the slight errors and peculiarities of style throw some light on the alleged debt which Wilde owed to Marcel Schwob, through whose hands the manuscript of 'Salome' passed before it was printed."[12] Schwob was one of several people who helped Wilde refine the French in his play *Salomé*, which was originally composed in French, and Birnbaum is here suggesting that the error-riddled state of Wilde's fragments shows that his French was not as strong as sometimes thought, at least at the time when he composed the notes.

Fragments as Epigrams

Following Birnbaum, the generic status of the fragments has always been in question: I refer to them as "fragments," for instance, despite the "epigrams" labels often attributed by archivists, librarians, or collectors. Yet there are some benefits to considering the pithy, quippy one-liners as epigrams. Birnbaum too points readers in this direction, when he refers to the fragments as "phrases and philosophies," in a nod to the title of one of Wilde's lists of epigrams: Wilde would go on to write and publish "A Few Maxims for the Instruction of the Over-Educated" (*Saturday Review*, November 1894) and "Phrases and Philosophies for the Use of the Young" (*The Chameleon*, December 1894), in addition to the "Preface" to *The Picture of Dorian Gray*, first published as a stand-alone catalogue of epigrams in the *Fortnightly Review* in March 1891.[13] Totalling around seventy-five epigrams across the three publications, this represents a relatively small output in terms of words; but these works are still considered representative of Wilde's command of the form.

Wilde's composition of the epigrams, as detailed in the many manuscripts that include them, might shed some light on his approach to the French fragments. Wilde's epigrams stand as a uniquely important genre for the author, written manifestations of his famously quick wit and spontaneous turn of phrase. Yet the archival corpus shows extensive evidence of his writerly process, which involved regular tinkering with the phrasing and ordering of his epigrams, with some undergoing serial revisions before arriving at their final iterations – evidence that undermines visions of a spontaneously ebullient, unlaboured ease which Wilde worked so hard to cultivate. To offer one example of the revision process that many of Wilde's epigrams underwent, consider the first epigram from *The Chameleon*'s "Phrases and Philosophies": "The first duty in life is to be as artificial as possible. What the second duty is no one has as yet discovered."[14] Variants of the line appear in four extant manuscript witnesses held at Princeton, the British Library, the Beinecke at Yale, and the William Andrews Clark Memorial Library at UCLA. None of the manuscript witnesses bears a definitive date, though one could imagine a progression from the single clause present in the Princeton manuscript:

> the only duty in life is to be as artificial as possible [15]

to the addition of the second clause and the ordinal pairing evident in the British Library's folio:

> The ~~only~~ first duty in life is to be as artificial as possible. What the second duty is no one has ~~ever~~ as yet discovered.[16]

Here, the "only" duty becomes the "first" duty, its singular status heightened by the addition of an unknown "second" duty. The Beinecke's manuscript shows the phrasing established, but Wilde emending the word order, inserting "The first duty in life" at the start of the epigram and striking it from its original position at the end:

> (The first duty in life is) To be as artificial as possible. ~~Is the first duty in life~~.[17]

The Clark manuscript is written without any changes, and only a slight variation from the published version ("The first duty of Life" versus "The first duty in life").[18] Evident throughout these manuscript pages are clear indications of process: words struck or overwritten, jottings in pen later amended in pencil, entire epigrams struck from a list, one might imagine, as he decided to include them in one publication or another. These variants document only minor changes, but they are indicative of the care that Wilde took in shaping the exact phrasing of his epigrams.

The earlier French fragments, however, show little of this compositional practice. One notable emendation occurs in Folio 3 of the NYPL holdings. One entry in a list of one-liners is credited to a worker at the Louvre museum: "Les maitres anciens, ~~L'art Grec~~, c'est la momie, n'est ce pas? – concierge at the Louvre."[19] Altering "Greek art" to "The ancient masters" makes the punchline – "that's the mummy, isn't it?" – funnier. This could be evidence of the same editorial impulse that marked the composition of his published epigrams, reworking phrasing to improve its flow or effect, or it could be a correction of a misremembered line. On balance, the French fragments do not show changes or the kind of careful development of drafts that lead to published works, but are instead likely scraps of cleverness to be remembered and perhaps used later; in that sense as well, the emendations and errors that feature in the French fragments appear less as indicators of the limitation of Wilde's fluency but rather the consequence of quickly writing without the knowledge that these notes would be later read by others.

French Fragments as Biographical Information

Birnbaum was not editing Wilde's work, so his caution about the publication of the fragments is particularly sensitive. Perhaps more interesting for Wilde's legacy as an authorial persona is the role that these French works play in the many memoirs or posthumous accounts of Wilde that circulated in the decades following his death. Robert H. Sherard provides an account of the interactions that seem to have given rise to the phrases in his *Story of an Unhappy Friendship* (1902).[20] Sherard, who met Wilde on the 1883 trip to Paris and would have been with him around the time of the conversations that are recorded in the fragments, would not have had access to the manuscript pages when he was writing his memoir, but his account nonetheless provides a narrative context for the fragments' contents. On Rollinat, for example, whose quip about his love for Japanese chairs not made for sitting was recorded by Wilde, Sherard described a poet in crisis: "it was drugs, drugs with him morning and night, drugs for food and drugs for sleep; cerebral excitement all the time."[21] Sherard notes that Wilde took "joy" in "the ravaged personality of the poet, who at that time seemed to be tottering, like a man on a tight-rope, between lunacy on the one side and death on the other"; Wilde's interest in Rollinat seemed to be "sincere, and mingled with admiration rather than pity."[22] The account counters one possible interpretation of the fragments: that of an author callously mining his companions for fodder to be later incorporated into his work.

Later writers did not have the advantage of having been present at Oscar Wilde's side, and have frequently adopted the pages' contents wholesale as factual evidence of Wilde's 1883 French visit, citing them to burnish Wilde's reputation as a bon vivant with ready access to bon mots, even if this means improving on Wilde's writing as he left it.[23] They also often fail to indicate the exact source of their information – whether they are consulting the manuscript or relying on others' accounts. Biographers, including Richard Ellmann and Matthew Sturgis, summarily correct Wilde's French when rendering these lines, and often tease out narrative implications well beyond the manuscript page. They are readings that embrace a view of Wilde that resists the evidence of revision, effort, or difficulty. Sturgis, for example, writes that "Wilde was delighted by the remark of one of the guards at the Louvre: when asked for directions to the Old Masters, they had replied, "Les maîtres anciens? C'est les momies, n'est-ce pas?" – directing the inquirer towards the Egyptian Mummies."[24] As we have seen, Wilde's lines are sparer than this narrative would suggest, and his words are missing the accents and punctuation that Sturgis restores. Wilde's edit to the lines, changing "Greek art" to "Ancient masters," also undercuts the spontaneous ease captured in Sturgis's retelling, but this would not have been obvious without access to the manuscript, and Sturgis does not mention it, privileging the fluency of the narrative over archivally informed accuracy, as would be expected in a biography.

In his still-standard (if flawed) 1987 biography, Ellmann draws on the fragments throughout his account of Wilde's 1883 sojourn, citing the lines as evidence of Wilde's brilliance at the table. About Wilde's dinners with the young Robert Sherard early in their acquaintance,

Ellmann writes that "There was no doubt who ruled the table that night. Wilde probably made use of some of the conversational gambits that he had begun to write down in his notebook ... He initialled these 'O.W.' to distinguish them from remarks he had heard from others."[25] Ellmann accurately describes the relevant manuscript page here, though his interpretation – that Wilde said these things while eating with Sherard – goes well beyond the evidence. Nevertheless, the accretion of accounts such as Ellmann's influences later biographers, who build further upon these suppositions. Jonathan Fryer extrapolates even further, embellishing the account: "[Wilde] kept a notebook in French of *bon mots* that he had used, or would use, in conversation, or wished he had thought of himself. He amused some of his Parisian acquaintances and outraged others with such remarks as 'In order to write, I must have yellow satin,' or 'I need lions in gilded cages. It's frightful; after human flesh, lions like bones, and people never give them any.'"[26] These biographies are typical and demonstrate the evolution of the narrative around Wilde away from the sparsity of the archival evidence of the French fragments to a more fluid account that bolsters existing ideas of Wilde's character: that his table talk was amusing and outrageous, and that he stood always prepared with a smart and pithy one-liner.

Wilde's French Fragments in France

As for the French reception of the excerpts, early renderings of the fragments, notably by the careful reader and translator of Wilde's work, Henry-D. Davray, hewed more to the caution demonstrated by Birnbaum than to the effusive glosses of later biographers. Davray, one of Wilde's best French translators, offered a nuanced appraisal of Wilde's manuscript pages when he reproduced the French lines for *Le Figaro* in 1927. Like the later biographers, Davray did correct Wilde's French grammar, but he offered a relatively comprehensive transcription, preceded by introductory comments. In those, he bemoaned the loss of the rest of the notebook pages, given the insight they might offer into Wilde's process. With a better understanding of that process, Davray concluded, "Peut-être y verrait-on que le caractère de spontanéité et d'aisance prime-sautière de son théâtre, de ses contes et de ses essais provient d'une élaboration réfléchie de la pensée" ("Perhaps we would see that the character of spontaneity and ease of his theatre, his tales, and his essays, comes from a reflective elaboration of thought").[27]

In contrast to the biographers who regard the French fragments as further evidence of Wilde's persona, extrapolating affective responses from the snippets of recorded speech, Davray expresses the caution of a careful editor, acknowledging that the partial manuscript materials are indicative of a writerly process as much as they are evidence of a personality. Not all later writers who engaged with Wilde's fragmentary manuscripts would adopt the same approach. One, Léon Guillot de Saix, had an enthusiasm for and commitment to Wilde's legacy that rivalled any of Wilde's better-known editors or champions. His methodologies, though, depend on the kind of wholesale embrace of an author's most inconsequential utterances that more careful editors eschew. Propelled by a seemingly limitless energy for publishing Wilde's anecdotes and short fiction – often stretching the idea of "table talk" to its very limits – Guillot de Saix oversaw the publication, from the late 1930s onward, of an extraordinary series of oral tales and short stories in French that were invariably attributed to Wilde.

One section of Wilde's French fragments appears in Guillot de Saix's 1942 collection *Le Chant du cygne*. It is not listed in the table of contents, but appears appended to the anecdote "Bienfaits et méfaits des mathématiques" with a preparatory comment:

> Lorsqu'il logeait à l'hôtel du quai Voltaire, Oscar Wilde notait chaque soir, sur un épais cahier de grand format, de son écriture aux élégants hiéroglyphes, des fragments de conversation, des traits d'esprit, des idées et des opinions glanés au long du jour. À la suite d'une rencontre avec Coquelin aîné, le grand Coq, Wilde traça en français sur son fidèle cahier ce fragment de dialogue: [28]

> When he was staying at the hotel on the quai Voltaire, Oscar Wilde wrote down each evening, in a thick large-scale notebook, in his writing of elegant hieroglyphs, fragments of conversation, witticisms, ideas, and opinions that he gleaned through the day. Following a meeting with Coquelin the elder, the great Rooster, Wilde recorded in French in his faithful notebook this fragment of dialogue:

Apparently drawing on published accounts of Sherard, Birnbaum, and Davray, Guillot de Saix then gives the line-by-line dialogue between "Ego" and "Coquelin," embellishing along the way. Further, only one of the folios of the fragments includes Coquelin's name, yet Guillot de Saix records a line from another folio – the one which includes lines attributed to Wilde, a waiter, and the concierge at the Louvre – as if it were a continuation of the dialogue with Coquelin: "Et lorsque l'acteur l'interroge sur la poésie, il réplique: – La poésie? c'est de la grammaire idéalisée" ("And when the actor asks him about poetry, he replies: – Poetry? It is idealized grammar).[29] Guillot de Saix closes the anecdote with an excerpt from still another folio, which is labeled by Wilde "Ego to Coquelin":

> Enfin, le comédien questionne l'auteur sur ses projets de théâtre, Oscar Wilde répond ironiquement: – Mon drame? du style seulement. Hugo et Shakespeare se sont partagé tous les sujets. Il ne nous reste plus que le style.[30]

> Finally, the actor questions the author about his theatrical projects, Oscar Wilde responds ironically: – My drama? It's only style. Hugo and Shakespeare have taken all the subjects. Only style remains.

Only the first two sentences that Guillot de Saix ascribes to Wilde appear in the manuscript pages or in Birnbaum's and Davray's transcriptions. The final line – "Il ne nous reste plus que le style" – does not appear anywhere in the holograph fragments. Wilde's response, as recorded by him in his notebook's pages, is also considerably longer than the version offered by Guillot de Saix, and the degree of irony present in it is debatable at best.[31] This kind of imprecision with sources, and ascribing words to Wilde without direct evidence of their having been uttered, is a hallmark of Guillot de Saix's approach to Wilde's work, and considering the extent of the publications he ascribed to Wilde, these choices are significant for the reception of Wilde in France in the mid-twentieth century.

Guillot de Saix's Recovery Project

Born in 1885, the French playwright, theatre director, and radio personality Guillot de Saix cultivated a varied career, though his abiding interest in Wilde's life and works remained a constant. His voluminous archives are presently housed in the Département des arts du spectacle of the Bibliothèque nationale de France, where the contents of many hundreds of binders, boxes, and folders are only minimally catalogued, in a single, bound typescript handlist. The extensive, unprocessed Wilde-related holdings reveal a hodgepodge of press clippings, handwritten notes, correspondence with members of Wilde's expansive circle, numerous drafts, typewritten radio scripts, and reams of correspondence with publishers. In a review of the contents of the collection, nothing in Wilde's hand was found.

From the morass of data, a few conclusions can be drawn. First, Guillot de Saix embraced a capacious view of Wilde's authorship: he would readily adopt the briefest anecdote or even passing comment as the genesis of an "oral tale," extrapolating as needed. Second, his efforts were sincere, devoted entirely to the preservation and propagation of the idea of Wilde's genius, if not his sainthood. Through sheer diligence of effort, and working towards a biography of Wilde that ultimately remained unfinished, he cultivated relationships with many of the more important figures in Wilde's life who were then still alive, including Robert Sherard, Montgomery Hyde, Vyvyan Holland, and Reginald Turner, whose long letters to Guillot de Saix were written as he was nearing the end of his life. Despite his dedication to Wilde's work and the prolific publications he produced and attributed to Wilde, Guillot de Saix has attracted almost no scholarly attention.[32]

For all of his genuine commitment to the idea of Wilde's authorial significance, Guillot de Saix's editorial practices demonstrate the degree to which even the smallest of Wilde's utterances could be turned to a completed "work." Extending the narrativizing on display in most English-language biographies to something more comprehensive, Guillot de Saix regularly attributed authorship status to works that Wilde never wrote, not just to lines that Oscar Wilde did not utter. Guillot de Saix's magnum opus on Wilde was *Le Chant du cygne: Contes parlés d'Oscar Wilde*, published by Mercure de France in 1942. While the title credits Wilde directly with the contents, the title page indicates the volume was "Recueillis et rédigés par Guillot de Saix" ("Compiled and edited by Guillot de Saix"). It contains over sixty short stories (termed "oral tales" in Guillot de Saix's title) purported to be Wilde's, many of which had appeared in print in English, often in variant form.

The transcription of the French fragments that appear in *Le Chant du cygne* has no introductory information or contextualization, so one can only assume that Guillot de Saix's source was Sherard's, Birnbaum's, or Davray's accounts. Many of the other stories, though, do feature some information on the works' provenance. In some cases, these prefaces are themselves embellished, as is the case in the note preceding "Bienfaits et méfaits des mathématiques," which is worth quoting in full:

> Oscar Wilde ne fut-il pas ce joueur de flûte obstiné dont les airs résonneront encore lorsque depuis longtemps nos voix se seront tues? Au temps de ses études, Oscar Wilde était à peu près nul en mathématiques, – trait qui lui est commun avec bon nombre d'hommes de lettres. Il eut jusqu'à sa mort la haine invétérée des chiffres. Oscar Wilde et Bernard Shaw se rencontrèrent un jour dans le quartier de Chelsea, à une exposition si dénuée de toute prétention que le seul fait de s'y voir les amusa énormément. Wilde, au lieu de son habituelle redingote à parements de soie, était vêtu d'un complet de lainage d'Écosse, et les deux auteurs, dont un seul parla,

s'entendirent magnifiquement. Ce fut la première fois que Wilde se révéla comme conteur à Bernard Shaw. Et voici quelle fut l'histoire racontée.[33]

Wasn't Oscar Wilde that stubborn pied piper whose tunes will still resound when our voices have long since fallen silent? When he was a student, Oscar Wilde was close to useless in mathematics – a trait which he has in common with a good number of men of letters. Until his death he had an inveterate hatred of figures. Oscar Wilde and Bernard Shaw met one day in Chelsea, at an exhibition so unpretentious that the very fact of seeing each other amused them enormously. Wilde, instead of his usual frock coat with silk facings, was dressed in a Scottish woolen suit, and the two authors, only one of whom spoke, got along splendidly. This was the first time that Wilde revealed himself as a storyteller to Bernard Shaw. And here is the story he told.

In the Guillot de Saix archive is a two-page typescript of the story as printed in *Le Chant du cygne*, with a handwritten note at the top in writing that appears to be Bernard Shaw's, dated 19 April 1950. His comment, written in English, noted that Wilde was a "superb raconteur" who "told me this story at a Naval Exhibition in the Chelsea Botanic Gardens in London." He also noted that the French translation of the story was good.[34] Shaw died just over six months after that comment would have been written, so this recollection would have been that of a very elderly man about events that had occurred over fifty years prior. There is no mention of Wilde's attire in Shaw's note, or that I could discover elsewhere in the archive. The details of Wilde's and Shaw's interaction included in the headnote, from the nature of the exhibition ("si dénuée de toute prétention") to Wilde's suit ("un complet de lainage d'Écosse") seem to be invented, while the actual details that Shaw provided – that the exhibition was at the Chelsea Botanic Garden, for example – are missing from Guillot de Saix's account.

In other cases, the headnotes are concerning rather than reassuring, and indicate the tenuousness of the editorial foundation of Guillot de Saix's stories: In the headnote to "Jean et Judas," he writes "Voici un autre conte rapporté par Eugène Tardieu, puis par son ami Léonard Sarluis. Il semble avoir été le départ d'une pièce intitulée *L'Immortel Péché* et qu'on a cru pouvoir attribuer à Wilde, alors qu'il s'agirait en réalité d'une paraphrase faite en Amérique, sous le pseudonyme de Dorian Hope, par un des neveux de sa femme" ("Here is another tale reported by Eugène Tardieu, then by his friend Léonard Sarluis. It seems to have been the start of a play entitled *L'Immortel Péché*, thought to be attributable to Wilde, though it would in fact be a paraphrase made in America under the pseudonym Dorian Hope, by one of his wife's nephews").[35] One might forgive Guillot de Saix not knowing the Dorian Hope works were forgeries, as they convinced many people, but while he acknowledges the dubious origin, he hedges by calling the forgery a "paraphrase." What is more, he includes the story – told at twice remove – in the collection even after his earlier correspondence with Vyvyan Holland should have put an end to it. Writing in response to Guillot de Saix's query about "L'Immortel Péché," Holland wrote in 1935, "I do not for a moment think that this was written by Oscar Wilde."[36]

Holland was not the only correspondent who sounded notes of caution about ascribing works to Wilde. Sherard, writing to Guillot de Saix in 1935 in an otherwise encouraging letter, noted that "90% des conversations mises en sa bouche par des biographes qui ne l'ont pas connu dont de contrefaçon" ("90% of the conversations put in his mouth by biographers who did not know him are counterfeit").[37] Such early remonstrances seem to have had little effect on Guillot de Saix's agenda, and he continued to publish stories. In "Six contes inédits d'Oscar Wilde" ("Six unpublished stories by Oscar Wilde"), for example, which appeared on 14 November 1946 in *Les Nouvelles littéraires*, Guillot de Saix included versions of "L'homme qui racontait des choses merveilleuses," "L'homme aux mains couvertes," "La valeur de la présence d'esprit," "Le Jeu des apparences," "L'Aimant et les limailles," and "Le Bal manqué." The title label "inédit" (unpublished) is misleading, as stated by John Waldorp, the agent for Wilde biographer Hesketh Pearson. Waldorp wrote to Guillot de Saix via the editors of *Les Nouvelles littéraires*, objecting that they had reprinted translations of stories first appearing in Pearson's then-recently published biography. While each of the stories features some gloss on its origin, it is only at the end of the piece that Guillot de Saix includes an acknowledgment: "Tels sont les contes que nous rélève, dans un de ses chapitres, le nouveau livre de M. Hesketh Pearson: *The Life of Oscar Wilde*" ("Such are the tales told to us, in one of its chapters, in the new book by Mr. Hesketh Pearson"), a postscript that undercuts the title claim that the pieces were unpublished. As is clear from Waldorp's letter, he and Pearson felt this was insufficient acknowledgment.

Further, Guillot de Saix's correspondence reveals that his attempts to publish Wilde's work were often rebuffed by presses. In light of the "large inequality in tone, sense, and literary interest" of the contents of a proposed follow-up volume to *Chant du cygne* that was to include thirty-three stories, the editor at Éditions Stock rejected the book, noting that while "certain passages reflect the fantasy and icy humour of Wilde well enough," others "could have been written by anyone," and the press would therefore not "blame Oscar Wilde for their authorship."[38] Undeterred, Guillot de Saix pressed on, and, for example, went to print with one of the stories from that collection, "L'Ouvrière de la dernière heure" in 1956, billing it as "an unpublished story by Oscar Wilde."[39] The planned follow-up collection to *Le Chant du cygne*, titled *Le Chant du phénix* or *L'Evangile de minuit* in draft versions, did not see print. Still, it is easy to underestimate the diffusion of Guillot de Saix's ostensible translations of Wilde's stories, which appear, attributed to Wilde, in countless French publications. Some of these efforts went to placing Wilde stories in unusual places. At least two of Wilde's stories ("conte parlé d'Oscar Wilde, recueilli et rédigé par Guillot de Saix") appeared in *Animaux*, the journal of the Association française pour la défense des animaux, "Le chien mort et ressuscité" and "L'homme et le chien." One of these, "Le chien mort ... " came through indirect means, as the head-notes indicates: "Voici un apologue, apparemment d'origine orientale, qu'une de ses compatriotes, Mrs. Jameson, de Dublin, rédigea différemment" ("Here is an apologue, apparently of Eastern origin, which one of his compatriots, Mrs. Jameson, of Dublin, wrote differently").[40] Others were translated into Italian, as evident from multiple clippings from *Realta* (1957 and 1958).

The precise motivation for Guillot de Saix's extensive efforts to publish Wilde's work is unclear. Unlike many of the people from Wilde's circle with whom he corresponded, Guillot de Saix himself never encountered Wilde. One of the archivists who compiled the catalogue to his collection at the BnF speculated that one reason for his investment in Wilde was Guillot de Saix's sexuality: "Homosexuel, sa défense de l'homosexualité se manifeste avant tout dans son attachement à Oscar Wilde, qu'il a beaucoup traduit et dont il s'est fait une mission de valoriser le talent et la mémoire" ("Homosexual, his defense of homosexuality is manifested above all in his attachment to Oscar Wilde, whom he has translated many times and whose talent and memory he has made it his mission to promote").[41] Whatever motivated the publications, once in print they become part of the scholarly and popular record. And Guillot de Saix's work, like the various textual speculations around the events and emotions that gave rise to the French fragments, contributes to the continual accumulation of stories by and of and around Oscar Wilde. Thomas Wright, for example, reprints some of Guillot de Saix's work, including his *Chant du cygne* stories, in the 2000 collection he titled *Table Talk*.[42] In adopting that title, Wright acknowledges the remove from Wilde's hand, and though the full extent of that remove remains opaque, it seems clear that even the faint echoes of Wilde that are present in the stories' retelling are, to many readers, valuable.

This chapter opens with an epigraph from Guillot de Saix's collection: he describes memory as "fragile," "fluid," and "pious," and notes that stories are resurrected in the mouths of those who have heard them. These sentiments are as applicable to Wilde's manuscript jottings in French as they are to Guillot de Saix's own works. Above all, the French fragments and their legacy demonstrate the investment readers can attach to the sparsest of textual witnesses – appropriating them to support a pre-existing idea of author or regarding them as a basis for even grander extrapolations – and to the passionate regard that Wilde and his memory still inspire.

NOTES

1 Léon Guillot de Saix, Headnote to Section 1, titled "La Vérité du mensonge," *Le Chant du cygne* (Paris: Mercure de France, 1942), 45. All translations are the author's.
2 Henry Davray discusses Wilde's fragments in "Le Carnet d'Oscar Wilde," in *Le Figaro supplément littéraire*, 22 October 1927, 1–2. See below.
3 Throughout this chapter, I have retained Wilde's errors and irregular capitalization when quoting from the manuscript pages.
4 Oscar Wilde, "Holograph Notes and Epigrams, unsigned and undated," NYPL 186814B: N5L, folio 2.
5 Oscar Wilde, *The Picture of Dorian Gray*, ed. Joseph Bristow (Oxford: Oxford World Classics, 2019), 165.
6 See Robert Sherard, *Oscar Wilde: The Story of an Unhappy Friendship* (London: Hermes Press), 47–50.
7 Oscar Wilde, *The Complete Letters of Oscar Wilde*, eds. Merlin Holland and Rupert Hart-Davis (London: Fourth Estate, 2000), 208.
8 Oscar Wilde, "Holograph Notes and Epigrams, unsigned and undated," NYPL 186814B: N5L, folio 1.
9 Walter Pater, "The School of Giorgione," in *The Renaissance: Studies in Art and Poetry*, ed. Donald L. Hill (Berkeley: University of California Press, 1980), 106.
10 Martin Birnbaum, *Oscar Wilde: Fragments and Memories* (New York: J.F. Drake, 1914), 9.
11 Birnbaum, *Oscar Wilde*, 13.
12 Birnbaum, *Oscar Wilde*, 13.
13 Because these epigrams appeared at the start of the novel in its volume form, they are treated in the critical literature almost uniformly as a part of the novel, as opposed to an independent text.
14 Oscar Wilde, "Phrases and Philosophies for the Use of the Young," *The Chameleon* 1 (December 1894), 1.

15 MS Princeton Wilde, Oscar, *Epigrams*, f.1r.
16 MS British Library "Draft Epigrams," Add MS 81636 A. The epigram is written in ink, and the emendation of "ever" to "as yet" is written in ink, but the strike through "only" and the insertion of "first" are in pencil, suggesting that this edit occurred at a different, likely later time.
17 MS Beinecke "Phrase and Philosophies," GEN MSS 275 Box 1 Folder 27, f.1r.
18 MS Clark, WILDE Uncatalogued Box 2, f.1.r.
19 Wilde, "Holograph Notes and Epigrams, unsigned and undated," NYPL 186814B: N5L, folio 3.
20 Sherard, *Oscar Wilde*, 48–55; 110. On Sherard, see Kevin H.F. O'Brien's "Robert Sherard: Friend of Oscar Wilde," *English Literature in Transition, 1880–1920* 28, no. 1 (1985): 3–29.
21 Sherard, *Oscar Wilde*, 47.
22 Sherard, *Oscar Wilde*, 48.
23 Sherard recounts Wilde's initial meeting with the younger Coquelin brother on Wilde's later visit in 1891, not 1883. See *Unhappy Friendship*, 114. Herbert Lottman, who records some of the fragments in *Oscar Wilde à Paris* (Paris: Fayard, 2007), 33–8, follows Davray's transcription, but is unclear about whether the contents date from 1883 or 1891.
24 Matthew Sturgis, *Oscar: A Life* (London: Knopf, 2022), 264.
25 Richard Ellmann, *Oscar Wilde* (London: Penguin, 1988), 203.
26 Jonathan Fryer, *André and Oscar: The Literary Friendship of André Gide and Oscar Wilde* (New York: Macmillan, 1998), 16.
27 Davray, "Le Carnet d'Oscar Wilde" *Le Figaro supplément littéraire*, 22 October 1927, 1–2.
28 Guillot de Saix, *Le Chant du cygne*, 265.
29 Guillot de Saix, *Le Chant du cygne*, 265. See Wilde, "Holograph Notes and Epigrams, unsigned and undated," NYPL 186814B: N5L, folio 3.
30 Guillot de Saix, *Le Chant du cygne*, 265.
31 "mon drame? du style seulement: Hugo et Shakespeare ont partage tous les sujets: il est impossible d'être original, même dans le péché: ainsi il n'y -a pas d'émotions, seulement des adjectifs extraordinaires. le fin est assez tragique, mon heros au moment de son triomphe fait un epigramme qui manque tout-a-fait d'effet, alors on le condamne a être academiciaen avec discours forcés. Ego to Coquelin." Wilde, "Holograph Notes and Epigrams, unsigned and undated," NYPL 186814B: N5L, folio 4.
32 One exception is a short article by Donald Mead, "Swan Song: Spoken Stories by Oscar Wilde Collected by Guillot de Saix" which appeared in *The Wildean*, no. 47 (July 2015): 101–8. Mead notes that Guillot de Saix's works "cannot have Wilde's authority and cannot be classified using the traditional textual criteria," but he argues for the value of the works: "His

approach is literary rather than 'scientific,' and, with considerable success, he reanimates the stories" (101, 104).

33 Guillot de Saix, *Le Chant du cygne*, 261–2.

34 Collection Guillot de Saix COL 31/302, box 1, folder 3. Bibliothèque nationale de France (BnF). Permission courtesy The Society of Authors, on behalf of the Bernard Shaw Estate.

35 Guillot de Saix, *Chant du cynge*, 112. For more on Dorian Hope, see Gregory Mackie, *Beautiful Untrue Things: Forging Oscar Wilde's Extraordinary Afterlife* (Toronto: University of Toronto Press, 2019), 68–123.

36 Letter dated 13 November 1935 from Vyvyan Holland to Guillot de Saix; original in English. Collection Guillot de Saix COL 31/302, box 2, folder 3. BnF. I am grateful to Merlin Holland for granting permission to print this quotation.

37 Letter from Robert Harborough Sherard to Guillot de Saix, 7 November 1935, Collection Guillot de Saix, COL-31/302, Folder 1 Box 1. BnF.

38 Letter 26 January 1949, from Éditions Stock: "Il règne dans ce manuscrit une grand inégalité de ton, de sens, d'intérêt littéraire. Un pareil recueil n'offre pas plus de garantie que n'en comporte le genre et qu'on ne saurait lui demander. Il nous a paru que certains passages reflètent assez bien la fantaisie, l'humour glacé d'Oscar Wilde. J'en ai trouvé de tout à fait remarquables comme esprit. Beaucoup d'autres pages pourraient être de n'importe qui; certaines des ces histoires ont traîné partout et on ne saurait en infliger la paternité à Oscar Wilde." Collection Guillot de Saix COL 31/302, box 2. BnF.

39 *Actualitiés littéraire*, November 1956. Collection Guillot de Saix COL 31/301, box 3. BnF.

40 Guillot de Saix (att. Oscar Wilde), "Le chien mort et ressuscité," *Animaux* (undated clipping), 4. One of these stories, "L'Homme et le chien" appeared at least one other time, as evidenced in a clipped page (with no identifying publication information) in the archive. Collection Guillot de Saix COL 31/301, box 3. BnF.

41 Emmanuelle Toulet, "Avant-propos," in *Collection Guillot de Saix inventaire sommaire*, eds. Marie-Thérèse Debuysscher, Catherine Ducrocq-Le Griffon, Claudette Joannis, Anita Mengozzi, and Emmanuelle Toulet (Paris: BnF, Département des arts du spectacle, 1999), 5.

42 Oscar Wilde, *Table Talk*, ed. Thomas Wright (London: Cassell, 2000).

PART FOUR

Literary Influence and Appropriation

7 Oscar Wilde and Pierre Louÿs: The Construction of a Literary Friendship

CLÉMENT DESSY AND STEFANO EVANGELISTA

It is new to me to think that friendship is more brittle than love is.
Wilde to Pierre Louÿs, 27 February 1893

Introduction

Writing to Alfred Douglas in *De Profundis*, Wilde contrasts different types of male friendships that had had a shaping influence on his life and work: "When I compare my friendship with you to my friendship with such still younger men as John Gray and Pierre Louÿs I feel ashamed. My real life, my higher life was with them and such as them."[1] Wilde opposes his destructive relationship with Douglas, which he now considers to have been poisoned by the latter's egotism and philistine materialism, with his friendship with two poets with whom he also became close in the early 1890s: the English John Gray and the French Pierre Louÿs. Looking back from prison to that pivotal period of his life, Wilde associates the friendships of Gray and Louÿs with the idealized notion of a "real" or "higher life" – a counterfactual construct marked by artistic and moral values that could have steered him away from the disastrous path that led him to the 1895 trials and Reading Gaol.

Starting from Wilde's belated idealization of his friendship with the French poet, this chapter explores the artistic and social dynamics that underpinned the connections between Wilde and Louÿs, in which Gray and Douglas also played important mediating roles. Between November 1891 and May 1893, Louÿs was for Wilde a key intermediary and companion in his dealings with literary Paris. The young Louÿs, who was born in 1870 – the same year as Douglas – was then one of the aspiring writers of the second Symbolist generation, alongside André Gide, Paul Valéry, and Alfred Jarry. In a striking act of artistic self-fashioning, he had recently changed his name from the very conventional Louis, adding an ornamental-looking, accented "y" ("i grec" in French) for exotic effect. Combined with this, Louÿs's keen interest in classical antiquity, his Anglophilia, and dandyism naturally attracted Wilde's attention. Their friendship developed at a fast pace. Barely a few weeks into their acquaintance, Wilde's inscription in Louÿs's copy of *A House of Pomegranates*, which was fresh off the press, recognized their shared love of beauty as the essence of their bond: "Au jeune homme qui adore la beauté. Au jeune homme que la beauté adore. Au jeune homme que j'adore" (To the young man who adores beauty. To the young man whom beauty adores. To the young man whom I adore).[2] The personal and literary relationship sanctioned here in such passionate terms received its most public symbolic consecration in 1893, when Wilde dedicated the French *Salomé* "À mon ami Pierre Louÿs"[3] – a formula in which the ideal of friendship to which Wilde would hark back in *De Profundis* stands out in its stark simplicity. Famously, however, Louÿs did not react as Wilde would have wished. In a letter, Wilde complained of being hurt by Louÿs's detached and possibly ironic reception. This is what prompted him to reflect that "friendship is more brittle than love is."[4] As several critics have noted, this episode marked a cooling in their relationship, a process that was also characterized by Louÿs's anxious withdrawal from Wilde's increasingly public homosexuality. It is telling that in the English translation of *Salomé*, issued roughly one year after its French original, Douglas replaced Louÿs as dedicatee – a symbolic switch that might well have been in Wilde's mind when he later reclaimed Louÿs's friendship over Douglas's in *De Profundis*.

The biographical connections between Wilde and Louÿs were mapped in detail by H.P. Clive in the late 1960s.[5] Building partly on that material, Matthew Sturgis, Wilde's latest biographer, has provided a sensitive account of the strain on their relationship as Wilde's reckless behaviour with Douglas became for Louÿs "the cause of real anguish."[6] In the French context, Louÿs's biographer Jean-Paul Goujon has also reconstructed Louÿs's ties with Wilde and his circle, drawing on sources that have been largely overlooked by English critics, such as Louÿs's translations from Wilde's *House of Pomegranates*.[7] Rather than aiming to correct existing biographical narratives, we are interested in exploring how their friendship was constructed across the private and public spheres through displays of intimacy and alliance in ephemera, books, and the media. This textual network reveals the traces of a dialogue that is otherwise occluded in the published works. Wilde's and Louÿs's practices of citation and translation, and their parallel and mutually informing performances of Francophilia and Anglophilia shed light on both authors' cosmopolitan orientation and internationalization strategies. Piecing together their dialogue therefore provides a unique perspective on how Wilde built and managed his French literary network, on how he constructed his presence on the Parisian scene, but also on how he transgressed social boundaries in France in ways that alienated him from his French literary allies.

In approaching this material, we need to be mindful of the fact that we are necessarily dealing with gaps in the archive caused by the fear generated by Wilde's public exposure and criminal conviction for homosexual offences. Partly as a result of these gaps, Louÿs's role as passive and/or disapproving spectator of Wilde's sexual excesses has become a staple ingredient of the Wilde mythology. Gide's ambivalent reclaiming of Wilde in his 1902 essay "In Memoriam" – a pivotal biographical document for Wilde's early reception – has also worked to deflect attention away from Wilde's arguably closer intimacy with Louÿs. This process was exacerbated by the fact that, while Louÿs was trying to sever his ties from Wilde's posthumous legacy, in the early twentieth century Gide needed Wilde – or, to be precise, the Wilde myth – to construct his own persona as queer writer. Gide's later testimony in *Si le grain ne meurt* (1924) was particularly influential in creating Wilde's image as a sexually transgressive Decadent by including a frank first-hand account of his dealings with boys in colonial Algeria. Gide, who was close to both authors in the early 1890s and also shared a history of Algerian sexual tourism with Louÿs, speculated on how aware Louÿs was of Wilde's sexual proclivities before the scandal broke out.[8]

Rumours about the nature of Louÿs's intimacy with Wilde were already circulating in the press several years before Gide, however. An early twentieth-century article in the French homophile periodical *Akademos*, edited by Jacques d'Adelswärd-Fersen, commented ironically on Louÿs's supposed naivety about Wilde's sexual behaviour, adding pointed remarks about Louÿs's own dandified tastes and literary interest in homosexuality: "Je suppose qu'à l'époque où Pierre Louÿs s'honorait de l'amitié d'Oscar Wilde (c'était *avant* le procès), il dut le prendre pour une petite fille, un peu perverse et beaucoup innocente. Car autrement, on ne s'expliquerait pas comment *après* le procès, qui sans doute dessilla ses yeux naïfs, il renia si complètement le magnifique artiste déchu ... " (I suppose that at the time when Pierre Louÿs prided himself on Oscar Wilde's friendship [that was *before* the trial], he must have taken him for a little girl, a little perverse and very naïve. Because otherwise it would be impossible to explain how *after* the trial, which undoubtedly opened his innocent eyes, he disowned so completely the magnificent fallen artist ...).[9] The article shows that, several years after Wilde's death, his friendship was still capable of turning Louÿs into an object of public scrutiny in ways that were clearly designed to make him uncomfortable. While his correspondence shows that Louÿs was capable of assuming a homophobic stance at times, we must consider that evidence as part of a difficult balancing act between public and private personae, which also informs the complexity of their literary relations.

Going Public

At the outset, the friendship between Wilde and Louÿs was based on imbalance, both in terms of age and literary standing: Louÿs was sixteen years younger than Wilde and much less experienced as an author, while Wilde was already somewhat of a literary celebrity in Britain. He was also very keen to expand his readership to France, where he believed audiences would be more favourably disposed towards his experiments with Symbolism. In order to achieve that, he worked hard to make his name known across the Channel, promoting his works with influential critics and attending literary gatherings. What brought the two writers together is precisely that they were intent on conquering the Parisian literary scene at the same time: they intuited that their profiles might complement each other rather than make them potential rivals.

In his early twenties, Louÿs was yet to publish a book of his own. However, he had already founded a literary journal, *La Conque*, where he had issued several of his poems. This short-lived review, active between 1891 and 1892, allowed Louÿs to build an impressive literary network and to acquire visibility by putting his name in print alongside established figures such as Leconte de Lisle (who opened the first issue), José-Maria de Heredia, Maurice Maeterlinck, and Stéphane Mallarmé. In July 1891, shortly after its launch, *La Conque* gave pride of place to A.C. Swinburne by printing his "The Ballad of Melicertes" in English, followed by an unsigned translation by the American-born Symbolist poet Francis Vielé-Griffin. Swinburne was a founding figure of English aestheticism and one of the best-known living English writers in France at the time. A few months later, Wilde's name featured in the short list of the journal's supporters that was published on the first page of every issue. This was November 1891, when Wilde was in Paris and starting to work on *Salomé*. The prominent presence of Swinburne's and Wilde's names in the pages of the journal signals Louÿs's cosmopolitan ambition for *La Conque*, highlighting at the same time his special interest in English literature.

From this point, their connection developed in the public sphere, as both writers attended salons and cafes, such as the Café d'Harcourt,

Paillard, or the Café de la Paix, where they were seen together. A private memorandum compiled by Louÿs at this point testifies to the intensity and visibility of their meetings in Paris: a dinner with Stuart Merrill on 2 December was followed by a rendezvous almost every day (on their own or with Gide) between 12 and 18 December, the day of Wilde's departure from the French capital.[10] Gide later contrasted Louÿs's habit of advertising his friendships with his own restrained attitude in that regard. In a letter to Eugène Rouart, to whom he admitted that he would rather not see their own friendship "épisodée" (chronicled), he explains: "Pierre Louÿs ne comprend pas cela; son grand tort (selon moi) c'est de vouloir créer des événements: il a, là-dessus, toutes les théories de Wilde et de Sherard; il veut troubler les sources et faire des vagues dans des cuvettes. Où je veux décanter, il agite" (Pierre Louÿs does not understand that; his great error [I think] is to want to cause a stir: he has, in this respect, all of Wilde's and Sherard's theories; he wants to muddy the waters and make a storm in a teacup. Where I want to allow things to settle, he stirs them up).[11] It is notable that Gide attributes Louÿs's ideas of advertising his friendships to his previous connections with Wilde, despite the fact that their friendship had ended by this point. It seems therefore that in Gide's eyes the visibility of the friendship between Wilde and Louÿs was the product of a deliberate strategy.

The two shaped their bond by publicly dedicating works to each other. In his debut poetry collection, *Astarté* (1892), Louÿs dedicated the poem "La Danseuse" to Wilde. A first version of the poem had already appeared in *La Conque* in May 1891. However, at that time, before their first encounter, the poem bore no dedication and the slightly different title "La Femme qui danse." Now Louÿs reworked the poem by giving it a more regular sonnet form, and he increased the eroticism by touching up some of the details in the physical descriptions (for instance, by changing "épaules dorées" [golden shoulders] into the more intimate "aisselles dorées" [golden armpits]).[12] The dedication in *Astarté* suggests that Louÿs drew a connection between his own fascination with the theme of the female dancer and Wilde's *Salomé*. Wilde's Symbolist play was still unpublished at that point, but Louÿs had read it in manuscript, helping Wilde with his written French and acting as intermediary with Edmond Bailly of the Librairie de l'Art indépendant, also the publisher of *Astarté*.[13] Louÿs's decision to enrich his poem's chromatic effects by adding striking primary colours ("ombre bleue," "rouge la bouche") enhances the Symbolist visual content in ways that are also reminiscent of Wilde's play.

Astarté is a highly intertextual collection, in which Louÿs builds a far-reaching literary network by means of paratexts such as dedications of individual poems and epigraphs that he either appends to poems or uses to introduce different sections of the book. This was not an unusual practice in the Parisian Symbolist scene, which thrived on public displays of artistic alliance – something that Wilde himself had emulated in *A House of Pomegranates*. However, what is striking is the extent of Wilde's presence. Beside the dedication, one of the epigraphs consists of a sentence from Wilde's "The Young King" in Louÿs's French translation: "On l'avait perdu plusieurs heures, et après une recherche prolongée, on l'avait découvert dans une petite chambre d'une des tourelles au nord du palais, regardant fixement, comme un extasié, une gemme grecque où était sculptée la figure d'Adonis" (He had been missed for several hours, and after a lengthened search had been discovered in a little chamber in one of the northern turrets of the palace gazing, as one in a trance, at a Greek gem carved with the figure of Adonis).[14] The story comes from *A House of Pomegranates*, the collection that Wilde had recently inscribed to Louÿs as a fellow aesthete and a "jeune homme que la beauté adore." Repurposed in *Astarté*, Wilde's epigraph discloses a shared interest in reviving classical antiquity as the medium for a timeless cult of beauty. Louÿs's act of fragmenting Wilde's text and transferring it to the alien context of a foreign language parallels the image of the Greek gem evoked in the original. Travelling from English to French, the reference to Adonis, an icon of male beauty, adds a homoerotic touch to the atmosphere of Louÿs's collection, where the erotic gaze is otherwise focused on the female body. Wilde's decision to dedicate *Salomé* to Louÿs the following year extends the exchange that the French poet had started in "La Danseuse," raising the stakes of their literary partnership.

The theme of the quest for beauty as a shared literary bond between the two writers comes out strongly in an unpublished co-authored manuscript that probably dates from around this period. Likely to have been intended as a private token of friendship rather than the draft of something to commit to print, it consists of two aphorisms written in the hands of the two poets on the same strikingly pink-coloured paper, signed with their first names only and glued together:

> Il ne faut regarder ni les choses ni les personnes. Il ne faut regarder que dans les miroirs.
> Car les miroirs ne nous montrent que des masques. Oscar
> Il faut montrer la Beauté aux hommes. Pierre[15]

> We should look neither at things nor at people. We should not look anywhere but in mirrors.

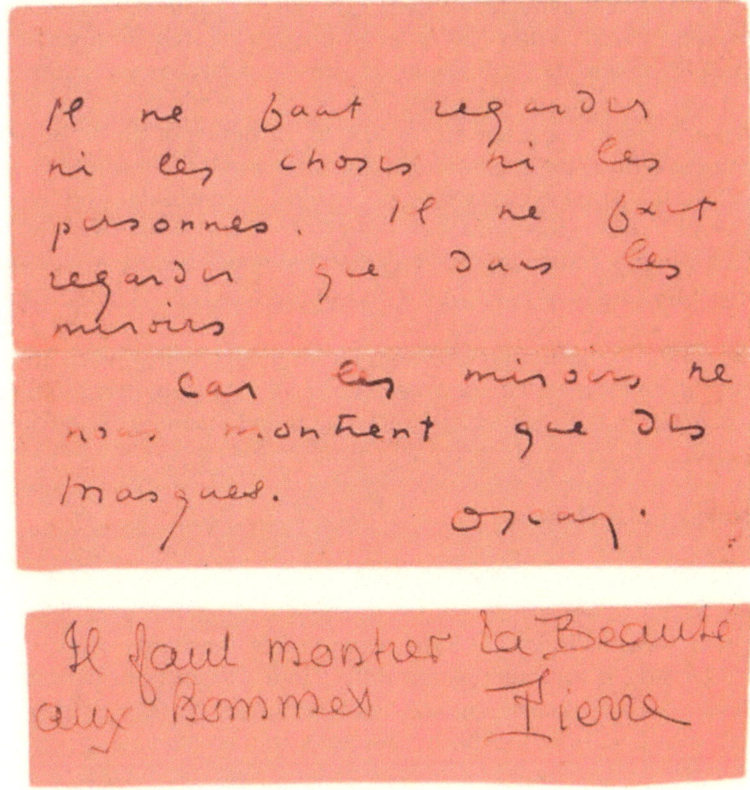

Il ne faut regarder
ni les choses ni les
personnes. Il ne faut
regarder que dans les
miroirs
car les miroirs ne
nous montrent que des
masques.
Oscar.

Il faut montrer la Beauté
aux hommes Pierre

Figure 7.1 Autograph manuscript with aphorisms by Oscar Wilde and Pierre Louÿs, in *Manuscrits de Pierre Louÿs et de divers auteurs contemporains: Claude Farrère, André Gide, Jean de Tinan, Oscar Wilde: Poésies et lettres autographes d'auteurs modernes et contemporains* (Paris: Léopold Carteret, 1926), 102–3.

Because mirrors show us nothing but masks. Oscar
We should show Beauty to mankind. Pierre

This short exchange replicates a mode of performative verbal interaction typical of salon settings, where invitees would trade witticisms and erudite pronouncements in a way that sits between collaboration and competition. Writing in French, Wilde symbolically takes on the role of the lead partner by initiating the exchange. His aphorism actually decontextualizes and repurposes parts of one of Herod's speeches in *Salomé*, where the king tries to distance himself from his desire for his stepdaughter: denying his own gaze, Herod fights his compulsive attraction towards Salomé in order to prevent himself from giving in to her perverse request for the head of the prophet. As we know, this act of restraint will prove useless. Taking on the role of Herod, Wilde portrays himself as equally susceptible to the power of the erotic gaze. At the same time, the symbolism of the mirror and the mask as proper objects of the gaze encourages us not to look for meanings and hidden truths underneath the surface of things. By way of response, Louÿs's almost Platonic statement about the need to reveal beauty to mankind partly upholds Wilde's sentiment and partly rejects it, playing Salomé to Wilde's Herod. Permeated by a Symbolist aesthetic, their exchange poses a philosophical problem about the ethics of beauty. But it can also be read in an intimate key, as an allusion to the game of revelation and concealment in their friendship, picking up on the image of Louÿs as a dispenser of beauty in the private dedication to *A House of Pomegranates*.

Aesthetic Entanglements

Echoes of this conversation can be heard in Louÿs's works from the 1890s, some of which he started writing during the period of his friendship with Wilde. In those years, Louÿs constantly refashioned and adapted his own works, not only moving them from periodicals to books but also across genres, transforming plays into poems and poems into fiction. In this body of writing that seems to stage its constant state of flux, Wilde's name is never mentioned, and it is difficult to claim precise and definite instances of influence. However, the dialogue between the two authors survives in Louÿs's choice of themes and literary forms. Wilde is never a clear source, but rather a diffuse presence. Private statements from this period show a mixture of admiration and critical distance from Wilde's works. Louÿs was particularly impressed by Wilde's prose poems and short stories, but he reacted sceptically to *A Woman of No Importance*, which he went to see on its opening night at London's Haymarket Theatre in April 1893. In a letter to his brother, he privately satirized the comedy as "*A Play of no importance*," explaining that he nonetheless intended to write a positive review that seems not to have been published in the end.[16] This episode shows that, while he admired the cosmopolitan and French Wilde, Louÿs developed a dislike for the comedian that English audiences would come to favour above and beyond all other aspects of the Irish author including, pointedly, his Symbolist experiments.

It is therefore not surprising to see that Louÿs tried his hand at a series of highly aestheticized short stories of his own inspired by classical myth.[17] These were mostly published as *plaquettes* with La Librairie de l'Art indépendant – the same publisher as *Salomé* and *Astarté*.[18] One of them, *La Maison sur le Nil ou les apparences de la vertu* (1894), contains echoes of Louÿs's conversation with Wilde in their joint manuscript on the ethics of beauty: at the end of the tale, the character Mélandryon argues that "il ne faut pas juger les choses sous le rapport du Bien et du Mal"; and later, that the "seule règle de la vie qui semble légitime, c'est le souci de la beauté" (one should not make judgments according to the relationship between Good and Evil; the only rule in life that seems legitimate is the concern for beauty).[19] Another story, which Louÿs left unfinished, *L'Amour et la mort d'Hermaphrodite*, revisits the well-known myth from Ovid's *Metamorphoses* following Swinburne's use of this same figure in *Poems and Ballads* (1866) to push the representation of eroticism and sexual desire outside the sphere of bourgeois sexual morality. Once again, the eroticization of the male body in this early story written around the time of his friendship with Wilde stands out as unusual when compared to Louÿs's later oeuvre, where eroticism will be heavily focused on the female body.

The dialogue suggested by these examples becomes closer to a form of collaboration when we consider side by side the genesis of *Salomé* and Louÿs's novel *Aphrodite* (1896), a commercial and popular success that made his name famous beyond the restricted circles of Symbolism. Like the short fiction, *Aphrodite* is also set in antiquity but now the action takes place on a much larger canvas that mixes historical material with elements of fantasy. The plot, set in Hellenistic Alexandria, develops around the self-destructive erotic relationship between an Egyptian sculptor named Demetrios and Chrysis, a Syrian courtesan and femme fatale who had already featured in Louÿs's early poetry. In June 1892, Louÿs started writing the novel as a three-act play in prose and verse intended for Sarah Bernhardt, who agreed to act as the title character in *Salomé* precisely around this time. He then adapted it into a short story that he published in the Belgian literary journal *La Wallonie* and then reprinted as one of the *plaquettes* discussed earlier.[20] The short story, entitled "Chrysis," would later become the first chapter of the novel. The delayed publication of *Aphrodite* obscures the fact that *Salomé* and Louÿs's novel had a common origin in their link with Bernhardt and the stage, and evolved in parallel as Louÿs disseminated fragments of his ongoing work at the same time as Wilde brought his French *Salomé* to publication. In this context, Wilde's dedication of *Salomé* must be seen as more than a mere acknowledgment of Louÿs's help with matters of linguistic fluency: rather, it was Wilde's way of paying homage to a shared literary endeavour – their ongoing, evolving dialogue about Symbolist poetics.

With these daring works centred on femme fatale figures resurrected from antiquity, both writers courted scandal by testing the boundary of the acceptable in contemporary literature. In a preface that he published separately in *La Revue blanche* prior to the first book publication of the entire novel (adopting a strategy that Wilde had used with *Dorian Gray*), Louÿs prepared the general public to be disturbed by his frank depictions of sensual excess. These, he claimed, played an essential part in a truthful reconstruction of a moral universe that was very different from the present. In the same piece, he also lamented the habit of white-washing classical culture in order to make it exemplary of modern ideas of virtue. While he did not mention Wilde, his acidic remarks on the hypocrisy of modern practices of dramatic and textual censorship were mindful of the debacle surrounding *Salomé*, which he had witnessed at close quarters:

> À juger les Grecs anciens d'après les idées actuellement reçues, *pas une seule* traduction exacte de leurs plus grands écrivains ne pourrait être laissée aux mains d'un collégien de seconde. Si M. Mounet-Sully jouait son rôle d'Oedipe sans coupures, la police ferait suspendre la représentation. Si M. Leconte de Lisle n'avait pas expurgé Théocrite, par prudence, sa version eût été saisie le jour même de la mise en vente.[21]

> If we judge the ancient Greeks according to current ideas, *not one single* exact translation of their greatest writers could be left in the hands of a high school pupil. If M. Mounet-Sully played his role of Oedipus without cuts, the police would ban the performance. If M. Leconte de Lisle had not expurgated Theocritus, as a precaution, his version would have been confiscated on the very day of its release.

When *Salomé* was banned from the stage, as when *Dorian Gray* was attacked for immorality, Wilde tried to turn his defeats into symbolic capital by publicly defending the author's role as custodian of higher artistic values that are quashed by philistine society. In the preface to *Aphrodite*, Louÿs did something similar ahead of the novel's public release (its erstwhile circulation in parts and serialized form in the Symbolist press would have exposed it to a much more limited degree of scrutiny, again not unlike *Dorian Gray*).

Louÿs's novel discloses other possible points of interaction between the two writers. In a letter to his brother from 1917, Louÿs would claim that Wilde's refrain from *The Ballad of Reading Gaol* – "Chacun tue ce qu'il aime" – was actually inspired by *Aphrodite*, as the novel hinged on the theory that "l'amour extrême tue son objet" (Each man kills the thing he loves; extreme love kills its object). He added that, when he knew Wilde, this idea "ne faisait pas partie de sa philosophie" (was not part of his philosophy).[22] While Louÿs's claim is hard to prove, an early version of the novel manuscript does show a possible trace of Wilde in an episode that Louÿs omitted from the published text. Consumed by jealousy, Chrysis reproaches Demetrios for having had a love affair with an ephebe:

> Tu m'as quittée parce qu'un bel éphèbe a passé. Tu vis avec lui, insoucieux de Chrysis et ses entrailles ont chaque nuit la rosée dont ma chair est tout altérée. Tu lui dis comme à moi qu'il a le ventre doux et les mains habiles, que ses yeux ressemblent à des fleurs de lotus sous l'eau, et ses cheveux à des averses illuminées de soleil. Tu le prends dans tes bras, dans tes cuisses, tu lui ouvres ta bouche, tu lui fais des caresses lentes ... [23]
>
> You have left me because a beautiful ephebe has walked by. You are living with him, caring nothing for Chrysis, and each night his entrails receive the dew for which my flesh thirsts. You say to him as you did to me that his abdomen is sweet and his hands skillful, that his eyes resemble lotus flowers beneath the water and his hair rain showers lit by the sun. You take him in your arms, between your thighs, you open your mouth to him, you caress him slowly ...

The graphic reference to the sexual union between Demetrios and the young boy – the "rosée" which now lands in the "entrailles" of the "bel éphèbe" instead of her own – shows that in the early stages of his novel Louÿs was flirting with images of male homosexuality and the eroticized passive male body – subjects that he self-censored as he moved to the final version of the text.

The deleted passage dates from around the summer of 1892, when Louÿs paid an extended visit to London. In the English capital Louÿs did what Wilde had done the previous autumn in Paris: he concentrated on perfecting his English and making his way into Decadent and Francophile literary networks. His most important literary contact was with John Gray, the poet with whom Wilde would associate Louÿs in *De Profundis* as an idealized counterpart to Douglas. Louÿs and Gray met through Wilde, and they remained on warm terms even after both of them had broken with the Irish author. The correspondence between them, mostly conducted in French, shows that Gray acted as a guide to London's cultural sights, such as galleries and theatres, as well as introducing Louÿs to literary society and giving him advice on his English reading (in a letter he mentions lending Louÿs a copy of a book by

Walter Pater).[24] As Louÿs had done with Wilde in *Astarté*, Gray made their personal and poetic alliance public by dedicating to Louÿs one of the poems in *Silverpoints* (1893). Following the practice prevalent among the French Symbolists, this iconic volume achieved a cosmopolitan character by including poems individually dedicated to a wide range of writers, from Verlaine to Wilde to Louÿs, as well as imitations and translation from the French. "On a Picture" is an ekphrastic rendering of Millais's *Ophelia*, which the two poets had seen together in 1892 as part of an exhibition of Pre-Raphaelite paintings in the Guildhall Library. As such, the poem commemorates a private occasion – it is likely that Louÿs had been particularly taken with this picture or that it had sparked a particularly memorable discussion during their visit – branding, as it were, their bond through the decadent mixture of eroticism and death captured by the painting.[25] Gray's use of the sonnet form responds to Louÿs's earlier dedication to Gray of his sonnet "La Prairie" (first published in *La Wallonie* in 1892, alongside "Chrysis"). Now, by associating Louÿs's name with this most English of subjects, linked to Shakespeare and the Pre-Raphaelites, Gray paid public homage to Louÿs's Anglophilia. In London, Wilde repaid the literary hospitality that Louÿs had shown him in Paris by facilitating such literary and personal connections. In a subsequent visit, for instance, on the occasion of the premiere of *A Woman of No Importance*, he made sure that Louÿs sat next to the future publisher of the English *Salome*, John Lane, to whom he introduced Louÿs as "a perfect English scholar."[26]

Tied in Translation

The literary friendship between Louÿs and Wilde grew in a polyglot context in which the two authors frequently adopted the other's language as a way of playing with different social and literary identities. Their bilingual correspondence gives us a flavour of how the two switched from English to French and vice versa to introduce particular nuances of meaning or for comic effect. This linguistic experiment came to a head with *Salomé*, where Wilde appropriated the literary idiom of Symbolism in order to write an idiosyncratic French that combines foreignness and assimilation – a cosmopolitan style that Louÿs helped him to refine when he collaborated on the manuscript's revisions.[27] And of course learning English at the time of his 1892 visit to London involved playing with translation. As Louÿs explained to his brother, he liked to practise different writing styles by turning into English fragments from Molière's *L'Avare* and Flaubert's *Tentation de St Antoine* – an important urtext of fin-de-siècle decadence that, incidentally, Wilde also fantasized about putting into English.[28] Some unpublished manuscript fragments that Louÿs composed directly in English display an altogether racier manner of linguistic exercise. These comprise a fictional letter to a young girl on the topic of flagellation and fragments that recall his own *Dialogues des courtisanes* – an erotic work of Louÿs's creation, with explicit sexual content, written in French, that, in its turn, alludes in the title to his translation of Lucian's *Scènes de la vie des courtisanes* (1894).[29] Switching to the unfamiliar literary medium of English is part and parcel of the erotic titillation of this letter, which enacts sexuality as masquerade and linguistic performance.

Wilde, for his part, liked to describe his crossing into French in *Salomé* as learning to play "a subtle instrument of music" – a metaphor of which he was very fond judging by how often he repeated it in the letters that accompanied his presentation copies of the French edition.[30] Wilde's musical comparison divorces literary language from narrow concerns with accuracy and indeed from referentiality altogether, maybe inspired by Pater's famous aphorism that "*[a]ll art constantly aspires towards the condition of music.*"[31] In any case, it shows that putting oneself in-between languages was a highly self-conscious literary practice that went beyond a desire to mediate between English and French: both Wilde and Louÿs adopted a translational voice in order to experiment with literary form, question standards of taste, push the boundaries of sexual morality, and write themselves into positions of strategic marginality vis-à-vis their national cultures.

At the turn of the twentieth century, few works manipulated the strategic power of translation better than Louÿs's *Chansons de Bilitis* (1894), a collection of sapphic poems that soon became famous as a literary hoax. Louÿs pretended that his prose poems were translations from an unknown Greek poetess, one of Sappho's disciples, which had come to light as part of a recent archaeological discovery. To create an aura of historical and scholarly authenticity, he added to the volume Bilitis's imaginary biography and a number of erudite footnotes. In fact, however, Louÿs's subterfuges did not fool many critics. In the *Mercure de France*, Camille Mauclair described the work as "prose poems" gathered together under a title that was subtle enough for "qui sait que Bilitis n'exista jamais" (those who know that Bilitis never existed).[32] Such scepticism was also echoed in the general press: in the newspaper *La Cocarde*, for instance, a reviewer introduced two "epigrams" from the collection as "subtils et jolis pastiches" (subtle and charming pastiches).[33] Nonetheless, as Lawrence Venuti has argued, *Bilitis* remains a testimony to how translation can be used as a means to demystify dominant cultural values. By cleverly parodying the conventions of scholarly translation, Louÿs undermined claims to historical truth and, at the same time, questioned prevailing ideas of authorship and originality.[34]

Through the medium of pseudo-translation, *Bilitis* interacts with a series of well-known provocations that Wilde put forward in his critical dialogues and short fiction, different though the latter are in form. To borrow one of Wilde's favourite metaphors, the translator of Bilitis put on a mask in order to reveal a deeper kind of truth about the ancient Greek world – a truth that is accessed through the channels of poetic sympathy rather than dry scholarship. Similar paradoxes defending the efficacy of falsification appear in "The Decay of Lying" and in "The Portrait of Mr W.H." In the latter story, Wilde makes use of an extended parody of historical criticism in order to recover the queer affect of Shakespeare's sonnets that was routinely erased in nineteenth-century scholarship.

Wilde's transgressive handling of Shakespeare might indeed have influenced Louÿs's decision to try his hand at putting into French the first five sonnets of *The Passionate Pilgrim*.[35] This octavo volume was issued in 1599 by the printer William Jaggard as authored by "W. Shakespeare" but in fact it also included poems by Richard Barnfield, Bartholomew Griffin, and, perhaps, Thomas Deloney. In 1891, Swinburne violently denounced Jaggard's book as a "worthless little volume of stolen and mutilated poetry, patched up and padded out with dirty and dreary doggerel."[36] But literary theft and adulteration were precisely what drew Louÿs to this first attempt to counterfeit "Shakespeare's authorial persona,"[37] as he himself trespassed aesthetic and ethical norms in his experiments with translation, imitation, and falsification.

It is important to remember that, at the time of publishing *Bilitis*, Louÿs already had a reputation as a translator of classical Greek poetry. His latest volume therefore appeared to all intents and purposes as an extension of his previous versions of Meleager and Lucian, which, like *Bilitis*, were also issued by the Librairie de l'Art indépendant.[38] These earlier works show that Louÿs already cultivated a translational style tailored to a Symbolist readership that was hungry for risqué subject matter and stylistic experimentation: he highlighted erotic content that was otherwise censored in erudite translations and modernized the poetic expression of the classical text in line with modern trends. For instance, he rendered Meleager's epigrams in the form of prose poems and put asterisks in the middle of his sentences to mark breaks in the original verses. However, the move from translation to pseudo-translation undoubtedly enabled Louÿs to exercise a greater degree of stylistic freedom in his handling of classical antiquity (to complicate matters even further, some of the verses in *Bilitis* were in fact based on actual classical fragments). Moreover, hiding behind the fiction of an original author allowed him greater latitude when treating the morally suspicious subject of lesbianism, which Louÿs undoubtedly did with a marked degree of voyeurism but also in a way that, again according to Venuti, exercised a positive influence on later lesbian writers such as Natalie Clifford Barney and Renée Vivien.[39]

It is easy to see that, both chronologically and artistically, Louÿs's translations and pseudo-translations from the Greek are closely intertwined with his "original" works from the 1890s. Louÿs used translation to forge his own individual style and authorial persona in dialogue with ancient and modern sources. Most notably, his translational practices fed into the long process of gestation of *Aphrodite*, where the character of Chrysis similarly took shape in transition across a variety of texts and genres, including drama, short stories, verse, and the novel. In content and tone, *The Songs of Bilitis* anticipates the cry against the punitive modern attitude towards sensualism that Louÿs made under his own signature in the preface to *Aphrodite*. If anything, the transgressive sexual content of *Bilitis* stood out even more than the issue of falsification: the question of sexual morality dominated the reception of both books, in France as much as in the English-speaking world.

In the first English version of *Bilitis* (1904), the translator Horace Manchester Brown commented nervously on "the marked flavour of sexualism" that, he argued, detracted from the beauty of Louÿs's poetic expression while not being untrue to "the social conditions among the Greeks in the period described."[40] He nonetheless defended his efforts to render the pseudo-translation on the grounds that it was addressed to an English-speaking readership that had been morally fortified by modern schooling. In other words, this was not a book for the "uneducated."[41] The compound of beauty and moral corruption was a familiar trope that made it easy to domesticate Louÿs's work within an English tradition of aestheticism ranging from Swinburne – from whom Louÿs had pointedly borrowed one of the epigraphs in *Bilitis* – to Wilde himself. Of course, in 1904, it would have been too compromising to mention the connection with Wilde. But Wilde is Louÿs's link to the English practices of reviving ancient Greek homosexuality, male and female, that Louÿs redeploys in *Bilitis* by means of his translational style.

Read against this background, it is easy to see that Louÿs's "Sonnet" published in Alfred Douglas's magazine, *The Spirit Lamp*, in May 1893 is part of this use of translation to unsettle prevailing ideas of authorship, authenticity, and sexual morality. As is well known, Louÿs's sonnet is a free poetic version of a love letter that Wilde had addressed to Douglas in extravagant praise of a poem – once again, a sonnet – written by the latter. The letter had fallen into the hands of a blackmailer who was threatening to make it public.[42] Turning Wilde's passionate words into a French literary text was therefore designed to show that those very words were no more than a literary exercise and that they could therefore not be interpreted as evidence of a homosexual relationship. Published only a few weeks before their final break, the sonnet can be seen as a hymn to their friendship with all its ambiguities. It was later to cause considerable anxiety to Louÿs when he heard that it had been cited in court during Wilde's trials, threatening to link his name with Wilde's scandal.[43]

The untitled sonnet, signed on the journal's title page, is prefaced with an epigraph that identifies it as a translation and directs readers to an absent and somewhat mysterious source text located in the private realm: "A letter written in prose poetry by Mr. Oscar Wilde to a friend, and translated into rhymed poetry by a poet of no importance."[44] In the verses that follow, the speaker, identified as Wilde, sings the love of one man for another in an ancient Greek setting. In the original letter, Wilde compared Douglas to Hyacinthus, eroticizing his "red-roseleaf lips [that] should be made no less for the madness of music and song than for the madness of kissing."[45] Louÿs's sonnet stresses the speaker's desire ("Je t'aime") for Hyacinthus (named four times in the course of the poem), evoking several of his erotically charged body parts ("yeux," "bouche," "cheveux," "mains," "beau corps étendu"). Loosening the connection with the present, it sets the action in a highly symbolic ancient Greek landscape ("lumière de la mer," "lyre," "acanthe," "houblon," "Porte d'Hercule," "âme antique" ...). The comparison between the source and target texts shows that Louÿs stretched the idea of translation, and even adaptation, to its limits: very little of Wilde's original is preserved in readily recognizable form as the letter makes its way into the highly constrained form of the sonnet. In matters of content, it is difficult to imagine that Louÿs – an expert, as we have seen, in ancient sexual customs – was too naive to understand the implications of his own verses. Transposing Wilde's homosexual eros to French, the translator mediates in the erotic exchange between Wilde and Douglas. The identification between author and translator is emphasized by Louÿs introducing himself as "a poet of no importance," which alludes to his private connection with Wilde and alerts us to possible subtexts suggested by the in-joke (as we know, Louÿs had attended the premiere of that play).

As Xavier Giudicelli has argued, translation and transposition in Louÿs's sonnet are part of a "staging of desire, based on performativity and performance."[46] We have seen that the same performative dynamics stretched all the way back to *Astarté*, where Louÿs had also played with Wilde's fascination with Greek homoerotic themes. The difference now was that in *The Spirit Lamp*, a little magazine edited by Douglas and printed in Oxford, the abstracted queer content of the translation (the myth of Hyacinthus and Apollo) was given concrete valence as it is textually networked into the homosocial milieu of the University and of Wilde's artistic circle. It is telling that the same issue contained a poem entitled "A Friend" by Lionel Johnson and was dominated by the presence of the recently deceased John Addington Symonds (it included an essay by Symonds as well as an anonymous obituary likely written by Douglas). Symonds was well known for his advocacy of homosexual emancipation, as well as for writings on ancient Greek homosexuality that were an important source of inspiration for Wilde. Through the medium of French, therefore, Louÿs's translation brought Oxford Hellenism back home via Paris, in a circular gesture.

The issue, moreover, closed with another classicizing poem, Douglas's own "A Sicilian Love Song," which, together with Louÿs's piece, bookended the issue on themes relating to homosexual love. In this poem, which evoked the homoerotic pastoral associated with Theocritus, the ungendered speaker articulates longing for the male body ("His lips are sweet and red") and fantasizes being united with her/his male lover in a "bridal bed."[47] Maybe it was this editorial manipulation on Douglas's part that caused Louÿs to issue his ultimatum to Wilde "to choose between his friendship and [the] fatal connection with A.D.," which seems to date from around this time.[48] Yet, an auction at Sotheby's brought to light Louÿs's own personal copy of the sonnet in *The Spirit Lamp*, torn out of the magazine and inscribed to Wilde "affectueusement."[49] Surprisingly, Louÿs had kept this together with the pages bearing Douglas's "Sicilian Love Song" and those Douglas devoted to Wilde's *Salomé*, as if he wanted to preserve in material form the ambiguous affect that linked poet, lover, and translator.

Conclusion

The sonnet in *The Spirit Lamp* is a fitting embodiment of a literary friendship that was played out through paratextual displays of affection and translational experiments, as well as a shared effort to push the boundaries of contemporary sexual morality. Wilde and Louÿs built together a highly performative cult of beauty based on the provocative idea that artificiality and illusion could open up a path to authenticity and "truth." Louÿs's writings helped to make Wilde known in Paris by circulating his name and broadcasting his ideas. Wilde, for his part, introduced Louÿs to English literary circles and exercised a subtle but formative influence on the writings of his French friend. Their biographical and textual entanglements reveal an emotionally charged collaboration as both were trying to break through the highly competitive Parisian Symbolist scene from somewhat marginal positions: Louÿs as a young author and Wilde as a foreign one.

The habit of linking their names in public, which had started in Parisian salons and cafes, became too dangerous for Louÿs when Wilde's taste for "feasting with panthers," as he would memorably put it in *De Profundis*, and his homosexual practices became too visible.[50] This is why an ephemeral text, published in a student magazine and smeared in court, was destined to remain their last joint venture. Louÿs's manuscript versions of "The Birthday of the Infanta" and "The Young King" did not see the light of day until many years after the authors' deaths. Indeed, after Loüys broke with Wilde, his interest in English literature seems to have waned. He abandoned the performative Anglophilia of the early '90s by turning his attention instead towards Spain for his second, successful, 1898 novel, *La Femme et le pantin* (translated into English by Arthur Symons and adapted by Luis Buñuel in 1977 as *Cet obscur objet du désir*). Wilde, for his part, continued to follow Louÿs and even to promote his work across the Channel. *Aphrodite* was one of the titles that Wilde requested straightaway when he was finally given permission to have books delivered to him in prison.[51] After he got out, he encouraged Ernest Dowson to translate Louÿs's novel for Leonard Smithers ("The Bacchic, the Dionysiac!"), who would soon publish his own *Ballad of Reading Gaol*.[52] And he later tried to persuade Smithers to bring out a private English edition of the *Chansons de Bilitis*, again in Dowson's translation.[53] Given Wilde's social disgrace and his loss of symbolic power in the literary world, it is little surprise that these efforts of mediation did not bear fruit.

NOTES

1 Oscar Wilde, *De Profundis* in *The Complete Works of Oscar Wilde*, ed. Ian Small (Oxford: Oxford University Press, 2005), 2:40.
2 Jean-Paul Goujon, *Pierre Louÿs: une vie secrète* (Paris: Fayard, 2002), 180. The citation is also in Matthew Sturgis, *Oscar: A Life* (London: Head of Zeus, 2018), 723.
3 Oscar Wilde, *Salomé* (Paris: Librairie de l'Art indépendant, 1893).
4 Wilde, "To Louÿs," [27 February 1893], in *The Complete Letters of Oscar Wilde*, ed. Merlin Holland and Rupert Hart-Davis (London: Fourth Estate, 2000), 557.
5 H.P. Clive, "Pierre Louÿs and Oscar Wilde: A Chronicle of Their Friendship," *Revue de littérature comparée* 43, no. 3 (July 1969): 353–84.

6 Sturgis, *Oscar*, 813.

7 Goujon, *Pierre Louÿs*, 170–180, 190–1, and 212–15. In the early 1890s, Louÿs tried his hand at translating at least two stories from *A House of Pomegranates*: "The Birthday of the Infanta" and "The Young King." Apart from the brief quotation from the latter that, as we shall see, Louÿs used in *Astarté*, these remained unpublished. The manuscript of "Le Jeune roy," dedicated to "Margaret Lady Brooke," has been published by Jean-Paul Goujon in "Le Jeune roy," *Chef-Lieu: revue de littérature* 2 (1994): 123–37. The current whereabouts of "L'Anniversaire de l'infante" are unknown but its first page has been reproduced in Goujon, *Pierre Louÿs*, 181.

8 André Gide, *Si le grain ne meurt*, in *Souvenirs et voyages*, ed. Pierre Masson, Daniel Durosay, and Martine Sagaert (Paris: Gallimard, 2001), 298–312.

9 Robert Scheffer, "Plumes d'oies et plumes d'aigles," *Akademos*, no. 6 (June 1909), 895. All translations are ours unless specified.

10 Jean-Paul Goujon, "Postface au Jeune roy," *Chef-Lieu: revue de littérature* 2 (1994), 140.

11 Gide to Rouart, 2 January 1895, in *André Gide–Eugène Rouart, Correspondance. Vol. I, 1893–1901*, ed. David H. Walker (Lyon: Presses universitaires de Lyon, 2006), 235.

12 "La Femme qui danse," *La Conque* 3 (May 1891), xxiv; "La Danseuse," in *Astarté* (Paris: Libraire de l'Art indépendant, 1892), n.p.

13 Wilde, *Salome* in *The Complete Works of Oscar Wilde, Vol. 1, Plays: The Duchess of Padua; Salomé: Drame en un acte*, ed. Joseph W. Donohue Jr. (Oxford: Oxford University Press, 2013), 5:335, 345.

14 Pierre Louÿs, *Astarté*, n.p. This was part of Louÿs's full translation of "Le Jeune roy" that remained unpublished during the author's lifetime.

15 The whereabouts of this manuscript are currently unknown; but we know that it was sold in 1926 and again in 2015. See the catalogue of the auction of 14 and 15 May 1926, *Manuscrits de Pierre Louÿs et de divers auteurs contemporains: Claude Farrère, André Gide, Jean de Tinan, Oscar Wilde: Poésies et lettres autographes d'auteurs modernes et contemporains* (Paris: Léopold Carteret, 1926), 102–3; and the auction catalogue of 22 May 2015 at Pierre Bergé & Associés (Paris), lot no. 377.

16 On 20 April 1893, he wrote to Georges Louis: "Je ne regrette pas Londres mais je regrette un peu la pièce. '*A Play of no importance*.' Et pourtant j'en ai dit tout le bien possible dans un article qui paraîtra samedi si on l'insère, ce qui est douteux." Then, on 22 April: "Sa pièce ne vaut vraiment rien et est attaquée par toute la presse. C'est un mauvais mélodrame parsemé de conversations charmantes qui n'ont rien à faire avec la pièce et qui seules sont intéressantes." Pierre Louÿs and Georges Louis, *Correspondance croisée, 1890–1917*, ed. Gordon Millan, 4 vols. (Paris: Honoré Champion, 2015), 1:199–200. (I don't regret London but I do regret

the play a little. *"A Play of no importance."* Nonetheless I said nothing but positive things in an article that's due to appear on Saturday, if they publish it, which is not sure ... That play is really not worth anything and it's being attacked everywhere in the press. It is a bad melodrama sprinkled with charming conversations that have nothing to do with the play and that are the only interesting thing in it.)

17 Louÿs praised *Dorian Gray* in a letter to his brother, who seems to have disliked the novel; Louÿs to Georges Louis, 6 July 1892, in *Correspondance croisée*, 1:125. The Bibliothèque nationale de France also keeps a mysterious bound volume collecting the pages of Wilde's "Poems in prose," as printed in *The Fortnightly Review* 56 (July 1894): 22–9, on which Louÿs wrote the following comment necessarily dating from after his argument with Wilde: "Je ne connais rien qui mérite le nom de Chef d'oeuvre comme ceci. Pour moi c'est la perfection même. C'est beau comme l'Évangile de St Jean" (I know nothing that deserves the name of Masterpiece more than this. For me it is perfection itself. It is as beautiful as the Gospel of St John). (BnF, Arsenal, RESERVE 4-PN-972 [BIS]). These comments were long wrongly associated with material dating from 1892, as in Carteret, *Manuscrits de Pierre Louÿs*, 99.

18 Five of the seven planned stories were written around this time and were gathered much later (1925) under the title *Le Crépuscule des nymphes*. The collection comprised *Lêda ou la louange des bienheureuses ténèbres*, *La Maison sur le Nil ou les apparences de la vertu*, *Ariane ou le chemin de la paix éternelle*, *Byblis ou l'enchantement des larmes*, and *Danaë ou le malheur*. For more information on this publisher, see the detailed account and publication catalogue in Denis Herlin, "À la Librairie de l'Art indépendant: musique, poésie, art et ésotérisme," *Histoires littéraires* 17, no. 68 (October–December 2016): 7–56.

19 Pierre Louÿs, *La Maison sur le Nil* (Paris: Librairie de l'Art indépendant), 30.

20 Although never published in the original form, the manuscript of the play has been preserved and is now in a private collection. It was sold in 1926 (Carteret, *Manuscrits*, 12–13), in 1936 (Hôtel Drouot, 21 November 1936, nr. 102), and in 2020 (Artcurial, Collections Aristophil, 18 November 2020, lot no. 523). For the complex textual history of *Aphrodite*, from play manuscript to novel, see the two lists of pre-publications and manuscripts in Pierre Louÿs, *Aphrodite*, ed. Jean-Paul Goujon (Paris: Gallimard, 1992), 330–4, 340–1.

21 Louÿs, *Aphrodite*, 36. The original periodical publication was in *La Revue blanche* 10 (1896): 256–9.

22 Louÿs to Georges Louis, 16 [February 1917], in *Correspondance croisée*, 4:2436.

23 First printed with other unpublished erotic parts in Pierre Louÿs, *Aphrodite*, ed. Pascal Pia (Paris: Tiflis, Bagration Davidoff [René Bonnel], 1928), quoted in Louÿs, *Aphrodite*, 348.

24 Gray to Louÿs, 16 July 1892, in Peter Vernon, "John Gray's Letters to Pierre Louÿs," *Revue de littérature comparée* 53, no. 1 (January 1979), 92. Vernon's article expands on the earlier work by Roger Lhombreaud, "Une amitié anglaise de Pierre Louÿs," *Revue de littérature comparée* 27 (1953), 343–57. Interestingly, Vernon notes that letters dating from the time of Wilde's trials are missing, surmising that this is the result of a deliberate effort to destroy references to Wilde during this sensitive period (88).

25 John Gray, "On a Picture," in *Silverpoints* (London: Elkin Mathews and John Lane, 1893), 21.

26 Wilde, "To John Lane," [? 19 April 1893], in Wilde, *Complete Letters*, 561.

27 See Stefano Evangelista, *Literary Cosmopolitanism in the English Fin de Siècle: Citizens of Nowhere* (Oxford: Oxford University Press, 2021), 63–71. On Wilde's use of French as a form of creative freedom and alternative to national belonging, see William A. Cohen, "Wilde's French," in *Wilde Discoveries: Traditions, Histories, Archives*, ed. Joseph Bristow (Toronto: University of Toronto Press, 2013), 233–59.

28 Louÿs to Georges Louis, 14 June 1892, in *Correspondance croisée*, 115; Wilde to W.E. Henley, [? December 1888], in *Complete Letters*, 372.

29 These fragments are now in private collections. Goujon, *Pierre Louÿs*, 191.

30 Wilde to Florence Balcombe Stoker, [postmarked 22 February 1893], in Wilde, *Complete Letters*, 552. Cf. letter to Edmond Gosse, [received 23 February 1893], in Wilde, *Complete Letters*, 553.

31 Walter Pater, *The Renaissance: Studies in Art and Poetry*, ed. Donald L. Hill (Berkeley: University of California Press, 1980), 106.

32 Camille Mauclair, "Les Livres," *Mercure de France* 14 (April 1895), 104.

33 "La Vie intellectuelle: lectures," *La Cocarde*, 8 January 1895, 2.

34 Lawrence Venuti, *The Scandals of Translation* (London: Routledge, 1998), 34.

35 Goujon, *Pierre Louÿs*, 190.

36 Algernon Charles Swinburne, "Social Verse," in *Studies in Prose and Poetry* (London: Chatto and Windus, 1894), 90. The essay had originally appeared in 1891.

37 Patrick Cheney, *Shakespeare, National Poet-Playwright* (Cambridge: Cambridge University Press, 2004), 160.

38 *Poésies de Méléagre* (1893) and the aforementioned *Les Scènes de la vie des courtisanes* by Lucian (1894). *Les Scènes de la vie des courtisanes* was later reprinted by the *Mercure de France* under the title *Mimes des courtisanes* (1899), with a rearranged chapter order.

39 Venuti, *Scandals*, 45.

40 H.M. Brown, Translator's Preface in *The Songs of Bilitis* by Pierre Louÿs (London: Privately Printed for Members of the Aldus Society, 1904), 8.

41 Brown, Translator's Preface in Louÿs, *Songs of Bilitis*, 11.

42 Richard Ellmann, *Oscar Wilde* (London: Penguin, 1988), 370; Sturgis, *Oscar*, 479.

43 "Tu ne peux pas te figurer dans quel affolement je vis depuis quinze jours à cause du 1845.7007 [code for London trial]. Je n'ai plus ni sommeil ni repos, et pourtant il faut que je sorte tous les jours tous les soirs et que je voie du monde afin d'observer quelle mine on me fait ... Quelle abomination! Et comme je me suis trompé! – Heureusement tout ce que j'ai écrit, toute ma vie sauf cela, et tous mes goûts démentent ce qu'on pourrait penser, mais cela suffit-il? ... Je me vois poursuivi jusqu'à la fin de ma vie par cette histoire. C'est à devenir fou." Louÿs to Georges Louis, 12 April 1895, *Correspondance croisée*, 1:300. (You can't imagine the state of panic in which I've been living for two weeks because of 1845.7007. I no longer know any sleep or rest, and yet I must go out every day and every night and I must see people in order to observe how they look at me ... What an abomination! And how wrong I was! – Fortunately everything I've written, all my life except that, and all my tastes refute what one might think, but is that enough? ... I can see this story haunting me until the end of my life. It is enough to drive one crazy.)

44 Pierre Louÿs, "Sonnet," *The Spirit Lamp* 4, no. 1 (May 1893), 1.

45 Wilde, *Complete Letters*, 544.

46 Xavier Giudicelli, "Butterflies, Orchids and Wasps. Polyglossia and Aesthetic Lives: Foreign Languages in *The Spirit Lamp* (1892–1893)," *Cahiers victoriens et édouardiens* 78 (Autumn 2013), https://journals.openedition.org/cve/930.

47 Alfred Douglas, "A Sicilian Love Song," *The Spirit Lamp* 4, no. 1 (May 1893), 46.

48 Wilde, "To More Adey," [25 September 1896], in Wilde, *Complete Letters*, 666.

49 Pierre Louÿs would have himself torn out the pages [1]–2, 19–28, and 45–6, and kept them bound together. See Sotheby's Auction, "Rimbaud, Verlaine, Mallarmé and Their Friends: Books, Manuscripts and Photographs from the Poetical Collection of Eric and Marie-Hélène B.," 15 December 2010, lot no. 174.

50 Wilde, *Complete Works*, 2:130. Tellingly, this expression also masks a literary translation from French, this time from Balzac's *Les Illusions perdues* (1837).

51 Wilde to Robert Ross, 6 April [1897], in Wilde, *Complete Letters*, 792.

52 Wilde to Dowson, 18 August [1897], in Wilde, *Complete Letters*, 926. On Dowson's involvement, see Colton Valentine, "Domesticating Decadence: Joris-Karl Huysmans, Pierre Louÿs, and Their Invisible English Translators," *Modern Language Quarterly* 82, no. 4 (2012), 454–5.

53 Wilde to Smithers, [9 March 1898], in Wilde, *Complete Letters*, 1034.

8 Oscar Wilde, Jacques d'Adelswärd Fersen, and Cross-Channel Decadence in the Twentieth Century

KRISTIN MAHONEY

In his foreword to Roger Peyrefitte's *L'Exile de Capri* (*The Exile of Capri*, 1961), a fictionalized account of the life of the early twentieth-century French Decadent writer Jacques d'Adelswärd Fersen[1] (1880–1923) (Figure 8.1), Jean Cocteau notes, "To be granted dreams but not genius must be the worst of tortures." He unfavourably compares Fersen, who was exiled from France following his prosecution for "incitement of minors to debauchery," to the "great damned," such as Oscar Wilde or Alfred Dreyfus, before whom he "[bows] his head." Fersen, on the other hand, demands no such reverence. He is an exemplar of "Preraphaelitico-Modernistic bric-à-brac," an "Icarus whose wings melt in the sun of vainglory."[2]

Referred to as *"le miserable disciple d'Oscar Wilde"* by André de Fouquières, Fersen worked throughout his career to attract comparisons between himself and Wilde, conceptualizing his own legal troubles as a repetition of Wilde's oppression and composing poetry and fiction that both honoured and appropriated the works of his predecessor.[3] His most well-known novel, *Lord Lyllian: messes noires* (*Lord Lyllian: Black Masses*, 1905), resembles a collage made from Wildean fragments, stitched together with explicit representations of love between men and age-differentiated eroticism, and his later prose and poetry indicate that he remained attuned and attached to Wilde until the end of his life. Fersen's life and writing illuminate the manner in which Wilde's influence enabled the expression of sexual dissidence and queer rebellion in twentieth-century France.

Mimicry of Wilde also, however, invited unflattering comparisons. Cocteau was not alone in finding Fersen in possession of the dreams but not the genius of Wilde. A whole host of Decadent modernists subjected Fersen, his work, his persona, and his conversation to ridicule. The post-Victorian Decadents and camp modernists who came into

Figure 8.1 Portrait of Jacques d'Adelswärd Fersen, 1905, private collection. Prismatic Pictures/Bridgeman Images.

contact with Fersen read his performance of Decadence as at once a reduction and a vulgar amplification of Wilde's ideas, as fundamentally a failure. However, the critical apprehension of his failure on the part of writers like Cocteau, Jean Lorrain, Norman Douglas, and Faith and Compton Mackenzie provided the opportunity for the practice of Decadent disdain as they dissected the manner in which Fersen fell short of his Wildean aspirations. Assessing Fersen's mindless and unsuccessful imitation of Wilde operated as a critical process by which camp modernists could clarify their understanding of Decadence. An echo chamber of cross-Channel Decadent contact and transmission – Fersen misapprehending and misappropriating Wilde, British writers dissecting Fersen's folly, Cocteau carrying their disdain forward to midcentury – enabled the distillation and revivification of Decadence. This set of cross-Channel volleys and returns illuminates how the Decadent aesthetic was cultivated, honed, and refined as it was passed between France and the United Kingdom. Emily Eells, discussing Cocteau's theatrical adaptation of *The Picture of Dorian Gray*, refers to French homages to Wilde as "of crucial importance in the complex cultural exchange which characterizes the arts in the *fin-de-siècle* period and the early 20th century, taking 'crucial' in the etymological sense of 'forming a cross.'"[4] Here am I interested in the fact that these crossings could at times go astray and, when they did, subjecting these misfires to critique could be just as generative, just as "crucial," in terms of defining and refining an aesthetic as the more clearly successful modes of transnational cross-pollination discussed by Eells. Attending to Fersen's failed approximation of Wilde along with the derision this failure elicited from camp modernists provides insight into how Wilde's legacy persisted in the conversations and connections between French and British modernists. The simulation of Wilde along with critical assessments of Wildean mimicry fine-tuned the Decadent aesthetic and solidified networks among Decadent writers into the twentieth century.

Wildean Masquerade: The Misfortunes of Jacques d'Adelswärd Fersen

As *The Exile of Capri* begins, Roger Peyrefitte imagines Jacques d'Adelswärd Fersen travelling to the Italian island of Capri with another young poet, Robert de Tournel, where they witness Wilde's humiliation following his release from prison. While dining at the Hotel Quisisana with Robert, Jacques sees a man with "a powerful head, long grey hair, heavy flaccid cheeks and ... fingers loaded with rings" appear in the doorway with a pale younger man who carries himself "insolently."[5] When the maître d'hôtel turns Wilde and Alfred Douglas away, informing them that every table is already reserved, Jacques with his "heart [beating] heavily, and in a voice hot with indignation," begs his companion to invite the two to join them. When Robert refuses, Jacques watches the pair depart, his eyes "bright with tears, as Wilde's had been."[6] While Will H.L. Ogrinc notes that there is not "one scrap of evidence" that Wilde and Fersen ever met, Peyrefitte's decision to open his chronicle of Fersen in this manner serves to highlight his subject's charged and reverential relationship to this tragic figure.[7]

Fersen did all that he could during his brief lifetime to link himself up with Wilde, and he seems to have understood himself as intimately connected with his predecessor both aesthetically and by their shared experiences of persecution. After being brought before the court on moral charges ("*outrages publics à la pudeur*" [public lewdness] and "*excitation des mineurs à la débauche*" [the corruption of minors]), he saw himself as a queer martyr like Wilde, whose life was upended by turn-of-the-century sexual legislation, and, as Nancy Erber notes, whose writing "like Wilde's, [underwent] scrutiny by state prosecutors and the press in search of incriminating lavender undertones."[8] As Erber argues, "Fersen was indebted to Wilde, who was a literary forebear and a model of a certain unconventional approach to life," and "Fersen's cultivation of his persona and the press's reception/dissemination of it," which emphasized his effeminacy, can be understood as evidence of "Wilde's legacy to cultural practices in France."[9]

In 1903, Fersen, who had published recently two collections of poetry as well as a novel, was living in Paris, mingling in Parisian literary salons and making plans to marry. However, his professional and romantic successes were disrupted when he was arrested in July on suspicion of indecent conduct with minors. As both Erber and Ogrinc recount, the periodical press in Paris made much of the event, featuring headlines concerning the "Satanic Masses" and "Orgies and Saturnalia" held at Fersen's "bachelor pad."[10] The papers reported that Fersen had involved "countless youngsters from the better circles of society," recruited from the local schools, in these orgies.[11] When Fersen, along with his friend and accomplice, Count Albert Hamelin de Warren, finally stood trial, the pattern of inquiry, as Erber notes, foregrounded the effects of "unhealthy literature," such as Baudelaire and Verlaine, on the young man. (When describing the *tableaux vivants* performed in his apartment, which had been sensationally described by the press as "black masses," Fersen stated that he had "wanted to put on stage what [he] had read in Baudelaire."[12]) Fersen's trial followed many of the patterns of Wilde's earlier trials. Like Wilde, he staged an aestheticist defense of illicit cultural objects, defending his possession of pornographic photos by declaring, "I considered them artistic. That's why I displayed them openly in my home!"[13] Fersen was also said to have exhibited a campy refusal to take the proceedings seriously, mimicking Wilde's lighthearted repartee during the first of his trials, exclaiming during an attorney's closing arguments, "Oh, how charming! It's just like being at the theater!"[14] Fersen and de Warren were in the end convicted on the charge of the corruption of minors and sentenced to six months in prison.[15] Fersen had already served this time pre-trial, so he was released upon the trial's completion. (His name, however, reappeared almost immediately in the Paris newspapers when he attempted suicide at the gateway to his ex-fiancée Mademoiselle Maupeiou's villa. The bullet had only grazed his temple.)

Echoes of Wilde's tragedy reverberate throughout Fersen's trials, but his cause, unlike Wilde's, as Erber notes, "attracted few advocates among Paris literati."[16] This must have had to do, at least in part, with the significant differences in the two men's literary reputations. In addition, the nature of the accusations against Fersen seems to have contributed to the distaste with which he was treated in the Parisian press. Wilde cannot be understood as innocent when it comes to the charge of age-differentiated eroticism, but press accounts of Fersen's arrest and trial centre pedophilia/ephebophilia in a manner that the popular representation of Wilde's trials did not. The Parisian papers placed significant emphasis on the fact that Fersen had been targeting children. "More than forty children corrupted," announced one headline.[17] The account of Fersen's arrest in *Le Journal* stated that when the police began their surveillance of his apartment, "Boys from the ages of 12 to 15 were seen; after the schoolday was over, they came and spent many hours in this meeting place."[18] Another court reporter found it "revolting to listen to these twelve and fourteen year-old youths lisp out their accusations" during the trial.[19] While the French legal code did not criminalize same-sex eroticism, Fersen's violation of laws against the corruption of minors attracted notice and derision. This, along with his perceived wealth and privilege, invited ridicule rather than outrage on the part of the Parisian press and Paris literary circles.[20] Pierre Louÿs, for example, condemned Fersen in private. Marcel Proust, according to Ogrinc, did advocate for Fersen's right to "love in his own way" during a conversation at the salon of Madame Marguerite de Pierrebourg, but he did not come to Fersen's defense in print.[21] Jean Lorrain was the only French writer willing to comment extensively to the public about the scandal at the time, and, while he certainly ridiculed the hysteria with which the Parisian press had responded to the scandal, he also communicated clearly his scorn for Fersen, whom he described as "pitiful" and a "snob." His comments, which appeared first in *Le Journal* in 1903 and were reprinted in *Pélleustres: Le Poison de la littérature* (1910), represent Fersen as pathetic, desperately attempting to reproduce the Black Masses of Joris-Karl Huysmans or Gilles de Rais and instead throwing "banal" costume parties.[22]

The pornographic novel, *Les Mémoires du Baron Jacques: Lubricités infernales de la noblesse décadente* (*The Memoirs of Baron Jacques: The Diabolical Debaucheries of Our Decadent Aristocracy*, 1904), which appeared in France the year after the trial, capitalized on the scandal of the trial and reinforced the sense that Fersen was indebted (and almost absurdly devoted) to his predecessor Oscar Wilde. Alphonse Gallais (writing under the pseudonym Doctor A.-S. Lagail) represents "Baron Jacques" as wild in his perversions, "deflowered" by his mother at age four, and involved in a sexual affair with her until her death.[23] One night, while musing upon his departed mother, he falls asleep and dreams of an orgy, the vision of which was to "have a telling influence on [his] later life," allowing him to sample "all the vices [he] was to pursue so single-mindedly and so enthusiastically."[24] He witnesses among the participants in the orgy "certain great men whose histories had been related to [him]," including Jean Lorrain and "Oscar Wilde, who was to make the trip from London to Paris for the sole purpose of giving it to me and having me give it to him."[25] Following this dream, he takes an oath "never to know any woman" and devotes himself to debauchery with his close friend Louis de Barden.[26] Erber argues that the representation of their exploits reinforced public suspicions concerning aristocratic arrogance, presenting the "insouciant young sinners" as flagrant in their disregard for law and morality, confident that their wealth insulates them from consequences.[27] The novel's primary aim certainly seems to be to satirize Fersen's haughtiness and decadence, but it also levels a sneer at his abject devotion to more accomplished men. While Baron Jacques insists that Lorrain is a superior lover to the "great Oscar," in the novel's concluding pages, he indicates that he has also named his dog, with whom he engages in sexual acts, Wilde.[28]

Following the trial, Fersen departed France and spent much of the remainder of his life on the Italian island of Capri, where he continued to perform a Wildean persona and did all he could to link himself imaginatively to the excesses of the Decadent Movement. He constructed for himself an ostentatious Art Nouveau Neoclassical home, the Villa Lysis, named for a dialogue by Plato that concerns the nature of friendship and, as Jamie James notes, "is framed as a wise elder's advice to a younger man about how to seduce boys."[29] The villa was equipped with an opium den, a dedication to love and sorrow, "AMORI ET DOLORI SACRUM," above the portico, and a nude statue of Nino, his companion and secretary whom he had taken from Naples at the age of fourteen, in the garden. Ogrinc notes that the Italian communist leader Giorgio Amendola writes in his autobiography that he and the other children on Capri understood the area near Villa Lysis to be a "forbidden zone" due to Fersen's "strange friendships."[30] The "Des Esseintes-like retreat" communicated to the world that Fersen wished to be understood as Decadent, sexually dissident, and debauched.[31]

Fersen began writing his most well-known novel, *Lord Lyllian: messes noires* (1905), while traveling to Ceylon as he waited for this home to be built, completing it upon his return.[32] The novel, like Villa Lysis, exhibits in an exaggerated and excessive fashion Fersen's desire to be understood as part of the Decadent tradition. Peyrefitte described the text as "inspired by [Fersen's] misfortunes, with some borrowings from Oscar Wilde," but it more properly resembles a French revision of *The Picture of Dorian Gray*, so loyal to the original that it borders on plagiarism.[33] Jeremy Reed notes accurately in his introduction to a recent edition of the novel that both Fersen and *Lord Lyllian* should be understood as "offshoots of a decadent *fin de siècle* sensibility that never transcended the influence of Huysmans and Wilde."[34] Fersen integrates Wilde's biography with his fiction, renders the mixture even more outrageous than its sources, and loosely translates Wilde's Decadence back into the French from which it came, in the process stripping the original material of its humour as well its elegance.

Lord Lyllian centres Wilde in every way, mimicking (or attempting to mimic) the style and the content of his major works and braiding together this content with representations of the key events in Wilde's life. Wilde looms large within the novel, appearing here as "Harold Skilde," author of *The Portrait of Miriam Green*, who has been "shocking London and Paris with his talent, fancies and aberrant behavior."[35] Skilde resembles not just Wilde but the characters Wilde invented as well, playing the role of both Lord Henry and Basil in relationship to the titular hero, making him aware of his beauty, inflaming his narcissism, and initiating his moral destruction. Lyllian first encounters Skilde as a youth when the celebrity author visits the region of Scotland that is his home. Seated beside the older man at a dinner, he is "charmed by the wit and repartees of his neighbor," and invites him to his estate.[36] During the visit, Skilde decides he has fallen in love with the "child" and begins immediately to operate as a teacher, mentor, and despoiler of innocence, encouraging Lyllian, in the vein of Lord Henry, to "have fun," to "[play] roles," to be aware of his beauty and potential, his "coquettish look of a bridegroom, as perverse as a demon and as pretty as an angel."[37] Skilde composes a play, *Narcissus*, inspired by Lord Lyllian, which, much like Basil's portrait, seems to exacerbate the beautiful young man's tendency to revel in his own attractiveness. After rehearsals, Lyllian strips and contemplates his form in the mirror, staring "ardently" at his reflection. One evening, Skilde interrupts these "exquisite pleasures" and bites him "from nape to heel" with "kisses he did not know existed," and the youth allows himself to "be raped like a pretty woman."[38] Following the play's premiere, Lyllian descends more thoroughly into self-absorption, "[arching] in front of the mirror and shivering with fever and pleasure," admiring his own body as it is covered in kisses by Skilde.[39] As he continues to engage with the older writer, he succumbs like Dorian Gray to the hedonistic influence of his mentor: "Skilde's paradoxes, which he developed skillfully with his usual loquaciousness, permeated his mind. His jaded pleasure-seeker's soul tainted Lord Lyllian."[40] When Skilde writes a new novel, *Isis*, inspired by his love for the younger man, Lyllian accuses the author of stealing his soul, but he nevertheless agrees to depart his home with his admirer and travel throughout the Mediterranean, growing increasingly debauched under Skilde's malignant influence.

The novel's second half integrates the plot line of *Dorian Gray* with an imaginative reconstruction of Wilde's suffering following his trials, remaining at once too close to its source material while falling short in the attempt to replicate its emotional register. In what may be the text's single innovation, Fersen forces Wilde into a confrontation with his most monstrous invention, Dorian Gray, allowing the icy, Dorianesque Lyllian to play the role of the unfeeling masses who witnessed Wilde's martyrdom and turned from his suffering. After splitting from his mentor following a row near Athens, Lyllian learns that Skilde has been arrested. Skilde's letter to Lyllian from prison reads like a maudlin approximation of *De Profundis*, transposing Lyllian from the position of Dorian Gray to that of Lord Alfred Douglas:

> When I recall those memories which continue to sing in my head, and am led astray by caresses from the past; when I remember our parties and our frenzies, our madness and our promises; when I see once again those moments when my soul became beautiful and pure as if to make itself like your eyes; when my memory shudders from the color of a look, from the sweetness of one of your smiles from the past; when I think of that, all of that, it seems, my Lord, that I have a dagger piercing my chest.[41]

Lyllian vows to forget Skilde and moves restlessly across Europe, taking his pleasures with an increasing sense of ennui. The dissipation begins to take a toll, and his beautiful visage conceals a depraved and decaying interiority that resembles Dorian's degenerating portrait: "I am an old man in the body of a child. Behind this face that some look at with what seems to be love, behind this face there lies a corpse, a corpse just like those found in the morning in dangerous neighborhoods, stabbed to death at the foot of a wall."[42] He becomes increasingly hard-hearted, thrilling at the knowledge that Skilde, following his release from prison, will never recuperate his reputation, that he is "finished."[43] In a moment that is, even among all these echoes of Wilde's work, strikingly derivative of *The Picture of Dorian Gray*, Lyllian returns to his childhood home and contemplates the portraits of his ancestors, much as Dorian "[strolled] through the gaunt cold picture-gallery of his country house" to "look at the various portraits of those whose blood flowed in his veins."[44] However, whereas Dorian finds in all he contemplates only a reflection of himself, seeing "the whole of history" as "merely the record of his own life," Lyllian is suddenly wrested from his self-absorption by this contact with the past, feeling his ancestors have judged him and recognized his evil, turning quite suddenly to remorse for "all the good he had ruined."[45] He nevertheless persists in his dissipation, staging parties with young boys reminiscent of Fersen's Parisian entertainments, until one night, while dining with friends before a ball, he encounters the ruined Skilde, "bloated, dirty and ugly."[46] In a scene reminiscent of Wilde's experiences of being "cut" by former acquaintances in Paris following his release from prison, Lyllian, though "deeply moved" and "hypnotized" by the sight of his former mentor and lover, flees suddenly when Skilde calls out to him, leaving him "grotesque and pitiable, alone."[47] The next day a friend reprimands Lyllian for passing Skilde by without a word, eliciting in the young man "an inexpressible melancholy," and he decides to visit his aging friend. Skilde, however, destroyed by the humiliation of the night before, suffered a heart attack in its wake and died, calling out with his last breath to the beloved younger man. Lyllian, much like Dorian, vows in the novel's final moments to reform, turning towards love for a woman as an antidote to his decline, but he is murdered finally by one of the boys from his parties, dying with the words "Harold Sk... " on his lips. As Ogrinc has argued, Lord Lyllian might be understood as an avatar of Fersen himself. Within the pages of the novel, Fersen imagines himself into a love affair with Wilde, attempting to entangle his persona with the figure upon which it is modeled, placing himself at the centre of Wilde's tragedy. Fersen reveals himself within the novel's pages to have been truly immersed in the details of Wilde's life and his oeuvre while at the same time indicating clearly why Cocteau might have found him wanting in comparison to the "great damned" he sought to replicate.

In the years following the publication of *Lord Lyllian*, Fersen lived an increasingly dissipated existence and continued to create scandal. According to Peyrefitte, he was at this point smoking thirty or forty pipes of opium a day. He published a fictionalized account of life on Capri, *Et le feu s'éteignit sur la mer ...* (*And the Fire Was Smothered by the Sea*, 1909), that deeply offended many of the island's inhabitants. He was soon after expelled temporarily from Capri. (The final straw was the Mithraic ceremony Fersen held in the Matermània grotto to commemorate Nino's entry into military service. Fersen outfitted himself as the "handsome youth" Hypatos, and two young servants Fersen had acquired from Ceylon, in the words of Ogrinc, played "the parts of slaves."[48] At daybreak, Nino stripped off his robe, and the Sinhalese boys delivered twenty lashes to his buttocks. A young peasant girl witnessed and reported the proceedings, and it was decided Fersen should leave the island.[49]) He was allowed to return to Capri in 1913, and he spent the final decade of his life oscillating between opium and cocaine addiction and drawing additional youths from Naples into his service at Villa Lysis. He died in 1923 of an overdose of cocaine dissolved in a glass of champagne.

Lord Lyllian represents Fersen's most sustained attempt to revivify and reincarnate Wilde, but his predecessor's influence remains present and visible in the works he produced during this later stage of his career. When he was cast out of Capri, he returned to Paris and turned his attention to his recently established (and short-lived periodical) *Akademos: revue mensuelle d'art libre et de critique* (1909), in which he published many significant Decadent, Symbolist, and modernist writers of the period, including F.T. Marinetti, Colette, Jean Moréas, and Arthur Symons. He maintained during his return to Paris his tendencies to lavish enjoyment and scandal, hosting Sunday receptions for *Akademos* collaborators at his home in rue Eugène Manuel and frequenting, with his companion Nino, Paris bars such as Le Scarabée d'Or, Maurice, and Palmyre. (One evening at the latter, he "insulted all those present," was boxed on the ears by the bar's owner, upon whom he poured a glass of wine, which led "all the homosexuals present" to throw him out of the bar. At the police station, Fersen dismissed the bar as "an odious tavern for lesbians and gays.")[50] He also continued to advertise his sense of affiliation to Wilde, weaving through *Akademos* multiple works that signaled his persisting investment in praising and defending his predecessor. In "Sur la glorification du Vierge dans la religion d'Oscar Wilde" ("On the glorification of the Virgin in the Religion of Oscar Wilde," 1909), for example, Fersen celebrates the queer Catholicism of *Salomé*, evidenced in John the Baptist's deep devotion to Christ.[51] His "L'Extase" [*Ecstasy*] (1909) is as an Orientalist fantasy in which two lovers, Rama and Kali, smoke opium together. As the two lie beside each other in a drug-induced haze, Rama murmurs an incantation to a poet crucified, subjected to a trial, imprisoned in Reading Gaol, forced to walk upon a treadmill, victim of the hypocrisies of his time. An aged and swollen man appears to them, his fingers covered in rings, wearing prison attire. He convinces Kali to pierce Rama's heart with a needle. Rama dies in ecstasy as the ghost of Wilde laps the blood from his heart.[52] Fersen has here integrated his knowledge of Wilde's life and writing and his fantasies about his sinister powers with his own colonialist eros and addiction.

In 1921, he published his final volume of poetry, *Hei Hsiang: le parfum noir* (Hei Hsang: the black perfume), focusing for the most part on the pleasures of opium. He continued in this collection, however, to bemoan the mistreatment of Wilde. "Tocca Alla Romanza" opens with an epigraph from the 1918 libel trial against Noel Pemberton Billing, who, in an article entitled "The Cult of the Clitoris," accused the performer Maud Allan of cultivating, through the staging of *Salome*, a homosexual conspiracy that might weaken the British effort during the First World War. Lord Alfred Douglas testified in support of Pemberton Billing, speaking of Wilde's diabolical influence, and the epigraph cites the moment when Justice Darling asked Lord Alfred Douglas if he regretted knowing Wilde and Lord Alfred Douglas responded, "Yes, I do. Most emphatically."[53] Beginning with an acknowledgment of Douglas's profound influence on Wilde, asserting Douglas was both Salome and John the Baptist to him all at once, the poem turns to Wilde's suffering both in prison and after, and states that the thought of Douglas's loyalty during this period had once brought him happiness. In the final stanza, however, Fersen derides Douglas's traitorous betrayal of Wilde during the Pemberton Billing trial, referring to him as *"ami traitre,"* [treacherous friend], wishing *"les crapauds de Judas viendront crever sur vous"* [Judas's toads will come croak on you].[54] While it is clear that his addictions overtook his imagination during the final years of his life, Fersen's reverence for and investment in Wilde remained with him until the end.

In the recent *Pagan Light: Dreams of Freedom and Beauty in Capri* (2019), Jamie James makes a case for the significance of Fersen's writing, arguing that "the particular interest of Fersen's works for the modern reader is the spectacle of the final decadence of Decadence, a bizarre efflorescence of hyperaesthetic attitudes of mind that shade provocatively into spiritual sickness."[55] The problem with this argument, however, is that this period, as many contemporary scholars of Decadence have argued, was not in fact the final decadence of Decadence.[56] Decadence was during this period reimagining itself, thriving, operating in conversation with the modernism of the 1910s and '20s, and many of the authors and artists who saw themselves as more properly and successfully carrying the Decadent tradition into the twentieth century were brought into contact with Fersen and had the opportunity to actively distinguish themselves from his brand of Wildean masquerade.

Disdain, Derision, and the Refining of Decadent Aesthetics

As much as Fersen insisted upon his connectedness to Wilde, the Decadent modernists of the early twentieth century did not agree to understand him on his own terms. His amplified and excessive repetition of Wilde was cast by these interlocutors as lacking something – the elegance, the intellect, the wit – that animated the dissidence of the original. He elicited an entire series of withering remarks, for example, from the notorious hedonist, novelist, and travel writer Norman

Douglas, whose writing about the pleasures of Capri in *Siren Land* (1911) and *South Wind* (1917) did much to contribute to the island's appeal for queer expatriates. In *Looking Back* (1934), Douglas notes ruefully in a chapter on Fersen, "It is one of my many crimes that I induced this apple of discord to establish himself on Capri."[57] The two met soon after Fersen arrived on the island seeking a location for his villa. Douglas took him to a favourite, remote spot of his, "high up, where you could dream through the summer evenings." "One could write poetry here," Fersen remarked and selected "the rocky stretch of ground" as the future site of Villa Lysis.[58] "'One could write poetry here,'" Douglas muses, "That summed him up sufficiently well. He wrote no poetry there; he smoked a good deal of opium."[59] Douglas speculates that Fersen was drawn to the spot because it was "remote yet conspicuous. People would be sure to enquire who could live, and build himself a palace, in such a situation; they would then learn that it was the retreat of a young and handsome French poet, who has turned his back on the world in disgust at the ill treatment he received at the hands of the Paris tribunals. He would be talked about."[60] Douglas sneers at Fersen's pretensions to literary genius, his overblown sense of himself as a tragic figure and suffering martyr for sexual freedoms, and his ostentation. He notes, "There was something theatrical about the fellow.... He could have made the impression he yearned to make if he had not always been over-tailored. That ruined everything – to my way of thinking, at all events."[61] Fersen has fallen short, it is clear, in relation to Wilde's axiom that one ought to compensate for being overdressed by being overeducated.[62] He is criticized, in addition, by Douglas for demanding more attention than he seems to deserve: "He was too noticeable an apparition.... In character, too, he was flamboyant and self-assertive. He had a passion for living on a stage, the Neronic love of exhibiting himself and being the centre of whatever was going on."[63] On Capri, enmeshed in a world of theatricality and excess, Fersen nevertheless emerged as entirely too much. This seemed to have something to do, in Douglas's eyes, with the fact that he was stupid: "He was a fluent but shallow talker. Vanity had made him even more empty-headed than he need have been."[64] His literary output is found similarly wanting. Fersen gifted to Douglas his novels and volumes of poetry, most of which he seems to have declined to read, but he does take a moment while musing about Fersen to "glance" into *Lord Lyllian* and notes its "musty, Dorian-Grayish flavor," derisively citing its opening lines with a withering "And so on" appended at the end of the citation.[65] Douglas casts Fersen's attempts to approximate Wilde as stale and silly, as musty and a bit off.

Douglas maintains this very same level of detachment and disdain even in discussing the more tragic elements of Fersen's existence – his addiction, his untimely death, and his desperate attempts to assert his own significance. Douglas does acknowledge a certain degree of intimacy with this dandy-aesthete who shared his tendencies to epicureanism and his taste for youths ("Fersen was attached to me in an idiotic and ineffectual sort of way") and recounts a morning spent doing cocaine with Fersen during which Douglas implored the younger man to stop ruining his own life.[66] Douglas's arguments were, of course, ineffective, and after "ten years' opium smoking" and "two years' cocaine sniffing," he "fell forward – dead" at the dinner table at the age of forty-two.[67] The circumstances of Fersen's death retain, in Douglas's narrative, his signature brand of failed camp and absurd pathos. The night he died was marked by a thunderstorm that lasted for twelve hours, and due to a disagreement between Nino and Fersen's family about how to handle the remains and suspicions of foul play on Nino's part, his body lay "pickled" in alcohol for months.[68] Douglas closes his recollection of Fersen wondering what, if the body was finally cremated, lies under the tombstone on Capri labeled "Baron J.A. Fersen," casting aspersions on Fersen's assertions concerning his familial connection to the friend of Marie Antoinette, Axel von Fersen, by noting the many names by which he called himself, "Count Fersen or de Fersen, Count Adelswärd Fersen, Count Fersen Adelwswärd, or simply Fersen. Funny not being able to make up your mind what your name is. Was he a Fersen at all?"[69] Fersen's shifting and malleable identity does not, in Douglas's recounting, reflect a successful enactment of Decadence's queer performativity and contestation of essentialism. It is read instead as absence, as complete and utter lack. Even in death, it seems, there was no there there.

Many of the Decadent modernists of the early twentieth century shared Douglas's estimation of Fersen, and one gets the sense that generating caustic quips concerning "the Count" was something of a shared and beloved pastime for the members of the queer network that emanated from Capri. The Anglo-Italian aesthete Harold Acton referred to him as "a poor little rich boy," a "third-rate exhibitionist," and "an irrepressible Captain Grimes under his thin veneer of greenery-yallery aestheticism."[70] E.F. Benson, author of *Mapp and Lucia* (1931), described an encounter in Fersen's opium den on Capri, where he stripped off most of his clothes and donned an embroidered Chinese robe, as "all rather like a charade."[71] Faith Mackenzie insisted "nothing made [Fersen] more socially impossible than his conversation, which was pretentious and never lit by a gleam of humor."[72] When she asked her close friend, the aesthete and translator John Ellingham Brooks, how he bore Fersen's conversation, he replied, "I just shut my ears."[73]

The most thoroughgoing lampoon of Fersen, however, was performed by Faith's partner Compton, who, along with Faith, stood at the centre of the Decadent community on Capri in the 1910s and '20s. Compton wrote an entire novel, *Vestal Fire* (1927), of which Fersen was the punchline. As I have discussed elsewhere, it is in the end the homophobic outsiders to Capri's queer community who are treated with the sharpest scorn by Mackenzie.[74] Fersen, or "Count Marsac," however, emerges as the comic through line of the text. Repeatedly within the novel, Marsac takes the excess of Decadence too far and in a slightly wrong direction. The "black dinner" of Huysmans's Des Esseintes becomes in Marsac's hands a pink dinner at which salmon, crayfish, borscht, and roast flamingos are served. The portrait Marsac commissions of his secretary Carlo di Fiore (Nino) being raped by the fountain nymphs makes entirely too clear and too explicit the "aesthetics of domination" and sexual violence that Decadence proper expresses as obliquely and indirectly as possible.[75] His *thé japonais*, for which "Japanese costume was indispensable" and at which he produces a "Cingalese boy" as his "*pièce de resistance*," renders Decadence's insidious yet muted Orientalism outré and absurd.[76] As the novel ends and Marsac becomes increasingly dependent on narcotics and Carlo's love for him dissipates, his writing grows monomaniacally devoted to the "hyperbolical expression of thwarted passion; and not the richest embroidery of words or phrases could make anything but disgusting the sores with which this beggar of love tried to win alms."[77] Whereas "Marsac's verse had formerly been inspired by the need to express his perpetual condition of being misunderstood by the mass of mankind, ... now he wrote entirely about Carlo's failure to understand him."[78] Decadence's melancholic treatment of unrequited love becomes within Marsac's verse transparently narcissistic and utterly abject. *Vestal Fire* is dedicated to the very same John Ellingham Brooks who felt it necessary to "shut [his] ears" while Fersen was speaking, and it is often understood to have been written under the influence of Douglas and his *South Wind*. It can be seen, then, as a consolidation of this group's shared efforts to place Fersen firmly outside their circle and apart from their approach to reinvigorating and revising late-Victorian Decadence.

Within the particular case study that I am considering, Fersen's poor return of Wilde's serve becomes a representative example of Decadence run afoul, of failed Decadence, embarrassing Decadence, pathetic Decadence. But Douglas, Acton, Benson, Brooks, and the Mackenzies along with Cocteau do not simply turn away from this botched attempt to reincarnate Wilde. They love to think about and talk about why it's wrong, and this practice is for them energizing and generative, getting them somewhere new in their vision of what Decadence might be in the twentieth century. This is intimately bound up, I would argue, with a developing sense of camp modernism. Fersen's failure to enact a compelling mode of queer rebellion, which is in their eyes tied to his earnestness, his lack of wit, his obviousness, his failed pathos, allows them to see backward more clearly at what made Wilde successful – his cleverness, his obliqueness, his capacity to articulate his fate effectively in tragic terms – and to see forward in terms of what they might wish to carry into the twentieth century, to treasure and reinvent elements of the Decadent past, as they collaborate in the production of a camp modernist ethos. Being at odds with Fersen, and enjoying watching others deride him, allows them to cohere into something new, something more than his mindless repetition of the Decadent past.

Camp, Decadence, and disdain operate in a complex and rich relationship to one another within this scenario. While camp may be associated with extravagance, exaggeration, flamboyance, and excess, there seems to be a shared recognition among the Decadent modernists of the early twentieth century, figures who positioned themselves as arbiters of camp taste, that Fersen's extravagance, exaggeration, flamboyance, and excess are all wrong. The camp aesthetic works so often to cast the concept of discrimination into question, to undermine the fixity of taste and "the good-bad axis of judgment."[79] The camp modernists who engage with Fersen, however, come to an agreement that he is too ridiculous to enjoy, that one cannot feel tenderly towards him. They encounter a persona designed to invite camp modes of consumption and they turn instead to disdain. According to Sontag's formulation of camp, the posture of disdain belongs to the "old-style dandy." Modern dandyism, camp connoisseurship, on the other hand, revels in vulgarity. Wilde is for Sontag a transitional figure, linked in her reading to both the elitism of the old dandy and the perpetual delight and enthusiasm of the new. The cross-Channel discourse between Decadent modernists concerning Fersen shows us, I would argue, a clarifying moment within the evolution of camp aesthetics, a renewed belief in the utility of disdain as a coterie of modernist dandies encounter a form of excess that defies appreciation. Speaking with one another about why they hate Fersen, returning for a moment to this earlier, withering mode of Decadent dandyism, furthers their understanding of what camp ought to be and what it is decidedly not. This then might be understood as a moment when the return to Decadence, and Decadent disdain in particular, can do something for camp, complicating our sense of the transition described by Sontag, allowing us to see how Decadent derision remained integral to camp modernist aesthetics in the twentieth century.

As we continue to think about the strata of Decadent literary history within a transnational framework, it might be helpful to turn our attention to these less enthusiastic, more discriminating modes of receiving and transmitting Decadence, to moments of generative derision. This particular case of Decadent transmission may operate, I would like to suggest, as a useful model as we continue to think in broader terms about the global circulation of Decadence. Considering Fersen's mimicry of Wilde along with the Decadent critiques it inspired might generate portable frameworks for thinking about the affects that guide transnational influence. I am interested in particular in what this case study might be able to teach us about the more complicated, less affirming, less receptive modes of affect that underwrite the transmission of aesthetics across national borders. How do derision and disdain burnish and clarify Decadence? How does hating something together engender a sense of aesthetic affinity and foster a concomitant fine-tuning of the sense of what is beloved? As we generate methods for tracing the transnational circulation of Decadence that do not treat influence as a unidirectional flow operating from privileged metropoles onto spaces abroad, that acknowledge the agency and critical capacity of the inheritors of the Decadent aesthetic in the twentieth century, we might wish to centre disdain or derision and attend to moments of rejection and repulsion, allowing for the positive power negative affects can have in the clarification and circulation of aesthetics.

NOTES

1 Born Jacques d'Adelswärd, the son of an Alsatian mother, Louise Emilie Alexandrine Vühret, and a father, Axel d'Adelswärd, of Swedish heritage whose wealth derived from the steel industry, Jacques added the "Fersen" to his name as a nod to his Swedish ancestor Count Hans Axel von Fersen, rumoured to have been a lover of Marie Antoinette.

2 Jean Cocteau, foreword to *The Exile of Capri* by Roger Peyrefitte, trans. Edward Hyams (London: Secker and Warburg, 1961), 5–6.

3 André de Fouquières, *Mon Paris et ses Parisiens* (Paris: Éditions Pierre Horay, 1953), 35.

4 Emily Eells, preface to *Two* Tombeaux *to Oscar Wilde: Jean Cocteau's* Le portrait surnaturel de Dorian Gray *and Raymond Laurent's Essay on Wildean Aesthetics* (Buckinghamshire, UK: Rivendale Press, 2010), 9.

5 Peyrefitte, *The Exile of Capri*, 16.

6 Peyrefitte, *The Exile of Capri*, 16.

7 Will H.L. Ogrinc, "Frère Jacques: A Shrine to Love and Sorrow: Jacques d'Adelswärd Fersen (1880–1923)," 2006, http://semgai.free.fr/doc_et_pdf/Fersen-engels.pdf, 3.

8 Nancy Erber, "Queer Follies: Effeminacy and Aestheticism in *fin-de-siècle* France, the Case of Baron d'Adelsward Fersen and Count de Warren," in *Disorder in the Court: Trials and Sexual Conflict at the Turn of the Century*, ed. George Robb and Nancy Erber (New York: New York University Press, 1999), 190.

9 Erber "Queer Follies," 190, 206.

10 Erber, "Queer Follies," 186–7.

11 Ogrinc, "Frère Jacques," 10.

12 Quoted in Erber, "Queer Follies," 200.

13 Quoted in Ogrinc, "Frère Jacques," 16.

14 Erber, "Queer Follies," 199, 202.

15 Fersen and de Warren were "convicted of only one charge, the corruption of minors. [The judge] Bondoux noted in his decision that after all, the acts the men were charged with had not occurred in public" (Erber, "Queer Follies," 202).

16 Erber, "Queer Follies," 190.

17 Quoted in Erber, "Queer Follies," 187.

18 Quoted in Erber, "Queer Follies," 187.

19 Quoted in Erber, "Queer Follies," 200.

20 Erber stresses that Fersen was represented in the press as a "idle and morally corrupt aristocrat" (Erber, "Queer Follies," 191).

21 Ogrinc, "Frère Jacques," 15.

22 Ogrinc, "Frère Jacques," 16.

23 Alphonse Gallais, *The Memoirs of Baron Jacques: The Diabolical Debaucheries of Our Decadent Aristocracy* (Vancouver: Ageneois Press, 1988), n.p. I quote here from this English translation (by Richard West) of the original pamphlet (A.-S. Lagail, *Les Mémoires du Baron Jacques: Lubricités infernales de la noblesse décadente* (Priapeville: Librairie Galante, [1904]).

24 Gallais, *Memoirs of Baron Jacques*, n.p.

25 Gallais, *Memoirs of Baron Jacques*, n.p.

26 Gallais, *Memoirs of Baron Jacques*, n.p.

27 Erber, "Queer Follies," 192.

28 Erber, "Queer Follies," 192.

29 Jamie James, *Pagan Light: Dreams of Freedom and Beauty in Capri* (New York: Farrar, Straus, and Giroux, 2019), 90.

30 Quoted in Ogrinc, "Frère Jacques," 27.

31 Whitney Davis, *Queer Beauty: Sexuality and Aesthetics from Winckelmann to Freud and Beyond* (New York: Columbia University Press, 2010), 146–7.

32 In my discussion of *Lord Lyllian: messes noires*, I will be quoting from the first English translation of the novel, *Lord Lyllian: Black Masses*, trans. Jeremy Reed (Norwich, VT: Elysium, 2005).
33 Peyrefitte, *Exile of Capri*, 110.
34 Jeremy Reed, introduction to Fersen, *Lord Lyllian*, iii.
35 Fersen, *Lord Lyllian*, 26.
36 Fersen, *Lord Lyllian*, 28.
37 Fersen, *Lord Lyllian*, 29–30.
38 Fersen, *Lord Lyllian*, 35.
39 Fersen, *Lord Lyllian*, 36.
40 Fersen, *Lord Lyllian*, 37.
41 Fersen, *Lord Lyllian*, 71. Jeremy Reed notes that, while the first edition of *De Profundis* appeared a year after *Lord Lyllian*'s publication, a German translation that Fersen may have encountered appeared in 1904. Alternately, Reed suggests, he could have heard tell of the letter's existence from friends of Wilde.
42 Fersen, *Lord Lyllian*, 94.
43 Fersen, *Lord Lyllian*, 107.
44 Oscar Wilde, *The Picture of Dorian Gray* (London: Ward, Lock, and Co., 1891), 213.
45 Wilde, *Dorian Gray*, 215; Fersen, *Lord Lyllian*, 121.
46 Fersen, *Lord Lyllian*, 141.
47 Fersen, *Lord Lyllian*, 142.
48 Ogrinc, "Frère Jacques," 27–8.
49 As Ogrinc notes, "The local authorities took advantage of this circumstance to rid themselves of d'Adelswärd. Fearing a new outburst in the press following the famous Krupp scandal in 1902, the police were kept out of the affair, and Jacques's brother-in-law, the Marquis di Bugnano, was asked to intervene. D'Adelswärd was summoned by the Marquis to Naples and given the choice of leaving the country voluntarily or being officially expelled. Jacques chose the former and returned to France" (Ogrinc, "Frère Jacques," 29).
50 Ogrinc, "Frère Jacques," 30.
51 Jacques d'Adelswärd Fersen, "Sur la glorification du Vierge dans la religion d'Oscar Wilde," *Akademos* 1, no. 10 (1909): 547–50.
52 Jacques d'Adelswärd Fersen, "L'Extase," *Akademos* 1, no. 9 (1909): 321–6.
53 Jacques d'Adelswärd Fersen, *Hei Hsiang: le parfum noir* (Paris: Albert Messein, 1921), 54.
54 Fersen, *Hei Hsiang*, 59.
55 James, *Pagan Light*, 111.
56 See, for example, Alex Murray, "Decadence Revisited: Evelyn Waugh and the Afterlife of the 1890s," *Modernism/modernity* 22, no. 3 (September

2015), 593–607; Vincent B. Sherry, *Modernism and the Reinvention of Decadence* (New York: Cambridge University Press, 2015); and Kate Hext and Alex Murray, eds., *Decadence in the Age of Modernism* (Baltimore: Johns Hopkins University Press, 2019).

57 Norman Douglas, *Looking Back: An Autobiographical Excursion* (London: Chatto and Windus, 1934), 358.

58 Douglas, *Looking Back*, 360.

59 Douglas, *Looking Back*, 360.

60 Douglas, *Looking Back*, 360.

61 Douglas, *Looking Back*, 361.

62 In *The Important of Being Earnest* (1895), Algernon states, "If I am occasionally a little over-dressed, I make up for it by being always immensely over-educated." Oscar Wilde, *The Importance of Being Earnest and Other Plays* (New York: Oxford University Press, 2008), 281.

63 Douglas, *Looking Back*, 361.

64 Douglas, *Looking Back*, 361.

65 Douglas, *Looking Back*, 362.

66 Douglas, *Looking Back*, 362.

67 Douglas, *Looking Back*, 365. In recounting the circumstances of Fersen's death, Douglas draws upon a letter from an unnamed friend.

68 Douglas, *Looking Back*, 365.

69 Douglas, *Looking Back*, 366.

70 Harold Acton, "Enfant Terrible," *New York Review of Books*, 14 October 1965.

71 E.F. Benson, *Final Edition: Informal Autobiography* (New York: Longmans Green and Co., 1940), 113.

72 Faith Compton Mackenzie, *As Much as I Dare: The Autobiography of Faith Compton Mackenzie* (London: Collins, 1938), 232.

73 Mackenzie, *As Much as I Dare*, 232.

74 See Chapter Three, "An Extraordinary Marriage: The Mackenzies and the Queer Cosmopolitanism of Capri" in Kristin Mary Mahoney, *Queer Kinship after Wilde: Transnational Decadence and the Family* (New York: Cambridge University Press, 2022).

75 Imani Perry, *Vexy Thing: On Gender and Liberation* (Durham, NC: Duke University Press, 2018), 76.

76 Compton Mackenzie, *Vestal Fire* (London: New Phoenix Library, 1951), 71, 74.

77 Mackenzie, *Vestal Fire*, 398.

78 Mackenzie, *Vestal Fire*, 400.

79 Susan Sontag, "Notes on 'Camp,'" *Partisan Review* 31, no. 4 (Fall 1964): 515–30.

PART FIVE

Legend and Legacy

9 Oscar Wilde's Tomb: *Silence* and the Aesthetics of Queer Memorial

ELLEN CROWELL

At the start of November 1900, an already-ill Oscar Wilde brushed off with characteristic wit and prescience a friend's warning that if he did not "pull himself up" he would not live much longer: "He of course laughed," recounted Wilde's literary executor and one-time lover Robert Ross, "and said he could never outlive the century as the English people would not stand it."[1] True to prediction, the Irish writer succumbed to complications of cerebral meningitis only three weeks later, on 30 November, at the age of forty-six. Wilde's death preceded that of Queen Victoria by less than two months. Consequently, at the start of 1901, the explosive case of R v. Wilde (1895) might reasonably have been considered at long last closed – firmly consigned to the nineteenth century by the passing of its two central adversaries. Yet the fallout from Wilde's trials, imprisonment, and early death-in-exile extended far into the twentieth century. The earliest manifestation of this battle over Wilde's place in the new century played out through heated debates over how the writer should be honoured and remembered through funerary monument.

Wilde's tomb at Père Lachaise Cemetery, Paris, is a living place; controversy still swirls around its conception, installation, suppression, desecration, veneration, and, most recently, sanitization. The history of this tomb highlights changing attitudes towards queer memorial practices over the course of the twentieth century and into the twenty-first. Jacob Epstein's monument to Wilde has elicited veneration and condemnation in equal measure since being transported in 1912 from the artist's London studio to its final resting place (Figure 9.1). Even today, this twenty-ton block of English stone – carved and chiselled into a strikingly stylized art deco variation on a fantastical, male sphinx – stands out like a sore thumb in a nineteenth-century cemetery whose sculptural aesthetic seems, to the modern visitor, overarchingly figurative

Figure 9.1 Jacob Epstein, *The Tomb for Oscar Wilde*, 1912. Printed in *The New Age*, 6 June 1912.

and representational. It is precisely this aesthetic alterity that has, for one hundred years, prompted viewers to regard Epstein's *Tomb for Oscar Wilde* as future- rather than past-oriented, more modernist than Victorian, a monument to enlightened pride rather than retrograde shame.

Seductive and reassuring, such "standard heroic narratives of the avant-garde"[2] nonetheless retroactively limit our apprehension of the complex aesthetic and sexual politics that informed late-Victorian British art. As Heather Love observes, late-Victorian and early-Modernist artists who seem to turn away from an avant-garde aesthetic of transcendence are no less challenging than their colleagues who, like Epstein, seem to anticipate such modern mandates: instead, we must see their "revolutionary imagination [as] bound not to the redeemed world but to the damaged world that it aims to repair."[3] As David Gesty reminds us, the artists of the "New Sculpture" movement in Britain were, from the 1880s onward, actively and variously looking to "renovate the very notion of the ideal" through innovative illuminations of the relationship between art and its immediate historical context. Whether they utilized or exploded the "formal vocabularies ... of figurative sculpture," artists working in Britain between 1880 and 1910 were united in their pursuit of a "new vision of sculpture, pushing its boundaries and examining its foundations."[4]

This chapter first explores the history of how Epstein's monument to Wilde came to be regarded as an embodiment of modernity – both in terms of sculptural aesthetics and queer politics – and how this collective sense of the monument's modernity has scripted the structures of mourning and ritual surrounding it for over a century. I then turn to a counterfactual yet suggestive consideration of how an alternate memorial – one designed not by an emerging avant-garde sculptor, but by a member of Wilde's queer circle – might have likewise (but differently) constituted a radical challenge to both prevailing sculptural aesthetics and attitudes towards queer memorial. By exposing the intricate personal, aesthetic, and queer cultural histories that swirl around Wilde's iconic Parisian tomb, this chapter meditates on the complex politics of queer memorialization within literary history to recover the radical potential of *Silence* in the face of communal trauma.

Monumental Advances

The many adulatory pilgrimages to Wilde's first tomb both before and after 1905 can be explained by the publication, in February of that year, of *De Profundis*. As I discuss below, when Wilde's long letter to Lord Alfred Douglas was published that year, with a cover design by Wilde's friend and artistic collaborator Charles Ricketts, this posthumous edition struck many as a monologue intoned from beyond the grave – one that, in manifesting what George Bernard Shaw termed "[t]he unquenchable spirit of the man," reiterated the tragic fact of Wilde's early death all the more poignantly. This phonographic aura – with its suggestion of having preserved a voice speaking "from the depths," as the volume's title suggests – helped fuel sales: *De Profundis* became the vehicle through which Wilde's estate was finally secured. The first run in January 1905 quickly sold out; by the end of the year Methuen was in its sixth printing.[5] In addition to significant proceeds from 1905/1906 productions of Richard Strauss's adapted *Salome*, royalties from *De Profundis* made it possible for Robert Ross to secure all copyrights for Wilde's published works. Ross then began work on an authorized "Complete Works" that would effectively halt the international market in pirated editions that had proliferated since Wilde's death.

Robert Ross's labour of love, *The Complete Works of Oscar Wilde,* was published in London by Methuen in 1908. In December of that year, this achievement, monumental in itself, was celebrated with an elaborate dinner for Ross at the London Ritz. Over one hundred of Wilde's friends, publishers, and admirers were in attendance to celebrate Ross's success. In a speech to the gathering, Ross thanked everyone present for their role in "giving back to Oscar Wilde's children the laurels of their distinguished father untarnished save by tears." At the end of his speech, Ross dropped an unexpected thanks into the mix: an anonymous donor (later identified as Helen Carew) had recently sent him a cheque for £2000, "to place a suitable monument to Oscar Wilde at Père-Lachaise." Ross continued: "The condition of this gift is not one to which I certainly have any objection – the condition is – that, the work should be carried out by the brilliant young sculptor, Mr. Jacob Epstein from whom Sir Charles Holyrod has already prophesied great things."[6] The choice of Epstein – a provocative, cutting-edge sculptor who had never known Wilde – was a bold, if impersonal one, and there was another artist in attendance on this occasion who likely took the impersonality of Ross's choice rather hard.

Charles Ricketts, who seating charts indicate was prominently seated across from Wilde's eldest son Cyril, had likely known for quite some time that a monument had been planned for Wilde's tomb. As he and his lifelong companion, the painter Charles Shannon, often socialized with Robert Ross, he may even have had advance knowledge of this monetary donation, whose equivalent value today would be close to $310,000 (USD). And, as Ross knew well, Ricketts was the artist with whom Wilde had most often collaborated, and this collaboration had continued posthumously with Ricketts's cover design for Wilde's *De Profundis*. Ricketts's journal records a January 1905 conversation between himself and Ross concerning Wilde's tomb, and by September of that year Ricketts had laboured over and produced a small bronze statuette entitled *Silence*. Two casts of this statuette are known to be in existence: one is housed at the William Andrews Clark Memorial Library, UCLA; the other is part of a private collection associated with the London Fine Art Society (Figure 9.2). Both are identified, although no clear provenance as yet has corroborated this identification, as having been designed for Wilde's tomb. In 1905 and 1906, Robert Ross had curated two exhibits of Ricketts's bronzes at London's avant-garde

Figure 9.2 Charles Ricketts, *Silence* (a memorial to Wilde), bronze sculpture, 1905. Courtesy of the William Andrews Clark Memorial Library, UCLA.

Carfax Gallery (of which he was part owner). Both exhibits featured *Silence*, and in published reviews many critics noted this bronze in particular as one of Ricketts's best. It is therefore hard to credit that Ross had not considered Ricketts as a contender for this commission; it is likewise difficult to imagine that Ricketts had not considered this himself. Therefore, on this evening in 1908, Ross's surprise announcement of a generous commission for Wilde's tomb likely surprised Charles Ricketts more than most.

Although their aesthetic styles could not have been more divergent, Charles Ricketts and Jacob Epstein were not adversaries; in fact, Ricketts played a key role in bringing him to the attention of Wilde's circle.

Earlier in 1908, Ricketts had been one of the many prominent London artists to defend Epstein's first major commission: a group of eighteen eight-foot stone nudes designed to grace the façade of central London's new British Medical Association Building. Once erected, these monuments prompted widespread outrage from conservative corners. Father Bernard Vaughan, secretary of the National Vigilance Society, opined that "[i]n no other city in Europe are figures in sculpture of the nature shown on the building in the Strand thrust upon the public gaze," and predicted that "[i]f photographs of the statues were sold in public streets or exposed for sale in any shop, proceedings would at once be taken."[7] The Strand Statues scandal brought Epstein to the attention of many in the London art world. To Ricketts, a queer artist whose "shock and stupor" over the Wilde trials gave way to a "mistrust of the British conscience, a mistrust of modern civilization,"[8] the threat of yet another artist falling prey to the forces of English moral censorship demanded prompt action. Successfully defended in the papers by Ricketts, Charles Holmes, and William Rothenstein, to name just a few, Epstein's provocative sculptures escaped demolition. Although the Strand Statues scandal may have, as many critics have noted, marked Epstein as a radical artist and thus limited his earning potential, the public debates his work engendered about the relationship between art and morality likely contributed to his being considered and ultimately chosen for a commission dedicated to the memory of an artist similarly radicalized through sexual scandal.

Jacob Epstein was as surprised as anyone to learn that he would be responsible for a permanent monument to Wilde's memory. In his *Autobiography* he records his shock upon receiving, the morning after the Ritz dinner, many congratulatory phone calls:

> I heard of the commission to do the tomb of Oscar Wilde the day after it had been announced at a dinner given to Robert Ross by his friends at the Ritz. I neither knew of this dinner nor of its being made the occasion for an announcement that I was to receive the commission ... The rumour was confirmed later in the day, and I believe the secrecy with regard to me can only be explained by the fact that other sculptors knew of the commission and expected it to be given them, and the trustee for the monument, Robert Ross, was too timid to let it be known that I would be offered the work for fear of what these sculptors might do to hinder the plan.[9]

Epstein's interpretation of why Ross chose this public event to announce the commission seems plausible; as Michael Pennington observes in his history of Epstein's monument, William Rothenstein (also present at the

1908 Ritz dinner) had, by 1908, become Epstein's most dedicated champion – and it was likely Rothenstein, not Helen Carew, who persuaded Ross to choose this controversial artist for the commission.[10] It is certainly curious that Ross, "a cautious man" who, as Wilde's reputed first male lover, had experienced his own share of scandal, in the end chose to offer this commission to an artist whose primary notoriety "was, in essence, a sexual one."[11]

But in some ways, Epstein *was* the cautious choice. As an artist trying to make it in turn-of-the-century London, Epstein shared with Wilde a certain outsider status: Wilde was an Irish sexual libertine, Epstein a Lower East Side Jewish New Yorker and sexual libertine. Yet Epstein had neither known Wilde, nor was he part of an extended circle of queer artists who might risk exposure by association if chosen for the commission. Ross may have chosen an artist unconnected with Wilde to shield his own queer community from collateral damage. Additionally, as a gallery owner who counted many artists among his close friends, Ross likely welcomed the plausible deniability against accusations of favouritism this less intimate allocation afforded him. It seems, then, that Epstein was correct in surmising that Ross likely chose this public occasion for his announcement because others did know about the commission and expected it to be assigned elsewhere. In particular, Ross made this announcement in the presence of Charles Ricketts, an artist and sculptor who had already himself created a memorial sculpture to Wilde, one quite unlike anything Epstein would create in both its symbolic power and its material execution.

Epstein's "Winged Demon-Angel"

Unlike *Silence,* Ricketts's comparatively quieter memorial to Wilde, Jacob Epstein's striking bas-relief tomb was executed through the direct carving techniques that would be so closely associated with twentieth-century avant-garde sculpture, and thus sutures Wilde's memory to the future. Epstein's *Tomb for Oscar Wilde* was heavily influenced by the ancient Indian, Egyptian, and Assyrian winged sphinxes the sculptor studied at length at the British Museum. As Stephen Gardiner observes, the works Epstein studied possessed an "immense vitality," and a "highly complex construction," but perhaps the most important element Epstein borrowed from these sculptures was the impression of a "sculpture in evolution – three-dimensional forms emerging from the graphic diagram of the relief: in almost every instance, there is a flat back, a front sculpture, and ... a stone frame for the whole."[12] Retaining the great heft and bas-relief aspects of these ancient sculptures as a starting point, Epstein added an almost brutal simplicity of line and a sensual, otherworldly androgyny to his execution of the front sculpture, making his *Tomb for Oscar Wilde* a radical and modern departure from the figural realism of nineteenth-century European sculpture. Epstein drew inspiration from Wilde's writing and personal history as well as from Charles Ricketts's decadent and intricate illustrations for Wilde's poem "The Sphinx" to imagine Wilde's tomb. The tension between ancient and modern sources, mediated through a grammar of ornament inspired largely by the Ricketts/Wilde collaboration, is used to great effect in the finished sculpture. Hewn from a twenty-ton block of Derbyshire Hopton-Wood limestone, Epstein's monument to Wilde seems comprised equally of lightness and heft. The winged angel that adorns the monument's face floats almost free from a squared-off backing. Its wings, which take up almost the whole of the monument's upper half, seem only partially up to the task of carrying the body beneath. This body, although sexed masculine, appears painfully fragile and about to break. Its face, carved into the side of the monument, is likewise delicate, the eyes as swollen shut, as if the figure had been abused. Although this side-facing design gives the impression of a figurehead breaking the waves into the future, the solid block behind the figure and the base on which it rests anchor the tomb in earth-bound permanence.

In June 1912, Epstein's provocative mix of ancient and modern was exhibited in his London studio to great general acclaim. Given that the choice of Epstein to carve Wilde's tomb represented a potentially explosive merger of two artists infamous for pushing the limits of artistic decency, the relative moral merits of Epstein's monument to Wilde – the naked figure adorning which struck many as uncannily resembling the deceased – prompted surprisingly little negative comment from the press. The *New York Times* London correspondent visited Epstein's studio to view the monument, and recorded: "It is a strange, weird, haunting conception, this massive, squarely-blocked-out tomb to which is attached a very archaic winged figure, with the somewhat conventionalized features of Oscar Wilde."[13] One month later, the paper reported again on Epstein's memorial, quoting another viewer's take on the figure:

> A demon-angel, nine feet in length ... is shown in flight. A go-between of earth and heaven, but with wings for flight stronger than the lithe earth limbs, the face wide, oval and full, with more of the earth than heaven in it, part-Isis, part-Celt, inexplicable, sensuous without being sensual, and as wholly secretive of its own thoughts as the eternal Sphinx – this is the spirit chosen to keep Wilde's memory green. Some of Wilde's friends

> declare that the face is reminiscent of him. But Mr. Epstein stoutly denies any intention of a resemblance.[14]

Considering that multiple viewers (including Wilde's friends) noted a physical resemblance between this fragile, sensuous, androgynous, Celtic "demon-angel" and Wilde himself, the *Pall Mall Gazette*'s positive response to Epstein's memorial, although open-minded regarding Wilde's legacy, seems intent on dislodging the viewer's understanding of the figure from any literal feelings they might have about the historical Wilde's ill-treatment or untimely death:

> It is obvious that Mr. Epstein did not propose to be either a literary or moral critic of Oscar Wilde. This brooding, winged figure, born long ago in primitive passions, is a child of marble, and ... has been created in anguish under the driving possession of an idea. The hand of the sculptor has groped in the block of marble impelled to the expression, without words or definition, of the haunting tragedy of a great career. How you are to apply this figure to the facts of Oscar Wilde's life – to his work or his character – is not a question that arises.[15]

Yet from the moment it was transported to Paris's Père Lachaise Cemetery, where Wilde's body waited after being exhumed, moved, and reinterred in 1909, Epstein's sexed sphinx was read by both admirers and detractors alike as a limestone embodiment of the embattled Celt, and this conflation of the monumental and the corporeal fueled the international scandal that marked the *Tomb*'s installation.

Once installed over Wilde's grave, Epstein's monument became inseparably entangled with biographical "facts." Arriving from London to complete the details of the elaborate headdress adorning his "flying demon-angel,"[16] Epstein found his creation covered and guarded – "[a]rrested," in the formulation of Ross, under whose direction the tomb had been commissioned and who would be interred there in 1950 along with his former lover and friend. Writing to the *Pall Mall Gazette* in September 1912, Ross caustically noted the irony of Wilde's tomb being censored for indecency not in England, but Paris: "I regard the arrest of the monument by the French authorities simply as a graceful outcome of the Entente Cordiale and a symptom on the part of our allies to prove themselves worthy of political union with our great nation, which rightly or wrongly they think has always put Propriety before everything. I hesitate to say that the rest lies in the lap of the gods, for that is exactly the part of the statue to which exception is taken."[17] Paris authorities attempted to solve the problem clumsily and with little respect for the artist: "Imagine my horror," Epstein wrote to a friend, "when arriving to the cemetery to find that the sex parts of the figure had been swaddled in plaster! and horribly." Consultation between the Prefect of the Seine and the Keeper of the Ecole des Beaux Arts resulted in a decree: "I must castrate or fig leaf the monument! What am I to do?"[18] Brought to Paris in August 1912, the monument remained in situ for almost two years, obscured from public view by "an enormous tarpaulin, and a gendarme standing beside it."[19]

To Epstein, this all felt like a repeat of the 1908 Strand Statues scandal. This was only his second major commission, and public morality was again interfering: "Here is the Strand business all over again," Epstein wrote. "You cannot imagine how terrible the monument looks now ... I feel quite sick over it but ridicule will do the work I think. Imagine a bronze fig leaf on the Oscar Wilde Tomb. For that is what the guardian of the cemetery suggested might be done."[20] Protests from English, French, Irish, and American artists and critics were to no avail; ultimately the fig-leaf solution was chosen. Eager to settle this issue and remove Wilde's name from the voracious press coverage of (yet another) sex scandal, Robert Ross pressed Epstein to allow a bronze cache-sexe in the shape of a butterfly to be affixed to the monument. Outraged, Epstein refused to attend the unveiling. The August 1914 ceremony was attended by a strange confluence of outcasts and was presided over by the occult leader Aleister Crowley. Legend has it that weeks later Crowley returned to the grave, removed the butterfly from the monument, and wore it around Paris as a codpiece.[21]

The tomb remained unadorned by any fig leaf or codpiece until 1961, when vandals chiselled off the genitals altogether. Giles Robertson, then joint executor of the estate of Robert Ross, offered historian Michael Pennington one rationale for this late act of censorship. Robertson observed that by the early 1950s, the tomb had become increasingly notorious as "a place of pilgrimage to the homosexual community" and that as a result, Epstein's sculpture was now covered with a layer of accumulated graffiti expressing that community's reverence for Wilde. "He noted, in particular," writes Pennington, "the extraordinarily polished, shiny quality of the angel's pendulous testicles by comparison with the dull, grainy texture of the rest of the tomb. He realized that their unusual appearance was due to the continual touching, stroking, and caressing by the hands of the homosexual admirers in worship and reverence to those parts of Oscar Wilde for which they believe he was martyred."[22] Whether or not this rationale holds water (we might question, for instance, whether only "homosexual admirers" paid homage at Wilde's tomb, or whether all of this "reverence" was in earnest), it leads directly to the urban legend accounting for who chiselled off "those parts." Pennington records the story, told by Michel Dansel in his book *Au Père Lachaise*, of two English ladies who enjoyed walking together in the cemetery but who were scandalized by the prominent display of male genitalia the burnished monument imposed upon them. The outraged ladies (who, it seems, were only selectively "proper" in their adherence to conventional morality) grabbed several rocks that lined the alley near the tomb and hacked away at the sculpture's genitals, finally removing them entirely. The severed stone member was then collected by the Père Lachaise conservation department, where it is said to have served as a paperweight for many years. This item is now missing, and the monument remains sexless.

Epstein's winged demon-angel has always, for better or worse, stood in as proxy for Wilde's physical body. Inspired by the sensuality of Wilde's writing and life, Epstein crafted a figure of erotic dignity that has inspired admirers to physical response. And such open, public affection for one imagined as a queer martyr – whose bruised, swollen, yet forward-looking stone countenance looks defiantly towards the future – has served as public protest against rigid sexual morality for over a century. Although methods of adulation have shifted over time, they always retain a sense of rebellious openness, one that responds to both the power and the fragility that marks Epstein's sculptural style. The "Wilde" being adored in Père Lachaise is a Wilde defiantly bold yet invested with fragility, imperious in his ability to resist any attempts to defile or contain him, yet powerfully seductive in his ability to solicit physical acts of both affection and outrage. In 1912 it was under wraps and guarded; up until 1914 it was the site of numerous public protests decrying the prudery behind the monument's suppression. Once freed of both butterfly codpiece and tarp, the monument was visited regularly and adored, even after its castration in the early 1960s. Kissing the Paris tomb became popular later in the century, and this rise in performative and public adulation might be productively mapped onto changing attitudes to both Wilde and the LGBTQ community in the aftermath of the AIDS crisis – for if, as the direct-action AIDS advocacy group ACT-UP demanded, "Silence = Death," what better way to break that silence than to openly adore one who died for the "love that dare not speak its name"?

Yet by November 2000, the one hundredth anniversary of Wilde's death, this practice of kissing Epstein's monument had so steadily damaged the English limestone out of which it is carved that many began calling for action. In November 2011, nearly one hundred years after the monument's installation, the Irish government partnered with

Wilde's grandson, Merlin Holland, to have the monument carefully cleaned and sealed from future displays of adoration. A glass barrier now encircles the monument, intended as insurance against further deterioration. Despite this prophylactic solution – which ensures that any graffiti can be wiped away with Windex – bold admirers still find ways to adorn the monument with kisses. And those who are less agile (or more law abiding) now throw written messages, flowers, and other items of remembrance over the glass barrier.

A lingering memory of the suppression of Epstein's monument – and the way that suppression recreated the public shaming and silencing of Wilde through his trial and early death – influenced the particular rituals of mourning and admiration that grew up around the tomb at Père Lachaise. Wilde's first grave at Bagneux had certainly been a place of pilgrimage for admirers at the start of the twentieth century, as had the Hotel d'Alsace. But it is with Epstein's monument and its history of passionate admiration from pilgrims assumed to be either queer or queer-friendly that we associate Wilde's memory; his status as queer martyr is inexorably bound up with the history of his Parisian tomb and its visitors. But how might this history have been different had Ross chosen not Epstein, but instead Charles Ricketts, as the sculptor to receive the Père Lachaise commission? It is to this experiment in counterfactual cultural history that the remainder of this chapter will be devoted in order to explore the ways in which diverging aesthetic modes might prompt different forms of queer memorial practice.

Ricketts, *Silence*, and Père Lachaise

Charles Ricketts, who had collaborated with Wilde on the designs for all but one of his books published before his imprisonment, took the news of his friend's death very hard. In a journal entry on 5 December 1900, he records the circumstances under which he heard the news and his initial response:

> [T. Sturge] Moore brought to-day the news, some days old, of Oscar's death. I feel too upset to write about it, and the end of that Comedy that was really Tragedy. There are days when one vomits one's nationality, when one regrets that one is an Englishman. I know I have not really felt the fact of his death, I am merely wretched, tearful, stupid, vaguely conscious that something has happened that stirs up old resentment and that one is not sufficiently reconciled to life and death. Moore had hardly finished giving us the news when a loud ringing was heard and Michael Field arrived, sobbing loudly in the hall.[23]

Two weeks later, he records a fitful night of grieving: "Dreamt all last night about Oscar Wilde, or what seems so to me, for I woke up and fell asleep again more than once." And on the eve of 1901, he notes that in a year otherwise marked with professional accomplishments there remained "One sorrow: the death, at first hardly felt, of poor Oscar Wilde; this affects one at stray moments, when one is off one's guard: at sundown, or at sunrise: moments, with me, of introspection, hesitation, or regret."[24] When Ricketts and Shannon travelled to Paris three months later to attend an exhibition at the Palais de l'École des Beaux Arts, the couple could not have avoided thoughts of their old friend: the entrance to the exhibition, at the intersection of the rue Bonaparte and the rue des Beaux-Arts, was a mere four doors up from the Hotel d'Alsace, Wilde's final residence. Ricketts and Shannon would have been aware of Wilde as they entered the exhibition, and given Ricketts's grief-stricken response to Wilde's death, it is not difficult to imagine the couple making their own pilgrimage to the Hotel, if not to Wilde's temporary grave at Bagneux. Both sites would have likely struck this aesthetically-minded pair as singularly and unsuitably inartistic.

When, four years later, Ricketts received from Robert Ross an advance copy of *De Profundis*, he was struck anew by the tragedy of Wilde's downfall and death: "Read Oscar Wilde's *De Profundis* ... It is tragic reading, tragic in statement and tragic between the lines, more tragic than the author seems to know."[25] Ross asked Ricketts to design the cover; Ricketts chose a simple gilt image, stamped on blue cloth boards, of a bird escaping from behind prison bars. On the eve of the volume's publication, Ricketts paid a visit to Ross, and the two spent the evening reminiscing about Wilde: "In the evening to see Ross, who is ill. He told me a charming story about Oscar. 'Ah Ross! When we are dead in our Porphyry tombs, when the trump of the last judgment is sounded, I shall turn and whisper to you, 'Robbie, Robbie, let us pretend we do not hear it.'"[26] From the work he produced over the course of 1905, it seems clear that Ricketts was listening to Ross's "charming story" about Wilde in his tomb with a working artist's ear. This image – two lovers huddled silently, evading final judgment in preference for an eternity entombed together – stayed with Ricketts. By the summer of 1904, Ricketts had, in his words, "turned sculptor," crafting several small figures in clay.[27] After a year spent intensely focused on Wilde's *De Profundis*, in September 1905 he produced a small bronze statue that, in the few times it has been catalogued or exhibited over the last hundred years, has been identified as a rejected design for the tomb of Oscar Wilde. Unlike Epstein's bold sculptural challenge to future generations, this alternative memorial echoes the evasively secretive spirit of Wilde's queer challenge to the concept of "last judgment." Entitled *Silence*, Ricketts's statue advocates radical reserve as posthumous protection against normative judgment.

Although Ricketts nowhere directly identifies *Silence* as a memorial to Wilde, his journals suggest that Wilde dominated his thoughts during its composition. On 7 September 1905, he records working all day on the "[f]igure of 'Silence' (a statuette)" following a night plagued by nightmares about death. Likewise, 8 September was spent working "nine hours on figure of 'Silence,'" and over the next few weeks he kept at it slowly. On 23 September, he returned home to his journal after attending the first revival of Wilde's *An Ideal Husband* at the Coronet Theatre: "Continued tinkering. Of this there is no end," he began, and then spent the rest of his entry thinking about Wilde:

> Oscar was always better than he thought he was, and no one in his lifetime was able to see it, including my clairvoyant self. It is astonishing that I viewed him as the most genial, kindly, and civilized of men, but it never entered my head that his personality was the most remarkable one that I should ever meet, that in intellect and humanity he is the largest type I have come across. Other men of my time were great in some one thing, not large in their very texture.[28]

Through this period of intense concentration Ricketts worked so hard on *Silence* that he often felt "dizzy from overwork";[29] this intensity produced a sculpture infused with the "texture" of Wilde and the history of the two artists' personal and working relationship.

Ricketts and Shannon shared with Wilde (and other artists of the late-Victorian period) an appreciation for the fluid modernity and sensual grace of Tanagra statuettes. These small Greek terracotta figurines from the fourth century, often covered in slip and vibrantly painted, depicted everyday women in draped, fluid clothing. These artists clearly delighted in their ability to reveal the contours of the human body through suggestive depictions of drapery's movement. *Silence*, in both its diminutive size and its sensitivity to sensuous physical movement beneath flowing drapery, pays homage to this common aesthetic interest. The majority of Ricketts's sculptures from this period are nudes; *Silence* is one of his only clothed bronzes. It was this Tanagra-like emphasis on drapery that was singled out for admiration by the *Athenaeum* in its review of a January 1906 exhibition at the New Gallery of work by the International Society of Sculptors, Painters and Gravers: "Mr. Charles Ricketts, who is perhaps the most varied and accomplished technician in England, has also of late turned his attention to sculpture, and his

Figure 9.3 Charles Ricketts, page decoration from Wilde, *A House of Pomegranates* (London: Osgood & McIlvaine, 1891). Beinecke Library, Yale.

bronzes have appeared from time to time in small exhibitions. Nothing that we have seen so far comes up to the level of the small figure of *Silence*. The form has great beauty and unity of silhouette, and the drapery is disposed with Mr. Ricketts' intense and instinctive feeling for rhythm."[30] Ricketts's design for *Silence* also draws upon several earlier drawings developed for Wilde's books before the author's tragic fall. As Stephen Calloway notes in *Charles Ricketts: Subtle and Fantastic Decorator*, in Ricketts's sculptures one often finds references to earlier designs, "such as in the beautiful single standing figure, *Silence*, which is based on one of the page ornaments in *A House of Pomegranates* [1891], drawn fifteen years earlier."[31]

In both its singular hand gesture and its winged headdress, *Silence* clearly remembers this page decoration from *A House of Pomegranates* (Figure 9.3). The statue's drapery and her barefooted stance also recall the imagery Ricketts designed for the volume's title page (Figure 9.4). Ricketts continued, however, to create variations on this figure for his Wilde illustrations. In the figure that adorns both the cover

FIgure 9.4 Charles Ricketts, title page from Wilde, *A House of Pomegranates* (London: Osgood & McIlvaine, 1891). Beinecke Library, Yale.

Figure 9.5 Charles Ricketts, cover design from *The Sphinx*, by Oscar Wilde (London: Elkin Mathews and John Lane, 1894). Beinecke Library, Yale.

and internal illustrations of the 1894 limited *edition deluxe* version of Wilde's *The Sphinx*, we find a draped figure in winged headdress gesturing – although the meaning of the gesture is here more ambiguous (Figure 9.5). This symbolic figure, loosely identified in the volume's

Figure 9.6 Charles Ricketts, detail illustration from *The Sphinx*, by Oscar Wilde (London: Elkin Mathews and John Lane, 1894). Beinecke Library, Yale.

frontispiece as "Melancholia," follows the androgynous sphinx as she searches for her dead lovers (Figure 9.6). Importantly, *The Sphinx* is a text that is echoed in *both* extant sculptural memorials to Wilde: Ricketts's *and* Epstein's. Whereas after surveying all of Wilde's written work, including this Ricketts-illustrated volume, Jacob Epstein chose the enigmatic, androgynous sphinx as the heraldic figure to preside over Wilde's tomb, Ricketts himself resurrected "Melancholia" – the one who follows, the one left behind – as the mournful figure to preside over Wilde's memory. Whereas Epstein's choice stresses a heroic solitude – the future-oriented figure in half-flight from a hostile present – Ricketts's choice highlights relationality, community, and loss.

What connects all of these interlocking Wildean aspects that together forged Ricketts's memorial to a dead friend is their common preference for suggestiveness, subtlety, quietude, and introspection. Ricketts's *Silence* is a sculpture that, above all, invokes privacy. Having shared with Wilde a fear of public exposure, Ricketts and his lover Charles Shannon had lived and worked together since their early twenties, and both their liberty and livelihood depended upon living a discreet existence. That Wilde had been less than discreet was certainly Ricketts's sense; Wilde's trials and imprisonment brought "widespread sorrow and suffering" to his entire community: "To me, the shock and stupor were slow to pass away ... something happened from which I have never quite recovered, a mistrust of the British conscience, a mistrust of modern civilization."[32] *Silence* is therefore a sculpture that seems to imply the viewer's participation in a shared secret history – which, given the anecdote about Wilde in his tomb, can be read as silence shared between lovers afraid that a final judgment will separate them forever. Whereas one might read the figure's appeal for silence as retrogressive turn back into the closet and therefore the past, the figure's mournful yet proud gesture might be more suggestively read as casting a protective, communal pall over Wilde's grave to ensure against future judgment or exposure.

The statue was first exhibited at the New Gallery in January 1906; it was subsequently shown with seven other bronzes at the Carfax Gallery in March of that year in a joint exhibition of Ricketts's sculptures and drawings by Ludwig von Hofmann, curated by Robert Ross. The Carfax catalogue for this exhibition lists the price for each bronze and number of plaster casts to be made from each sculpture; *Silence* was listed at £25, with up to twenty-five plaster casts permissible.[33] At least two bronze casts of *Silence* are in existence; one is in private hands. The other is held at the William Andrews Clark Memorial Library, UCLA. The privately owned cast was displayed as part of the Victoria and Albert Museum's "Cult of Beauty" exhibition (2 April–17 July 2011); the V & A exhibition catalogue identifies *Silence* as a "figure for the tomb of Oscar Wilde."[34] The Clark Library bronze was purchased in 1954 from the London rare book dealers G.F. Sims; the original card catalogue entry for the item unambiguously identifies *Silence* as having been "submitted" (and rejected) as a design for Wilde's tomb.

An undated letter from Ricketts to the great Edwardian actor Sir John Martin Harvey, also at the Clark, is annotated by another hand identifying Harvey as having once owned *Silence*: "Ricketts designed and made a bronze figure named 'Silence,' which he designed and made for his old friend Oscar Wilde, and which was bought by Sir John Martin Harvey, now in the possession of his daughter."[35] The two bronze casts known today to exist are both identified as having been designed, and rejected, for Wilde's tomb at Père Lachaise.

Additionally, one plaster cast of *Silence* exists, and I suggest that it too should be identified as a memorial to Wilde. Although no record of its purchase or acquisition exists, an uncatalogued, damaged, but provocatively painted plaster cast of *Silence* is housed at the Clark. Done in rich blues, pinks, and golds, this plaster cast recalls all the more strongly Ricketts's interest (shared with Wilde) in Tanagra statuettes. However, the statue's colour scheme also provocatively links *Silence* to another shared queer history. Although we know from a 1906 Carfax Gallery exhibition catalogue that Ricketts authorized the manufacture of up to twenty-five plaster casts of *Silence,* Ricketts biographer J.G.P. Delaney is the only scholar to mention the existence of any such cast. Delaney records that in 1910, Ricketts learned that his friend Edith Cooper was dying of cancer. Ricketts and Shannon had long counted Katharine Bradley and Edith Cooper – the literary aunt/niece lesbian partnership known under the collective penname "Michael Field" – among their closest friends. And as I mention above, Bradley and Cooper, along with T. Sturge Moore, were the first to mourn with Ricketts the death of their mutual friend Oscar Wilde. In Ricketts's memory, Bradley and Cooper would have been closely associated with the extended queer circle that was affected by and mourned Wilde's downfall and untimely death.

During her final illness, Edith Cooper looked forward to Ricketts's regular visits, to which he always brought gifts. This was a generosity that surprised Cooper, who observed in her journal: "I never thought the freakish aesthete of the Vale could be so brotherly in sweetness and charity to those stricken by sorrow and disease."[36] One of these gifts was, as Delaney records, "a plaster cast of 'Silence,' his memorial to Wilde, which, as Sturge Moore later told them, was modeled on Miss Cooper."[37] Because Ricketts and Cooper mourned Wilde's death together, he seems to have associated her with his grief and therefore incorporated her image into his memorial sculpture. This plaster cast of *Silence*, which Ricketts may have painted after hearing that Cooper was ill, is carefully composed in colours that remember the warm pink, blue, and gold palette Ricketts chose for a 1901 miniature portrait of Cooper herself (Figure 9.7) – whose fair skin and pale reddish hair Ricketts had admired as "exactly like" the women of Renaissance paintings.[38] This palette also recalls that of the Pre-Raphaelite painters Ricketts and Cooper mutually appreciated. Taken together, these details compellingly suggest a rich history for this plaster-cast-with-no-provenance, long hidden away in the Clark Library archives (Figure 9.8). This version of *Silence* was likely one decorated by Ricketts to honour a cherished,

Figure 9.7 Miniature of Edith Cooper, 1901. Ricketts-Shannon Collection, Fitzwilliam Museum, Cambridge.

dying member of a fast-dwindling late-Victorian queer circle – one that once included Wilde. The statuette's evocative gesture commemorates multiple events within this circle: the Wilde trials and the threat of exposure they represented to his queer friends; Wilde's death and the end of suffering many who cared deeply for him felt death offered; and this most recent tragedy – Cooper's diagnosis of inoperable cancer, that would end another partnership, the true nature of which needed to be covered in silence until the end.

Silence then, is a sculpture complexly entwined not only with Wilde's memory, but with what Wilde's tragedy represented to those in his extended queer circle. Ricketts's own carefully recorded preoccupation with Wilde during the creation of the sculpture, as well as clear iconographic details linking *Silence* to earlier aesthetic collaborations between Ricketts and Wilde, suggest that *Silence* was indeed created as a memorial to Wilde, as numerous sources have suggested but have never verified. But perhaps verifying Ricketts's intentions behind this sculpture is less important than one might think, given that the statue is today widely identified as having been so intended. Ricketts's *Silence*, whether or not it was intended to one day adorn the tomb at Père Lachaise, offers us a glimpse into a pivotal moment in queer history, and into how the medium of sculpture in the Edwardian period marshalled the symbolic to express layered, if opaque, erotic histories.

Figure 9.8 Plaster cast of *Silence*. Courtesy of the William Andrews Clark Memorial Library, UCLA. Photograph by the author.

If such a reticent aesthetic seems at odds with the more confrontational avant-garde expressionism of a sculptor like Epstein, whose work, despite being contemporaneous with that of Ricketts, is more readily categorized under the heading "modernist," this may be a problem of vantage point. In cultural moments that measure the success of queer activism by increasing benchmarks of openness, we perhaps find it difficult to see the radical aesthetic potential in silence, secrecy, and refusal during eras scarred by queer scandal.

Had *Silence* been the statue brought to Paris to adorn the tomb at Père Lachaise, Wilde's gravesite would not stand out from most other monuments in the cemetery, as it does so resolutely now. Wilde's tomb might therefore not have become the site of creatively physical demonstrations of love and respect; it is difficult to imagine throngs of admirers kissing *Silence,* even more difficult to conceive of any puritanical shows of outrage over the sculpture's mode of memorializing a dead friend. Ricketts's design would seem to fit comfortably into the dominant aesthetic of the cemetery, looking serenely backwards towards the nineteenth century rather than defiantly forwards towards the twenty-first. Yet such an orientation does not, as narratives of queer progress so often maintain, necessarily indicate shame, repression, or closeted self-preservation. Although Ricketts's sculpture seems to advocate sealing Wilde's memory in "Silence," that silence speaks volumes about the constitutive histories of secrecy, shame, and loss that shaped an entire generation, of which Wilde and Ricketts were a part.

NOTES

An earlier version of this chapter appeared in *BRANCH: Britain, Representation and Nineteenth-Century History*, ed. Dino Franco Felluga, November 2012, https://branchcollective.org/?ps_articles=ellen-crowell-oscar-wildes-tomb-silence-and-the-aesthetics-of-queer-memorial.

1 Robert Ross, "To Adela Schuster," 23 December 1900, in *The Complete Letters of Oscar Wilde*, ed. Merlin Holland and Rupert Hart-Davis (New York: Henry Holt, 2000), 1227.

2 David Getsy, ed., *Sculpture and the Pursuit of a Modern Ideal in Britain, c. 1880–1930* (Aldershot, UK: Ashgate, 2004).

3 Heather Love, *Feeling Backward: Loss and the Politics of Queer History* (Cambridge, MA: Harvard University Press, 2007), 132.

4 Gesty, *Sculpture*, 4–5.

5 Joseph Bristow, Introduction to *Oscar Wilde and Modern Culture: The Making of a Legend*, ed. Joseph Bristow (Athens: Ohio University Press, 2008), 1–45.

6 Robert Ross, "Remarks on the Occasion of the 1908 Methuen Complete Works of Wilde," 1 December, 1908, MS Wilde box 58, Folder 3, William Andrews Clark Memorial Library, University of California, Los Angeles.

7 Quoted in Jacob Epstein, *Epstein, an Autobiography* (New York: Dutton, 1955), 238.

8 Charles Ricketts, *Self Portrait: Taken from the Letters and Journals of Charles Ricketts, R.A.* (London: Peter Davies, 1939), 300.

9 Epstein, *Autobiography*, 51.

10 Michael Pennington, *An Angel for a Martyr: Jacob Epstein's Tomb for Oscar Wilde* (Reading, UK: Whiteknights, 1987), 14.

11 Pennington, *Angel*, 14.

12 Stephen Gardiner, *Epstein: Artist against the Establishment* (New York: Viking, 1993), 84. See also Simon Wilson, "From Greek Youth to Flying Demon Angel: Jacob Epstein's Studies for his *Tomb for Oscar Wilde*," *The Wildean*, no. 56 (January 2020): 3–62.

13 "Art Notes from London," *The New York Times*, 30 June 1912, SM15.
14 "Memorial to Oscar Wilde: Sculptor's Work a Demon-Angel with the Face of a Sphinx," *The New York Times*, 25 February 1912, C4.
15 Quoted in Epstein, *Autobiography*, 251.
16 Epstein, *Autobiography*, 51.
17 Quoted in Pennington, *Angel*, 52.
18 Quoted in Pennington, *Angel*, 49.
19 Epstein, *Autobiography*, 52.
20 Quoted in Pennington, *Angel*, 49.
21 Pennington, *Angel*, 55.
22 Pennington, *Angel*, 60–1.
23 Ricketts, *Self Portrait*, 49.
24 Ricketts, *Self Portrait*, 50.
25 Ricketts, *Self Portrait*, 112–13.
26 Ricketts, *Self Portrait*, 114.
27 J.G. Paul Delaney, *Charles Ricketts: A Biography* (Oxford: Clarendon, 1990), 190.
28 Ricketts, *Autobiography*, 124–5.
29 Ricketts, *Autobiography*, 124.
30 "The New Gallery," *Athenaeum* (London), 13 January 1906.
31 Stephen Calloway, *Charles Ricketts: Subtle and Fantastic Decorator* (London: Thames and Hudson, 1979), 22.
32 Ricketts, *Autobiography*, 299–300.
33 *British Sculpture 1850–1914: Catalogue of a Loan Exhibition of Sculpture and Medals Sponsored by the Victorian Society, 30th September–30th October 1968* (London: Fine Art Society, 1968), 16.
34 Stephen Calloway and Lynne Orr, eds. *The Cult of Beauty: The Aesthetic Movement, 1860–1900* (London: V&A Publishing, 2011), 230.
35 Charles Ricketts to Sir John Martin-Harvey, 1912, MS Wilde Box 54. Folder 1. William Andrews Clark Memorial Library, University of California, Los Angeles.
36 Quoted in Delaney, *A Biography*, 274.
37 Delaney, *A Biography*, 272.
38 Delaney, *A Biography*, 140.

10 *Un faux parisien*: Sylvestre Dorian and *Oscar Wilde's Letters to Sarah Bernhardt*

GREGORY MACKIE

There are no surviving letters from Oscar Wilde to the great French actress Sarah Bernhardt (1844–1923) – that is to say, there are no authentic ones. It would stand to reason that the two corresponded, and in French (Bernhardt did not speak English). Wilde, after all, was an enthusiastic admirer. He had first seen Bernhardt perform in Racine's *Phèdre* in 1879, and the experience inspired him to compose a sonnet that imagines Bernhardt as a revenant spirit of classical beauty.[1] Wilde's regard for the French stage star extended to displaying her inscribed portrait in his London house.[2] Shortly before his death in Paris, Wilde was still musing lyrically about her, describing Bernhardt, in a witty conflation of Shakespeare and Pater, as an ageless Cleopatra: "that 'serpent of old Nile,' older than the Pyramids."[3] Wilde and Bernhardt, of course, will be forever linked in theatre history by the abortive production of the biblical drama *Salomé*. With Bernhardt cast in the title role, the play's public performance was banned in England in 1892. Much of the play had been written during Wilde's extended stay in Paris in late 1891, where he made numerous contacts with members of the literary intelligentsia. By writing a Decadent, one-act play in the French language and dedicating *Salomé* to the Symbolist writer Pierre Louÿs, Wilde attempted to style himself, as Jacques de Langlade has observed, an *écrivain français*.[4]

Many of Wilde's friends abandoned him after the scandal occasioned by his sex trials in 1895, and although Bernhardt remained tacitly supportive,[5] she nevertheless declined to purchase the rights to the play that had linked her name with Wilde's. Wilde lived mainly in France after his release from prison, and despite Bernhardt's lack of financial support, he still managed a tearful 1898 reunion with his "dear Sarah" after seeing her perform in Nice.[6] Writing to Robert Ross, Wilde vividly related that after the performance "I went round to see Sarah and she embraced me and wept, and I wept, and the whole evening was wonderful."[7] That reunion was to be their last.

Wilde died in 1900, and Bernhardt lived until 1923. By the 1920s, a sustained revival of interest in Wilde's legacy had begun to supersede the opprobrium in which his name had formerly been held, and that revival's central site was the world of print. This resurgence of recollections of Wilde is evidenced by the publication of multiple memoirs about his life and selections from his extensive correspondence, along with imaginative reconstructions of his characteristically epigrammatic conversation, such as Laurence Housman's *Echo de Paris* (1923). Auction sales of Wilde manuscripts and private letters during this period, complete with elaborate catalogues (the best known of which is probably the Stetson sale, which took place in New York in 1920), attracted significant attention and realized vast sums. Such sales, when viewed in combination with the growing bibliography of titles memorializing the Irish writer who fashioned himself as French, indicate that a robust market for Wilde memorabilia had developed in the 1920s.[8] Into this framework of nostalgia, curiosity, and celebrity publishing, an apparently rediscovered epistolary archive, eventually published in book form as *Oscar Wilde's Letters to Sarah Bernhardt*, emerged in print in 1924. There was only one problem: the "letters" were fakes. By assessing the peculiar creative investments that went into manufacturing this audacious and gossipy forgery of Wilde's letters to the Parisian actress, this chapter uncovers the queer, Francophilic mythmaking about Wilde's early twentieth-century afterlife that was mediated by print and archive and embodied by a little-known literary adventurer who went by the name Sylvestre Dorian. He is the *faux parisien* of my title. Sylvestre Dorian's activities allow us to glimpse the transnational coordinates of the Wilde in Paris myth at the moment of their consolidation. This chapter turns not to Paris itself, but instead to the celebrity-hungry print culture of the United States in the 1920s.

Oscar Wilde's Paris *à l'américain*

Wilde's lost letters to the French stage star were a transatlantic, not simply a European, print phenomenon. They were presented to American readers in two different, albeit similarly ephemeral, formats: the newspaper serial and the ten-cent booklet. The circulation of this trove of celebrity information registers the extraordinary degree to which the name Oscar Wilde and the cultural history of Paris had become firmly linked in the popular imagination – at least in the United States. When we ask how, why, and by whom *Oscar Wilde's Letters to Sarah Bernhardt* were contrived, we become immersed in an intriguing story that not only connects the legacies of both Wilde and Bernhardt, but also the celebrity culture of the 1920s United States and that culture's investment in a familiar notion of Paris as the site of glamorous sophistication and sexual decadence.

The compilation of letters, diary extracts, and interviews that appeared under the heading "Oscar Wilde's Letters to Sarah Bernhardt" in both newsprint and subsequently in booklet form purported to record the decades-long friendship between the dramatist and the actress. In the first instalment that appeared in the *Detroit Free Press* on 6 January 1924, the compilation's editor and translator, a self-proclaimed "Parisian dramatist"[9] called Sylvestre Dorian, linked the pair by emphasizing two prominent and shared sources of their fame: quotable outspokenness and sexual nonconformity. These common characteristics, it would seem, defined the friendship of the "two geniuses." Wilde's "missives to 'Naughty Sarah,'" claimed the Detroit newspaper, "are filled with the brilliant epigram and characteristic philosophy of the noted Irish author."[10] (What a treat for *Free Press* readers, then, to be able to sample such a candid insider scoop, and in an English translation at that!)

After appearing in multiple weekly instalments in the *Free Press*'s Sunday Magazine section, Wilde's letters were promptly republished in a diminutive, ten-cent pulp booklet by the Haldeman-Julius Company of Girard, Kansas.[11] The populist, left-wing publishing house was the brainchild of the freethinking socialist entrepreneur Emanuel Haldeman-Julius. His press's "Little Blue Books" series offered readers a wide variety of (sometimes controversial) subjects in an affordable format, reaching millions of Americans by mail order in the 1920s.[12] During the "peak period" for the "Little Blue Books" from 1924–6, "impressions generally varied between 10,000 and 30,000 depending on the popularity of each title."[13] Haldeman-Julius also became the publishing venue of choice for a number of Sylvestre Dorian's subsequent Francophile journalistic productions, which included *Sarah Bernhardt as I Knew Her* and *Sarah Bernhardt's Philosophy of Love*, which is alternately, and more enticingly, entitled *The Love Code of a Parisian Actress*.

As for the physically modest volume of *Oscar Wilde's Letters to Sarah Bernhardt*, it was never again republished, and in his introduction to the *Complete Letters of Oscar Wilde*, Wilde's grandson Merlin Holland drily observes that "embedded within its sixty-four pages of rambling gossip and quotation are what purport to be eight letters from Oscar Wilde to Sarah Bernhardt, translated from their original French. Although some of them may have been partially based on genuine originals ... they are too spurious for inclusion here."[14] In light of such an authoritative repudiation, I do not propose that the letters are genuine, and worthy of editorial reconsideration.[15] But to dismiss them (and the moment of their irruption into public view) entirely on the basis of their spuriosity is, however, to misunderstand the roguish creativity involved in generating what Wilde himself, in critical essays such as "The Decay of Lying," might more generously champion as works of art – that is, imaginative creations that tell lies. In point of fact, the fake status of *Oscar Wilde's Letters to Sarah Bernhardt* does little to negate the "spurious" compilation's interest to scholars of Wilde or the history of celebrity culture and its lengthy historical connections to the city of Paris. Rather, the sequential publication of a gossipy newspaper serial and a cheap booklet in America can best be understood as a literary performance, centred upon Sylvestre Dorian's fantasy of becoming a "Parisian dramatist" like Wilde himself desired to become when he wrote *Salomé*. Indeed, this print performance is essentially theatrical, and defined by what we might describe as neo-Wildean imposture.

The very name Sylvestre Dorian suggests Wildean imposture. The surname "Dorian" recalls the protagonist of *The Picture of Dorian Gray*, and "Sylvestre" or Sylvester is derived from a Latin root (*silva*) meaning woodland or forest, or – in a more provocative and punning construal – "wild." The alias Sylvestre Dorian thus conflates Oscar Wilde's most (in)famous fictional character with a pun on the writer's surname – and, crucially, in French. This "Parisian dramatist" may have been a Francophile Wilde enthusiast, as we shall see, but he wasn't actually French. Rather, "Sylvestre Dorian" was one of many identities assumed by a daring, queer American writer and impostor whose real name was Brett Holland (1898–1934). The son of a prominent bourgeois family in Gastonia, North Carolina, Brett Holland displayed a knack for garnering journalistic notice – while editing his own origins – from an early age. At eighteen, he "attracted much attention" performing in drag in Delaware, and was "considered one of the best woman impersonators in the country," all the while claiming that he has a native of Bordeaux, France.[16] Prior to his reinvention as Sylvestre Dorian, Holland's activities had been strongly inspired by Wilde. Under the name "Dorian Hope," Holland had issued a volume of plagiarized poetry in New York with the Wildean title *Pearls and Pomegranates* (1920); he had also circulated a vast array of ingeniously forged Wilde manuscripts from Paris in 1921 and directed them at the London rare book market. Moving between London and Paris in 1922, he re-emerged in his native country with the new identity of "Sylvestre Dorian" by 1923. The research and painstaking work that went into the Dorian Hope forgeries was immense, and they fooled and embarrassed the most prominent Wilde experts in the world at the time. There is no reason not to think that Brett Holland/Dorian Hope/Sylvestre Dorian did not put the same creativity and effort into his other publishing feats, which, as the 1920s progressed, came to include a series of nostalgic, diva-worshipping titles related to recently deceased female performers such as Bernhardt, Eleonora Duse, and Isadora Duncan.

In embroidering the posthumous celebrity mythology surrounding both the author and the actress, Sylvestre Dorian's practice as a literary forger is, I argue, artistic in a Wildean sense. The material lie of the printed correspondence – evidently the product of considerable knowledge about both Wilde and Bernhardt – presents a platform for promoting the persona of Sylvestre Dorian as *un homme de lettres*. Dorian's approach to this forgery was both daring and unconventional, just as his earlier literary delinquencies had been. His strategy with the Wilde-Bernhardt letters was not marked by the caution of a shadowy forger with straightforwardly financial motivations, eager to protect his anonymity. Instead, Dorian engages in a far riskier enterprise by widely broadcasting his claims. Unlike a batch of forged manuscript letters that might purport to record the two celebrities' friendship with the tactile intimacy of handwriting, the mass-produced falsehood of *Oscar Wilde's Letters to Sarah Bernhardt* is not something that could be considered unique, exclusive, or expensive; the compilation is not a collector's item. By 1924, multiple forgers (including Dorian Hope) had managed to introduce fake Wilde letters into the collectors' market for rare books and manuscripts. Such acts of literary larceny did not reach a great many people, however, since their effects were confined to a limited audience of collectors (and later, institutions).[17] By going to print in his chosen venues, Sylvestre Dorian's aim was instead to engineer a deception that was accessible and diffused as widely as possible.

Sylvestre Dorian's forgery of *Oscar Wilde's Letters to Sarah Bernhardt* represents fiction masquerading as nonfiction, and print performing as archive, an enterprise enhanced by the credibility (we could also say credulousness) of a publication venue that unwittingly promoted and sustained the hoax. Indeed, there is no reason to believe that the newspaper acted in anything but good faith and in complete ignorance of the fraud. The *Detroit Free Press* provided the platform for launching the career of Sylvestre Dorian, who posed as the voluble friend and confidant to deceased French celebrities. He fashioned himself an interpreter of the French capital's unique combination of the stylish and the risqué for his American readers. In doing so, he practiced a neo-Wildean form of media manipulation at its most audacious and exuberant.

Faking a Friendship

Dorian Hope's media manipulation began by labelling the fraud with a plausible title. The title *Oscar Wilde's Letters to Sarah Bernhardt* is something of a misnomer, as Merlin Holland correctly points out. The so-called letters are embedded in the framework of a memoir stitched together from interviews and conversations that apparently took place between Bernhardt and Dorian, whom the *Detroit Free Press* describes – in a phrase supplied by Dorian himself – as "a close friend of Bernhardt during the last five years of her life."[18] In its textually identical serial and booklet forms, the compilation is punctuated by sequences of anecdotes and quotations, some of which are authentic, while others are newly manufactured by their ostensible editor in order to enhance the credibility of the assemblage. In one example of the latter manoeuvre, Dorian attributes to Bernhardt a version of a Wildean epigram from *A Few Maxims for the Instruction of the Over-Educated* (1894). Wilde's "Friendship is far more tragic than love. It lasts longer" becomes Bernhardt's "friendship is far more durable than love. It is far more difficult to like than to love."[19] Wilde's stylistic technique of inverting expected terms and values is retained in the new epigram that affirms Bernhardt's reputed promiscuity and her friendly bond with Wilde, while subtly eroding the distinction between the two personalities. If they both talk (or write) in the same manner, we begin to wonder: who is the author, and who the diva?

The compilation's appeal rests on its promise of plausible revelations about two of the previous generation's most mythologized figures. This sales pitch is built into the *Detroit Free Press*'s editorial framing. When Dorian promises his readers the fantasy of privileged access to Wilde and Bernhardt with the tantalizing claim that "some of the finest things ever written by Oscar Wilde – one of the intellectual and artistic geniuses of the last generation, whose life ended in tragedy – are revealed in his private letters to Sarah Bernhardt,"[20] he is curating an experience: a time-travelling excursion to "naughty" belle époque Paris – a locale remote from Prohibition-era Michigan. These "private letters" were 1920s fake news, a miniature archive of imaginary gossip that was promoted with such roguish ingenuity that Dorian quickly followed it up with two subsequent series of faux Bernhardt memoirs in the *Free Press* (and from which Wilde's name was rarely absent): the ostensibly biographical "Sarah Bernhardt as I Knew Her" and, even more daringly, "King Edward's Love Affair with Bernhardt." Amazingly, Dorian seems to have succeeded in persuading Detroit of his credibility in interpreting a bygone Paris to such an extent that he added book reviewing, public speaking, and hobnobbing with local high society to his résumé. In one announcement for a speaking engagement at a Detroit Women's Club, for instance, Dorian is credentialed as a French *homme de lettres* whose portfolio of writings strongly recalls the earlier stages of Wilde's own career: "M. Dorian, a Parisian, is the author of two plays in French ... besides numerous critical articles on the stage and contemporary art."[21]

That Sylvestre Dorian was none of these things should come as no surprise, given the assiduous care with which he cultivated this fictitious persona. Again, he takes his lead from Wilde, who once apparently said about his embodied performance of extreme aestheticism in sauntering down London's Piccadilly carrying a lily: "to have done it was nothing, but to make people think one had done it was a triumph."[22] *Oscar Wilde's Letters to Sarah Bernhardt* thus represents the attempt to achieve a similar "triumph" of mediated self-fashioning. The circulation of Wilde's Bernhardt letters among American readers in multiple publication formats suggests that both theatrical luminaries' legacies could continue to inspire desires and performances of their own – for Sylvestre Dorian as much as for the audiences who consumed his fictional translations of celebrity gossip.

Oscar Wilde's Letters to Sarah Bernhardt were first promoted in an impressive quarter-page panel in the 4 January 1924 issue of the *Free Press* (Figure 10.1). "Gay, daring and personal," the notice enthuses, before going on to situate these documents in a flurry of superlatives: "From England's most spectacular dramatist to the world's greatest actress. Their relationship was close and frank. They concealed nothing from each other. Wilde therefore wrote to her in an open and brilliant manner. Epigrams resound! Confessions abound!"[23] Although both putative correspondents achieved their greatest successes in the theatre, the ostensible subject of *Oscar Wilde's Letters to Sarah Bernhardt* is not stage drama, but rather fame and its secrets. The compilation's contents, moreover, are perhaps less interesting than is Dorian's careful mobilization of contextual framing to support the hoax. The rhetorical mechanics of confirmation bias constitute the raw materials of literary forgery, by appealing to what readers already know, or what they are inclined to believe. The false, once situated in a network of the familiar, thus becomes plausible.

This gambit is readily apparent in the putative origin of the letters. Dorian established the source of his Wilde cache by locating it in an economically inflected nexus of privacy and suppression. According to this story, the elderly Bernhardt retained Wilde's letters for decades. Only "when pressed for money" did she permit them to be published – and then only after her death. If we think about Sylvestre Dorian's creative

Oscar Wilde's Letters to Sarah Bernhardt

GAY, DARING and personal. From England's most spectacular dramatist to the world's greatest actress. Their relationship was close and frank. They concealed nothing from each other. Wilde therefore wrote to her in an open and brilliant manner.

Epigrams Resound!

Confessions Abound!

These letters have only just been released since the actress's death. Bernhardt, when pressed for money, sold them with the understanding that they should not be published until her demise.

NO SUCH SERIES HAS COME OUT IN YEARS

Begin them in the Magazine Section of

SUNDAY'S DETROIT

Free Press

"Michigan's Greatest Newspaper"

Figure 10.1 Promotion for "Oscar Wilde's Letters to Sarah Bernhardt" in the *Detroit Free Press* (4 January 1924).

practice as a forger, one of the more striking aspects of such a claim is the conjuring of an imaginary archive accruing value over time. Dorian insists that the "confessions" on offer to his readers are derived not only from actual material sources, but also from lived economic realities, such as Bernhardt's periods of impecuniousness. The Wilde cache, in other words (and the friendship it represents), has a history, a monetary value, and a chain of custody – all of which are as fictitious as the contents of the correspondence. And yet they do sound plausible. According to Dorian, who cannily appeals to the aura of the archive, Bernhardt not only "preserved every line she ever received from Wilde," in some cases she even "made" "note[s]" on certain letters, which are, of course, helpfully transcribed in print.[24] Unsurprisingly, neither the *Detroit Free Press* series nor the Haldeman-Julius "Little Blue Book" was illustrated with a facsimile of these missives.

In curating and exhibiting this fake archive, Dorian establishes the documents' provenance in an elaborate story that anticipates and attempts to neutralize any suspicions about their authenticity. Readers might reasonably wonder: how could these letters have remained unknown for so long? Fortunately, Sylvestre Dorian had an answer. Two weeks into the serial's four-week run in the *Free Press*, readers were reminded that the archival traces of Wilde's legacy had been cloaked in secrecy and shame: "the notorious end of Oscar Wilde's life has scared every letter with any revelation about it into a hiding-place, and no one has had the courage to let them be made public lest his name should suffer something by the connection, and the correspondence of Oscar Wilde has up until now been buried more effectively than were the manuscripts of the writings of Sappho!"[25] Wilde's troubled reputation, in combination with French reticence, is apparently responsible for the letters' delayed disclosure. And by invoking Sappho, Dorian implies that the letters' revelations are connected to queer sexuality. Bernhardt's recent death has obviated the need for any further concealment, thus conveniently explaining the timing of the publication of this "buried" correspondence. Prior to their publication, we are told, the letters were in the possession of a "Madame Claudine Champsaur," to whom Bernhardt sold them. "The rights of translation into English," we are informed, "were secured from Mme. Champsaur by Sylvestre Dorian, a young French author ... Mr. Dorian was a close friend of Bernhardt during the last five years of her life."[26] These vaguely plausible claims are sustained, again, by careful reference to fictitious documents and relationships remote from 1924 Detroit.

The biographical literature on Bernhardt is (unsurprisingly) voluminous, and yet no account of her life mentions this "close friend" who transcribed and translated her memories of Oscar Wilde, and ultimately published the writer's letters to her. [27] Again, Dorian keenly anticipates scepticism on this point. If Wilde's name does not appear in the actress's 1907-published memoirs,[28] it is because, as Dorian explains, celebrity status is vulnerable to sexual revelations. Needing the income from American sales of her memoirs, Bernhardt suppressed her greatest friendship: "she had been told ... that if she enlarged upon her admiration for Wilde, the Americans would ... put her in the same category, and believe all the ugly reports about her character." As the self-styled confidant of her last years, Dorian is well placed to relieve the actress of this reticence by interviewing her, for once "Sarah Bernhardt found herself in the presence of an admirer of Wilde, a seemingly inexhaustible fountain of absorbing reminiscence came into life, and the recaptured echoes of past conversations with that enigmatic poet-dramatist scintillated with the wittiest dialogue since Aristophanes."[29]

For her part, Claudine Champsaur appears to be as fictional as this last of Bernhardt's friendships. She first emerged in print as the keeper of another theatrical archive, "Sarah Bernhardt's Love Letters to Sardou," which was published in several American newspapers, including the *San Francisco Examiner* and the *Buffalo Courier*, in August 1923 – and all of which, of course, were translated and edited by Sylvestre Dorian. This initial foray into Parisian mythmaking by Sylvestre Dorian established Madame Champsaur as a celebrity archivist, and as the precious, singular source of all of these sensational documents. (Victorien Sardou, the French master of the well-made play, had died in 1908, making him unavailable for comment on the publication of these "love letters.") Described in those newspapers as a former lover of Sardou's, the name of the fictitious Madame Champsaur is most likely derived from Félicien Champsaur, a French writer and journalist whose 1881 novel *Dinah Samuel* was based on Bernhardt's life. (His wife, Jeanne Marie Chazotte, was not named Claudine.) An imaginative forger, Sylvestre Dorian is careful to authenticate his claims about Wilde and Bernhardt by leavening his Parisian fictions with elements of fact, for just as much as Wilde and Bernhardt were indeed connected (although not in the ways that Dorian claims), so too did Sardou write plays for Bernhardt, and the name Champsaur is, in itself, a name with an honest-to-goodness Bernhardt connection.

The compilation omits some of the best-known aspects of the Wilde-Bernhardt relationship, probably because that relationship was mostly a professional, as opposed to an intensely personal, one. Readers are not presented with a fake letter discussing the non-appearance of *Salomé* on the London stage, for instance, although it is easy to imagine a lively conversation between Wilde and Bernhardt on a topic that speaks to artistic integrity and national (and linguistic) affiliation simultaneously. Bernhardt had long imagined herself as "an unofficial ambassador of French cultural grandeur,"[30] and Wilde's indignation at the play's banning was such that he threatened to make her nationality his, as he announced his intention "to settle in France" in protest against such "narrowness of artistic judgement."[31] (Wilde's Symbolist play was eventually produced, sans Bernhardt, in Paris in 1896 while the playwright was in prison.) Instead of insights into theatre history, readers are privileged with an apparently insider view into the two artists' lives – or more precisely, their public personas – in a manner that interweaves fact with fiction. We are told that Wilde invented Bernhardt's appellation "the divine Sarah"; that *he* suggested one of her greatest eccentricities – that she sleep in a coffin; that she sought out and treasured his advice in matters of the heart; and that, crucially, he confided in her.

The airing of confidences and secrets, enlivened by Wilde's "fine" style, as we have seen, is the *Letters'* main selling point for readers. In the record of their imaginary closeness, preserved in an alternate archival reality, "Oscar" and "Sarah" are fictional characters as much as historical personages. In this fiction, Oscar Wilde's "dear Sarah" plays a Victorian version of a later twentieth-century stereotype: the gay man's adoring female confidante. She opines, for example, in an invented extract that "Oscar Wilde is always so kind to me when I am in London ... when he says he is glad to see you, so significant is his manner and so respected are his name and genius, you feel as if the queen herself had told you that you were to be her guest while in town."[32] Although Wilde's longtime admiration for Queen Victoria was well known, the double entendre on "queen," the slang term for an effeminate male homosexual,[33] is far from accidental.

Wilde's confidences gain in credibility insofar as they confirm what the readers of 1924 know to have been concealed from public view before his trials – namely the secret of his sexuality. That sexual scandal is the core of the Wilde legend is elliptically referenced throughout the compilation, with special emphasis placed on the "tragedy" of Wilde's downfall, imprisonment, and death in Paris. This manoeuvre is quite common in many of the Wilde forgeries that proliferated in print and in manuscript in the early 1920s. Forgery theorist K.K. Ruthven describes its operation as an "authenticatory device" – that is, a piece of authoritative information that is deployed strategically to enhance the credibility of a forgery.[34] Having fabricated an entire archive of Wilde/Bernhardt documents (or rather, having reported their existence) Sylvestre Dorian embellishes the Wilde record with new and outrageous information. He effectively promotes the "divine Sarah" to the status of Wilde's ultimate secret-keeper. "In the heart of Oscar Wilde," the *Letters'* editor writes with breathless anticipation, "was a secret that fostered all his views on life and love, a zealously-guarded secret which he confided only to Sarah Bernhardt, whose death makes possible its publication now, along with all his marvelously brilliant letters to her, heavily charged with passion, poetry, and revelation. That secret was Oscar Wilde's desire to be a woman."[35] By disclosing Wilde's "zealously-guarded secret" in a specious conflation of transgender identity and homosexuality, the forger amplifies the association of Oscar Wilde with both gender and sexual nonconformity. In his lost letters to Bernhardt, the world's most (in)famous male homosexual is now not only trans, but this revelation is also central to "fostering" Wilde's thought. The letters' "views on life and love" expounded in Wildean aphorisms are thus the direct result of this hitherto concealed cross-gender identification.

Such devices in the rhetoric of forgery can be undermined, however, by factual errors. "Even as a boy," Oscar writes to Sarah, "I had the most inordinate delight in putting on my sister's clothes and looking at myself in a long glass in feminine vestiture, fan in hand, like a capricious demoiselle or a grand lady ... "[36] The problem with this drag fantasia (Oscar as Lady Windermere; Oscar as Lady Bracknell) is that Wilde's younger sister Isola had died at the age of ten. Her clothes would not have fit her physically much larger (and elder) brother. Bernhardt, having kept this secret from Wilde's childhood, tried to carry it to her grave, which, according to the newspaper, was "so near to [Wilde's] grave [in Paris's Père Lachaise Cemetery] that the trees falling over their respective resting-places divide their shadows and falling leaves equally between them."[37] In point of fact, Bernhardt's tomb in that cemetery is rather distant from Wilde's, but Sylvestre Dorian's fable shrewdly assumes that readers of the *Detroit Free Press*'s Sunday Magazine will not be fact-checking.

To speculate on the success or failure of Dorian's Wilde/Bernhardt deception depends on how one measures success. It is unclear that Sylvestre Dorian made all that much money from the *Letters'* publication. Although it is probably impossible to gauge the remuneration he received from the *Detroit Free Press* for his series of articles, he seems to have parlayed their popularity into a period of solid journalistic employment, as he inserted himself into an imagined and mythic past. Further series of articles about Bernhardt followed in its pages, where he also reviewed books and wrote a column with advice on versification for aspiring juvenile poets that continued until 1931. As we have seen, his Bernhardt material also appeared under the Haldeman-Julius imprint, but that company paid "Little Blue Book" authors only $50 for producing the fifteen thousand words of text that came out as sixty-four-page pamphlets.[38] As far as I have been able to ascertain, Sylvestre Dorian also succeeded in avoiding being accused of making it all up, which is no small feat. He came closest to exposure when a reader identified a plagiarized passage in the compilation, but he managed to rise to the challenge with aplomb.

The contretemps began when a reader wrote to the newspaper, "intimating that Wilde plagiarized from Robert Louis Stevenson."[39] This is a lucky, as much as a perilous accusation, for it is not Dorian who is accused of literary misappropriation, but Wilde. In replying to the charge, Dorian manages to turn this brush with danger into an opportunity for, again, enhancing his own credibility – in this instance, as an expert on Wilde. "Wilde was an arch plagiarist, and I am not defending him ... at least nine-tenths of all Wilde ever wrote was plagiarized" Dorian opines, "and as he has never been severely indicted for the bigger offences, I feel like urging clemency for him in the minor ones."[40] The accusation further afforded Dorian with the subject for another very well-informed article on Wilde's life, work, and taste for plagiarism, which duly appeared in the *Free Press* as the Bernhardt serial was progressing.[41] Never one to let serviceable prose go to waste, Dorian republished this piece verbatim as "The Plagiarism of Oscar Wilde" in the "Little Blue Book" publisher's *Haldeman-Julius Monthly* magazine in January 1925.[42]

Transitive Personalities

Verbal copying and imitation are themselves a running theme in the epistolary compilation, in which Bernhardt emulates Wilde's quotable and aphoristic style, and Dorian merges their personalities as he elaborates the Francophilic myth of Wilde. According to Dorian, the two celebrities were united by their favourite style of utterance: the witty epigram. The compilation is positively bursting with these, noting of Bernhardt, "in nothing did she share [Wilde's] personality so much as in her love for paradox and aphorism."[43] Here are a few examples, credited to Bernhardt, and all in a decidedly neo-Wildean vein:

> A woman should never marry a man who lives beyond her means.
>
> French women dress; American women upholster. That is the only difference between French and American women.
>
> Laws and hearts are made but to be broken.[44]

This last aperçu was economically recycled from the earlier Sylvestre Dorian compilation, "Sarah Bernhardt's Love Letters to Sardou."[45]

A shared affinity for Wilde's characteristic mode of expression, as we have seen, has the effect of eroding the distinction between these two personalities. "The influence that Bernhardt and Wilde exerted over each other is incalculable," Dorian enthuses. "They became almost identical."[46] If Wilde wished to become a woman, it would appear he inspired Bernhardt – who famously played male parts, such as Hamlet – with transgender aspirations of her own. As Dorian observes, "Sarah Bernhardt had long ago taken Oscar Wilde as a model personality, imitated him so regularly and faithfully that she quite naturally assumed his views and became a veritable second Oscar Wilde."[47] Wilde and Bernhardt are thus presented as doubles, or mirror images that enable the one to inhabit the personality of the other. Sylvestre Dorian clearly adores them both – or at least the versions of the two figures that he has created. Their verbal talent and witty nonconformity bind them together, and operate as authenticatory devices for the entire hoax at the level of style.

It is not merely that Sarah Bernhardt's personality is informed, and ultimately subsumed by Wilde's, however; these charismatic individuals possess a degree of enchantment for the forger that permits him to revise history, and to imagine its re-enactment in an alternate reality (c. 1924). Imitating Wilde's verbal style is one manner in which the forger costumes his own writing, and imaginatively transforms it – and himself – by performing a different persona. His fantastical wordsmithing, in other words, constitutes a form of verbal drag. On 18 January 1924, Dorian actually dressed in public as Wilde. He attended the annual masquerade ball organized by Detroit's Scarab Club – a meeting place for artists and members of local high society – that "has come down the past few years as Detroit's largest and most talked of event."[48] Despite that year's Orientalist theme of "Scarabian Nocturne," Sylvestre Dorian attended in more European attire, costumed as Oscar Wilde, with a colleague – Mary Humphreys, the *Free Press*'s book review editor – on his arm. A brief notice in the newspaper's Society column namechecks them and their costumed promotion of Dorian's gossipy series, which was running at the time: "Miss Mary Humphrey went dressed as Sarah Bernhardt, while her escort, Sylvestre Dorian, represented Oscar Wilde."[49] By becoming a "Parisian dramatist" in print and dressing up as Oscar Wilde, Sylvestre Dorian is living out an alternative history of Wilde's final Parisian years. In this fantasy, Wilde succeeds (via Dorian's impersonation) in re-establishing his literary career by becoming a dramatist in Paris – something he had been unable to achieve in real life.[50] But the Wilde legend possesses enough magic for Dorian that such "trammelling accidents and limitations of real life" can (for a time) be swept away, and Wilde thus lives on through fantasy and illusion.[51] And in a sense Dorian is indeed a "Parisian dramatist," in that he dramatizes, with his words and with his own body, a fantasy about fin-de-siècle Paris in the chilly winter of 1924 Detroit.

The forgery of *Oscar Wilde's Letters to Sarah Bernhardt* and this publicity stunt can perhaps best be understood with reference to a burgeoning culture of fandom in the early twentieth century. According to Sharon Marcus, fans are "happ[y] to commune with *representations* of their favourite stars ... ": they "pursue intimacy, connection, and proximity, not with real people, but with the heaps of stuff generated by celebrity culture."[52] These observations are eminently applicable to this instance of (false) representation, where the celebrities are – and in Bernhardt's case recently – deceased: newspaper stories and mass-market pamphlets are all that remain of these charismatic individuals. Inventing and re-inventing himself while generating new myths about famous people founded on a fake and fantastic archive full of secrets, Sylvestre Dorian appears dazzled by the mediated representations he generated. And at the centre of this project was an obsession with Oscar Wilde, whose legacy of theatrically self-generated fame authorizes his roguishly imaginative forays into print. Fans, according to Marcus, generally "recycle pre-existing representations" instead of generating new ones;[53] as a fan *and* a forger of Oscar Wilde, Sylvestre Dorian generates the fantasy – secured by published materials, however ephemeral – that such representations could have existed at all. Crucially, this fantasy could not exist without drawing on the powerfully resonant mystique and allure of Paris. In so doing, Dorian briefly inhabits the place of the celebrities he adores, broadcasting their Parisian secrets for new circuits, and new generations, of fans.

NOTES

1 Originally entitled "To Sarah Bernhardt," the sonnet appeared as "Phêdre" in Wilde's volume *Poems* (London: D. Bogue, 1881).

2 See Matthew Sturgis, *Oscar: A Life* (London: Head of Zeus, 2018), 147.

3 See Wilde, *The Complete Letters of Oscar Wilde*, eds. Merlin Holland and Rupert Hart-Davis (New York: Henry Holt, 2000), 1196.

4 See Jacques de Langlade, *Oscar Wilde: ecrivain français* (Paris: Stock, 1975).

5 See Karl Beckson, *The Oscar Wilde Encyclopedia* (New York: AMS Press, 1998), 29.

6 Wilde, *Complete Letters*, 1115.

7 Wilde, *Complete Letters*, 1116.

8 Major auctions of Wilde's books manuscripts to this period include the Tite Street sale (1895), the Glaenzer sales (1905 and 1911), and the Stetson sale (1920).

9 See "Tells of Sarah's Loves," *Detroit Free Press*, 25 January 1924, 12. Variations of this phrase appear throughout the newspaper's promotion of the Wilde letters.

10 See Sylvestre Dorian, "Oscar Wilde's Letters to Bernhardt," Sunday Magazine, *Detroit Free Press*, 6 January 1924, 3.

11 See Sylvestre Dorian, ed., *Oscar Wilde's Letters to Sarah Bernhardt*, Little Blue Book No. 664 (Girard, KS: Haldeman-Julius Company, 1924).

12 On Haldeman-Julius, see Richard Colles Johnson and G. Thomas Tanselle, "The Haldeman-Julius 'Little Blue Books' as a Bibliographical Problem," *Papers of the Bibliographical Society of America* 64, no. 1 (1970): 29–78; and R. Alton Lee, *Publisher for the Masses, Emanuel Haldeman-Julius* (Lincoln: University of Nebraska Press, 2017).

13 Johnson and Tanselle, "Haldeman-Julius 'Little Blue Books,'" 41.

14 Merlin Holland, Introduction to *The Complete Letters of Oscar Wilde*, ed. Holland and Hart-Davis xv.

15 Genuine unpublished, and previously uncollected, Wilde letters continue to appear on the market, making a new edition of the *Complete Letters* desirable. See, for instance, Donald Mead, "More Unpublished Oscar Wilde Letters," *The Wildean* 61 (July 2022): 79–104.

16 See "Woman Impersonator Demonstrates Gas Range," *Wilmington Evening Journal*, 18 August 1916, 7.

17 See my *Beautiful Untrue Things: Forging Oscar Wilde's Extraordinary Afterlife* (Toronto: University of Toronto Press, 2019), especially Chapter 2, "The Picture of Dorian Hope."

18 Sunday Magazine, *Detroit Free Press*, 6 January 1924, 3.

19 Sunday Magazine, 3.

20 Sunday Magazine, 3.

21 See "Sylvestre Dorian to Tell City Club of Bernhardt," Sunday Magazine, *Detroit Free Press*, 20 January 1924, 8.

22 The veracity of this much-circulated quip might well serve as an illustration of its own argument. It is often cited as having originated in an interview with a reporter from the *New York World* on 8 January 1882, shortly after Wilde's arrival in that city. However, according to *Oscar Wilde in America*, the phrase did not appear. See Matthew Hofer and

Gary Scharnhorst, eds. *Oscar Wilde in America: The Interviews* (Urbana: University of Illinois Press, 2013), 22–5.

23 *Detroit Free Press*, 4 January 1924, 10.

24 Sunday Magazine, *Detroit Free Press*, 6 January, 1924, 3.

25 Sunday Magazine, *Detroit Free Press*, 20 January, 1924, 3.

26 Sunday Magazine, *Detroit Free Press*, 6 January, 1924, 3.

27 See, for instance, Thérèse Berton and Basil Woon's *The Real Sarah Bernhardt, Whom Her Audiences Never Knew* (New York: Boni and Liveright, 1924).

28 In connection with the actress's debut in London, Wilde's name actually does figure in Bernhardt's memoirs, which appeared with different titles on either sides of the Atlantic in 1907. See Bernhardt's *Memories of My Life: Being My Personal, Professional, and Social Recollections as Woman and Artist* (New York: D. Appleton, 1907), 311.

29 Sunday Magazine, *Detroit Free Press*, 6 January 1924, 4.

30 Lenard R. Berlanstein, *Daughters of Eve: A Cultural History of French Theater Women from the Old Regime to the Fin de Siècle* (Cambridge, MA: Harvard University Press, 2001), 219.

31 Quoted in Richard Ellmann, *Oscar Wilde* (Harmondsworth, UK: Penguin, 1988), 352.

32 Sunday Magazine, *Detroit Free Press*, 6 January 1924, 3.

33 The *OED* traces the earliest slang usage of "queen" in the sense of "a homosexual man, typically one regarded as ostentatiously effeminate" to 1729; it also appears as a synonym for "an obvious homosexual male" as early as 1924 in the *New Partridge Dictionary of Slang and Unconventional English*, 2nd ed. (London: Routledge, 2013). George Chauncey cites the term as an equivalent of the more common "fairy" in the 1910s and 1920s. See Chauncey, *Gay New York: Gender, Urban Culture, and the Makings of the Gay Male World* (New York: Basic Books, 1994), 16.

34 See K.K. Ruthven, *Faking Literature* (Cambridge: Cambridge University Press, 2001), 146–70.

35 Sunday Magazine, *Detroit Free Press*, 6 January 1924, 4.

36 Sunday Magazine, 4.

37 Sunday Magazine, *Detroit Free Press*, 3 February 1924, 3.

38 See Johnson and Tanselle, "Haldeman-Julius 'Little Blue Books,'" 39.

39 See "Author Refutes Wilde Plagiarism Charge," *Detroit Free Press*, 12 January 1924, 13.

40 "Author Refutes Wilde Plagiarism Charge," 13.

41 See "Plagiarism: Translator's Answer to the Comment on Bernhardt's Letters from Wilde," Book Review Section, *Detroit Free Press*, 20 January 1924, 5, 9.

42 See Sylvestre Dorian, "The Plagiarism of Oscar Wilde," *Haldeman-Julius Monthly* 1, no. 2 (January 1925): 95–8. The same issue also features another article of his, "Blackmail – America's Most Popular Crime," 125–7.

43 Sunday Magazine, *Detroit Free Press*, 27 January 1924, 3.

44 Sunday Magazine, *Detroit Free Press*, 27 January 1924, 4.

45 On the Sardou material, see "Bernhardt's Love Letters to Sardou" *San Francisco Examiner*, 26 August 1923, 29; and *Sarah Bernhardt's Love-Letters to Sardou*, ed. Sylvestre Dorian, Little Blue Book No. 665 (Girard, KS: Haldeman-Julius Company, 1924).

46 Sunday Magazine, *Detroit Free Press*, 27 January 1924, 3.

47 Sunday Magazine, *Detroit Free Press*, 3 February 1924, 3.

48 See "Dinner Parties Precede Annual Scarab Ball," *Detroit Free Press*, 20 January 1924, 1.

49 See "Russian Costume," *Detroit Free Press*, 19 January 1924, 3.

50 Despite many plans for new plays, none came to fruition, and he published no new work after *The Ballad of Reading Gaol* in 1898.

51 See Wilde, "The Incomparable and Ingenious History of Mr. W.H.," in *The Complete Works of Oscar Wilde*, vol. 8, *The Short Fiction*, ed. Ian Small (Oxford: Oxford University Press, 2017), 197.

52 Sharon Marcus, *The Drama of Celebrity* (Princeton, NJ: Princeton University Press, 2019), 95, 96. Emphasis added.

53 Marcus, *Drama of Celebrity*, 95.

Bibliography

Libraries and Archives

British Library, London; Beinecke Library, Yale University; Bibliothèque nationale de France, Paris; Fitzwilliam Museum, Cambridge; The National Archives, Kew Gardens, London; New York Public Library, New York; Princeton University Library, Princeton; William Andrews Clark Memorial Library, University of California, Los Angeles.

Newspapers

Ajalbert, Jean. "Article additionnel." *Gil Blas* (Paris), 31 May 1895.

– "L'avocat d'Oscar." *Gil Blas* (Paris), 3 May 1895.

"Art Notes from London." *The New York Times*, 30 June 1912.

"À travers Paris." *Le Figaro* (Paris), 15 June 1895.

"Author Refutes Wilde Plagiarism Charge." *Detroit Free Press*, 12 January 1924.

Baüer, Henry. "Oscar Wilde en prison." *L'Echo de Paris*, 15 June 1895.

Boyer, Michelle de. "Oscar Wilde mourait dans mes bras." *L'Intransigeant* (Paris), 30 November 1900.

"The Censure and *Salomé*." *Pall Mall Budget* (London), 30 June 1892.

"Crime et châtiment," *Gil Blas* (Paris), 9 January 1895.

Daurelle, Jacques. "Un Poète anglais à Paris." *L'Echo de Paris*, 6 December 1891.

Davray, Henry. "Le Carnet d'Oscar Wilde." *Le Figaro supplément littéraire* (Paris), 22 October 1927.

Despretz, Julien. "Oscar Wilde littérateur." *Gil Blas* (Paris), 25 April 1895.

– "Le procès Oscar Wilde." *Gil Blas* (Paris), 15 April 1895.

"Dinner Parties Precede Annual Scarab Ball." *Detroit Free Press*, 20 January 1924.

Docquois, George. "Entretien avec Lord Alfred Douglas." *Le Journal* (Paris), 25 May 1895.

Dorian, Sylvestre. "Oscar Wilde's Letters to Bernhardt." Sunday Magazine, *Detroit Free Press*, 6 January 1924.

Douglas, Lord Alfred. "Oscar Wilde: His Last Book and His Last Years." *St. James's Gazette* (London), 2 March 1905.

"'Dur travail': Le châtiment d'Oscar Wilde." *Le XIX siècle* (Paris), 4 June 1895.

"Échos de Paris, Interview-express." *Le Gaulois* (Paris), 26 November 1895.

Fouquier, Henry. "La barbarie." *L'Echo de Paris*, 30 May 1895.

Fouquier, Marcel. "Chronique, par Marcel Fouquier." *Le XIX siècle* (Paris), 3 December 1895.

Guillot de Saix, Léon. "Souvenirs inédits sur Oscar Wilde." *L'Européen* (Paris), 8 May 1929.

"Le 'Hard Labour.'" *Le Temps* (Paris), 28 May 1895.

Huret, Jules. "Petite chronique des lettres." *Le Figaro supplément littéraire* (Paris), 13 April 1895.

Lorrain, Jean. "Salomé et ses poètes." *Le Journal* (Paris), 11 February 1896.

"Marquis and Son Come to Blows." *New York Herald* (European Edition), 22 May 1895.

Mauclair, Camille [pseud. Séverin Faust]. "Les Livres." *Mercure de France* 14, April 1895.

– "Le Portrait de Dorian Gray, par Oscar Wilde (Savine)." *Mercure de France*, August 1895.

"Memorial to Oscar Wilde: Sculptor's Work a Demon-Angel with the Face of a Sphinx." *The New York Times*, 25 February 1912.

Millot, Léon. "Hard Labour." *La Justice* (Paris), 7 June 1895.

Mirbeau, Octave. "A propos du 'Hard Labour.'" *Le Journal* (Paris), 16 June 1895.

"Mr. Oscar Wilde at Pentonville." *Galignani's Messenger* (Paris), 25 June 1895.

"The New Gallery." *Athenaeum*, 13 January 1906.

"Oscar Wilde, à la prison de Pentonville." *Le Gaulois* (Paris), 13 June 1895.

"Oscar Wilde, au moulin de discipline." *Quotidien illustré* (Paris), 7 June 1895.

"Oscar Wilde in Prison." *St. James's Gazette* (London), 23 February 1905.

"Oscar Wilde's Death-Bed Jest." *St. James's Gazette* (London), 28 February 1905.

"Oscar Wilde's Prison Cry." *Reynolds's Newspaper* (London), 26 February 1905.

"Our Dark Places." *Daily Chronicle* (London), 23, 25, 29 January 1894.

"Pages from the Prison Diary of Oscar Wilde." *Daily Mirror* (London), 23 February 1905.

"Plagiarism: Translator's Answer to the Comment on Bernhardt's Letters from Wilde." Book Review Section, *Detroit Free Press*, 20 January 1924.

Rebell, Hugues. "La Défense d'Oscar Wilde." *Mercure de France*, August 1895.

Roche, Paul. "Oscar Wilde jugé par le docteur Max Nordau." *Le Gaulois* (Paris), 10 April 1895.

Rochefort, Henri. "Supplicieurs et suppliciés." *L'Intransigeant* (Paris), 30 May 1895.

Ross, Robert. "The Lessee of the Grave at Bagneux." *Reynolds's Newspaper* (London), 7 August 1904.

– "The Writer of the Preface to 'De Profundis.'" *St. James's Gazette* (London), 8 March 1905.

"Russian Costume." *Detroit Free Press*, 19 January, 1924.

Samuel, Henry. "Parisians Say City Will Be 'As Ugly As London' if Romantic Newspaper Kiosks Replaced with Modern 'Sardine Tins.'" *Telegraph* (London), 8 July 2016. https://www.telegraph.co.uk/news/2016/07/08/parisians-say-city-will-be-as-ugly-as-london-if-romantic-newspap/.

Sherard, Robert H. "At Oscar Wilde's Grave." *Reynolds's Newspaper* (London), 21 June 1903.

– "Oscar Wilde." *St. James's Gazette* (London), 9 March 1905.

– "Oscar Wilde's Tomb." *Reynolds's Newspaper* (London), 31 July 1904.

Sisley, Maurice. "La *Salomé* de M. Oscar Wilde." *Le Gaulois* (Paris), 29 June 1892.

"Sylvestre Dorian to Tell City Club of Bernhardt." Sunday Magazine, *Detroit Free Press*, 20 January 1924.

Tavernier, Adolphe. "Chronique parisienne." *Gil Blas* (Paris), 11 April 1895.

Teixeira, Lily. "Oscar Wilde." *St. James's Gazette* (London), 11 March 1905.

"Tells of Sarah's Loves." *Detroit Free Press*, 25 January 1924.

Tinan, Jean de. Review of Oscar Wilde's *Salomé*. *Mercure de France*, March 1896.

"La Torture en Angleterre." *Le Jour* (Paris), 29 May 1895.

"La Vie intellectuelle: lectures." *La Cocarde* (Paris), 8 January 1895.

"Une visite à Oscar Wilde." *La Presse* (Paris), 26 June 1895.

"Woman Impersonator Demonstrates Gas Range." *Wilmington Evening Journal* (DE), 18 August 1916.

Zola, Émile. "J'Accuse ... !" *L'Aurore* (Paris), 13 January 1895.

Other Sources

Acton, Harold. "Enfant Terrible." *New York Review of Books*, 14 October 1965.

Adut, Ari. "A Theory of Scandal: Victorians, Homosexuality, and the Fall of Oscar Wilde." *Journal of Sociology* 111, no. 1 (July 2005): 213–48. https://doi.org/10.1086/428816.

Aquien, Pascal. *Oscar Wilde: Les mots et les songes*. Croissy-Beaubourg: Aden, 2006.

Baedeker's Paris and Its Environs. Leipzig: Karl Baedeker, 1881, 1891, 1896.

Barker, Michael. "Brasseries, Restaurants and Cafés in Paris, and a Gazetteer of Establishments of Decorative Interest." *The Journal of the Decorative Arts Society 1850–the Present*, no. 22 (1998): 82–9.

Barnaby, Paul. "Timeline of the European Reception of Oscar Wilde." In *The Reception of Oscar Wilde in Europe*, edited by Stefano Evangelista, xxi–lxxxii. London: Bloomsbury, 2010.

Baudelaire, Charles. *The Painter of Modern Life and Other Essays*, edited and translated by Jonathan Mayne. New York: Phaidon Press, 1995.

Beckson, Karl. *The Oscar Wilde Encyclopedia*. New York: AMS Press, 1998.

Bell, T.H. "Oscar Wilde's Unwritten Play." *Bookman* 71 (April/May 1930): 139–50.

Benjamin, Walter. "Paris, Capital of the Nineteenth Century." In *Reflections: Essays, Aphorisms, Autobiographical Writings*, translated by Edmund Jephcott. New York: Schoken Books, 1978.

Benson, E.F. *Final Edition: Informal Autobiography*. New York: Longmans, Green and Co., 1940.

Berlanstein, Lenard R. *Daughters of Eve: A Cultural History of French Theater Women from the Old Regime to the Fin de Siècle*. Cambridge, MA: Harvard University Press, 2001.

Bernhardt, Sarah. *Memories of My Life, Being My Personal, Professional, and Social Recollections as Woman and Artist*. New York: D. Appleton, 1907.

Berton, Thérèse, and Basil Woon. *The Real Sarah Bernhardt, Whom Her Audiences Never Knew*. New York: Boni and Liveright, 1924.

Birnbaum, Martin. *Oscar Wilde: Fragments and Memories*. New York: J.F. Drake, 1914.

Boltanski, Luc, et al. *Affaires, scandales et grandes causes: de Socrate à Pinochet*. Paris: Stock, 2007.

Bourdieu, Pierre. "The Field of Cultural Production; or, The Economic World Reversed." In *The Field of Cultural Production: Essays on Art and Literature*, edited and translated by Randal Johnson, 29–74. New York: Columbia University Press, 1993.

Bristow, Joseph. Introduction to *Oscar Wilde and Modern Culture: The Making of a Legend*, edited by Joseph Bristow, 1–45. Athens: Ohio University Press, 2008.

Bristow, Joseph, and Rebecca N. Mitchell. "On Oscar Wilde and Plagiarism." *The Public Domain Review*, 13 January 2016. https://publicdomainreview.org/essay/on-oscar-wilde-and-plagiarism.

Brown, H.M. Translator's Preface to *The Songs of Bilitis* by Pierre Louÿs, 7–11. London: Privately Printed for Members of the Aldus Society, 1904.

Calloway, Stephen. *Charles Ricketts: Subtle and Fantastic Decorator*. London: Thames and Hudson, 1979.

Calloway, Stephen, and Lynne Orr, eds. *The Cult of Beauty: The Aesthetic Movement 1860–1900*. London: V & A Publishing, 2011.

Carteret, Léopold. *Manuscrits de Pierre Louÿs et de divers auteurs contemporains: Claude Farrère, André Gide, Jean de Tinan, Oscar Wilde: poésies et lettres autographes d'auteurs modernes et contemporains*. Paris: Carteret, 1926.

Casanova, Pascale. *La république mondiale des lettres*. Paris: Éditions du Seuil, 1999.

– *The World Republic of Letters*. Translated by M.B. DeBevoise. Cambridge, MA: Harvard University Press, 2004.

Charle, Christophe. *Paris, fin de siècle: culture et politique*. Paris: Éditions du Seuil, 1998.

Chauncey, George. *Gay New York: Gender, Urban Culture, and the Makings of the Gay Male World, 1890–1940*. New York: Basic Books, 1994.

Cheney, Patrick. *Shakespeare, National Poet-Playwright*. Cambridge: Cambridge University Press, 2004.

Clark, T.J. *The Painting of Modern Life: Paris in the Art of Manet and His Followers*. Princeton, NJ: Princeton University Press, 1984.

Claverie, Élisabeth. "Procès, affaire, cause. Voltaire et l'innovation critique." *Politix*, no. 26 (1994): 76–85. https://doi.org/10.3406/polix.1994.1843.

Clive, H.P. "Pierre Louÿs and Oscar Wilde: A Chronicle of Their Friendship." *Revue de littérature comparée* 43, no. 3 (July 1969): 353–84.

Cocks, H.G. *Nameless Offences: Homosexual Desire in the Nineteenth Century*. London: I.B. Tauris, 2003.

Cocteau, Jean. Foreword to *The Exile of Capri* by Roger Peyrefitte, translated by Edward Hyams. London: Secker and Warburg, 1961.

Cohen, William A. "Wilde's French." In *Wilde Discoveries: Traditions, Histories, Archives*, edited by Joseph Bristow, 60–70. Toronto: University of Toronto Press, 2013.

Colligan, Colette. *A Publisher's Paradise: Expatriate Literary Culture in Paris, 1890–1960*. Amherst: University of Massachusetts Press, 2014.

Collins, Ross F. "Traitorous Collaboration: The Press in France, 1815–1914." In *The Rise of Western Journalism, 1815–1914*, edited by Ross F. Collins and E.M. Palmegiano, 71–105. Jefferson, NC: McFarland, 2007.

Crowell, Ellen. "Oscar Wilde's Tomb: *Silence* and the Aesthetics of Queer Memorial," *BRANCH: Britain, Representation and Nineteenth-Century History*, edited by Dino Franco Felluga, November 2012, https://branchcollective.org/?ps_articles=ellen-crowell-oscar-wildes-tomb-silence-and-the-aesthetics-of-queer-memorial.

Cvetkovitch, Ann. *An Archive of Feelings: Trauma, Sexuality, and Lesbian Public Cultures*. Durham, NC: Duke University Press, 2003.

d'Adelswärd-Fersen, Jacques. "L'Extase," *Akademos* 1, no. 9 (1909): 321–6.

– *Hei Hsiang: le parfum noir*. Paris: Albert Messein, 1921.

– *Lord Lyllian: Black Masses*. Translated by Jeremy Reed. Norwich, VT: Elysium, 2005.

– *Messes Noires: Lord Lyllian*. Paris: Léon Vanier, 1905.

– "Sur la glorification du Vierge dans la religion d'Oscar Wilde." *Akademos* 1, no. 10 (1909): 547–50.

Dampierre, Eric de. "Thèmes pour l'étude du scandale." *Annales:economies, sociétés, civilizations* 9, no. 3 (1954): 328–36. https://doi.org/10.3406/ahess.1954.2291.

Dauphiné, Claude. "Rachilde et le 'Mercure.'" *Revue d'Histoire littéraire de la France* 92, no. 1 (January–February 1992): 17–28.

Davis, Michael F., and Petra Dierkes-Thrun. "Wilde's Other Worlds: An Introduction." In *Wilde's Other Worlds*, edited by Michael F. Davis and Petra Dierkes-Thrun, 1–15. New York: Routledge, 2018.

Davis, Whitney. *Queer Beauty: Sexuality and Aesthetics from Winckelmann to Freud and Beyond*. New York: Columbia University Press, 2010.

Davray, Henry-D. [Henry-Durand]. Review of *The Ballad of Reading Gaol*. In "Lettres anglaises," *Mercure de France*, April 1898, 323.

– Obituary of Oscar Wilde. In "Lettres anglaises," *Mercure de France*, February 1901, 555–60.

– *Oscar Wilde: la tragédie finale, suivi de épisodes et souvenirs et des apocryphes*. Paris: Mercure de France, 1928.

de Blic, Damien, and Cyril Lemieux. "Le Scandale comme épreuve: Éléments de sociologie pragmatique." *Politix* 3, no. 71 (2005): 9–38.

de Fouquières, André. *Mon Paris et ses Parisiens*. Paris: Éditions Pierre Horay, 1953.

Delaney, J.G. Paul. *Charles Ricketts: A Biography*. Oxford: Clarendon, 1990.

de Langlade, Jacques. *Oscar Wilde: écrivain français*. Paris: Stock, 1975.

Denby, Elaine. *Grand Hotels: Reality and Illusion. An Architectural and Social History*. London: Reaktion, 1998.

Dierkes-Thrun, Petra. "Decadent Sensuality in Rachilde and Wilde." In *Decadence and the Senses*, edited by Jane Desmarais and Alice Condé, 51–65. London: Legenda, 2017.

– "Oscar Wilde, Rachilde, and the *Mercure de France*." In *Wilde's Other Worlds*, edited by Michael F. Davis and Petra Dierkes-Thrun, 220–41. New York: Routledge, 2018.

– *Salome's Modernity: Oscar Wilde and the Aesthetics of Transgression*. Ann Arbor: University of Michigan Press, 2011.

Dorian, Sylvestre, ed. *Oscar Wilde's Letters to Sarah Bernhardt*. Little Blue Book No. 664. Girard, KS: Haldeman-Julius Company, 1924.

– "The Plagiarism of Oscar Wilde." *Haldeman-Julius Monthly* 1, no. 2 (January 1925).

Douglas, Lord Alfred. *Oscar Wilde and Myself*. New York: Duffield, 1914.

– "A Sicilian Love Song." *The Spirit Lamp* 4, no. 1 (May 1893): 46.

Douglas, Norman. *Looking Back: An Autobiographical Excursion*. London: Chatto and Windus, 1934.

Edwards, H. Sutherland. *Old and New Paris: Its History, Its People, and Its Places*. London: Cassell, 1893.

Eells, Emily. "Naturalizing Oscar Wilde as an *homme de lettres*: The French Reception of *Dorian Gray* and *Salomé* (1895–1922)." In *The Reception of Oscar Wilde in Europe*, edited by Stefano Evangelista, 80–95. London: Continuum, 2010.

– *Two* Tombeaux *to Oscar Wilde: Jean Cocteau's* Le Portrait surnaturel de Dorian Gray *and Raymond Laurent's Essay on Wildean Aesthetics*. Buckinghamshire, UK: Rivendale Press, 2010.

– "Wilde's French *Salomé*." *Cahiers victoriens et édouardiens* 72 (Autumn 2010): 115–30.

Ellmann, Richard. *Oscar Wilde*. Harmondsworth, UK: Penguin, 1988.

Epstein, Jacob. *Epstein: An Autobiography*. New York: E.P. Dutton, 1955.

Erber, Nancy. "The French Trials of Oscar Wilde." *Journal of the History of Sexuality* 6, no. 4 (April 1996): 549–88.

– "Queer Follies: Effeminacy and Aestheticism in *fin-de-siècle* France, the Case of Baron d'Adelsward Fersen and Count de Warren." In *Disorder in the Court: Trials and Sexual Conflict at the Turn of the Century*, edited George Robb and Nancy Erber, 186–208. New York: New York University Press, 1999.

Escuret, Annie. "Henry-D. Davray and the *Mercure de France*." In *The Reception of H.G. Wells in Europe*, edited by Patrick Parrinder and John S. Partington, 28–47. New York: Continuum, 2005.

Evangelista, Stefano, ed. *Literary Cosmopolitanism in the English Fin de Siècle: Citizens of Nowhere*. Oxford: Oxford University Press, 2021.

– *The Reception of Oscar Wilde in Europe*. London: Bloomsbury, 2010.

Ferguson, Priscilla Parkhurst. *Paris as Revolution: Writing the Nineteenth-Century City*. Berkeley: University of California Press, 1994.

Fort, Paul. *Mes mémoires: toute la vie d'un poète, 1872–1943*. Paris: Flammarion, 1944.

Frankel, Nicholas. *Oscar Wilde's Decorated Books*. Ann Arbor: University of Michigan Press, 2000.

– *Oscar Wilde: The Unrepentant Years*. Cambridge, MA: Harvard University Press, 2017.

– Review of *Salome: A Tragedy in One Act*, by Oscar Wilde, translated by Joseph W. Donohue, illustrated by Barry Moser, *Journal of Pre-Raphaelite Studies*, n.s. 22 (Spring 2013): 110–14.

Fryer, Jonathan. *André and Oscar: The Literary Friendship of André Gide and Oscar Wilde*. New York: Macmillan, 1998.

Gallais, Alphonse. *The Memoirs of Baron Jacques: The Diabolical Debaucheries of Our Decadent Aristocracy*. Vancouver: Ageneois Press, 1988.

Gardiner, Stephen. *Epstein: Artist Against the Establishment*. New York: Viking, 1993.

Getsy, David, ed. *Sculpture and the Pursuit of a Modern Ideal in Britain, c. 1880–1930*. Aldershot, UK: Ashgate, 2004.

Gide, André. *Oscar Wilde: In Memoriam*. Paris: Mercure de France, 1910.

– *Oscar Wilde: In Memoriam*, translated by Bernard Frechtman. New York: Philosophical Library, 1949.

– *Si le grain ne meurt*. 3 vols. Paris: Gallimard, 1924.

– *Si le grain ne meurt*. In *Souvenirs et voyages*, edited by Pierre Masson, Daniel Durosay, and Martine Sagaert, 298–312. Paris: Gallimard, 2001.

Gide, André, and Eugène Rouart. *André Gide – Eugène Rouart, Correspondance I, 1893–1901*, edited by David H. Walker. Lyon: Presses universitaires de Lyon, 2006.

Gillespie, Michael Patrick. *Branding Oscar Wilde*. New York: Routledge, 2018.

Giudicelli, Xavier. "Butterflies, Orchids and Wasps. Polyglossia and Aesthetic Lives: Foreign Languages in *The Spirit Lamp* (1892–1893)." *Cahiers victoriens et édouardiens* 78 (Autumn 2013). https://doi.org/10.4000/cve.930.

Gluckman, Max. "Papers in Honor of Melville J. Herskovits: Gossip and Scandal." *Current Anthropology* 4, no. 3 (June 1963): 307–16. https://doi.org/10.1086/200378.

Goujon, Jean-Paul. "Le Jeune Roy." *Chef-Lieu: revue de littérature* 2 (1994): 123–37.

– *Pierre Louÿs: une vie secrete, 1879–1925*. Paris: Fayard, 2002.

– "Postface au Jeune Roy." *Chef-Lieu: revue de littérature* 2 (1994): 140.

Gray, John. *Silverpoints*. London: Elkin Mathews and John Lane, 1893.

Griffiths, Richard. "The Château-Rouge and the Père Lunette: Insights into the 'Slumming' Culture of Late Nineteenth-Century France." *French Cultural Studies* 24, no. 1 (2013): 3–26. https://doi.org/10.1177/0957155812464160.

Guillot de Saix, Léon. *Le Chant du cygne*. Paris: Mercure de France, 1942.

– *Rien n'est vrai que le beau: oeuvres choisies, lettres*, edited by Pascal Aquien. Paris: Gallimard, 2019.

Guy, Josephine M., and Ian Small. *Oscar Wilde's Profession: Writing and the Culture Industry in the Late Nineteenth Century*. Oxford: Oxford University Press, 2000.

Hare, Augustus J.C. "Walks in Old Paris." *Good Words* 28 (December 1887): 48–51.

Harper's Guide to Paris and the Exposition of 1900. London: Harper and Brothers, 1900.

Harris, Frank. "New Preface to 'The Life and Confessions of Oscar Wilde.'" In *New Preface to "The Life and Confessions of Oscar Wilde,"* by Frank Harris and Alfred Douglas. London: Fortune Press, 1925.

– *Oscar Wilde: His Life and Confessions*. 2 vols. New York: Privately printed, 1916.

– *La vie et les confessions d'Oscar Wilde*, translated by Henry-D. Davray and Madeleine Vernon. Paris: Mercure de France, 1928.

Harrold, Pauline, Una Rota, and Thomas Stainton, comps. *British Sculpture 1850–1914: Catalogue of a Loan Exhibition of Sculpture and Medals Sponsored by the Victorian Society, 30th September–30th October 1968*. London: Fine Art Society, 1968.

Herlin, Denis. "À la Librairie de l'Art indépendant: musique, poésie, art, et ésotérisme." *Histoires littéraires* 17, no. 68 (2016): 7–56.

Hext, Kate, and Alex Murray, eds. *Decadence in the Age of Modernism*. Baltimore: Johns Hopkins University Press, 2019.

Hibbitt, Richard. "The Artist as Aesthete: The French Creation of Wilde." In *The Reception of Oscar Wilde in Europe*, edited by Stefano Evangelista, 65–79. London: Continuum, 2010.

Hofer, Matthew, and Gary Scharnhorst, eds. *Oscar Wilde in America: The Interviews*. Urbana: University of Illinois Press, 2013.

Holland, Merlin. Introduction to *The Complete Letters of Oscar Wilde*, edited by Merlin Holland and Rupert Hart-Davis, xiii–xxi. London: Fourth Estate, 2000.

Housman, Laurence. *Echo de Paris: A Study from Life*. London: Jonathan Cape, 1923.

Hunter-Blair, Rt. Rev. Sir David. *In Victorian Days, and Other Papers*. London: Longmans, Green, and Co., 1939.

Iandoli, Louis J. "The Palace of the Tuileries and Its Demolition: 1871–1883." *The French Review* 79, no. 5 (April 2006): 986–1008.

James, Jamie. *Pagan Light: Dreams of Freedom and Beauty in Capri*. New York: Farrar, Straus and Giroux, 2019.

Johnson, Richard Colles, and G. Thomas Tanselle. "The Haldeman-Julius 'Little Blue Books' as a Bibliographical Problem." *Papers of the Bibliographical Society of America* 64, no. 1 (1970): 29–78. https://doi.org/10.1086/pbsa.64.1.24301793.

Jordan, David P. "Haussmann and Haussmanisation: The Legacy for Paris." *French Historical Studies* 27, no. 1 (Winter 2004): 87–113. https://doi.org/10.1215/00161071-27-1-87.

– *Transforming Paris: The Life and Labors of Baron Haussmann*. New York: Free Press, 1995.

Joseph-Renaud, J. Preface to *Intentions* by Oscar Wilde, translated by J. Joseph-Renaud. Paris: P.-V. Stock, 1905.

Kaspi, André, and Antoine Marès, eds. *Le Paris des étrangers: depuis un siècle*. Paris: Imprimerie nationale, 1989.

Kiberd, Declan. *Inventing Ireland: The Literature of a Modern Nation*. London: Jonathan Cape, 1995.

Killeen, Jarlath. *The Faiths of Oscar Wilde: Catholicism, Folklore and Ireland*. Basingstoke, UK: Palgrave Macmillan, 2005.

Kolbert, Elizabeth. "Why Facts Don't Change Our Minds." *The New Yorker*, 20 February 2017.

Lagail, Dr. A.-S. [Alphonse Gallais, pseud.]. *Les Mémoires du Baron Jacques: Lubricités infernales de la noblesse décadente*. Priapeville [Paris?]: Librairie Galante, 1904.

La Jeunesse, Ernest. "Oscar Wilde." In *Oscar Wilde: Interviews and Recollections*, vol. 2, edited by E.H. Mikhail, 477–80. London: Macmillan, 1979.

Lee, R. Alton. *Publisher for the Masses, Emanuel Haldeman-Julius*. Lincoln: University of Nebraska Press, 2017.

Lemieux, Cyril. "L'Accusation tolérante. Remarques sur les rapports entre commérage, scandale et affaire." *Affaires, scandales et grandes causes: de Socrate à Pinochet*, edited by Luc Boltanski, Elisabeth Claverie, Nicolas Offenstadt, and Stéphane Van Damme, 367–94. Paris: Stock, 2007.

Lemonnier, Léon. *La Vie d'Oscar Wilde*. Paris: Éditions de la Nouvelle Revue Critique, 1931.

Lewis, Lloyd, and Henry Justin Smith. *Oscar Wilde Discovers America, 1882*. New York: Harcourt Brace, 1935.

Lhombreaud, Roger. "Une amitié anglaise de Pierre Louÿs." *Revue de littérature comparée* 27 (1953): 343–57.

Lobrano, Alec. *Hungry for Paris: The Ultimate Guide to the City's 109 Best Restaurants*. New York: Random House, 2014.

Lord, Rev. Daniel A. *The Pure of Heart*. Dublin: Catholic Truth Society, 1945.

Lottman, Herbert R. *Oscar Wilde à Paris*. Paris: Fayard, 2007.

Louÿs, Pierre. *Aphrodite*, edited by Pascal Pia. Paris: Tiflis, Bagration Davidoff [René Bonnel], 1928.

– *Aphrodite*, edited by Jean-Paul Goujon. Paris: Gallimard, 1992.

"La Danseuse." In *Astarté*. Paris: Librairie de l'Art indépendant, 1892.

– "La Femme qui danse." *La Conque* 3 (May 1891): xxiv.

– *La Maison sur le Nil*. Paris: Librairie de l'Art indépendant, 1894.

– Preface to *Aphrodite*. *La Revue blanche* 10 (1896): 256–9.

– "Sonnet." *The Spirit Lamp* 4, no. 1 (May 1893): 1.

Louÿs, Pierre, and Georges Louis. *Correspondance croisée, 1890–1917*, edited by Gordon Millan. 4 vols. Paris: Honoré Champion, 2015.

Love, Heather. *Feeling Backwards: Loss and the Politics of Queer History*. Cambridge, MA: Harvard University Press, 2007.

Loyer, François. *Paris Nineteenth Century: Architecture and Urbanism*, translated by Charles Lynn Clark. New York: Abbeville Press, 1988.

Machado, Manuel. "La última balada del poeta inglés." In *Los amigos españoles de Oscar Wilde*, edited by José Esteban, 49–59. Madrid: Reino de Cordelia, 2013.

Mackenzie, Compton. *Vestal Fire*. London: Chatto & Windus, 1951.

Mackenzie, Faith Compton. *As Much As I Dare: The Autobiography of Faith Compton Mackenzie*. London: Collins, 1938.

Mackie, Gregory. *Beautiful Untrue Things: Forging Oscar Wilde's Extraordinary Afterlife*. Toronto: University of Toronto Press, 2019.

Maguire, J. Robert. *Ceremonies of Bravery: Oscar Wilde, Carlos Blacker, and the Dreyfus Affair*. Oxford: Oxford University Press, 2013.

Mahoney, Kristin Mary. *Queer Kinship after Wilde: Transnational Decadence and the Family*. Cambridge: Cambridge University Press, 2022.

Marcus, Sharon. *The Drama of Celebrity*. Princeton, NJ: Princeton University Press, 2019.

Marjoribanks, Edward. *Carson the Advocate*. New York: Macmillan, 1932.

McCormack, Jerusha, ed. *Wilde the Irishman*. New Haven, CT: Yale University Press, 1998.

Mead, Donald. "More Unpublished Oscar Wilde Letters." *The Wildean* 61 (July 2022): 79–104.

– "Swan Song: Spoken Stories by Oscar Wilde Collected by Guillot de Saix." *The Wildean*, no. 47 (July 2015): 101–8.

Mendelssohn, Michèle. *Making Oscar Wilde*. Oxford: Oxford University Press, 2018.

Mercier, Hugo, and Dan Sperber. *The Enigma of Reason*. Cambridge, MA: Harvard University Press, 2017.

Merle, Robert. *Oscar Wilde, ou la "destinée" de l'homosexuel*. Paris: Gallimard, 1955.

Merrill, Stuart. "Some Unpublished Recollections of Oscar Wilde." In *Oscar Wilde: Interviews and Recollections*, vol. 2, edited by E.H. Mikhail, 468–72. London: Macmillan, 1979.

Mikhail, E.H., ed. *Oscar Wilde: Interviews and Recollections*. 2 vols. London: Macmillan, 1979.

Mitchell, Rebecca N. "Oscar Wilde and the French Press, 1880–91." *Victorian Periodicals Review* 49, no. 1 (Spring 2016): 123–48. https://doi.org/10.1353/vpr.2016.0007.

Morel, Dominique, and Merlin Holland, eds. *Oscar Wilde: L'impertinent absolu*. Paris: Paris-Musées, 2016.

Moretti, Franco. *Atlas of the European Novel, 1800–1900*. London: Verso, 1998.

Murray, Alex. "Decadence Revisited: Evelyn Waugh and the Afterlife of the 1890s." *Modernism/modernity* 22, no. 3 (September 2015): 593–607. https://doi.org/10.1353/mod.2015.0052.

Murray's Handbook for Visitors to Paris. London: John Murray, 1879, 1890.

Navas, Ana Rodríguez, and Nathalie Bouzaglo. "Oscar Wilde's Forgotten Legacy in Latin America." *Journal of Latin American Cultural Studies* 28, no. 3 (2019): 321–8. https://doi.org/10.1080/13569325.2019.1712790.

Nordau, Max Simon. *Dégénérescence*. Paris: Alcan, 1894.

– *Entartung*. Berlin: Duncker, 1892.

O'Brien, Kevin H.F. "Robert Sherard: Friend of Oscar Wilde." *English Literature in Transition, 1880–1920* 28, no. 1 (1985): 3–29.

Ogrinc, Will H.L. "Frère Jacques: A Shrine to Love and Sorrow: Jacques D'Adelswärd Fersen (1880–1923)." 2006. http://semgai.free.fr/doc_et_pdf/Fersen-engels.pdf.

Oscar Wilde in America: The Definitive Resource of Oscar Wilde's Visits to America. https://www.oscarwildeinamerica.org.

O'Sullivan, Vincent. *Aspects of Wilde*. New York: Henry Holt, 1936.

Palmer, Michael B. *Des Petits journaux aux grandes agences: naissance du journalism modern, 1863–1914*. Paris: Aubier, 1983.

Partridge, Eric. *New Partridge Dictionary of Slang and Unconventional English*, 2nd ed. London: Routledge, 2013.

Pater, Walter. *The Renaissance: Studies in Art and Poetry*, edited by Donald L. Hill. Berkeley: University of California Press, 1980.

Pennington, Michael. *An Angel for a Martyr: Jacob Epstein's Tomb for Oscar Wilde*. Reading, UK: Whiteknights Press, 1987.

Perry, Imani. *Vexy Thing: On Gender and Liberation*. Durham, NC: Duke University Press, 2018.

Peyrefitte, Roger. *The Exile of Capri*. Translated by Edward Hyams. London: Secker & Warburg, 1961.

Pinkney, David H. *Napoleon III and the Rebuilding of Paris*. Princeton, NJ: Princeton University Press, 1972.

Pinson, Guillaume. *La Culture médiatique francophone en Europe et en Amérique du Nord*. Montreal: Presses de l'Université Laval, 2016.

Potolsky, Matthew. *The Decadent Republic of Letters: Taste, Politics, and Cosmopolitan Community from Baudelaire to Beardsley*. Philadelphia: University of Pennsylvania Press, 2013.

Quignard, Marie-Françoise, ed. *Le Mercure de France: cent un ans d'édition*. Paris: Bibliothèque nationale de France, 1995.

Rachilde [pseud. Marguerite Eymery Vallette]. *Alfred Jarry: ou le surmâle de lettres*. Paris: Bernard Grasset, 1928.

– *Monsieur Vénus: A Materialist Novel*. Translated by Melanie Hawthorne after the 1929 translation by Madeleine Boyd. New York: Modern Language Association of America, 2004.

– "Oscar Wilde et lui." *Mercure de France*, July–August 1918, 59–68.

– "Questions brûlantes." *La revue blanche*, September 1896, 193–200.

Ransome, Arthur. *Oscar Wilde*, translated by G. de Lautrec and H.-D. Davray. Paris: Mercure de France, 1914.

– *Oscar Wilde: A Critical Study*. London: Martin Secker, 1912.

– "Oscar Wilde in Paris." *Bookman* 33, no. 3 (1911): 268–73.

– "Oscar Wilde in Paris." *T.P.'s Magazine* (London), 2, no. 9 (June 1911): 427–35.

Rebell, Hugues. "La Défense d'Oscar Wilde." *Mercure de France* (August 1895), 182–90.

– *Pour Oscar Wilde: des écrivains français au secours du condamné*. Rouen: Elisabeth Brunet; Association des amis d'Hugues Rebell, 1994.

Reed, Jeremy. Introduction to *Lord Lyllian: Black Masses* by Jacques d'Adelswärd Fersen. North Pomfret, VT: Asphodel, 2005.

Rice, Shelley. *Parisian Views*. Cambridge, MA: MIT Press, 1997.

Richmond-Garza, Elizabeth. "The Double Life of *Salomé*." In *Refiguring Wilde's Salomé*, edited by Michael Y. Bennett, 21–36. New York: Rodopi, 2011.

Ricketts, Charles. *Self Portrait: Taken from the Letters and Journals of Charles Ricketts, R.A*, edited by Cecil Lewis. London: Peter Davies, 1939.

Robins, Ahley H., and Sean L. Sellars. "Oscar Wilde's Terminal Illness: Reappraisal after a Century." *The Lancet* 356, no. 9244 (November 2000): 1841–3. https://doi.org/10.1016/S0140-6736(00)03245-1.

Roden, Frederick S., ed. *Palgrave Advances in Oscar Wilde Studies*. New York: Palgrave Macmillan, 2004.

Rose, David Charles. *Oscar Wilde's Elegant Republic: Transformation, Dislocation and Fantasy in Fin-de-Siècle Paris*. Newcastle upon Tyne: Cambridge Scholars, 2015.

Ross, Iain. *Oscar Wilde and Ancient Greece*. Cambridge: Cambridge University Press, 2013.

Ross, Margery. *Robert Ross, Friend of Friends*. London: Jonathan Cape, 1952.

Rosteck, Jens. *Die Sphinx verstummt: Oscar Wilde in Paris*. Berlin: Propyläen, 2000.

Rothenstein, William. *Men and Memories: A History of the Arts 1872–1922*. New York: Coward-McCann, 1931.

Ruthven, K.K. *Faking Literature*. Cambridge: Cambridge University Press, 2001.

Sala, George Augustus. *Paris Herself Again in 1878–9*. London: Vizetelly and Co., 1884.

Scheffer, Robert. "Plumes d'oies et plumes d'aigles: les trois gendres." *Akademos* 6 (June 1909): 895.

Schroeder, Horst. "Oscar Wilde's and Stéphane Mallarmé's First Meeting and Mallarmé's Presentation Copy." *The Wildean*, no. 41 (2012): 75–82.

Scott, Kathleen. *Self-Portrait of an Artist: from the Diaries and Memoirs of Lady Kennet, Kathleen, Lady Scott*. London: John Murray, 1949.

Sherard, Robert Harborough. *Bernard Shaw, Frank Harris and Oscar Wilde*. London: T. Werner Laurie, 1937.

– *Oscar Wilde: The Story of an Unhappy Friendship*. London: Greening and Co., 1905.

– *The Real Oscar Wilde*. London: T. Werner Laurie, 1917.

– *Twenty Years in Paris: Being Some Recollections of a Literary Life*. London: Hutchinson, 1905.

Sherry, Vincent B. *Modernism and the Reinvention of Decadence*. Cambridge: Cambridge University Press, 2015.

Sontag, Susan. "Notes on Camp." *Partisan Review* 31, no. 4 (1964): 515–30.

Stokes, John. *Oscar Wilde: Myths, Miracles and Imitations* (Cambridge: Cambridge University Press, 1996).

– "Wilde and Paris." In *Oscar Wilde in Context*, edited by Peter Raby and Kerry Powell, 60–70. Cambridge: Cambridge University Press, 2013.

Sturgis, Matthew. *Oscar: A Life*. London: Head of Zeus, 2018.

– *Oscar Wilde: A Life*. New York: Alfred A. Knopf, 2022.

Swinburne, Algernon Charles. "Social Verse." In *Studies in Prose and Poetry*, 84–109. London: Chatto & Windus, 1894.

Toulet, Emmanuelle. "Avant-propos." In *Collection Guillot de Saix inventaire sommaire*, edited by Marie-Thérèse Debuysscher, Catherine Ducrocq-Le Griffon, Claudette Joannis, Anita Mengozzi, and Emmanuelle Toulet. Paris: BnF, Département des arts du spectacle, 1999.

The Trial of Oscar Wilde: From the Shorthand Reports. Paris: Privately printed [Charles Carrington], 1906 [1905].

Valentine, Colton. "Domesticating Decadence: Joris-Karl Huysmans, Pierre Louÿs, and Their Invisible English Translators." *Modern Language Quarterly* 82, no. 4 (2021): 441–72. https://doi.org/10.1215/00267929-9365957.

Van Puymbroeck, Birgit. "Cross-Channel Mediations: Henry-D. Davray and British Popular Fiction in the *Mercure de France*." In *Transitions in Middlebrow Writing, 1880–1930*, edited by Kate Macdonald and Christoph Singer, 183–200. Basingstoke, UK: Palgrave Macmillan, 2015.

Venuti, Lawrence. *The Scandals of Translation: Towards an Ethics of Difference*. London: Routledge, 1998.

Vernadakis, Emmanuel. "Oscar Wilde et Julien Green: marges, espaces et interlignes." *Études Greeniennes* 10 (2018) : 11–26.

Vernon, Peter. "John Gray's Letters to Pierre Louÿs." *Revue de littérature comparée* 53, no. 1 (1979): 88–107.

Wan, Marco. "From the Rack to the Press: Representation of the Oscar Wilde Trials in the French Newspaper *Le Temps*." *Law and Literature* 18, no. 1 (2006): 47–67.

Wilde, Oscar. *Ballade de la gêole de Reading*, translated by Henry-D. Davray. Paris: Mercure de France, 1898.

– "Les Ballons." In *The Complete Works of Oscar Wilde*, vol. 1, *Poems and Poems in Prose*, edited by Bobby Fong and Karl Beckson. Oxford: Oxford University Press, 2000.

– *The Collected Works*, 14 vols., edited by Robert Ross. London: Methuen, 1908.
– *The Complete Letters of Oscar Wilde*, edited by Merlin Holland and Rupert Hart-Davis. London: Fourth Estate, 2000.
– *The Critical Writings of Oscar Wilde: An Annotated Selection*, edited by Nicholas Frankel. Cambridge, MA: Harvard University Press, 2022.
– "The Decay of Lying." In *The Complete Works of Oscar Wilde*, vol. 4, *Criticism*, edited by Josephine M. Guy. Oxford: Oxford University Press., 2007.
– *De Profundis, précédé de lettres écrites de la prison*. Paris: Mercure de France, 1905.
– *De Profundis*, edited by Robert Ross. London: Methuen, 1905.
– *De Profundis*. In *The Complete Works of Oscar Wilde*, vol. 2, *De Profundis; Epistola: In Carcere et Vinculis*, edited by Ian Small. Oxford: Oxford University Press, 2005.
– *The Importance of Being Earnest and Other Plays*. Oxford: Oxford University Press, 2008.
– "The Incomparable and Ingenious History of Mr. W.H." In *The Complete Works of Oscar Wilde*, vol. 8, *The Short Fiction*, edited by Ian Small. Oxford: Oxford University Press, 2017.
– "Le Jardin des Tuileries." In *The Complete Works of Oscar Wilde*, vol. 1, *Poems and Poems in Prose*, edited by Bobby Fong and Karl Beckson. Oxford: Oxford University Press, 2000.
– *Lady Windermere's Fan*. London: Elkin Mathews and John Lane, 1893.
– "Phrases and Philosophies for the Use of the Young." *The Chameleon* 1 (December 1894), 1.
– *The Picture of Dorian Gray*. London: Ward, Lock and Co., 1891.
– *The Picture of Dorian Gray*, edited by Joseph Bristow. Oxford: Oxford World Classics, 2019.
– "Poems in Prose." *The Fortnightly Review* 56, no. 331 (July 1894): 22–9.
– *Salomé*. Paris: Librairie de l'Art indépendant, 1893.
– *Salome*. In *The Complete Works of Oscar Wilde*, vol. 5, *Plays 1: The Duchess of Padua; Salomé: Drame en un acte; Salome: Tragedy in One Act*, edited by Joseph Donohue Jr. Oxford: Oxford University Press, 2013.
– *The Sphinx*. London: Elkin Matthews and John Lane, 1894.
– *The Sphinx*. In *The Complete Works of Oscar Wilde*, vol. 1, *Poems and Poems in Prose*, edited by Bobby Fong and Karl Beckson. Oxford: Oxford University Press, 2000.
– "The Sphinx without a Secret." In *The Complete Works of Oscar Wilde*, vol. 8, *The Short Fiction*, edited by Ian Small. Oxford: Oxford University Press, 2017.
– *Table Talk*, edited by Thomas Wright. London: Cassell, 2000.

Wilde Trials International News Archive. https://dhil.lib.sfu.ca/wilde/index.html.

Williams, Raymond. "The Metropolis and the Emergence of Modernism." In *Unreal City: Urban Experience in Modern European Literature and Art*, edited by Edward Timms and David Kelley, 13–24. Manchester: Manchester University Press, 1985.

Wilson, Simon. "From Greek Youth to Flying Demon Angel," *The Wildean*, no. 56 (January 2020): 3–62.

Wright, Thomas. *Built of Books: How Reading Defined the Life of Oscar Wilde*. New York: Henry Holt, 2009.

Yeats, William Butler. *The Collected Letters of W.B. Yeats*, vols. 1–5, edited by John Kelly and Ronald Schuchard. Oxford: Oxford University Press, 1986– .

Contributors

Joseph Bristow is Distinguished Professor of English at the University of California, Los Angeles. His most recent books are *Oscar Wilde on Trial: The Criminal Proceedings, from Arrest to Imprisonment* (Yale University Press, 2022) and an edited collection, *Extraordinary Aesthetes: Decadents, New Women, and Fin-de-Siècle Culture* (University of Toronto Press, 2023).

Colette Colligan is Professor of English Studies at the Université d'Angers (France). She is the author of *A Publisher's Paradise: Expatriate Literary Culture in Paris, 1890–1960* (University of Massachusetts Press, 2014), as well as *The Traffic in Obscenity from Byron to Beardsley: Sexuality and Exoticism in Nineteenth-Century Print Culture* (Palgrave Macmillan, 2008).

Ellen Crowell is an Associate Professor of English and Director of the University Core at Saint Louis University. She has published numerous articles on Oscar Wilde and fin-de-siècle queer cultures, and is the author of *The Dandy in Irish and American Southern Fiction: Aristocratic Drag* (Edinburgh University Press, 2007).

Clément Dessy is FNRS Research Associate and Professor of French and Comparative Literature, Université libre de Bruxelles. His research focuses on text/image relations and transnational literary exchanges at the fin de siècle. He is currently preparing a monograph on the cultural relations between Belgium and Britain at the turn of the century. He is the author of *Les Écrivains et les Nabis: la littérature au défi de la peinture* (Presses universitaires de Rennes, 2015), and co-editor of several volumes, including *(Bé)vues du futur: les imaginaires visuels de la dystopie (1840–1940)* (Presses universitaires du Septentrion, 2015) and *L'Artiste* *en revues: arts et discours en mode périodique* (Presses universitaires de Rennes, 2019).

Petra Dierkes is Lecturer in Comparative Literature and Undergraduate Advising Director at Stanford University. She has published widely on Symbolism, Decadence, and Oscar Wilde, and is the author of *Salome's Modernity: Oscar Wilde and the Aesthetics of Transgression* (University of Michigan Press, 2011) and the co-editor, with Michael F. Davis, of *Wilde's Other Worlds* (Routledge, 2018).

Stefano Evangelista is Professor of English and Comparative Literature at Oxford University and Fellow of Trinity College. His research interests include aestheticism and Decadence, the reception of classical antiquity, and the relationship between literature and visual culture. He is the author of *British Aestheticism and Ancient Greece: Hellenism, Reception, Gods in Exile* (Palgrave Macmillan, 2009) and *Literary Cosmopolitanism in the English Fin de Siècle: Citizens of Nowhere* (Oxford University Press, 2021), both of which include chapters on Oscar Wilde. He currently holds an Einstein Visiting Fellowship at the Centre for British Studies in the Humboldt University, Berlin.

Nicholas Frankel is Professor of English at Virginia Commonwealth University. His many books about Wilde include *The Invention of Oscar Wilde* (Reaktion Books, 2021), *Oscar Wilde: The Unrepentant Years* (Harvard University Press, 2017), and *Oscar Wilde's Decorated Books* (University of Michigan Press, 2000).

Gregory Mackie is Associate Professor of English and Norman Colbeck Curator of Rare Books at the University of British Columbia. He is most recently the author of *Beautiful Untrue Things: Forging Oscar Wilde's Extraordinary Afterlife* (University of Toronto Press, 2019).

Kristin Mahoney is a Professor in the Department of English at Michigan State University. She is the author of *Literature and the Politics of Post-Victorian Decadence* (Cambridge University Press, 2015) and *Queer Kinship after Wilde: Transnational Decadence and the Family* (Cambridge University Press, 2022), which received Honourable Mention for the North American Victorian Studies Association Book Prize. She co-edited, with Dustin Friedman, *Nineteenth-Century Literature in Transition: The 1890s* (Cambridge University Press, 2023). She co-founded and co-edits *Cusp: Late 19th-/Early 20th-Century Cultures*, which is published by Johns Hopkins University Press and won the Council of Editors of Learned Journals award for Best New Journal in 2024.

Paisley Mann is an Instructor in the Department of English at Langara College, Vancouver. Her research focuses on Victorian engagements with the city of Paris, and her article "A Paris of Their Own: Guidebooks for Anglo-American Female Travellers, and the Rewriting of Mainstream Guidebook Culture" recently appeared in the *Journal of Victorian Culture.*

Rebecca N. Mitchell is Reader in Victorian Literature and Culture, University of Birmingham. She is the author of *Victorian Lessons in Empathy and Difference* (The Ohio State University Press, 2011) and the co-author, with Joseph Bristow, of *Oscar Wilde's Chatterton: Literary History, Romanticism, and the Art of Forgery* (Yale University Press, 2015).

Index

Italicized page numbers indicate illustrations (figures and photographs).